M. A. Sridhar
January 9, 1989

EATCS
Monographs on Theoretical Computer Science

Editors: W. Brauer G. Rozenberg A. Salomaa

Kurt Mehlhorn

Data Structures and Algorithms 3:

Multi-dimensional Searching and Computational Geometry

With 134 Figures

Springer-Verlag
Berlin Heidelberg New York Tokyo 1984

Editors
Prof. Dr. Wilfried Brauer
FB Informatik der Universität
Rothenbaum-Chausee 67–69, 2000 Hamburg 13, Germany

Prof. Dr. Grzegorz Rozenberg
Institut of Applied Mathematics and Computer Science
University of Leiden, Wassenaarseweg 80, P.O. Box 9512
2300 RA Leiden, The Netherlands

Prof. Dr. Arto Salomaa
Department of Mathematics, University of Turku
20500 Turku 50, Finland

Author
Prof. Dr. Kurt Mehlhorn
FB 10, Angewandte Mathematik und Informatik
Universität des Saarlandes, 6600 Saarbrücken, Germany

With the permission of B. G. Teubner publishers, Stuttgart, arranged, solely authorized and revised English translation of the original German edition: Effiziente Allgorithmen (1977)

ISBN 3-540-13642-8 Springer-Verlag Berlin Heidelberg New York Tokyo
ISBN 0-387-13642-8 Springer-Verlag New York Heidelberg Berlin Tokyo

Offsetprinting: Beltz Offsetdruck, Hemsbach/Bergstrasse
Binding: J. Schäffer OHG, Grünstadt
2145/3140-543210

For Ena, Uli, Steffi, and Tim

Preface to Volume 3

The design and analysis of data structures and computer algorithms has gained considerable importance in recent years. The concept of "algorithm" is central in computer science and "efficiency" ist central in the world of money.

This book treats multi-dimensional searching and computational geometry amd comprises chapters VII and VIII of the three volume series "Data Structures and Efficient Algorithms". The material covered in this book is all very recent and derives its importance from its implications for various application areas such as database systems amd computer graphics. The other two volumes treat sorting and searching (chapters I to III) and graph algorithms and NP-completeness (chapters IV to VI). All three volumes are organized according to problem areas. In addition, a chapter IX is included in all three volumes which gives a paradigm oriented view of the entire series and orders the material according to algorithmic methods.

In chapter VII we deal with multi-dimensional searching problems. Let U be an ordered set, e.g. the real numbers, and let $S \subseteq U^d$ be a set of d-tuples over U. We treat

exact match queries: given $x = (x_0, \ldots, x_{d-1}) \in U^d$ decide whether x belongs to S

partial match queries: given $x = (x_0, \ldots, d_{d-1}) \in (U \cup \{*\})^d$ find all $y = (y_0, \ldots, y_{d-1}) \in S$ with $x_i = y_i$ for all i with $x_i \neq *$.

orthogonal range queries: given $x = (x_0, \ldots, x_{d-1}) \in U^d$ and $z = (z_0, \ldots, z_{d-1}) \in U^d$ find all $y = (y_0, \ldots, y_{d-1}) \in S$ with $x_i \leq y_i \leq z_i$ for all i.

polygon queries: given a polygon P in U^2 find all points in $S \cap P$.

Multi-dimensional searching is a natural generalization of one-dimensional searching which is covered extensively in chapter III. We discuss three data structures for multi-dimensional searching in detail, namely d-dimensional trees, range trees, and polygon trees. We also treat multi-dimensional divide-and-conquer techniques in general. Most data structures for multi-dimensional searching problems cannot deal with dynamic or weighted data directly. We therefore consider (in section VII.1) general methods for converting data structures for static sets into data structures for dynamic and weighted sets. These methods are applicable to a wide range of searching problems, the so called decomposable searching problems. The search for efficient algorithms also implies the search for the optimum; we therefore have to ask for lower bounds. Lower bounds are dealt with in section 2.3. It is shown that the data structures mentioned above are essentially optimal with respect to a wide class of possible solutions.

Chapter VIII is devoted to computational geometry. We start by reviewing the use of binary search in a geometric setting. This method leads us first to hierarchical representations of convex polygons, and then to logarithmic algorithms for various problems about convex polygons (section 1). It also yields an efficient implementation of the scan line (plane) in plane (space) sweep algorithms (section 4). We use sweep algorithms for problems like intersection of various objects (line segments, polygons, convex polyhedra) and triangulation of plane figures. The convex hull problem is treated in section 2. Closest point problems, Voronoi diagrams, and searching in planar subdivisions are the subject of section 3. Iso-oriented objects, i.e., objects whose sides are parallel to the axes, are the topic of section 5. Plane sweep algorithms for these objects lead to three new data structures, namely interval trees, segment trees, and priority search trees. Many of the algorithms initially designed for iso-oriented objects can also be used for general polygons if we employ path decompositions. Path decompositions are also useful for searching planar subdivisions. Iso-oriented objects are amenable to divide and conquer algorithms, too; this is the subject of section 5.2. The chapter is closed by a treatment of two geometric transforms, namely duality and inversion, including their usefulness in designing efficient algorithms for geometric tasks.

Chapter IX gives an orthogonal view of all three volumes. Whilst the material in chapters I to VIII is organized according to problem areas, it is organized according to algorithmic paradigms (e.g. divide and conquer, dynamic programming, ...) in Chapter IX.

The book covers advanced material and leads the reader to very recent results and current research. It is intended for a reader who has some previous knowledge in algorithm design and analysis. More precisely, there are the following prerequisites. The reader must be familiar with the fundamental data structures, such as queues, stacks, static trees, linked list structures, and with one more advanced data structure, namely, the balanced tree. Any kind of balanced tree, e.g. AVL-tree, BB[α]-tree, 2–3-tree, red-black-tree, ... will do. This material is covered in sections III.5.1, III.5.2 and III.5.3.1 of volume 1 but also in many other books on algorithm design. Knowledge of this material allows the reader to appreciate most of the book. The notable exceptions are *dynamic* (not static) range, interval, and segment trees. The dynamic versions of these trees require advanced material about BB[α]-trees and D-trees which is covered in sections III.5.2 and III.6.2 of volume 1.

The organization of the book is quite simple. There are three chapters which are numbered using roman numerals. Sections and subsections of chapters are numbered using arabic numberals. Within each section, theorems and lemmas are numbered consecutively. Cross references are made by giving the identifier of the section (or subsection) and the number of the theorem. The common prefix of the identifiers or origin and destination of a cross reference may be suppressed, i. e., a cross reference to section VII.1.2 in section VII.2 can be made by either referring to section VII.1.2 or to section 1.2.

Each chapter has an extensive list of exercises and a section of bibliographic remarks. The exercises are of varying degrees of difficulty. In many cases hints are given, or a reference is provided in the section on bibliographic remarks.

Most parts of the book were used as course notes either by myself or by my colleagues N. Blum, Th. Lengauer, and A. Tsakalidis. Their comments were a big help. I also want to thank H. Alt, O. Fries, St. Hertel, B. Schmidt, and K. Simon who collaborated with me on several sections and I want to thank the many students who helped to improve the presentation by their criticism. Discussions with many colleagues helped to shape my ideas: B. Becker, J. Berstel, B. Commentz-Walter, H. Edelsbrunner, B. Eisenbarth, Ph. Flajolet, M. Fontet, G. Gonnet, R. Güttler, G. Hotz, S. Huddleston, I. Munro, J. Nievergelt, Th. Ottmann, M. Overmars, M. Paterson, F. Preparata, A. Rozenberg, M. Stadel, R. E. Tarjan, J. van Leeuwen, D. Wood, and N. Ziviani.

The drawings and the proof reading were done by my student Hans Rohnert. He did a fantastic job. Of course, all remaining errors are my sole responsibility. Thanks to him, there should not be too many left. The typescript was prepared by Christel Korten-Michels, Martina Horn, Marianne Weis and Doris Schindler under sometimes hectic conditions. I thank them all.

Saarbrücken, April 1984 Kurt Mehlhorn

Contents Vol. 3: Multi-dimensional Searching and Computational Geometry

VII. Multidimensional Data Structures

Chapter III was devoted to searching problems in one-dimensional space. In this chapter we will reconsider these problems in higher dimensional space and also treat a number of problems which only become interesting in higher dimensions. Let U be some ordered set and let $S \subseteq U^d$ for some d. An element $x \in S$ is a d-tuple $(x_o,\ldots,x_{d-1})$. The simplest searching problem is to specify a point $y \in U^d$ and to ask whether $y \in S$; this is called an exact match query and can in principle be solved by the methods of chapter III. Order U^d by lexicographic order and use a balanced search tree. A very general form of query is to specify a region $R \subseteq U^d$ and to ask for all points in $R \cap S$. General region queries can only be solved by exhaustive search of set S. Special and more tractable cases are obtained by restricting the query region R to some subclass of regions. Restricting R to polygons gives us polygon searching, restricting it further to rectangles with sides parallel to the axis gives us range searching, and finally restricting the class of rectangles even further gives us partial match retrieval. In one-dimensional space balanced trees solve all these problems efficiently. In higher dimensions we will need different data structures for different types of queries; d-dimensional trees, range trees and polygon trees are therefore treated in VII.2.. There is one other major difference to one-dimensional space. It seems to be very difficult to deal with insertions and deletions; i.e. the data structures described in VII.2. are mainly useful for static sets. No efficient algorithms are known as of today to balance these structures after insertions and deletions. However, there is a general approach to dynamization which we treat in VII.1.. It is applicable to a wide class of problems and yields reasonably efficient dynamic data structures.

In section VII.2.3 we discuss lower bounds. We will first prove a lower bound on the complexity of partial match retrieval where no redundancy in storage space is allowed. The lower bound implies the optimality of d-dimensional trees. The second lower bound relates the complexity of insertions, deletions, and queries with a combinatorial quantity. The spanning bound implies the optimality of range trees and near-optimality of polygon trees.

Multidimensional searching problems appear in numerous applications, most notably database systems. In these applications U is an arbitrary ordered set, e.g. a set of names or a set of possible incomes. Region queries arise in these applications in a natural way; e.g. in a database containing information about persons, say name, income, and number of children, we might ask for all persons with

# children = 3, , a partial match query
# children = 3, 1000 ≤ income ≤ 2000 , a range query
income = 1000 + 1000· # children , a polygon query

VII. 1. A Black Box Approach to Data Structures

In chapter III we designed clever data structures for variants of the dictionary problem. With a little bit of unfairness one might say that all we did in chapter III is the following: We started with binary search on sorted arrays and generalized it in two directions. First we generalized to weighted static trees in order to cope with access frequencies and then to unweighted dynamic trees in order to cope with insertions and deletions. Finally we combined both extensions and arrived at weighted dynamic trees. Suppose now that we want to repeat the generalization process for a different data structure, say interpolation search. Do we have to start all over again or can we profit from the development of chapter III? In this section we will describe some general techniques for generalization: dynamization and weighting. We start out with a static solution for some searching problem, i.e. a solution which only supports queries, but does support neither insertion and deletions nor weighted data. Then dynamization is a method which allows us to also support insertions and deletions, weighting is a method which allows us to support queries to weighted data and finally weighted dynamization combines both extensions. Of course, we cannot hope to arrive at the very best data structures by only applying general principles. Nevertheless, the general principles can give us very quickly fully dynamic solutions with reasonable running times. Also there are data structures, e.g. d-dimensional trees, where all special purpose attempts of dynamization have failed.

Binary search on sorted arrays will be our running example. Given a set of n elements one can construct a sorted array in time O(n log n)(preprocessing time is O(n log n)), we can search the array in time O(log n) (query time is O(log n)), and the array consumes space O(n)(space requirement is O(n)). Dynamization produces a solution for the dictionary problem (operations Insert, Delete, Member) with running time O(log n) for Inserts and Deletes and $O(\log^2 n)$ for Member. Thus Inserts and Deletes are as fast as in balanced trees but queries are less efficient. Weighting produces weighted static dictionaries with access time $O(\log 1/p)$ for an element of probability p. This is the same order of magnitude as the special purpose solution of section III.4., the factor of proportionality is much larger though. Finally weighted dynamization produces a solution for the weighted, dynamic dictionary problem with running time $O((\log 1/p)^2)$ for Member operations and running time $O(\log 1/p)$ for Insert, Delete, Promote and Demote operations. Note that only access time is worse than what we obtained by dynamic weighted trees in III.6..

Although sorted arrays are our main example, they are not an important application of our general principles. The most important applications are data structures for higher dimensional searching problems described in this chapter. In many of these cases only static solutions are known and all attempts to construct dynamic or weighted solutions by special purpose methods have failed so far. The only dynamic or weighted solutions known today are obtained by applying the general principles described in this section.

VII. 1.1 Dynamization

We start with a definition of searching problem.

Definition: Let T_1, T_2, T_3 be sets. A searching problem Q of type T_1, T_2, T_3 is a function $Q: T_1 \times 2^{T_2} \to T_3$. □

A searching problem takes a point in T_1 and a subset of T_2 and produces an answer in T_3. There are plenty of examples. In the member problem we have $T_1 = T_2, T_3 = \{\underline{true}, \underline{false}\}$ and $Q(x,S)$ = "$x \in S$". In the nearest neighbour problem in the plane we have $T_1 = T_2 = \mathbb{R}^2$, $T_3 = \mathbb{R}$ and $Q(x,S) = \delta(x,y)$, where $y \in S$ and $\delta(x,y) \le \delta(x,z)$ for all $z \in S$. Here δ is some metric. In the inside the convex hull problem we have $T_1 = T_2 = \mathbb{R}^2$, $T_3 = \{\underline{true}, \underline{false}\}$ and $Q(x,S)$ = "is x inside the convex hull of point set S". In fact, our definition of searching problem is so general that just about everything is a searching problem.

A static data structure S for a searching problem supports only query operation Q, i.e. for every $S \subseteq T_2$ one can build a static data structure S such that function $Q(x,S): T_1 \to T_3$ can be computed efficiently. We deliberately use the same name for set S and data structure S because the internal workings of structure S are of no concern in this section. We associate three measures of efficiency with structure S, query time Q_S, preprocessing time P_S and space requirement S_S.

$Q_S(n)$ = time for a query on a set of n points using data structure S.

$P_S(n)$ = time to build S for a set of n points.

$S_S(n)$ = space requirement of S for a set of n points.

We assume throughout that $Q_S(n)$, $P_S(n)/n$ and $S_S(n)/n$ are nondecreasing.

A semi-dynamic data structure D for a searching problem supports in addition operation Insert, i.e. we can not only query D but also insert new points into D. A dynamic structure supports Insert and Delete. We use the following notation for the resource requirements of D.

$Q_D(n)$ = time for a query on a set of n points using structure D.

$S_D(n)$ = space requirement of D for a set of n points.

$I_D(n)$ = time for inserting a new point into a set of n points stored in D.

$\overline{I}_D(n)$ = amortized time for n-th insertion, i.e. (maximal total time spent on executing insertions in any sequence of n operations starting with the empty set)/n.

$D_D(n)$ = time for deleting a point from a set of n points stored in D.

$\overline{D}_D(n)$ = amortized time for n-th deletion, i.e. (maximal total time spent on executing deletions in any sequence of n operations (insertions, deletions, queries) starting with the empty set)/n.

We will next describe a general method for turning static data structures into semi-dynamic data structures. This method is only applicable to a subclass of searching problems, the decomposable searching problems.

Definition: A searching problem Q of type T_1, T_2, T_3 is decomposable if there is a binary operation $\square : T_3 \times T_3 \to T_3$ such that for all $S \subseteq T_2$ and all partitions A,B of S, i.e. $S = A \cup B$, $A \cap B = \emptyset$, and all $x \in T_1$.

$$Q(x,S) = \square\ (Q(x,A),\ Q(x,B))$$

Moreover $\square$ is computable in constant time. □

In decomposable searching problems we can put together the answer to a query with respect to set S from the answers with respect to pieces A and B of S using operator $\square$. We note as a consequence of the definition of decomposability that T_3 with operation $\square$ is basically a commutative semigroup with unit element $Q(x,\emptyset)$. The member problem is decomposable with $\square$ = or, the nearest neighbour problem is decomposable with $\square$ = min. However, the inside the convex hull problem is not decomposable.

Theorem 1: Let S be a static data structure for a decomposable searching problem Q. Then there is a semi-dynamic solution D for Q with

$$Q_D(n) = O(Q_S(n) \log n)$$
$$S_D(n) = O(S_S(n))$$
$$\overline{I}_D(n) = O((P_S(n)/n) \log n)$$

Proof: The proof is based on a simple yet powerful idea. At any point of time the dynamic structure consists of a collection of static data structures for parts of S, i.e. set S is partioned into blocks S_i. Queries are answered by querying the blocks and composing the partial answers by $\square$. Insertions are dealt with by suitably combining blocks.

The details are as follows. Let S be any set of n elements and let $n = \sum_{i=0} a_i 2^i$, $a_i \in \{0,1\}$, be the binary representation of n. Let $S_0, S_1, \ldots$ be any partition of S with $|S_i| = a_i 2^i$, $0 \le i \le \log n$. Then structure D is just a collection of static data structures, one for each non-empty S_i.

The space requirement of D is easily computed as

$$S_D(n) = \sum_i S_S(a_i 2^i) = \sum_i (S_S(a_i 2^i)/a_i 2^i)\ a_i 2^i$$
$$\le \sum_i (S_S(n)/n) a_i 2^i = S_S(n)$$

The inequality follows from our basic assumption that $S_S(n)/n$ is non-decreasing.

Next note that $Q(x,S) = \square_{0\le i\le \log n} Q(x,S_i)$ and that there are never more than log n non-empty S_i's. Hence a query can be answered in time

$$\log n + \sum_i Q_S(a_i 2^i) \le \log n(1+Q_S(n)) = O(\log n\ Q_S(n)).$$

Finally consider operation Insert(x,S). Let $n + 1 = \sum \beta_i 2^i$ and let j be such that $\alpha_j = 0$, $\alpha_{j-1} = \alpha_{j-2} = \dots = \alpha_o = 1$. Then $\beta_j = 1$, $\beta_{j-1} = \dots = \beta_o = 0$. We process the (n+1)-th insertion by taking the new point x and the $2^j-1 = \sum_{i=0}^{j-1} 2^i$ points stored in structures $S_o, S_1, \dots, S_{j-1}$ and constructing a new static data structure for $\{x\} \cup S_o \cup S_1 \cup \dots \cup S_{j-1}$. Thus the cost of the (n+1)-st insertion is $P_S(2^j)$. Next note that a cost of $P_S(2^j)$ has to be paid after insertions $2^j(2\ell+1)$, $\ell = 0,1,2,\dots,$ and hence at most $n/2^j$ times during the first n insertions. Thus the total cost of the first n insertions is bounded by

$$\sum_{j=0}^{\lfloor \log n \rfloor} P_S(2^j)\ n/2^j \le n \sum_{j=0}^{\lfloor \log n \rfloor} P_S(n)/n \le P_S(n)(\lfloor \log n \rfloor +1).$$

Hence $\overline{I}_D(n) = O((P_S(n)/n)\log n)$. □

Let us apply theorem 1 to binary search on sorted arrays. We have $S_S(n) = n$, $Q_S(n) = \log n$ and $P_S(n) = n \log n$. Hence we obtain a semi-dynamic solution for the member problem with $S_D(n) = O(n)$, $Q_D(n) = (\log n)^2$ and $\overline{I}_D(n) = (\log n)^2$. Actually, the bound on $\overline{I}_D(n)$ is overly pessimistic. Note that we can merge two sorted arrays in linear time. Hence we can construct a sorted array of size 2^k out of a point and sorted arrays of size $1,2,4,8,\dots,2^{k-1}$ in time $O(2^k)$ by first merging the two arrays of length 1, obtaining an array of length 2, merging it with the array of length 2, ... Plugging this bound into the bound on $\overline{I}_D(n)$ derived above yields $\overline{I}_D(n) = O(\log n)$.

There are other situations where the bounds stated in theorem 1 are overly pessimistic. If either $Q_S(n)$ or $P_S(n)/n$ grows fast, i.e. is of order at least n^ε for some $\varepsilon > 0$, then better bounds hold. Suppose for example that $Q_S(n) = \Theta(n^\varepsilon)$ for some $\varepsilon > 0$. Then (cf. the proof of theorem 1)

$$Q_D(n) = \sum_i Q_S(a_i 2^i)$$

$$= Q_S(2^{\lfloor \log n \rfloor}) \sum_{i=0}^{\lfloor \log n \rfloor} Q_S(a_i 2^i)/Q_S(2^{\lfloor \log n \rfloor})$$

$$= \Theta(n^{\varepsilon} \sum_{i=0}^{\lfloor \log n \rfloor} 2^{(i-\lfloor \log n \rfloor)\varepsilon}) = \Theta(n^{\varepsilon}) = \Theta(Q_S(n)).$$

Thus if either $Q_S(n)$ or $P_S(n)/n$ grows fast then the log n factor in the corresponding bound on $Q_D(n)$ or $\bar{I}_D(n)$ can be dropped.

The bound on insertion time derived in theorem 1 is amortized. In fact, the time required to process insertions fluctuates widely. More precisely, the 2^k-th insertion takes time $P_S(2^k)$, a non-trivial amount of time indeed. Theorem 2 shows that we can turn the amortized time bound into a worst case time bound without increasing the order of query time and space requirement.

Theorem 2: Let S be a static data structure for a decomposable searching problem. Then there is a semi-dynamic data structure D with

$$Q_D(n) = O(Q_S(n) \log n)$$

$$S_D(n) = O(S_S(n))$$

$$I_D(n) = O(P_S(n)/n \log n)$$

Proof: The basic idea is to use the construction of theorem 1, but to spread work over time. More precisely, whenever a structure of size 2^k has to be constructed we will spread the work over the next 2^k insertions. This will have two consequences. First, the structure will be ready in time to process an overflow into a structure of size 2^{k+1} and second, the time required to process a single insertion is bounded by $\sum_{k=0}^{\lfloor \log n \rfloor} P(2^k)/2^k = O(P(n)/n \log n)$. The details are as follows.

The dynamic structure D consists of bags $BA_0, BA_1, \ldots$. Each bag BA_i contains at most three blocks $B_i^u[1]$, $B_i^u[2]$ and $B_i^u[3]$ of size 2^i that are "in use" and at most one block B_i^c of size 2^i that is "under construction". More precisely, at any point of time blocks $B_i^u[j]$, $i \geq 0$, $1 \leq j \leq 3$, form a partition of set S, and static data structures are available for them. Furthermore, the static data structure for block B_i^c is under construction. Block B_i^c is the union of two blocks $B_{i-1}^u[j]$. We proceed as follows. As soon as two B_i^u's are available, we start building a B_{i+1}^c of size 2^{i+1} out of them. The work is spread over the next 2^{i+1} insertions, each time doing $P_S(2^{i+1})/2^{i+1}$ steps of the construction. When B_{i+1}^c is finished it becomes a B_{i+1}^u and the two B_i^u's are discarded. We have to show that there will be never more than three non-empty B_i^u's.

Lemma 1: When we complete a B_i^c and turn it into a block in use there are at most two non-empty B_i^u's.

Proof: Consider how blocks in BA_i develop. Consider the moment, say after the t-th insertion, when BA_i contains two B_i^u's and we start building a B_{i+1}^c out of them. The construction will be finished 2^{i+1} insertions later. Observe that BA_i got a second B_i^u because the construction of B_i^c was completed after the t-th insertion and hence B_i^c was turned into a B_i^u. Thus B_i^c was empty after insertion t and it will take exactly 2^i insertions until it is full again and hence gives rise to a third B_i^u and it will take another 2^i insertions until it gives rise to a fourth B_i^u. Exactly at this point ot time the construction of B_{i+1}^u is completed and hence two B_i^u's are discarded. Thus we can start a new cycle with just two B_i^u's completed. □

It follows from lemma 1 then there will be never more than three B_i^u's and one B_i^c for any i. Hence $S_D(n) = O(S_S(n))$, $Q_D(n) = O(Q_S(n) \log n)$ and $I_D(n) = \sum_{i=0}^{\lfloor \log n \rfloor} O(P_S(2^i)/2^i) = O(P_S(n)/n) \log n)$. □

The remarks following theorem 1 also apply to theorem 2. The "logarithmic" dynamization method described above has a large similarity to the binary number system. The actions following the insertion of a point into a dynamic structure of n elements are in complete analogy to adding a 1 to integer n written in binary. The main difference is the cost of processing a carry. The cost is $P(2^k)$ for processing a carry from the (k-1)-th to the k-th position in logarithmic dynamization, whilst it is O(1) in processing integers. The analogy between logarithmic dynamization and the binary number system suggests that other number systems give rise to other dynamization methods. This is indeed the case. For example, for every k one can uniquely write every integer n as

$$n = \sum_{i=1}^{k} \binom{a_i}{i}$$

with $i-1 \le a_i$ and $a_1 < a_2 < \ldots < a_k$ (Exercise 1). This representation gives rise to the k-binomial transformation. We represent a set S of n elements by k static structures, the i-th structure holding $\binom{a_i}{i}$ elements. Then $Q_D(n) = O(Q_S(n) \cdot k)$ and $\bar{I}_D(n) = O(k \cdot n^{1/k} P_S(n)/n)$. (Exercise 1). More generally, we have

Theorem 3: Let S be any static data structure for a decomposable searching problem and let k: $\mathbb{N} \to \mathbb{N}$ be any "smooth" function. Then there is a semi-dynamic data structure D such that

a) if $k(n) = O(\log n)$ then
$Q_D(n) = O(k(n)\ Q_S(n))$
$\bar{I}_D(n) = O(k(n)\ n^{1/k(n)}\ P_S(n)/n)$

b) if $k(n) = \Omega\ (\log n)$ then
$Q_D(n) = O(k(n)\ Q_S(n))$
$\bar{I}_D(n) = O(\log n/\log(k(n)/\log n)\ P_S(n)/n)$

Proof: The proof can be found in K. Mehlhorn, M.H. Overmars: Optimal Dynamization of Decomposable Searching Problems, IPL 12(1981), 93-98. The details on the definition of smoothness can be found there; functions like log n, log log n, log log log n, n , $(\log n)^2$ are smooth in the sense of theorem 3. The proof is outlined in exercise 2. □

Let us look at some examples. Taking k(n) = log n gives the logarithmic transformation (note that $n^{1/\log n} = 2$), k(n) = k yields an analogue to the k-binomial transformation, $k(n) = kn^{1/k}$ yields a transformation with $Q_D(n) = O(kn^{1/k}\ Q_S(n))$ and $\bar{I}_D(n) = O(k\ P_S(n)/n)$, a dual to the k-binomial transformation, and $k(n) = (\log n)^2$ yields a transformation with $Q_D(n) = O((\log n)^2 Q_S(n))$ and $\bar{I}_D(n) = O((\log n/\log\log n)\ P_S(n)/n)$. Again it is possible to turn amortized time bounds into worst case time bounds by the techniques used in the proof in theorem 2. The interesting fact about theorem 3 is that it describes exactly how far we can go by dynamization.

Theorem 4: Let h,k: $\mathbb{N}$ be functions. If there is a dynamization method which turns every static data structure S for any decomposable searching problem into a dynamic data structure D with $Q_D = k(nK\ Q_S(n)$ and

$\bar{I}_D(n) = h(n)\ P(n)/n$ then $h(n) = \Omega(OP(k)(n))$ where

$$OP(k)(n) = \begin{cases} \log n/\log(k(n)/\log n) & \text{if } k(n) > 2 \log n \\ k(n)^{1/k(n)} & \text{if } k(n) \le 2 \log n \end{cases}$$

Proof: The proof can be found in K. Mehlhorn: Lower Bounds on the Efficiency of Transforming Static Data Structures into Dynamic Data Structures, Math. Systems Theory 15,1-16(1981). □

Theorem 4 states that there is no way to considerably improve upon the results of theorem 3. There is no way to decrease the order of the query penalty factor (= $Q_D(n)/Q_S(n)$) without simultaneously increasing the order of the update penalty factor (= $\bar{I}_D(n)\cdot n/P_S(n)$) and vice versa. Thus all combinations of query and update penalty factor described in theorem 3 are optimal. Moreover, all optimal transformations can be obtained by an application of theorem 3.

Turning static into semi-dynamic data structures is completely solved by theorems 1 to 4. How about deletions? Let us consider the case of the sorted array first. At first sight deletions from sorted arrays are very costly. After all, we might have to shift a large part of the array after a deletion. However, we can do a "weak" deletion very quickly. Just mark the deleted element and search as usual. As long as only a few, let's say no more than 1/2 of the elements are deleted, search time is still logarithmic in the number of remaining elements. This leads to the following definition.

Definition: A decomposable searching problem together with its static structure S is deletion decomposable iff, whenever S contains n points, a point can be deleted from S in time $D_S(n)$ without increasing the query time, deletion time and storage required for S. □

We assume that $D_S(n)$ is non-decreasing. The Member problem with static structure sorted array is deletion decomposable with $D_S(n) = \log n$, i.e. we can delete an arbitrary number of elements from a sorted array of length n and still keep query and deletion time at log n. Of course, if we delete most elements then log n may be arbitrarily large as a function of the actual number of elements stored.

Theorem 5: Let searching problem Q together with static structure S be deletion decomposable. Then there is a dynamic structure D with

$$Q_D(n) = O(\log n \; Q_S(8n))$$
$$S_D(n) = O(S_S(8n))$$
$$\bar{I}_D(n) = O(\log n \; P_S(n)/n)$$
$$\bar{D}_D(n) = O(P_S(n)/n + D_S(n) + \log n)$$

Proof: The proof is a refinement of the construction used in the proof of theorem 1. Again we represent a set S of n elements by a partition $B_0, B_1, B_2, \ldots$. We somewhat relax the condition on the size of blocks B_i; namely, a B_i is either empty or $2^{i-3} < |B_i| \le 2^i$. Here $|B_i|$ denotes the actual number of elements in block B_i. B_i may be stored in a static data structure which was originally constructed for more points but never more than 2^i points. In addition, we store all points of S in a balanced tree T. In this tree we store along with every element a pointer to the block B_i containing the element. This will be useful for deletions. We also link all elements belonging to B_i, $i \ge 0$, in a linear list.

Since $|B_i| \ge 2^{i-3}$ there are never more than log n + 3 non-empty blocks. Also since the structure containing B_i might have been constructed for a set eight times the size we have $Q_D(n) \le Q_S(8n)(\log n + 3) = O(Q_S(8n) \log n)$. Also $S_D(n) \le \sum_i S_S(8|B_i|) = \sum_i S_S(8|B_i|)/8|B_i|) 8|B_i| \le S_S(8n)/8n \sum_i 8|B_i| = S_S(8n)$.

It remains to describe the algorithms for insertions and deletions. We need two definitions first. A non-empty block B_i is deletion-safe if $|B_i| \ge 2^{i-2}$ and it is safe if $2^{i-2} \le |B_i| \le 2^{i-1}$.

Insertions are processed as follows. After an insertion of a new point x we find the least k such that $1 + |B_0| + \ldots + |B_k| \le 2^k$. We build a new static data structure B_k for $\{x\} \cup B_0 \cup \ldots \cup |B_k|$ in time $P_S(2^k)$ and discard the structures for blocks $B_1, \ldots, B_k$. In addition we have to update the dictionary for a cost of $O(\log n + 2^k)$, log n for inserting the new point and 2^k for updating the information associated with the points in the new B_k. Note that time O(1) per element suffices if we chain all elements which belong to the same block in a linked list.

Lemma 1: Insertions build only deletion-safe structures.

Proof: This is obvious if $k = 0$. If $k > 0$ then $1 + |B_0| + \ldots + |B_{k-1}| > 2^{k-1}$ by the choice of k and hence the claim follows. □

The algorithm for deletions is slightly more difficult. In order to delete x we first use the dictionary to locate the block, say B_i, which contains x. This takes time $O(\log n)$. Next we delete x from B_i in time $D_S(2^i)$. If $|B_i| > 2^{i-3}$ or B_i is empty after the deletion then we are done. Otherwise, $|B_i| = 2^{i-3}$ and we have to "rebalance". If $|B_{i-1}| > 2^{i-2}$ then we interchange blocks B_i and B_{i-1}. This will cost $O(|B_i| + |B_{i-1}|) = O(2^i)$ steps for changing the dictionary; also B_i and B_{i+1} are safe after the interchange. If $|B_{i-1}| \le 2^{i-2}$ then we join B_{i-1} and B_i -- the resulting set has size at least 2^{i-3} and at most $2^{i-3} + 2^{i-2} \le 2^{i-1}$ -- and construct either a new B_{i-1} (if $|B_{i-1} \cup B_i| < 2^{i-2}$) or a new B_i (if $|B_{i-1} \cup B_i| \ge 2^{i-2}$). This will cost at most $P_S(2^i) + O(2^i) = O(P_S(2^i))$ time units; also B_{i-1} ans B_i are safe after the deletion.

Lemma 2: If a deletion from B_i causes $|B_i| = 2^{i-3}$ then B_{i-1} and B_i are safe after restructuring.

Proof: Immediate from discussion above. □

Lemma 3: $\bar{D}_D(n) = O(P_S(m)/m + D_S(m) + \log m,)$, here m is the maximal size of set S during the first n updates.

Proof: By lemmas 1 and 2 only deletion-safe blocks are built. Hence at least 2^{i-3} points have to be deleted from a Block B_i before it causes restructuring after a deletion. Hence the cost for restructuring is at most $8P_S(m)/m$ per deletion. In addition, log m time units are required to update the dictionary and $D_S(m)$ time units to actually perform the deletion. □

Lemma 4: $\bar{I}_D(n) = 4P_S(m)/m \log m$.

Proof: Consider any sequence of n insertions and deletions into an initially empty set. Suppose that we build a new B_k after the t_o-th update operation and that this update is an insertion. Then $B_o, B_1, \ldots, B_{k-1}$ are empty after the t_o-th update. Suppose also that the next time a B_ℓ, $\ell \ge k$, is constructed after an insertion is after the t_1-th update operation. Then immediately before the t_1-th update $1 + |B_o| + \ldots + |B_{k-1}| > 2^{k-1}$.

We will show that $t_1 - t_o \ge 2^{k-2}$. Assume otherwise. Then at most $2^{k-2} - 1$ points in $B_o \cup \ldots \cup B_{k-1}$ are points which were inserted after time t_o. Hence at least 2^{k-2} points must have moved from B_k into $B_o \cup \ldots \cup B_{k-1}$ by restructuring after a deletion. However, the restructuring algorithm constructs only deletion-safe structures and hence B_k can underflow ($|B_k| = 2^{k-3}$) at most once during a sequence of 2^{k-2} updates. Thus at most $2^{k-3} < 2^{k-2}$ points can move from B_k down to $B_o \cup \ldots \cup B_{k-1}$ between the t_o-th and the t_1-th update, a contradiction. Thus $t_1 - t_o \ge 2^{k-2}$.

In particular, a new B_k is constructed at most $n/2^{k-2}$ times after an insertion during the first n updates. The construction of a new B_k has cost $P_S(2^k)$ for building the B_k, $O(2^k)$ for updating the dictionary and log m for inserting the new point into the dictionary. Hence

$$\bar{I}_D(n) = O\Big(\Big(\sum_{k=o}^{\log m} (P_S(2^k)\, n/2^{k-2} + 2^k n/2^k) + n \log m\Big)/n$$

$$= O(\log m\, P_S(m)/m). \qquad \square\square$$

In our example (binary search on sorted arrays) we have $Q_S(n) = D_S(n) = \log n$ and $P_S(n) = n$ (cf. the remark following theorem 1). Hence $Q_D(n) = O((\log n)^2)$ and $\bar{I}_D(n) = \bar{D}_D(n) = O(\log n)$. There is something funny happening here. We need balanced trees to dynamize sorted arrays. This is not a serious objection. We could do away with balanced trees if we increase the time bound for deletes to $O((\log n)^2)$. Just use the Member instruction provided by the data structure itself to process a Delete.

Theorem 5 can be generalized in several ways. Firstly, one can turn amortized bounds into worst case bounds and secondly one can choose any of the transformations outlined in theorem 3. This yields.

Theorem 6: Let searching problem Q together with static structure S be deletion-decomposable, and let k(n) be any smooth function. Then there is a dynamic structure D with

$Q_D(n) = O(k(n)\ Q_S(n))$

$D_D(n) = O(\log n + P_S(n)/n + D_S(n))$

$$I_D(n) \begin{cases} O(\log n/\log(k(n)/\log n)\ P_S(n)/n & \text{if } k(n) = \Omega(\log n) \\ O(k(n)\ n^{1/k(n)}\ P_S(n)/n) & \text{if } k(n) = O(\log n) \end{cases}$$

Proof: The proof combines all methods described in this section so far. It can be found in M.H. Overmars/J.v. Leeuwen: Worst Case Optimal Insertion and Deletion Methods for Decomposable Searching Problems, IPL 12 (1981), 168-173. □

VII. 1.2 Weighting and Weighted Dynamization

In this section we describe weighting and then combine it with dynamization described in the previous section. This will give us dynamic weighted data structures for a large class of searching problems.

Definition: A searching problem $Q: T_1 \times 2^{T_2} \to T_3$ is monotone decomposable if there are functions $q: T_3 \to \{\underline{true}, \underline{false}\}$ and $\square : T_3 \times T_3 \to T_3$ such that for all $x \in T_1$, $S \subseteq T_2$ and all partitions A,B of S, i.e. $A \cup B = S$, $A \cap B = \emptyset$:

$Q(x,S) = \underline{if}\ q(Q(x,A))\ \underline{then}\ Q(x,A)\ \underline{else}\ \square\ (Q(x,A), Q(x,B))\ \underline{fi}$ □

Again, there are plenty of examples. Member is monotone decomposable with q the identity and □ = or. ε-diameter search, i.e. $Q((x,\varepsilon),S)$ = true if $\exists\ y \in S: \delta(x,y) \le \varepsilon$ is monotone decomposable with q the identity and □ = or. Also orthogonal range searching is monotone decomposable. Here $T_2 = \mathbb{R}^2$, T_1 = all rectangles with sides parallel to the axis and $Q(R,S) = (|R \cap S| \ge 1)$.

A query Q(x,S) is successful if there is a $y \in S$ such that $q(Q(x,\{y\}))$. If Q(x,S) is successful then any $y \in S$ with $q(Q(x,\{y\}))$ is called a witness for x (with respect to S). If y is a witness for x then $Q(x,S) = Q(x,\{y\} \cup (S-\{y\})) = \underline{if}\ q(Q(x,\{y\}))\ \underline{then}\ Q(x,\{y\})\ \underline{else}\ \ldots\ \underline{fi} = Q(x,\{y\})$.

Weighting is restricted to successful searches (but cf. exercise 6). Let $S = \{y_1,\ldots,y_n\} \subseteq T_2$ and let μ be a probability distribution on

$Suc = \{x \in T_1;\ Q(x,S)$ is successful$\}$. We define a reordering π of S and a discrete probability distribution $p_1,\ldots,p_n$ on S as follows. Suppose that $\pi(1),\ldots,\pi(k-1)$ and $p_1,\ldots,p_{k-1}$, are already defined. For $y_j \in S - \{y_{\pi(1)},\ldots,y_{\pi(k-1)}\}$ let $p(y_j) = \mu\ \{x \in Suc;\ y_j$ is a witness for x but none of $y_{\pi(1)},\ldots,y_{\pi(k-1)}$ is$\}$. Define $\pi(k) = j$ such that $p(y_j)$ is maximal and let $p_k = p(y_{\pi(k)})$. Then $p_1 \geq p_2 \geq \ldots \geq p_n$. We assume from now on that S is reordered such that π is the identity. Then p_k is the probability that y_k is witness in a successful search but none of $y_1,\ldots,y_{k-1}$ is.

<u>Theorem 7:</u> Let Q be any monotone decomposable searching problem and suppose that we have a static data structure with query time $Q_S(n)$, $Q_S(n)$ non-decreasing, for Q. Let $S = \{y_1,\ldots,y_n\} \subseteq T_2$, and let $\mu, p_1,\ldots, p_n$ be defined as above. Then there is a weighted data structure W for Q where the expected time of a successful search is at most $4\cdot\sum_i p_i\ Q_S(i) \leq 4\ \sum_i p_i\ Q_S(1/p_i)$.

<u>Proof:</u> Define $f: \mathbb{N}_0 \to \mathbb{N}_0$ by $f(0) = 0$ and $Q_S(f(i)) = 2^i$ for $i \geq 1$. Then $f(i)$ is increasing. We divide set S into blocks $B_1, B_2, \ldots$, where $B_i = \{y_j;\ f(i-1) < j \leq f(i)\}$. Then W consists of a collection of static data structures, one for each B_i. A query $Q(x,S)$ is answered by the following algorithm.

> $i \leftarrow 0$;
> <u>repeat</u> $i \leftarrow i + 1$ <u>until</u> $Q(x,B_i)$ is successful <u>od</u>;
> output $Q(x,B_i)$

The correctness of this algorithm is immediate from the definition of monotone decomposability. It remains to compute the expected query time of a successful query. Let $Suc_j = \{x \in T_1;\ y_j$ is a witness for x but $y_1,\ldots,y_{j-1}$ are not$\}$. Then $p_j = \mu(Suc_j)$. The cost of a query $Q(x,S)$ for $x \in Suc_j$ and $f(i-1) < j \leq f(i)$ is

$$\sum_{h=1}^{i} Q_S(f(h) - f(h-1)) \leq \sum_{h=1}^{i} Q_S(f(h)) = \sum_{h=1}^{i} 2^h \leq 4\cdot 2^{i-1}$$

$$= 4\cdot Q_S(f(i-1)) \leq 4\ Q_S(j).$$

Thus the expected cost of a successful query is $4\ \sum_j p_j\ Q_S(j) \leq$

$4 \sum_j p_j Q_S(1/p_j)$. The last inequality follows from $p_1 \ge p_2 \ge \dots$ and hence $1/p_j \ge j$. □

It is worthwhile to go through our examples at this point. Let us look at the member problem first. If we use sorted arrays and binary search then $Q_S(n) = \log n$ and hence the expected time for a successful search is $4 \sum_i p_i \log i \le 4 \sum_i p_i \log 1/p_i$. This bound relates quite nicely with the bounds derived in chapter III.4. on weighted trees. There we derived a bound of $\sum_i p_i \log 1/p_i + 1$ on the expected search time in weighted trees. Thus the bound derived by weighting is about four times as large as the bound derived by special methods. However, this is not the entire truth. The bound of 4 log i derived now on individual searches can sometimes be considerably better than the bound of $\log 1/p_i$ derived in III.4. (cf. exercise 3).

Binary search is not the only method for searching sorted arrays. If the keys are drawn from a uniform distribution then interpolation search is a method with O(log log n) expected query time. If the weights of keys are independent of key values then every block B_i is a random sample drawn from a uniform distribution and hence the expected time of a successful search is $O(\sum_i p_i \log\log i) = O(\sum_i p_i \log\log 1/p_i)$ (cf. exercise 4).

Let us finally look at orthogonal range searching in two-dimensional space. 2-dimensional trees (cf. VII.2.1. below) are a solution with $Q_S(n) = \sqrt{n}$. Then weighting yields an expected search time of $\sum_i p_i \sqrt{i}$.

The construction used in the proof of theorem 7 is optimal among a large class of algorithms, namely all algorithms which divide set S into blocks, construct static data structures for each block, and search through these blocks sequentially in some order independent of the query. Note first that the division into blocks should certainly be according to probability. If an element in the i-th block has higher probability than an element in the (i-1)-st block then interchanging the elements will reduce average search time. Thus a search with witness y_i (recall that S is reordered such that $p_1 \ge p_2 \ge \dots$) must certainly have cost $Q_S(n_1) + \dots + Q_S(n_k)$ where $n_1 + \dots + n_k \ge i$. If we assume that $Q_S(x+y) \le Q_S(x) + Q_S(y)$ for all x,y, i.e. Q is subadditive, then $Q(n_1) + \dots + Q_S(n_k) \ge Q_S(n_1 + \dots + n_k) \ge Q_S(i)$. Hence a search with witness y_i has cost at least $Q_S(i)$ under the modest assumption of subadditivity of Q_S. Thus the construction used in the proof of theorem 7 is optimal because it achieves query time $O(Q_S(i))$ for a search with witness y_i for all i.

We close this section by putting all concepts together. We start with a static data structure for a monotone and deletion decomposable searching problem Q and then use dynamization and weighting to produce a dynamic weighted data structure W for Q. W supports queries on a weighted set S, i.e. a set $S = \{y_1,\dots,y_n\}$ and weight function $w: S \to \mathbb{N}$, with query time depending on weight. It also supports operations Promote(y,a) and Demote(y,a), $y \in T_2$, $a \in \mathbb{N}$. Promote(y,a) increases the weight of element y by a and Demote(y,a) decreases the weight of y by a. Insert and Delete are special cases of Promote and Demote (cf. III.6. for the special case: Q = Member).

We obtain W in a two step process. In the first step we use dynamization and turn S into a dynamic data structure D with $Q_D(n) = Q_S(n) \log n$ and $U_D(n) = \max(I_D(n), D_D(n)) = O(P_S(n)/n \log n + D_S(n))$ (cf. theorem 6). $U_D(n)$ is the time to perform an update (either Insert or Delete) on D. In the second step we use weighting and turn D into a weighted structure W. More precisely, we define f by $Q_D(f(n)) = 2^n$ and store a set $S = \{y_1,\dots,y_n\}$ by cutting it into blocks as described in theorem 7, i.e. block B_i contains all y_j with $f(i-1) < j \le f(i)$. Here we assumed w.l.o.g. that $w(y_1) \ge w(y_2) \ge \dots \ge w(y_n)$. This suffices to support queries. A query in W with witness $y \in S$ takes time $O(Q_D(w(S)/w(y)))$ by theorem 7. Here $w(S) = \Sigma\ \{w(y); y \in S\}$.

We need to add additional data structures in order to support Promote and Demote. We store set S in a weighted dynamic tree (cf. III.6.) T. Every element in tree T points to the block B_i containing the element. Furthermore, we keep for every block B_i the weights of the points in B_i in a balanced tree. This allows us to find the smallest and largest weight in a block fast.

We are now in a position to describe a realization of Promote(y,a). We first use the weighted dynamic tree to find the block with contains y. This takes time $O(\log w(S)/w(y))$. Suppose that block B_i contains y. We then run through the following routine.

(1) delete y from block B_i; $h \leftarrow i$;
(2) <u>while</u> $w(y) + a >$ maximal weight of any element in B_h
(3) <u>do</u> delete the element with minimal weight from B_{h-1} and insert it into B_h;
(4) $h \leftarrow h - 1$
<u>od</u>
(5) insert y into B_h

The algorithm above is quite simple. If the weight of y is increased it might have to move to a block with smaller index. We make room by deleting it from the old block and moving the element with minimal weight down one block for every block. We obtain the following time bound for Promote(y,a):

$$O[\log(w(S)/w(y)) + \sum_{h=o}^{i} \log(f(h)) + U_D(f(h))]]$$

Here $\log w(S)/w(y)$ is the cost of searching for y in tree T and $\log f(h) + U(S(h))$ is the cost of inserting and deleting an element from a structure of size h and updating the balanced tree which holds the weights. Observing $U(n) \geq \log n$ for all n, $i \leq \lceil f^{-1}(w(S)/w(y)) \rceil$, and $U_D(\lceil f^{-1}(w(S)/w(y)) \rceil)) \geq U_D(w(S)/w(y)) \geq \log w(S)/w(y)$ this bound simplifies to

$$O(\sum_{0 \leq h \leq \lceil f^{-1}(w(S)/w(y)) \rceil} U_D(f(h)))$$

The algorithm for Demote(y,a) is completely symmetric. The details are left for the reader (exercise 5). We obtain exactly the same running time as for Promote, except for the fact that w(y) has to be replaced by the new weight $w(y) - a$.

<u>Theorem 8:</u> A static data structure with query time Q_S, preprocessing time P_S, and weak deletion time D_S for a monotone deletion decomposable searching problem can be extended to a dynamic weighted data structure W such that:

a) A query in weighted set S (with weight function $w: S \rightarrow \mathbb{N}$) with witness $y \in S$ takes time $O(Q_D(w(S)/w(y)))$. Here $Q_D(n) = Q_S(n) \log n$.

b) Promote(y,a) takes time

$$O\left(\sum_{0\le h\le \lceil f^{-1}(w(S)/w(y))\rceil} U_D(f(h))\right)$$

d) Demote(y,a) takes time

$$O\left(\sum_{0\le h\le \lceil f^{-1}(w(S)/(w(y)-a))\rceil} U_D(f(h))\right)$$

Proof: Immediate from the discussion above. □

Let us look again at binary search in sorted arrays as a static data structure for Member. Then $Q_S(n) = D_S(n) = O(\log n)$ and $P_S(n) = O(n)$ (cf. the remark following theorem 1). Hence $Q_D(n) = O((\log n)^2)$, $U_D(n) = O(\log n)$, and $f(n) = 2^{\sqrt{2}^n}$ A query for y with weight w(y) takes time $O((\log w(S)/w(y))^2)$, the square of the search time in weighted dynamic trees. Also Promote(y,a) takes time $U_D(f(\lceil f^{-1}(w(S)/w(y))\rceil)) = O(\log w(S)/w(y))$ and Demote(y,a) takes time $O(\log w(S)/(w(y)-a))$. This is the same order as in weighted dynamic tees. Of course, weighted dynamic trees are part of the data structure W considered here. Again (cf. theorem 5) this is not a serious objection. Since Member is the query considered here we can replace the use of weighted dynamic trees by a use of the data structure itself. This will square the time bounds for Promote and Demote. Also binary search in sorted arrays is not a very important application of weighted dynamization. In the important applications in this chapter the use of a weighted, dynamic dictionary is negligable with respect to the complexity of the data structure itself.

Dynamization and weighting are powerful techniques. They provide reasonably efficient dynamic weighted data structures very quickly which can then be used as a reference point for more special developments. Tuning to the special case under consideration is always necessary, as weighting and dynamization tend to produce somewhat clumsy solutions if applied blindly.

VII. 1.3. Order Decomposable Problems

In sections 1 and 2 we developed the theory of dynamization and weighting for decomposable searching problems and subclasses thereof. Although a large number of problems are decomposable searching problems, not all problems are. An example is provided by the inside the convex hull problem. Here we are given a set $S \subseteq \mathbb{R}^2$ and a point $x \in \mathbb{R}^2$ and are asked to decide whether $x \in CH(S)$ (= the convex hull of S). In general, there is no relation between CH(S) and CH(A), CH(B) for arbitrary partition A,B of S. However, if we choose the partition intelligently then there is a relation. Suppose that we order the points in S according to x-coordinate and split into sets A and B such that the x-coordinate of any point in A is no larger than the x-coordinate of any point in B. Then

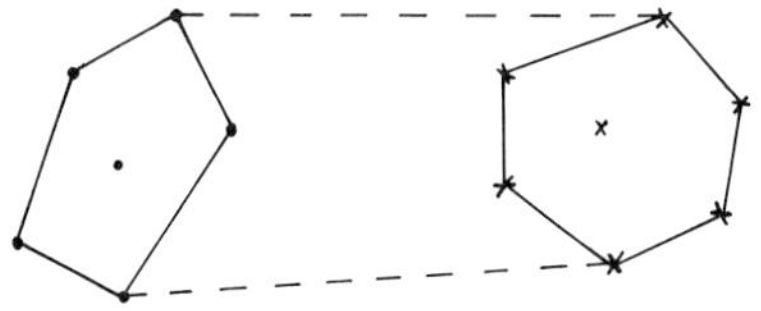

the convex hull of S can be constructed from CH(A) and CH(B) by adding a "low" and the "high" tangent. These tangents can be constructed in time O(log n) given suitable representations of CH(A) and CH(B). The details are spelled out in VIII.2. and are of no importance here. We infer two things from this observation. First, if we choose A and B such that $|A| = |B| = |S|/2$ and apply the same splitting process recursively to A and B then we can construct the convex hull in time $T(n) = 2T(n/2) + O(\log n) = O(n)$. This does not include the time for sorting S according to x-coordinate. The details are described in theorem 9. Second, convex hulls can be maintained efficiently. If we actually keep around the recursion tree used in the construction of CH(S) then we can insert a new point in S by going down a single path in this tree and redoing the construction along this path only. Since the path has length O(log n) and we spent time O(log n) in every node for merging convex hulls this will consume $O((\log n)^2)$ time units per insertion and deletion of a new point. The details are described in theorem 1o below.

<u>Definition:</u> Let T_1 and T_2 be sets and let $P: 2^{T_1} \to T_2$ be a set problem. P is <u>order decomposable</u> if there is a linear order < on T_1 and an operator $\square : T_2 \times T_2 \to T_2$ such that for every $S \subseteq T_1$, $S = \{a_1 < a_2 < \ldots < a_n\}$ and every i

$$P(\{a_1,\ldots,a_n\}) = \square(P(\{a_1,\ldots,a_i\}), P(\{a_{i+1},\ldots,a_n\}))$$

Moreover, $\square$ is computable in time $C(n)$ in this situation. $\square$

We assume throughout that $C(n)$ is non-decreasing. In the convex hull example we have $T_1 = \mathbb{R}^2$, T_2 = the set of convex polygons in $\mathbb{R}^2$ (suitable presented), $<$ is the lexicographic order on $\mathbb{R}^2$, $\square$ merges two convex hulls, and $C(n) = O(\log n)$. We outlined above that convex hulls can be constructed efficiently by divide and conquer. This is true in general for order decomposable problems.

<u>Theorem 9:</u> Let P be order decomposable. Then $P(S)$, $S \subseteq T_1$ can be computed in time $Sort(|S|) + T(|S|)$ where $Sort(n)$ is the time required to sort a set of n elements according to $<$, and $T(n) = T(\lfloor n/2 \rfloor) + T(\lceil n/2 \rceil) + O(C(n))$ for $n > 1$ and $T(1) = c$ for some constant c.

<u>Proof:</u> The proof is a straightforward application of divide and conquer. We first sort S in time $Sort(|S|)$ and store S in sorted order in an array. This will allow us to split S in constant time. Next we either compute $P(S)$ directly in constant time if $|S| = 1$ or we split S into sets A and B of size $\lfloor n/2 \rfloor$ and $\lceil n/2 \rceil$ respectively in constant time (if $S = \{a_1 < a_2 < \ldots < a_n\}$ then $A = \{a_1,\ldots,a_{\lfloor n/2 \rfloor}\}$ and $B = \{a_{\lfloor n/2+1 \rfloor},\ldots,a_n\}$), compute $P(A)$ and $P(B)$ in time $T(\lfloor n/2 \rfloor)$ and $T(\lceil n/2 \rceil)$ respectively by applying the algorithm recursively, and then compute $P(S) = \square\,(P(A),P(B))$ in time $C(n)$. Hence $T(n) = T(\lfloor n/2 \rfloor) + T(\lceil n/2 \rceil) + O(1) + C(n) = T(\lfloor n/2 \rfloor) + T(\lceil n/2 \rceil) + O(C(n))$. $\square$

Recurrence $T(n) = T(\lfloor n/2 \rfloor) + T(\lceil n/2 \rceil) + C(n)$ is easily solved for most C (cf. II.1.3.). In particular, $T(n) = O(n)$ if $C(n) = O(n^{\varepsilon})$ for some $\varepsilon < 1$, $T(n) = O(C(n))$ if $C(n) = \Theta(n^{1+\varepsilon})$ for some $\varepsilon > 0$, and $T(n) = O(C(n)(\log n)^{k+1})$ if $C(n) = \Theta(n(\log n)^k)$ for some $k \geq 0$.

The proof of theorem 9 reflects the close relation between order decomposable problems and divide and conquer. A non-recursive view of divide and conquer is to take any binary tree with $|S|$ leaves, to write the elements of S into the leaves (in sorted order), to solve the basic problems in the leaves and then to use operator $\square$ to compute P for larger subsets of S. What tree should we use? A complete binary tree will give us the most efficient algorithm, but any reasonably weight-balanced tree will not be much worse. If we want to support insertions and deletions this is exactly what we should do. So let D be a $BB[\alpha]$-tree with $|S|$ leaves for some α. (Exercise 9 shows that we <u>cannot</u> obtain the same efficiency by using (a,b)-trees, or AVL-trees, or ...). We store the elements of S in sorted order (according to <) in the leaves of D and use D as a search tree for S. What should we store in the internal nodes of D beside the search tree information? A first idea is to store P(S(v)) in node v where S(v) is the set stored in the leaves below v. P(S(v)) is easily computed bottom-up starting at the leaves and working towards the root. Not quite, if v has sons x,y and we compute $P(S(v)) = \square\,(P(S(x)), P(S(y)))$ then application of □ will in general destroy (the representation of) P(S(x)) and P(S(y)). Making a copy of P(S(x)) and P(S(y)) before applying □ might cost a lot more than C(|S(v)|) and is therefore excluded. A different strategy is called for.

We store P(S(r)) only in the root r. In internal nodes $v \neq r$ we store two things. First, the sequence a(v) of actions executed to compute □ applied to P(S(x)) and P(S(y)). This sequence has length O(C(n)). Second, the piece $P^*(S(v))$ which is leftover from P(S(v)) when P(S(father(v))) is computed by applying □ to P(S(v)) and P(S(brother(v)). We call tree D augmented by this additional information an augmented tree.

<u>Lemma 1:</u> An augmented tree D for set S has space requirement T(|S|) and can be constructed in time Sort(|S|) + T(|S|) where T(n) =

$$\max_{\alpha \le \beta \le 1-\alpha} [T(\beta n) + T((1-\beta)n) + O(C(n))].$$

<u>Proof:</u> The recursion for T(n) follows from the fact that $\alpha \le |S(x)|/|S(v)|,\ |S(y)|/|S(v)| \le 1 - \alpha$ for any node v with sons x,y in a BB[α]-tree D. The space bound follows since at most t storage cells can be used in t time units for any t. □

The remark following theorem 9 also applies to lemma 1. In particular, $T(n) = O(n)$ if $C(n) = O(n^{\varepsilon})$ for some $\varepsilon < 1$, and ... . The space bound stated in lemma 1 is usually overly pessimistic. One does not use a new storage cell every time unit in general.

We will next describe how to insert into and delete from an augmented tree. We describe insertion in detail and leave deletion for the reader, deletion being very similar to insertion. Let a be a new point which we want to insert in S. Let D be an augmented tree for S. We first use D as a search tree. This will outline a path p down tree D. Let

$p = v_0, v_1, \ldots, v_k$ with v_0 being the root. We walk down this path and reconstruct the $P(S(v_i))$'s as we walk down. More precisely, we start in root v_0 with $P(S(v_0))$ in our hands and use the sequence of actions $a(v_0)$ stored in v_0 and the leftover pieces $P^*(S(v_1))$ and $P^*(S(brother(v_1)))$ stored in v_1 and its brother to reconstruct $P(S(v_1))$ and $P(S(brother(v_1)))$ by running $a(v_0)$ backwards. This will take time $O(C(|S(v_0)|)$. Next we repeat this process with $v_1, \ldots, v_k$. At the end we have reconstructed $P(S(brother(v_i)))$, $1 \le i \le k$, and $P(S(v_k)))$.

Lemma 2: Let D be an augmented tree for S, $|S| = n$ and let $p = v_0, \ldots, v_k$ be a path from the root v_0 to a leaf. Then $P(S(brother(v_i)))$, $1 \le i \le k$, and $P(S(v_k))$ can be reconstructed in time $O(C(n)\log n)$.

Proof: The algorithm outlined above has running time

$$\sum_i C(|S(v_i)|) \le \sum_i C(n(1-\alpha)^i) \le \sum_i C(n) = O(C(n)\log n)$$

since the depth of the tree is $O(\log n)$ and $|S(v_i)| \le n(1-\alpha)^i$. □

If $C(n) = \Theta(n^\varepsilon)$ for some $\varepsilon > 0$ then $\sum_i C(n(1-\alpha)^i) = n^\varepsilon \sum_i (1-\alpha)^{i\cdot\varepsilon} = O(n^\varepsilon) = O(C(n))$. In (a,b)-trees this improved claim is not true in general, i.e. there are (a,b)-tree where reconstruction along a path has cost $O(n^\varepsilon \log n)$ if $C(n) = \Theta(n^\varepsilon)$ (cf. exercise 9).

The remainder of the insertion algorithm is now almost routine. We insert the new point a, walk back to the root and merge the P's as we go along. More precisely, we first compute $P(a)$, then merge it with $P(S(v_k))$, then with $P(S(brother(v_k)))$, ... The time bound derived in lemma 2 applies again except that we forgot about rotations and double-rotations. Suppose that we have to rotate at node v_i.

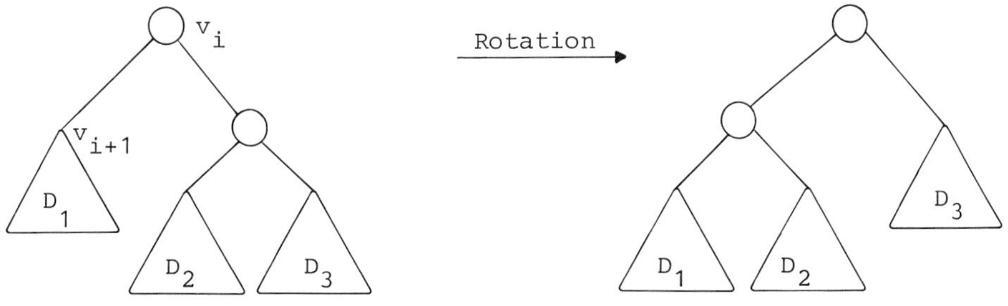

and assume that v_{i+1} is the root of subtree D_1. As we walk back to the root we have already computed $P(S(v_{i+1}))$. Also $P(S(brother(v_{i+1})))$ is available from the top-down pass. We reverse the construction at brother(v_{i+1}) and thus compute P for the roots of D_2 and D_3. It is then easy to compute P for the relevant nodes after the rotation. Double rotations are treated similarly, the details are left to the reader. Also it is obvious that the time bound derived in lemma 2 does still apply, because rotations and double rotations at most require to extend the reconstruction process to a constant vicinity of the path of search. We summarize in:

Theorem 1o: Let P be an order decomposable problem with merging operator □ computable in time C(n). Then P can be dynamized such that insertions and deletions take time $O(C(n))$ if $C(n) = \Theta(n^\varepsilon)$ for $\varepsilon > 0$ and time $O(C(n)\log n)$ otherwise.

Proof: By the discussion above. The time bound follows from lemma 2 and the remark following it. □

In the convex hull problem we have $C(n) = O(\log n)$. Thus we can maintain convex hulls under insertions and deletions with time bound $O(\log n)^2)$ per update. More examples of order decomposable problems are discussed in exercises 1o-12.

VII. 2. Multi-dimensional Searching Problems

This section is devoted to searching problems in multi-dimensional space. Let U_i, $0 \le i < d$, be an ordered set and let $U = U_o \times U_1 \times \ldots \times U_{d-1}$. An element $x = (x_o,\ldots,x_{d-1}) \in U$ is also called point or record or d-tuple; it is customary to talk about points in geometric applications and about records in database applications. No such distinction is made here. Components x_i are also called coordinates or attributes.

A region searching problem is specified by a set $\Gamma \subseteq 2^U$ of regions in U. The problem is then to organize a static set $S \subseteq U$ such that queries of the form "list all elements in $S \cap R$" or "count the number of points in $S \cap R$" can be answered efficiently for arbitrary $R \in \Gamma$. We note that region searching problems are decomposable searching problems and hence the machinery developed in VII.1.1. and VII.1.2. applies to them. Thus we automatically have dynamic solutions for region searching problems once a static solution is found.

We address four types of region queries.

a) Orthogonal Range Queries: Here Γ is the set of hypercubes in U , i.e.

$$\Gamma_{OR} = \{R;\ R = [\ell_0,h_0] \times [\ell_1,h_1] \times \ldots \times [\ell_{d-1},h_{d-1}] \text{ where } \ell_i,h_i \in U_i \text{ and } \ell_i \le h_i\}.$$

b) Partial Match Queries: Here Γ is the set of degenerated hypercubes where every side is either a single point or all of U_i, i.e.

$$\Gamma_{PM} = \{R;\ R = [\ell_0,h_0] \times [\ell_1,\ h_1] \times \ldots \times [\ell_{d-1},h_{d-1}] \text{ where } \ell_i,h_i \in U_i \text{ and either } \ell_i = h_i \text{ or } \ell_i = -\infty \text{ and } h_i = +\infty \text{ for every } i\}$$

If $\ell_i = h_i$ then the i-th coordinate is specified, otherwise it is unspecified.

c) Exact Match Queries: Here Γ is the set of singletons, i.e.

$$\Gamma_{EM} = \{R;\ R = \{x\} \text{ for some } x \in U\}$$

d) Polygon Queries: Polygon queries are only defined for $U = \mathbb{R}^2$. We have

$$\Gamma_P = \{R;\ R \text{ is a simple polygonal region in } \mathbb{R}^2\}$$

Exact match queries are not really a new challenge; however the three other types of problems are. There seems to be no single data structure doing well on all of them and we therefore describe three data structures: d-dimensional trees, polygon trees, and range trees. d-dimensional trees and polygon trees use linear space and solve partial match queries and polygon queries in time $O(n^{\varepsilon})$ where ε depends on the type of the problem. Range trees allow us to solve orthogonal range queries in time $O((\log n)^d)$ but they use non-linear space $O(n(\log n)^{d-1})$. In fact they exhibit a tradeoff between speed and space.

In view of chapter III these results are disappointing. In one-dimensional space we could solve a large number of problems in linear space and logarithmic time, in higher dimensions all data structures mentioned above either use non-linear space or use "rootic" time $O(n^{\varepsilon})$ for some ε, $0 < \varepsilon < 1$. Section VII.2.3. is devoted to lower bounds and explains this behaviour. We show that partial match requires rootic time when space is restricted to its minimum and that orthogonal range queries and polygon queries either require large query or large update time. Large update time usually points to large space requirement, although it is not conclusive evidence.

VII. 2.1 D-dimensional Trees and Polygon Trees

We start with d-dimensional trees and show that they support partial match retrieval and orthogonal range queries with rootic search time. However, they do not do well for arbitrary polygon queries. A discussion of why they fail for polygon retrieval leads to polygon trees.

D-dimensional trees are a straightforward, yet powerful extension of one-dimensional search trees. At every level of a dd-tree we split the set according to one of the coordinates. Fairness demands that we use the different coordinates with the same frequency; this is most easily achieved if we go through the coordinates in cyclic order.

Definition: Let $S \subseteq U_o \times \dots \times U_{d-1}$, $|S| = n$. A dd-tree for S (starting at coordinate i) is defined as follows

1) if $d = n = 1$ then it consists of a single leaf labelled by the unique element $x \in S$.

2) if $d > 1$ or $n > 1$ then it consists of a root labelled by some element $d_i \in U_i$ and three subtrees $T_<$, $T_=$, and $T_>$. Here $T_<$ is a dd-tree starting at coordinate $(i+1) \bmod d$ for set $S_< = \{x \in S;\ x = (x_o,\dots,x_{d-1})$ and $x_i < d_i\}$, $T_>$ is a dd-tree starting at coordinate $(i+1) \bmod d$ for set $S_> = \{x \in S;\ x = (x_o,\dots,x_{d-1})$ and $x_i > d_i\}$ and $T_=$ is a $(d-1)$-dimensional tree starting at coordinate $i \bmod (d-1)$ for set $S_= = \{(x_o,\dots,x_{i-1},x_{i+1},\dots,x_{d-1});\ x = (x_o,\dots,x_{i-1},d_i,x_{i+1},\dots,x_d) \in S\}$ □

The figure below shows a 2d-tree for set S = {(1,II), (1,III), (2,I), (2,III), (3,I), (3,II)} starting at coordinate 0.

Here $U_o = U_1 = \{1,2,3\}$

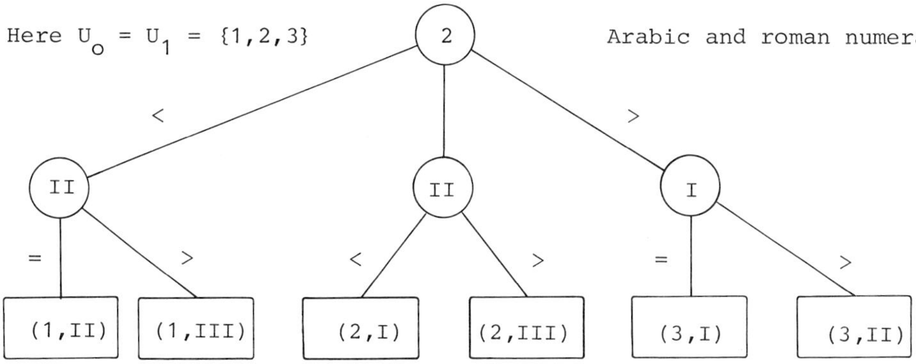

Arabic and roman numerals are used to distinguish coordinates. It is very helpful to visualize 2d-trees as subdivisions of the plane. The root node splits the plane by vertical line $x_o = 2$ into three parts:

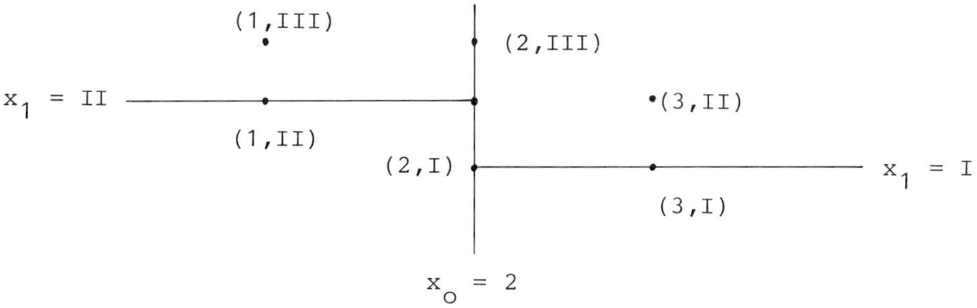

left halfplane, right halfplane and the line itself. The left son of the root then splits the left halfplane by horizontal line $x_1 = 2$, ...

The three sons of a node v in a dd-tree do not all have the same quality. The root of $T_=$ (the son via the = - pointer) represents a set of one smaller dimension. In general we will not be able to bound the size of this set. The roots of $T_<$ and $T_>$ (the sons via the <-pointer and the >-pointer) represent sets of the same dimension but generally smaller size. Thus every edge of a dd-tree reduces the complexity of the set represented: either in dimension or in size. In 1d-trees, i.e. ordinary search trees, only reductions in size are required.

It is clear how to perform exact match queries in dd-trees. Start at the root, compare the search key with the value stored in the node and follow the correct pointer. Running time is proportional to the height of the tree. Our first task is therefore to derive bounds on the height of dd-trees.

<u>Definition:</u> a) Let T be a dd-tree and let v be a node of T. Then S(v)

is the set of leaves in the subtree with root v, d(v) is the depth of node v, and sd(v), the number of <-pointers and >-pointers on the path from the root to v, is the strong depth of v. Node x is a proper son of node v if it is a son via a <- or >-pointer.

b) A dd-tree is <u>ideal</u> if $|S(x)| \le |S(v)|/2$ for every node v and all proper sons x of v.]

Ideal dd-trees are a generalization of perfectly balanced 1d-trees.

<u>Lemma 1:</u> Let T be an ideal dd-tree for set S, $|S| = n$.

a) $d(v) \le d + \log n$ for every node v of T

b) $sd(v) \le \log n$ for every node v of T

<u>Proof:</u> a) follows from b) and the fact that at most d =-pointers can be on the path to any node v. Part b) is immediate from the definition of ideal tree. □

<u>Theorem 1:</u> Let $S \subseteq U = U_0 \times \ldots \times U_{d-1}$, $|S| = n$.

a) An exact match query in an ideal dd-tree for S takes time $O(d + \log n)$.

b) An ideal dd-tree for S can be constructed in time $O(n(d + \log n))$.

<u>Proof:</u> a) Immediate from lemma 1,a.

b) We describe a procedure which constructs ideal dd-trees in time $O(n(d + \log n))$. Let $S_0 = \{x_0; (x_0,\ldots,x_{d-1}) \in S\}$ be the <u>multi</u>-set of 0-th coordinates of S. We use the linear time median algorithm of II.4. to find the median d_0 of S_0. d_0 will be the label of the root. Then clearly $|S_<| \le |S|/2$ and $|S_>| \le |S|/2$ where $S_< = \{x \in S; x_0 < d_0\}$ and $S_> = \{x \in S; x_0 > d_0\}$. We use the same algorithm recursively to construct dd-tree for $S_<$ and $S_>$ (starting at coordinate 1) and a (d-1)-dimensional tree for $S_=$. This algorithm will clearly construct an ideal dd-tree T for S. The bound on the running time can be seen as follows. In every node v of T we spend $O(|S(v)|)$ steps to compute the median of a set of size $|S(v)|$. Furthermore, $S(v) \cap S(w) = \emptyset$ if v and w are nodes of the same depth and hence $\sum_{d(v)=k} |S(v)| \le n$ for every k,

$0 \le k < d + \log n$. Thus the running time is bounded by

$$\sum_{v \text{ node of } T} O(|S(v)|) = O(\sum_{0 \le k \le d+\log n} \sum_{d(v)=k} |S(v)|) = O(n(d + \log n))$$
□

Insertions into dd-trees are a non-trivial problem. A first idea is to use an analogue to the naive insertion algorithm into one-dimensional trees. If x is to be inserted into tree T, search for x in T until a leaf is reached and replace that leaf by a small subtree with two leaves. Of course, the tree will not be ideal after the insertion in general. We might define weight-balanced dd-trees to remedy the situation, i.e. we choose some parameter α, say $\alpha = 1/4$, and require that $|S(x)| \le (1-\alpha)|S(v)|$ for every node v an all proper sons x of v. This is a generalization of BB[α]-trees. Two problems arise. Both problems illustrate a major difference between one-dimensional and multi-dimensional searching. The first problem is that although theorem 1 is true for weight-balanced dd-trees, theorems 2 and 3 below are false, i.e. query time in near-ideal dd-trees may have a different order than query time in ideal trees. More precisely, partial match in ideal 2d-trees has running time $O(\sqrt{n})$ but it has running time $\Omega(n^{1/\log 8/3}) = \Omega(n^{0.706})$ in weight-balanced dd-trees, $\alpha = 1/4$. (Exercise 14). Thus weight balanced dd-trees are only useful for exact match queries. A second problem is that weight-balanced dd-trees are hard to rebalance. Rotations are of no use since splitting is done with respect to different coordinates on different levels. Thus it is impossible to change the depth of a node as rotations do. There is a way out. Suppose that we followed path $p = v_0, v_1, \ldots$ to insert point x. Let i be minimal such that v_i goes out of balance by the insertion. Then rebalance the tree by replacing the subtree rooted at v_i by an ideal tree for set $S(v_i)$. This ideal tree can be constructed in time $O(m(d + \log m))$ where $m = |S(v_i)|$. Thus rebalancing is apparently not as simple and cheap as in one-dimensional trees. The worst case cost for rebalancing after an insertion is clearly $O(n(d + \log n))$ since we might have to rebuild the entire tree. However, amortized time bounds are much better as we will sketch now. We use techniques developed in III.5.1. (in particular in the proof of theorem 4). We showed there (lemmas 2 and 3 in the proof of theorem 4), that the total number of rebalancing operations caused by nodes v with $1/(1-\alpha)^i \le |S(v)| \le 1/(1-\alpha)^{i+1}$ during the first n insertions (and deletions) is $O(n(1-\alpha)^i)$. A rebalancing operation caused by such a node has cost $O((1-\alpha)^{-i}(d+1))$ in weight-balanced dd-trees. Hence the total cost of restructuring a weight-balanced dd-tree during a sequence of n insertions and deletions is

$$\sum_{0 \le i \le O(\log n)} O(n(1-\alpha)^{i}(1-\alpha)^{-i}(d+i)) = O(n \log n(d + \log n))$$

Thus the amortized cost of an insertion or deletion is $O(\log n(d + \log n))$. The details of this argument are left for exercise 13.

Dynamization (cf. VII.1.) also gives us dynamic dd-trees with $O((d + \log n) \log n))$ insertion and deletion time. Query time for exact match queries is $O((d + \log n) \log n)$ which is not quite as good as for weight-balanced dd-trees. However, dynamization has one major advantage. The time bounds for partial match and orthogonal range queries (theorem 2,3 and 4 below) stay true for dynamic dd-trees.

It is about time that we move to partial match queries. Let $R = [\ell_0,h_0] \times \ldots \times [\ell_{d-1},h_{d-1}]$ with $\ell_i = h_i$ or $\ell_i = -\infty$, $h_i = +\infty$ be a partial match query. If $\ell_i = h_i$ then the i-th coordinate is called specified. We use s to denote the number of specified coordinates. The algorithm for partial match queries is an extension of the exact match algorithm. As always we start searching in the root. Suppose that the search reached node v. Suppose further that we split according to the i-th coordinate in v and that key d_i is stored in v. If the i-th coordinate is specified in query R, then the search proceeds to exactly one son of v, namely the son via the <-pointer if $\ell_i = h_i < d_i$, the son via the =-pointer if $\ell_i = h_i = d_i$, and ... . If the i-th coordinate is unspecified in query R then the search proceeds to all three sons of v. Once we reach a leaf, we return it if it belongs to region R. The correctness of this algorithm is obvious. The running time of this algorithm heavily depends on set S. We treat a favourable special case first: invertible sets.

<u>Definition</u>: $S \subseteq U = U_0 \times U_1 \times \ldots \times U_{d-1}$ is <u>invertible</u> if for all $x = (x_0,\ldots,x_{d-1}) \in S$, $y = (y_0,\ldots y_{d-1}) \in S$: $x_i = y_i$ for some i implies $x = y$. □

A set is invertible if all projection functions are injective when restricted to S.

<u>Theorem 2:</u> Let T be an ideal dd-tree for invertible set $S \subseteq U = U_0 \times U_1 \times \ldots \times U_{d-1}$. Then a partial match query with $s < d$ specified components takes time $O(d\ 2^{d-s}\ n^{1-s/d})$.

Proof: Let T' be the subtree of T consisting of all nodes visited by the search. It suffices to show that the number of nodes of T' is bounded by $O(d2^{d-s}\ n^{1-s/d})$. A node of T' is called branching if it has a proper son and non-branching otherwise. Since S is invertible all descendants of non-branching nodes are non-branching. Hence all branching nodes can be reached by following <- and >-pointers only. A branching node of T' is a proper branching node if it has two proper sons. We claim that there are at most $2^{\lceil(\log n)/d\rceil(d-s)}$ proper branching nodes in T'. This follows from the fact that at most (d-s) out of any d consecutive nodes on any path through T' are proper branching nodes, because only d-s out of d consecutive nodes split according to unspecified components. Also $d(v) = sd(v) \le \log n$ for all branching nodes. Hence there are at most $\lceil(\log n)/d\rceil(d-s)$ proper branching nodes on any path through T' and thus the bound follows. It remains to count the improper branching nodes and the non-branching nodes in T'. Again consider any path through T'. Then there can be at most d consecutive nodes which are not proper branching nodes and hence the total number of nodes of T' is $O(d2^{\lceil(\log n)/d\rceil(d-s)}) = O(d2^{d-s}\ n^{(d-s)/d}) = O(d2^{d-s}\ n^{1-s/d})$. □

The behaviour of the partial match algorithm on general sets is harder to analyse. Let us look at an example first. Let $U_i = \mathbb{R}$, $0 \le i < d$, and let $S = \{0\}^k \times \{0,\ldots,m-1\}^{d-k}$ for some m and k. Then $|S| = m^{d-k}$. Consider first partial match query R_1 which specifies the first s = k coordinates as being 0 and leaves the remaining coordinates unspecified. Then the answer to the query is the entire set S and hence the running time of any algorithm must be at least linear. Consider next partial match query R_2 which specifies the first s = k+1 coordinates a being 0 and leaves the remaining coordinates unspecified. Then the query is "equivalent" to a partial match query in a d-k = d-s+1 dimensional set with one specified coordinate. In view of theorem 2 we therefore cannot hope to do better than $O(n^{1-1/(d-s+1)})$ time units. This is indeed the bound.

Theorem 3: Let T be an ideal dd-tree for S, $|S| = n$. Then a partial match query with s specified components takes time $O(f(d,d-s)n^{\max(1/2,1-1/(d-s+1))} + (d+1)|A|)$. Here A is the set of answers to the query and f(d,d-s) is some function increasing in both arguments. f is independent of T and S.

Proof: Let T' be the subtree of T consisting of all nodes visited in the search. We split the set of nodes of T' into three classes which we count seperately. A node is a tertiary node (belongs to the third class) if all descendants of v belong to A, i.e. if $S(v) \subseteq A$. The number of tertiary nodes is clearly bounded by $(d+1)|A|$. A non-tertiary node is a primary node if it is reachable without using an =-pointer. All other nodes of T' are secondary nodes. We will show that the number of primary and secondary nodes is bounded by $f(d,d-s)n^{\max(1/2,1-1/d-s+1))}$ for some siutable function f. The proof is by induction on d-s and for fixed d-s by induction on s and n.

If $d = s$ then partial match is equivalent to exact match and the claim follows from theorem 1,a. So let us assume $d > s$. If $s = 0$ then all the nodes are tertiary and the claim is trivial. This leaves the case $d > s \geq 1$. If n is small then the claim is certainly true by suitable choice of $f(d,d-s)$.

The primary nodes are easy to count. We have shown in the proof of theorem 2 that their number is $O(d2^{d-s}\, n^{1-s/d})$. It remains to count the secondary nodes.

We group the secondary nodes into maximal subtrees. If v is the root of such a subtree then v is reached via an =-pointer and there is no other =-pointer on the path to v. Thus $sd(v) = d(v)-1$ and $|S(v)| \leq n/2^{sd(v)} \leq 2n/2^{d(v)}$. Also there can be at most $2^{\lceil j/d \rceil (d-s)}$ such nodes v with $d(v) = j$. This follows from the fact that all nodes on the path to v are primary nodes and hence at most $\lceil j/d \rceil (d-s)$ of these nodes can be proper branching nodes; cf. the proof of theorem 2.

In the subtree with root v we have to compute a partial match query on a (d-1)-dimensional set with s' specified components. Here $s' = s$ or $s' = s-1$. Also, $s' \geq 1$. Note that v and all its descenadants are tertiary nodes if $s' = 0$. By induction hypothesis there are at most $f(d-1,d-1-s')\ m^{\max(1/2,1-1/d-1-s'+1)}$ non-tertiary nodes visited in the subtree with root v where $m = |S(v)|$. For the reminder of the argument we have to distinguish two cases, $s = 1$ and $s \geq 2$.

<u>Case 1</u>: $s \geq 2$.
Since $d-1-s' \leq d-s$, f is increasing, and $d-s \geq 1$ we conclude that the number of non-tertiary nodes below v is bounded by $f(d-1,d-s)\ m^{1-1/(d-s+1)}$.

We finish the proof by summing this bound for all roots of maximal subtrees of secondary nodes. Let RT be the set of such roots. Then

$$\sum_{v\in RT} f(d-1,d-s) \ |S(v)|^{1-1/(d-s+1)}$$

$$\le f(d-1,d-s) \sum_{j\ge 1} 2^{\lceil j/d\rceil (d-s)} (2n/2^j)^{1-1/(d-s+1)}$$

$$\le (2n)^{1-1/(d-s+1)} f(d-1,d-s)\ 2^{(d-s)} \sum_{j\ge 1} [2^{(d-s)/d-1+1/(d-s+1)}]^j$$

$$\le (f(d,d-s) - d2^{d-s}) n^{1-1/(d-s+1)}$$

for suitable choice of $f(d,d-s)$. Note that $(d-s)/d-1+1/(d-s+1) = -s/d + 1/(d-s+1) < 0$ for $2 \le s \le d$. Adding the bound for the number of primary nodes proves the theorem.

Case 2: $s = 1$

Define RT as in case 1. Since $s \ge s' \ge 1$ we have $s' = 1$. Consider the case $d = 2$ first. Then the query below v degenerates to an exact match query in a one-dimensional set, and hence there are at most $d + \log |S(v)|$ non-tertiary nodes below v. Summing this bound for all nodes in RT we obtain

$$\sum_{v\in RT} (d + \log |S(v)|)$$

$$\le \sum_{j=1}^{d+\lceil \log n\rceil} 2^{\lceil j/d\rceil (d-s)} (d + \log (2n/2^j))$$

$$\le 2^{(d-s)} \sum_{k=-d}^{\lceil \log n\rceil -1} 2^{(\lceil \log n\rceil -k)/d} (d+1+k)$$

where we used the substitution $k = \lceil \log n\rceil - j$

$$\le 2^{(d-s+1)} n^{1/d} \sum_{k=-d}^{\lceil \log n\rceil} (d+1+k)/2^{k/d}$$

$$\le (f(2,1) - d2^{d-s})\ n^{\max(1/2,1-1/(d-s+1))}$$

Theorem 3 shows that d-dimensional trees support partial match queries with rootic running time. In particular if $d = 2$ and $s = 1$ then the running time is $O(\sqrt{n} + |A|)$ even in the case of general sets. We will see in section VII.4.1. that this cannot be improved without increasing storage. However it is trivial to improve upon this result by using $O(d!n)$ storage.

Let $S \subseteq U = U_0 \times \ldots \times U_{d-1}$. For any of the d! possible orderings of the attributes build a search tree as follows:

Order S lexicographically and build a standard one-dimensional search tree for S. A partial match query with s specified components is then easily answered in time $O(d \log n + |A|)$. Assume w.l.o.g. that the first s attributes are specified, i.e. $R = [\ell_0, h_0] \times \ldots \times [\ell_{d-1}, h_{d-1}]$ with $\ell_i = h_i$ for $0 \le i < s$ and $\ell_i = -\infty$, $h_i = +\infty$ for $s \le i < d$. Search for key $(\ell_0, \ldots, \ell_{s-1}, -\infty, \ldots, -\infty)$ in tree T corresponding to the natural order of attributes. This takes time $O(d \log n)$. The answer to the query will then consist of the next $|A|$ leaves of T in increasing order. Thus logarithmic search time can be obtained at the expense of increased storage requirement. For small d, say $d = 2$, this approach is feasible and in fact we use it daily. After all, there is a German-English and an English-German dictionary and no one ever complained about the redundancy in storage.

Another remark about theorem 3 is also in order at this place. The running time stated in theorem 3 is for the enumerative version of partial match retrieval: "Enumerate all points in $S \cap R$". A simpler version is to count only $|S \cap R|$. If we store in every node v of a dd-tree the cardinality $|S(v)|$ of $S(v)$ then the counting version of partial match retrieval has running time $O(f(d,d-s)\, n^{\max(1/2,1-1/(d-s+1))})$; cf. exercise 15.

The next harder type of queries are orthogonal range queries. Let $R = [\ell_0, h_0] \times \ldots \times [\ell_{d-1}, h_{d-1}]$ be a hypercube in $U_0 \times \ldots \times U_{d-1}$. Before we can explain the search algorithm we need to introduce one more concept; the range of a node. We can associate a hypercube Reg(v) with every node of a dd-tree in a natural way, namely $Reg(v) = \{x \in U_0 \times \ldots \times U_{d-1}$; an exact match query of x goes through v$\}$.

by suitable choice of $f(2,1)$; recall that $d = 2$ and $s = 1$. Adding the bound for the number of primary nodes proves the theorem.

It remains to consider the case $d \geq 3$. We infer from the induction hypothesis that the number of non-tertiary nodes below $v \in RT$ is bounded by $f(d-1,d-2)|(S(v)|^{1-1/(d-1)}$ in this case. Summing this bound for all $v \in RT$ we obtain

$$\sum_{v \in RT} f(d-1,d-2)|S(v)|^{1-1/(d-1)}$$

$$\leq \sum_{j=1}^{d+\lceil \log n \rceil} f(d-1,d-2) \quad 2^{\lceil j/d \rceil (d-1)} (2n/2^j)^{1-1/(d-1)}$$

$$\leq (2n)^{1-1/(d-1)} f(d-1,d-2)\ 2^{d-1} \sum_{j=1}^{d+\lceil \log n \rceil} [2^{(d-1)/d + 1/(d-1)-1}]^j$$

$$\leq (2n)^{1-1/(d-1)} f(d-1,d-2)\ c\ (2n)^{1/((d-1)d)}$$

where c is a constant depending on d

$$\leq (f(d,d-1)-d2^{d-s})\ n^{1-1/d}$$

by suitable choice of $f(d,d-1)$. Adding the bound for the number of primary nodes proves the theorem. □

Reg(v) is easily determined recursively. If v is the root then Reg(v) = $U_0 \times \dots \times U_{d-1}$. If v is a son of w, say via the <-pointer, and w is labelled with $d \in U_i$ then $\mathrm{Reg}(v) = \mathrm{Reg}(w) \cap \{(x_0,\dots,x_{d-1});\ x_i < d\}$.

We are now in a position to describe the search algorithm for orthogonal range queries. Let R be the query hypercube. As always we start the search in the root r. Then $R \cap \mathrm{Reg}(r) \neq \emptyset$. Assume for the inductive step that the search has reached node v with $R \cap \mathrm{Reg}(v) \neq \emptyset$. Then the search proceeds to all sons x of v with $R \cap \mathrm{Reg}(x) \neq \emptyset$. There is at least one such son and all sons with that property can be found in time O(1). Finally, if v is a leaf then we output the leaf if $v \in R$.

We analyse the running time of this algorithm only in two dimensions and leave the higher-dimensional case to the reader. The proof for the higher-dimensional case is completely analogous but somewhat more tedious.

<u>Theorem 4:</u> Let T be an ideal 2d-tree for $S \subseteq U_0 \times U_1$, $|S| = n$. Then an orthogonal range query takes time $O(d4^d\, n^{1-1/d} + d|A|)$ where A is the set of answers.

<u>Proof:</u> Let $R = [\ell_0,h_0] \times [\ell_1,h_1]$ be a rectangle in $U_0 \times U_1$ and let T' be the subtree of all nodes visited when answering query R. Observe first that $\mathrm{Reg}(v) \cap R \neq \emptyset$ iff v is visited in the search. Observe next that $\mathrm{Reg}(v) \subseteq R$ implies $S(v) \subseteq A$. Hence the number of nodes v of T' with $\mathrm{Reg}(v) \subseteq R$ is certainly bounded by $d|A|$. It remains to count the number of nodes v with $\mathrm{Reg}(v) \cap R \neq \emptyset$ and $\mathrm{Reg}(v) - R \neq \emptyset$. Let N be the set of such nodes. If $v \in N$ then there must be one of the four bounding line segments of R which intersects Reg(v) but does not contain Reg(v). Thus $|N| \le 4 \cdot t$ where t is the maximal number of nodes such that Reg(v) intersects with but is not contained in any fixed horizontal or vertical line segment.

<u>Claim:</u> Let T be an ideal 2d-tree with n leaves and let $L = \{(x,y) \in U_0 \times U_1;\ x = \ell_0,\ \ell_1 \le y \le h_1\}$ be a vertical line segment. Then the number of nodes v such that Reg(v) intersects L but is not contained in L is $O(\sqrt{n})$.

<u>Proof:</u> A node v of T is called a primary node if there is no =-pointer on the path from the root to v. Let P_d be the number of primary nodes v

of depth k such that Reg(v) intersets L (but is not contained in L). Then $P_0 \le P_1 \le 2$ and $P_{k+2} \le 2P_k$. Inequality $P_{k+2} \le 2P_k$ follows from the observation that a vertical line can intersect at most two of the four Regions R_1, R_2, R_3, R_4 associated with the proper grandsons of any node v. This fact is illustrated in the diagram. From $P_0 \le P_1 \le 2$ and $P_{k+2} \le 2P_k$ we infer $P_k \le 2 \cdot 2^{k/2}$.

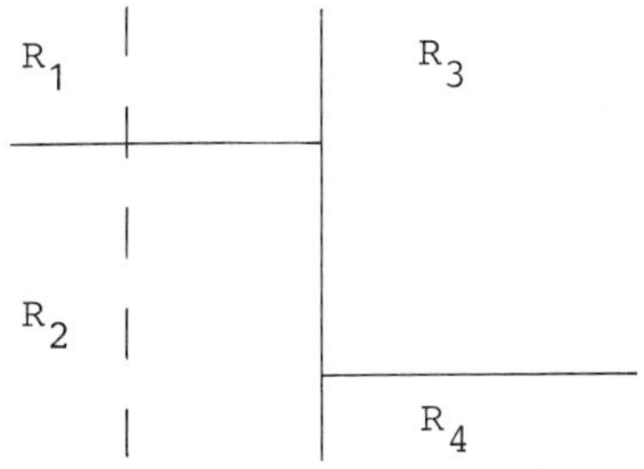

Next consider any primary node v of depth k such that Reg(v) intersects L. Let x be the son of v via the =-pointer. Then $S(x) \subseteq S(v)$ and hence $|S(x)| \le |S(v)| \le n/2^k$. Also there are at most 2 log S(x) descendants w of x such that Reg(w) intersects L but is not contained in L. This can be seen as follows.

The tree with root x is a one-dimensional search tree for a set of nodes which lie either on a horizontal or a vertical line. If they lie on a horizontal line then the search below x follows exactly one path down the tree. If they lie on a vertical line (which then must be the line $x = \ell_o$) then Reg(w) intersects L but is not contained in L iff either $\ell_1 \in \text{Reg}(w)$ or $h_1 \in \text{Reg}(w)$. The set of nodes w with $\ell_1 \in \text{Reg}(w)$ ($h_1 \in \text{Reg}(w)$) form a path in the tree with root x. Thus there are at most 2 log |S(x)| descendants w of x such that Reg(w) intersects L but is not contained in L.

Pulting everything together we have shown that the number of nodes v in T such that Reg(v) intersects L but is not contained in L is at most

$$\sum_{0 \le k \le \log n} 2 \cdot 2^{k/2}\, 2 \log n/2^k = 4\sqrt{n} \sum_{0 \le k \le \log n} 2^{(k-\log n)/2} (\log n - k)$$

$$= O(\sqrt{n})$$

This proves the claim and the theorem. □□

So in two dimensions (d = 2) 2d-trees support even orthogonal range queries with running time $O(\sqrt{n})$. Can we stretch the use of dd-trees even further? If we want to talk about more complicated queries we have to make some additional assumptions about the U_i's. Let us assume for the sequel that $d = 2$ and $U_o = U_1 = \mathbb{R}$. It is then natural to generalize orthogonal range queries to arbitrary polygon queries. In a database which contains persons stored by income and number of children we might ask for all persons where the income exceeds \$ 1000 plus \$ 200 for every child. This query describes a triangle in two-space. Do 2d-trees support efficient polygon searching? The answer is no (cf. exercise 18) and the reason for this can be seen clearly in the proof of theorem 4. A line segment in arbitrary position can intersect the regions associated with all four proper grandsons of a node v and in fact can intersect the regions of all nodes of a 2d-tree. What can we do to overcome this difficulty? First, every node v of the tree should define a subdivision of Reg(v) such that any line segment can intersect only a proper subset of the regions in the subdivision. One possible way of achieving this is to divide Reg(v) into four regions by two straight lines. Then any

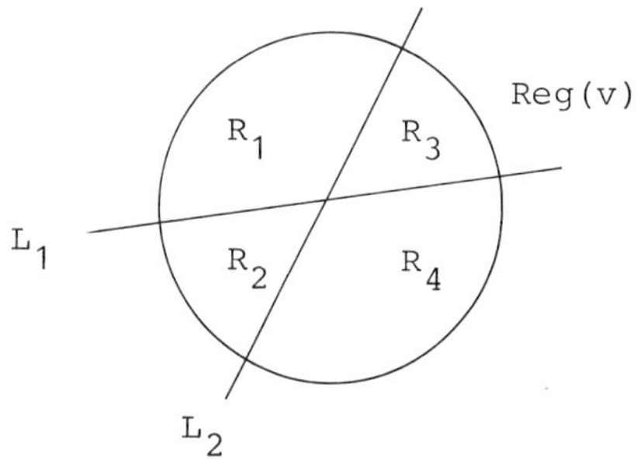

straight line can intersect at most three of the four regions R_1, R_2, R_3, R_4 plus a number of the "one-dimensional" regions defined by the lines themselves. With the notation of the claim in the proof of theorem 4 we would obtain $P_{k+1} \le 3P_k$ and hence could hope for a search time of $3^{\log n/\log 4} = n^{\log 3/\log 4} \le n^{0.8}$. Note that the depth of the tree will be log n/log 4 because we divide into four pieces in every step. However, we have to be careful. The argument above is only correct if the depth of the tree is indeed log n/log 4, i.e. if the tree is ideal. Thus lines L_1 and L_2 above have to be chosen such that $|R_i \cap S(v)| \le \lceil |S(v)|/4 \rceil$ for $1 \le i \le 4$. The following lemma shows that this is always possible.

Lemma 2: Let $S \subseteq \mathbb{R}^2$, $|S| = n$ and let n_1, n_2, n_3, n_4 be such that $n_1 + n_2 + n_3 + n_4 \le n$. If L_1 is a line such that $n_1 + n_2$ points of S are on one side of L_1 and $n_3 + n_4$ points of S are on the other side of L_1 then there is a line L_2 such that the four open regions R_1, R_2, R_3 and

R_4 defined by L_1 and L_2 contain at most n_1,n_2,n_3,n_4 points of S respectively. Also L_2 can be computed in time $O(n^2)$.

<u>Proof:</u> For any point P on L_1 let f(P) be the minimum angle α between L_1 and L_2 such that regions R_1,R_2 contain at most n_1,n_2 points respectively. Then f(P) is a continuous function of P. Also $\lim_{P\to-\infty} f(P) = 0$ and $\lim_{P\to+\infty} f(P) = \pi$

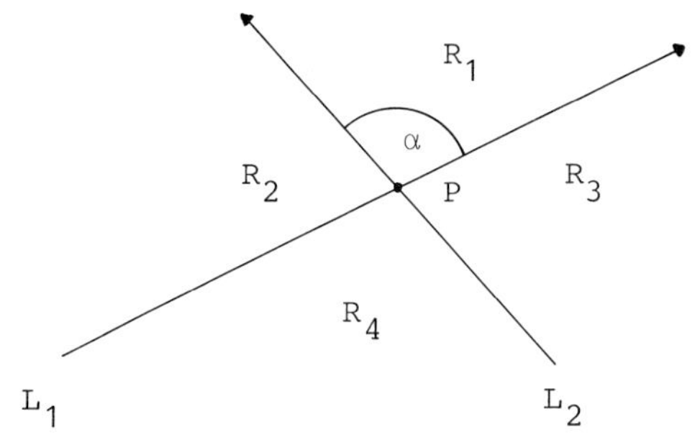

Similarly define g(P) be the minimum angle α between lines L_1 and L_2 such that regions R_3,R_4 contain at most n_3 and n_4 points respectively. Then g(P) is a continuous function of P and $\lim_{P\to-\infty} g(P) = \pi$ and $\lim_{P\to+\infty} g(P) = 0$. Hence there is a point P such that f(P) = g(P). Then P and f(P) define line L_2 with the desired property. This shows the existence of line L_2. It also shows that line L_2 can be assumed to go through two points of S. Thus there are only n^2 candidates for L_2.

Let $K_1,\ldots,K_k$, $k = n(n-1)/2$ be the lines defined by all pairs of points of S ordered according to their intersection point with L_1. Let P_i be the point of intersection of K_i and L_1. Consider any fixed P_i. Express all points of S in polar coordinates with respect to P_i and find among the $n_1 + n_2$ points "above" L_1 two points which define the n_1-th and $(n_1 + 1)$-th largest angle between line L_1 and the line defined by P_i and the point. This can be done in time $O(n_1 + n_2)$ by the linear time selection algorithm II.4.. In this way we have computed a sector S_1 through which line L_2 must go if it were to intersect L_1 in P_i. In a similar way we compute sector S_2 based on the points "below" L_2. If there is a line which goes through sectors S_1 and S_2 then we are done and have found line L_2.

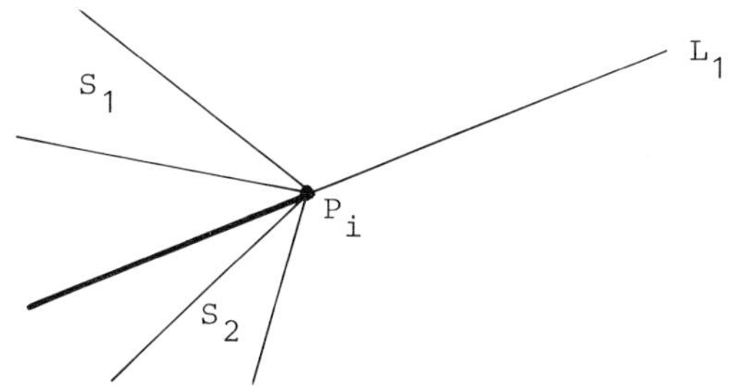

If sectors S_1 and S_2 do not have a line in common (as it is the case in the diagram) then we can restrict the search to one of the halflines defined by L_1 and P_i. In the diagram this halfline is shown bold. We summarize. In time $O(n)$ we can either determine that L_2 goes through P_i or exclude one of the half-lines defined by L_1 and P_i.

This suggests that we can use binary search to find line L_2. We first compute in time $O(n^2)$ lines $K_1,\dots,K_k$ and points $P_1,\dots,P_k$. Next we find the median point of $P_1,\dots,P_k$ in time $O(n^2)$. Then we are either done or can restrict the search to $k/2$ points. This decision takes time $O(n)$. Thus line L_2 can be found in $O(\log n^2)$ iterations and the cost of the i-th iteration is $O(k/2^i + n)$. Total cost is thus $O(n^2)$. □

Lemma 2 and the preceding discussion lead to:

Definition: a) A 4-way polygon tree T for set $S \subseteq \mathbb{R}^2$, $|S| = n$ is defined as follows: If set S is collinear then T is an ordinary one-dimensional search tree for S. If set S is not collinear then T consists of a root r and six subtrees. There are two lines L_1 and L_2 associated with r and there is one subtree for each of the six sets $S \cap R_1$, $S \cap R_2$, $S \cap R_3$, $S \cap R_3$, $S \cap L_1$, $S \cap L_2$. Here R_1,R_2,R_3,R_4 are the four open regions defined by lines L_1 and L_2.

b) A 4-way polygon tree T is ideal if for every node v of T and son x of v: If S(v) is collinear then $|S(x)| \le \lceil |S(v)|/2 \rceil$ and if S(v) is not collinear and x is one of the four sons corresponding to regions $R_1,\dots,R_4$ then $|S(x)| \le \lceil |S(v)|/4 \rceil$. □

Theorem 5: Let $S \subseteq \mathbb{R}^2$, $|S| = n$.

a) An ideal 4-way polygon tree for set S can be constructed in time $O(n^2)$.

b) If T is an ideal 4-way polygon tree for S and R is a polygonal region with s sides then $A = R \cap S$ can be computed in time $O(s \cdot n^{\log 3/\log 4} + |A|)$.

Proof: a) If S is collinear then an ideal tree can be constructed in time $O(n \log n)$, the time required to sort S. If S is not collinear then lines L_1,L_2 dividing the plane into four open regions containing at most $\lceil n/4 \rceil$ points of S each can be computed in time $O(n^2)$ by lemma 2. Hence T(n), the time required to build a 4-way polygon tree for n points, satisfies the recurrence

$$T(n) \le O(n^2 + n \log n) + 4T(\lceil n/4 \rceil)$$

Thus $T(n) = O(n^2)$ by theorem II.1.3.4..

b) Let R be a polygonal region with s sides. We triangulate R (cf. section VIII.4.2) and compute $R' \cap S$ seperately for each of the s-1 triangles R' in the triangulation. It therefore suffices to show that $A' = R' \cap S$ can be computed in time $O(n^{\log 3/\log 4} + |A'|)$ for a triangle R'. This shows that we may assume w.l.o.g. that R is a triangle.

We describe the search algorithm next. The search reaches only nodes v of the polygon tree T' with $Reg(v) \cap R \ne \emptyset$. Let us assume inductively that when the search reaches node v we have determined $Reg(v) \cap e_i$, $1 \le i \le 3$, for each of the three sides of triangle R. Note that Reg(v) is convex and hence $Reg(v) \cap e_i$ is a line segment. Also note that $Reg(v) \subseteq R$ iff $Reg(v) \cap e_i = \emptyset$ for $1 \le i \le 3$ or $Reg(v) \subseteq e_i$ for some i (recall that we assume $Reg(v) \cap R \ne \emptyset$). If $Reg(v) \subseteq R$ then the search proceeds to all six (two, if Reg(v) is one-dimensional) sons of v and clearly $Reg(w) \subseteq R$ for all sons w of v.

The case $Reg(v) \not\subseteq R$ is slightly more complicated. Let w be a son of v. Then $Reg(w) = Reg(v) \cap C$ where C is either a line or a cone-shaped region, as indicated in the daigram below

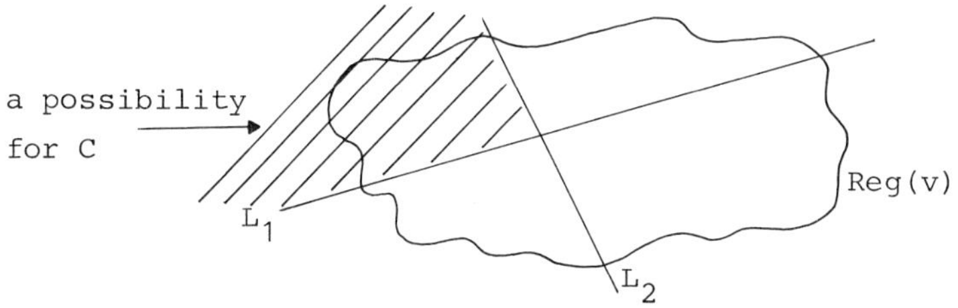

Then $e_i \cap Reg(w) = (e_i \cap Reg(v)) \cap (e_i \cap C)$ and hence $e_i \cap Reg(w)$ is readily computed for $1 \le i \le 3$. If $e_i \cap Reg(w) \ne \emptyset$ for some i then certainly $R \cap Reg(w) \ne \emptyset$ and hence the search proceeds to node w. If $e_i \cap Reg(w) = \emptyset$ for all i then the search proceeds to node w iff $c \in R$ where $c = L_1 \cap L_2$ is the intersection of the two lines which are associated with node v. Note that $Reg(w) \subseteq R$ if $c \in R$ and that $Reg(w) \cap R = \emptyset$ if $c \notin R$.

It remains to estimate the complexity of this algorithm. Let T' be the subtree of all nodes visited in the search. It suffices to bound the number of nodes of T'. If $v \in T'$ then $Reg(v) \cap R \neq \emptyset$ and hence either $Reg(v) \subseteq R$ or $Reg(v) \cap R \neq \emptyset$ and $Reg(v) - R \neq \emptyset$. In the former case we have $S(v) \subseteq A$ and hence the number of nodes with $Reg(v) \subseteq R$ is $O(|A|)$. In the latter case there must be an edge e of region R such that $Reg(v) \cap e \neq \emptyset$ but Reg(v) is not contained in e. It therefore suffices to bound t wherer t is the maximal number of nodes v such that Reg(v) intersects but is not contained in any fixed line segment L.

<u>Claim:</u> $t \leq O(n^{\log 3/\log 4})$.

<u>Proof:</u> Let L be any line segment. Let P_k be the number of primary nodes v, i.e. Reg(v) is not a line segment, of depth k such that $Reg(v) \cap L \neq \emptyset$. Then $P_1 = 1$ and $P_{k+1} \leq 3P_k$ since L can intersect at most 3 of the four open regions associated with the sons of any primary node. Thus $P_k \leq 3^k$.

Let v be a primary node of depth k. Then v has two sons x and y which are not primary nodes. We have $S(x) \cup S(y) \subseteq S(v)$ and $|S(v)| \leq \lceil n/4^k \rceil$ since T is an ideal 4-way tree. The argument used in the proof of theorem 4 shows that there are at most $2 \log S(x)$ descendants w of x such that Reg(w) intersects L but is not contained in L. The analogous claim holds true for y. Putting both bounds together we conclude that

$$t \leq \sum_{0 \leq k \leq \log n/\log 4} 4 \cdot P_k \log \lceil n/4^k \rceil$$

$$\leq 3^{\log n/\log 4} \sum_{0 \leq k \leq \log n/\log 4} 8 \cdot 3^{k-\log n/\log 4} (\log n - 2k)$$

$$= O(3^{\log n/\log 4}) = O(n^{\log 3/\log 4})$$

□

Can we improve upon 4-way polygon trees? Exercise 19 shows that one can always cut any set of n non-collinear points into 2j open regions such that any straight line will intersect at most j + 1 out of these regions and such that no region contains more than $\lceil n/2j \rceil$ points. Here $j \geq 2$ is any integer. Polygon trees based on subdivisions of this form allow us to do polygon retrieval in time $O(n^{\log(j+1)/\log 2j})$. The exponent is minimized for j = 3 and is 0.77 in this case.

VII. 2.2 Range Trees and Multidimensional Divide and Conquer

D-dimensional trees support orthogonal range queries with linear space O(n) and rootic time $O(n^{1-1/d})$. Range trees will allow us to trade space for time. More specifically, we can obtain polylogarithmic query time at the expense of non-linear storage or rootic query time $O(n^{\varepsilon d})$ and space $O((1/\varepsilon)^d\ n)$ for any $\varepsilon > 0$. Also range trees support insertions and deletions in a natural way.

Orthogonal range queries in one-dimensional space are particularly simple. If $S \subseteq U_0$ then any ordinary balanced tree will do. We can compute $S \cap [\ell_0,h_0]$ by running down two paths in the tree (the search path according to ℓ_0 and the search path according to h_0) and then listing all leaves between those paths. Thus query time is $O(\log n + |A|)$ and space requirement is O(n). The counting version, i.e. to compute $|S \cap [\ell_0,h_0]|$, only takes time O(log n) if we store in every node the number of leaf descendants. This comes from the fact that we have to add up at most O(log n) counts to get the final answer, namely the counts of all nodes which are sons of a node on one of the two paths and which lie between the two paths. It is very helpful at this point to interpret search trees geometrically. We can view a search tree as a hierarchical decomposition of S into intervals, namely sets $Reg(v) \cap S$. The decomposition process is balanced, i.e. we try to split set S evenly at every step, and it is continued to the level of singleton sets. The important fact is that for every conceivable interval $[\ell_0,h_0]$ we can decompose $S \cap [\ell_0,h_0]$ into only O(log n) pieces from the decomposition. Hence the O(log n) query time for counting $S \cap [\ell_0,h_0]$.

This idea readily generalizes into two-dimensional (and d-dimensional space). Let $S \subseteq U_0 \times U_1$. We first project S onto U_0 and build a balanced decomposition of the projection as described above. Suppose now that we have to compute $S \cap ([\ell_o,h_o] \times [\ell_1,h_1])$. We can first decompose $[\ell_o,h_o]$ into $O(\log n)$ intervals. For each of these intervals we only have to solve a one-dimensional problem. This we can do efficiently if we also have data structures for all these one-dimensional problems around. Each one-dimensional problem will cost $O(\log n)$ steps and so total run time is $O((\log n)^2)$. However, space requirement goes up to $O(n \log n)$ because every point has to be stored in log n data structures for one-dimensional problems. The details are as follows.

Definition: Let $S \subseteq U_o \times U_1 \times \ldots \times U_{d-1}$ and let $P = \{i_1,\ldots,i_k\} \subseteq \{0,\ldots,d-1\}$. Then $p(S,P) = \{(x_{i_1},\ldots,x_{i_k});\ x \in S\}$ is the projection of S onto coordinates P. If $P = \{i\}$ then we also write $p_i(S)$ instead of $p(S,\{i\})$. □

Definition: Let $m \in \mathbb{N}$ and let $\alpha \in (1/4, 1-\sqrt{2}/2)$. m is a slack parameter and α is a weight-balancing parameter. A d-fold range tree for multiset $S \subseteq U_o \times U_1 \times \ldots \times U_{d-1}$, $|S| = n$ is defined as follows. If $d = 1$ then T is any BB[α]-tree for S. If $d > 1$ then T consists of a BB[α]-tree T_o for $p_o(S)$. T_o is called the primary tree. Furthermore, for every node v of T_o with $\text{depth}(v) \in m\mathbb{Z}$ there is an auxiliary tree $T_a(v)$. $T_a(v)$ is a (d-1)-fold tree for set $p(S(v), \{1,\ldots,d-1\})$. Here S(v) is the set of $x = (x_o,\ldots,x_{d-1}) \in S$ such that leaf x_o is descendant of v in T_o. □

The precise definition of range trees differs in two respects from the informal discussion. First, we do not insist on perfect balance. This will slightly degrade query time but will allow us to support insertions and deletions directly. Also we introduced slack parameter m which we can use to control space requirement and query time.

Lemma 1: Let $S_m(d,n)$ be the space requirement of a d-fold tree with slack parameter m for a set of n elements. Then $S_m(d,n) = O(n(c \log n/m)^{d-1})$ where $c = 1/\log(1/(1-\alpha))$.

Proof: Note first that the depth of a BB[α]-tree with n leaves is at most c log n. Thus every point $x \in S$ is stored in the primary tree, in at most c log n/m primary trees of auxiliary trees, in at most $(c \log n/m)^2$ primary trees of auxiliary-auxiliary trees, ... Thus the total number of nodes (counting duplicates) stored in all trees and hence space requirement is $O(n \sum_{0 \le i \le d-1} ((c \log n)/m)^i) = O(n((c \log n)/m)^{d-1})$. □

We will use two examples to illustrate the results about range trees: $m = 1$ and $m = \varepsilon \log n$ for some $\varepsilon > 0$. If $m = 1$ then $S_m(d,n) = O(n(c \log n)^{d-1})$ and if $m = \varepsilon \log n$ then $S_m(d,n) = O((c/\varepsilon)^{d-1} n)$.

Lemma 2: Ideal d-fold range trees, i.e. $|S(x)| \leq \lceil S(v)/2 \rceil$ for all nodes v (primary or otherwise) and sons x of v, can be constructed in time $O(d\, n \log n + n\, ((\log n)/m)^{d-1})$. Here m is the slack parameter.

Proof: We start by sorting S d-times, once according to the o-th coordinate, once according to the first coordinate, ... This will take time $O(d\, n \log n)$. Let $T_m(d,n)$ be the time required to build an ideal d-fold tree for a set of n elements if S is sorted according to every coordinate. We will show that $T_m(d,n) = O(n((\log n)/m)^{d-1})$. This is clearly true for $d = 1$ since $O(n)$ time units suffice to build an ideal $BB[\alpha]$-tree from a sorted list. For $d > 1$ we construct the primary tree in time $O(n)$ and we have to construct auxiliary trees of sizes $n_1,\dots,n_t$. We have $n_1 + \dots + n_t \leq n(\log n)/m$ since every point is stored in $(\log n)/m$ auxiliary trees. Note that the primary tree has depth $\log n$ since it is ideal. Hence

$$\begin{aligned} T_m(d,n) &= O(n) + \sum_i T_m(d-1,n_i) \\ &= O(n) + O(\sum_i n_i (\log n/m)^{d-2}) \\ &= O(n(\log n/m)^{d-1}) \end{aligned}$$ □

If $m = 1$ then ideal d-fold trees can be constructed in time $O(n(\log n)^{\max(1,d-1)})$ and if $m = \varepsilon \log n$ then they can be constructed in time $O(d\, n \log n)$.

Lemma 3: Let $Q_m(d,n)$ be the time required to answer a range query in a d-fold tree for a set of n elements. Then $Q_m(d,n) = O(\log n(c(2^m/m)\log n)^{d-1} + |A|)$. Here c and m are as in lemma 1.

Proof: The claim is obvious for $d = 1$. So let $d > 1$ and let $R = [\ell_o,h_o] \times \dots \times [\ell_{d-1},h_{d-1}]$ be an orthogonal range query. We search for ℓ_o and h_o in the primary tree T_o. This will define two paths of length at most $c \log n$ in T_o. Consider one of these paths. There are at most c log n nodes v such that v is a son of one of the nodes on the paths and v is between two paths. Every such node represents a subset of points of S whose O-th coordinate is contained in $[\ell_o, h_o]$. We have to solve (d-1)-dimensional problems on these subsets. Let v be any such node and let $v_1, \ldots, v_t$ be the closest descendants of v such that m divides depth(v_i). Then $t \le 2^{m-1}$ and auxiliary trees exist for all v_i's. Also we can compute $S \cap R$ by forming the union of $S(v_i) \cap ([\ell_1 \times h_1] \times \ldots \times [\ell_{d-1}, h_{d-1}])$ over all v_i'. Since the number of v_i's is bounded by $2c((\log n)/m)2^{m-1}$ we have:

$$Q_m(d,n) \le c(2^m/m) \log n \; Q_m(d-1,n) + |A|$$

This proves lemma 3. □

If m = 1 then $Q_m(d,n) = O(\log n(2\ c \log n)^{d-1} + |A|)$ and if $m = \varepsilon \log n$ then $Q_m(d,n) = O(\log n(c/\varepsilon)^{d-1}\ n^{\varepsilon d})$.

We close our discussion of range trees by discussing insertion and deletion algorithms. We will show that the amortized cost of an insertion or deletion is polylogarithmic. Suppose that point $x = (x_o, x_1, \ldots, x_{d-1})$ has to be inserted (deleted). We search for x_o in the primary tree and insert or delete it whatever is appropriate. This has cost O(log n). Furthermore, we have to insert x into (delete x from) at most (c log n)/m auxiliary trees, $((c \log n)/m)^2$ auxiliary-auxiliary trees, ... Thus the total cost of an insertion or deletion is $O(\log n(c \log n/m)^{d-1})$ not counting the cost for rebalancing. Rebalancing is done as follows. For every (primary or auxiliary or auxiliary-auxiliary or ...) tree into which x is inserted (from which x is deleted) we find a node v of minimal depth which goes out of balance. We replace the subtree rooted at v by an ideal d'-fold tree for the set S(v) of descendants of v. Here d' = d if v is a node of the primary tree of an auxiliary tree, ... ; d-d' is called the level of node v. This will take time $O(d'\ q \log q + q(\log q/m)^{d'-1})$ by lemma 2 where $q = |S(v)|$. Rebalancing on the last level (d' = 1) is done differently. On level 1 we use the standard algorithm for rebalancing BB[α]-trees.

Worst case insertion/deletion cost is now easily computed. It is $O(d^2\ n \log n + n(\log n/m)^{d-1})$, essentially the cost of constructing a new d-fold tree from scratch. Amortized insertion/deletion cost is much smaller as we demonstrate next. We use theorem III.5.1.4. to obtain a polylogarithmic bound on amortized insertion/deletion cost.

Note first that a point x is inserted into (deleted from) at most $((c \log n)/m)^{d-1}$ trees of level 1 for a (worst case) cost of $O(\log n)$ each. Thus total rebalancing cost on level 1 is $O(\log n(c \log n/m)^{d-1})$.

We next consider levels ℓ, $2 \le \ell \le d$. We showed (lemmas 2 and 3 in the proof of theorem III.5.1.4.) that the total number of rebalancing operations caused by nodes v at level ℓ with $1/(1-\alpha)^i \le |S(v)| \le 1/(1-\alpha)^{i+1}$ during the first n insertions/deletions is $O(TA_{i,\ell}(1-\alpha)^i)$, where $TA_{i,\ell}$ is the total number of transactions which go through nodes v at level ℓ with $1/(1-\alpha)^i \le |S(v)| \le 1/(1-\alpha)^{i+1}$; here $0 \le i \le c \log n$. The cost of a rebalancing operation caused by such node v is $O(\ell(1-\alpha)^{-(i+1)}(i+1 + ((i+1)/m)^{\ell-1})$ by lemma 2. Also $TA_{i,\ell} \le n((c \log n)/m)^{d-\ell}$ by a simple induction on ℓ starting with $\ell = d$. Thus total rebalancing cost at levels $\ell \ge 2$ is at most

$$\sum_{2\le\ell\le d} \sum_{0\le i\le c \log n} n((c \log n)/m)^{d-\ell}(1-\alpha)^i \, \ell(1-\alpha)^{-(i+1)}(i+1 + (i+1)/m)^{\ell-1})$$

$$= O(\sum_{2\le\ell\le d} n((c \log n)/m)^{d-\ell} \, \ell((c \log n)^2 + (c \log n/m)^{\ell} (m/\ell))$$

$$= O(n(m^2 + m\, d) \, ((c \log n)/m)^d)$$

We summarize in

<u>Lemma 4:</u> Amortized insertion/deletion cost in d-fold range trees with slack parameter m is $O((m^2 + md)((c \log n)/m)^d)$.

<u>Proof:</u> By preceding discussion. □

<u>Theorem 6:</u> d-fold range trees with slack parameter $m \ge 1$ and balance parameter $\alpha \in (1/4, 1-\sqrt{2}/2)$ for a set of n elements take space $O(n(c(\log n)/m)^{d-1})$, support orthogonal range queries with time bound $O(\log n(c(2^m/m)\log n)^{d-1} + |A|)$, and have amortized insertion/deletion cost $O((m^2 + md)(c(\log n)/m)^d)$. Here $c = 1/\log(1/(1-\alpha))$. In particular, we have:

slack/parameter	space	query time	insertion/deletion time
1	$n(c \log n)^{d-1}$	$\log n(2c \log n)^{d-1}$	$d(c \log n)^d$
$\varepsilon \log n$	$n(c/\varepsilon)^{d-1}$	$(c/\varepsilon)^{d-1} n^{\varepsilon d} \log n$	$(c/\varepsilon)^d((\varepsilon \log n)^2 + d\varepsilon \log n)$

Proof: Immediate from lemmas 1 to 4. □

Search trees are always examples for divide and conquer. Range trees and dd-trees exemplify a variant of divide and conquer which is particular useful for multidimensional problems: multidimensional divide and conquer. A problem of size n in d-space is solved by reducing it to two problems of size at most n/2 in d-space and one problem of size at most n in (d-1)-dimensional space. Range trees (with slack parameter m = 1) fit well into this paradigm. A set of size n is split into two subsets of size n/2 each at the root. In addition, an auxiliary tree is associated with the root which solves the (d-1)-dimensional range query problem for the entire set. Other applications of multidimensional divide and conquer are dd-trees and polygon trees, domination problems (exercises 22,23) and closest point problem (exercises 24,25).

In the fixed radius near neighbours problem we are given a set $S \subseteq \mathbb{R}^d$ and a real $\varepsilon > 0$ and are asked to compute the set of all pairs $(x,y) \in S \times S$ such that $dist_2(x,y) < \varepsilon$. Here $dist_2(x,y) = (\sum_{0 \le i < d} (x_i - y_i)^2)^{1/2}$ is the Euclidian or L_2-norm, but similar approaches work for orther norms. We denote the set of such pairs by $\varepsilon NN(S)$. Of course, $\varepsilon NN(S)$ might be as large as n^2, $n = |S|$, if the points of S lie very dense. In most applications dense sets do not arise. We therefore restrict our considerations to sparse sets.

Definition: Let $\varepsilon > 0$, $c > 0$. Set $S \subseteq \mathbb{R}^d$ is (ε,c)-sparse if for every $x \in \mathbb{R}^d$ we have $|\{y \in S;\ dist_2(x,y) < \varepsilon\}| < c$, i.e. any sphere of radius ε contains at most c points of S. □

If S is (ε,c)sparse then $|\varepsilon NN(S)| \le cn$, i.e. the size of the output is at most linear. We apply the paradigm of multidimensional divide and conquer to solve the fixed radius near neighbours problem.

If d = 1 then a simple method will do. Sort set S in time $O(n \log n)$ and then make one linear scan through (the sorted version of) S. For every point $x \in S$ look at the c preceding points in the linear order and find out which of them have distance at most ε from x. In this way, we can produce εNN(S) in time O(cn) from the sorted list. Altogether we have an O(n log n + cn) algorithm in one-dimensional space.

If $d \geq 2$ then we project S onto the o-th coordinate and find the median of the multiset $p_o(S)$ of projected points. Let that median be m. We split S into two sets A and B of n/2 points each, namely A contains only points $x \in S$ with $x_o \leq m$ and B contains only points $x \in S$ with $x_o \geq m$. We apply the algorithm recursively to d-dimensional point sets A and B. This will compute all pairs $(x,y) \in \varepsilon NN(S)$ where both points are in either A or B. It remains to compute pairs $(x,y) \in \varepsilon NN(S)$ with $x \in A$ and $y \in B$. If $x \in A$, $y \in B$ and $(x,y) \in \varepsilon NN(S)$ then x and y both belong to the slab SL of width 2ε around hyperplane $x_o = m$, i.e. $SL = \{x = (x_o,\ldots,x_{d-1}) \in S;\ |x_o - m| < \varepsilon\}$. So all we have to do is to solve εNN on point set SL. SL is not quite (d-1)-dimensional. We make it (d-1)-dimensional by projecting the points in SL onto hyperplane $x_o = m$, i.e. we compute $S' = \{x';$ there is $x = (x_o,\ldots,x_{d-1}) \in SL$ such that $x' = (x_1,\ldots,x_{d-1})\}$. The crucial observation is that S' is still sparse, and that εNN(S') "contains" εNN(SL).

Lemma 5: a) If S is (ε,c)-sparse then S' is $(\varepsilon,(1+2^d)c)$-sparse.

b) If $x,y \in SL$ and $dist_2(x,y) < \varepsilon$ then $dist_2(x',y') < \varepsilon$.

Proof: a) Consider any point $x' = (m,x_1,\ldots,x_{d-1})$ on hyperplane $x_o = m$. We have to compute a bound on the number of points in the "strange" sphere $SSPH(x') = \{y \in S;\ |y_o - m| < \varepsilon$ and $(\sum_{1 \leq c < d} (x_i - y_i)^2)^{1/2} < \varepsilon\}$ with center x' because exactly the projections of the points in SSPH(x') have distance at most ε from x' in (d-1)-dimensional set S'. It is easy to see (cf. the diagram for an illustration in 2-space)

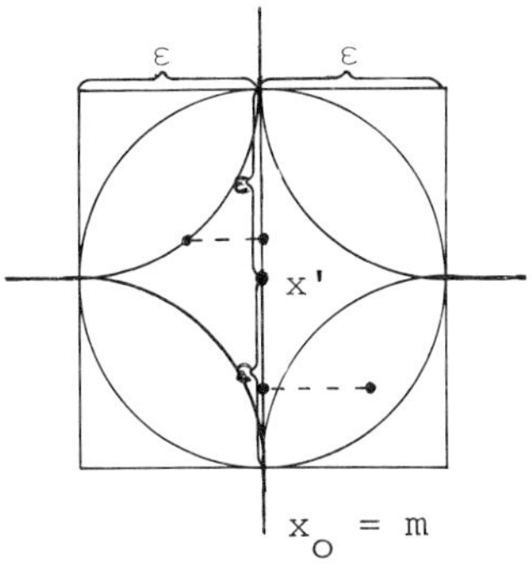

that SSPH(x') can be covered with $(1+2^d)$ d-dimensional spheres of radius ε. Any such sphere can contain at most c points of S and hence $|SSPH(x')| \le (1+2^d)c$. This shows that S' is $(\varepsilon,(1+2^d)c)$ sparse.

b) obvious. □

Lemma 5 holds true for other norms as well; however, factor $(1+2^d)$ in 5a depends on the norm. We infer from lemma 5 that we can compute $\varepsilon NN(SL)$ by solving the (d-1)-dimensional problem on S' and then going through list $\varepsilon NN(S')$ and throwing out some pairs. This leads to

Theorem 7: Let d be fixed and let $S \subseteq \mathbb{R}^d$ be (ε,c)-sparse. Then $\varepsilon NN(S)$ can be computed in time $O(n (\log n)^d/d! + (1+\hat{c})n (\log n)^{d-1}/(d-2)!)$, where $\hat{c} = \prod_{2\le i\le d} (1+2^i)\, c$ and $n = |S|$.

Proof: We will first derive a recurrence on T(i,n), the time to compute $\varepsilon NN(S)$ for any (ε,c)-sparse set S, $|S| = n$ and $S \subseteq R^i$, $i \le d$. We have

$$T(i,n) \le 2T(i,n/2) + T(i-1,n) + O(n)$$

since in order to solve an i-dimensional problem on n points we spend O(n) time on computing the median and splitting the set and then solve two i-dimensional problems on n/2 points each and one (i-1)-dimensional problem on at most n points. Also

$$T(i,1) = 0$$

since subproblems of size 1 are trivial and

$$T(1,n) = O(n \log n + \hat{c}n)$$

since all one-dimensional problems generated are $(\varepsilon,\hat{c})$-sparse by lemma 5a and therefore can be solved in time $O(n \log n + \hat{c}n)$. It is not too hard to verify by induction on n and i that $T(i,n) = O(n (\log n)^i/i! + (i+\hat{c})n (\log n)^{i-1}/(i-1)!)$. We leave this for exercise 25. We will rather show how one arrives at the bound for T(i,n).

Observe first that it suffices to study recurrence

$$\begin{aligned} U(i,n) &= 2U(i,n/2) + U(i-1,n) + n && \text{for } i \ge 2,\ n \ge 2 \\ U(i,1) &= 0 && \text{for } i \ge 1 \\ U(1,n) &= n \log n + \hat{c}n && \text{for } n \ge 2 \end{aligned}$$

because we have $T(i,n) = O(U(i,n))$. We solve this recurrence for n a power of two. Let $V(i,k) = U(i,2^k)/2^k$. By substitution we obtain

$$\begin{aligned} V(i,k) &= V(i,k-1) + V(i-1,k) + 1 && \text{for } i \ge 2,\ k \ge 1 \\ V(i,0) &= 0 && \text{for } i \ge 1 \\ V(1,k) &= k + \hat{c} && \text{for } k \ge 1 \end{aligned}$$

This is further simplified by setting $V(i,k) = W(i,k) - 1$. Then

$$\begin{aligned} W(i,k) &= W(i,k-1) + W(i-1,k) && \text{for } i \ge 2,\ k \ge 1 \\ W(i,0) &= 1 && \text{for } i \ge 1 \\ W(1,k) &= k + 1 + \hat{c} && \text{for } k \ge 1 \end{aligned}$$

If the boundary conditions were simpler, namely all equal to one, then this recursion has a simple combinatoric interpretation. It counts a set of paths. More precisely, if

$$\begin{aligned} X(i,k) &= X(i,k-1) + X(i-1,k) && \text{for } i \ge 1,\ k \ge 1 \\ X(i,0) &= X(0,k) = 1 && \text{for } i,k \ge 0 \end{aligned}$$

then $X(i,k)$ is exactly the set of paths from the origin $(0,0)$ to point (i,k) where the set of edges consists of unit length horizontal and vertical lines.

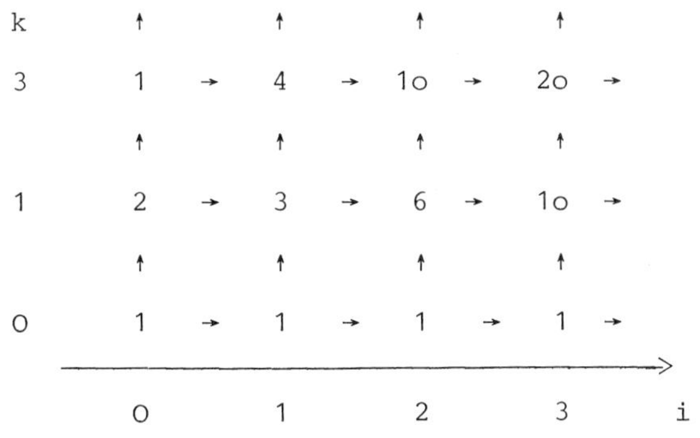

Every path from $(0,0)$ to (i,k) has length (number of edges) $i + k$ and contains exactly i horizontal edges. Hence $X(i,k) = \binom{i+k}{i}$. In particular, $X(1,k) = k + 1$. It is now easy to express W in terms of X. Write $W(i,k) = W_1(i,k) + W_2 i,k)$ where

$$\begin{array}{lll} W_j(i,k) = W_j(i-1,k) + W_j(i,k-1) & & j = 1,2,\ i \geq 2,\ k \geq 1 \\ W_1(1,k) = k + 1 & W_2(1,k) = \hat{c} & \text{for } k \geq 1 \\ W_1(i,0) = 1 & W_2(i,0) = 0 & \text{for } i \geq 1 \end{array}$$

Then $W_1(i,k) = X(i,k)$ and $W_2(i,k) = \hat{c}\ X(i-1,k-1)$ and therefore $W(i,k) = X(i,k) + \hat{c}\ X(i-1,k-1)$. Reversing all substitutions we obtain.

$$T(i,n) = O(n[\binom{i + \log n}{i} + \hat{c}\binom{i-1 + \log n - 1}{i-1}]-n)$$

for n a power of two. Finally using the approximation $\binom{a+b}{a} = \frac{b^a}{a!} + \Theta(\frac{b^{a-1}}{(a-2)!})$ for a fixed and b growing we have

$$T(d,n) = O(n(\log n)^d/d! + (1 + \hat{c})n(\log n)^{d-1}/(d-2)!)$$

for n a power of two. It is now tedious but straight forward to verify by induction that this formula holds for all n (Exercise 25). □

We will next describe two improvments upon the basic algorithm for the fixed radius near neighbours problem. Presorting, the first improvement, is of general interest and was used already in the proof of lemma 2; the strategy of finding good dividing lines, the second improvement, helps only in a few situations.

We observed already that the one-dimensional problem can be solved in linear time if set S is sorted, but that it takes time $O(n \log n)$ for general inputs. When we solve a two-dimensional problem we reduce it to a collection of one-dimensional problems of total size $O(n \log n)$. (The recurrence for the total size $S(n)$ of all one-dimensional problems generated from a two-dimensional problem is $S(n) = n + 2S(n/2)$ which solves for $S(n) = O(n \log n)$. We have to sort all these problem instances for a total cost of $O(n(\log n)^2)$. A better strategy is to sort all of S according to y-coordinate once and then to pull out only sorted subproblems in the divide-step. If we proceed according to this strategy then all one-dimensional problem instances generated are sorted and hence can be solved in linear time. Thus two-dimensional problems can be sorted in time $O(n \log n)$. This generalizes to

Theorem 8: Let $d \geq 2$ be fixed and let $S \subseteq \mathbb{R}^d$ be (ε,c)-sparse. Then $\varepsilon NN(S)$ can be computed in time $O((1+\hat{c})n(\log n)^{d-1}/(d-2)!)$ where $n = |S|$ and $\hat{c} = c \prod_{2\leq i\leq d} (1+2^i)$.

Proof: We sort S once according to the last coordinate in time $O(n \log n)$. Then we proceed as described above. With a little care all subproblems generated are also sorted. Hence we obtain the same recurrence as in the proof of theorem 7 with the only change that $T(1,n) = O(n+\hat{c}n)$ now. This will save one factor of log n throughout. □

Theorems 7 and 8 derive upper bounds on the performance of a multi dimensional divide and conquer algorithm for the fixed radius near neighbours problem. Are there any sets $S \subseteq \mathbb{R}^d$ where this upper bound is actually achieved? Let us look at the two-dimensional case. If the points of S crowd into a very narrow, say width $< \varepsilon$, vertical slab then all subproblems generated will have indeed maximal size and so our algorithm will run very long. A similar observation holds true in higher dimensional space. However, this observation also suggests a major improvement upon the basic algorithm. There is no a-priori reason for only looking at vertical dividing lines, we can also look for horizontaldividing lines and choose whatever is better. A "good" dividing line is a line which divides set S into (nearly) equal parts, defines a small (size o(n)) lower dimensional subproblem and which is easy to find. Good dividing lines always exist. We content ourselves to a discussion in the two-dimensional space and leave the general case to the reader.

Lemma 6: Let $S \subseteq \mathbb{R}^2$, $|S| = n$, be (ε,c)-sparse. Then there exists a line L orthogonal to one of the axes such that

1) no half-space defined by L contains more than 4n/5 points of S;

2) the slab of width 2ε around L contains at most $\sqrt{36cn/5}$ points of S.

Proof: For i,i = 0,1, let $\ell_i = \min\{a;\ x_i \leq a$ for at least n/5 points of $S\}$ and $h_i = \min\{a;\ x_i \leq a$ for at least 4n/5 points x of $S\}$. Next consider lines $L_{ij} = \{y \in \mathbb{R}^2;\ y_i = \ell_i + (2j+1)\varepsilon\}$, $0 \leq j \leq (h_i-\ell_i)/2\varepsilon - 1$, and the slabs of width 2ε around them, i.e. $SL_{ij} = \{y \in \mathbb{R}^2;\ \ell_i + 2j\varepsilon < y_i < \ell_i + 2(j+1)\varepsilon\}$.

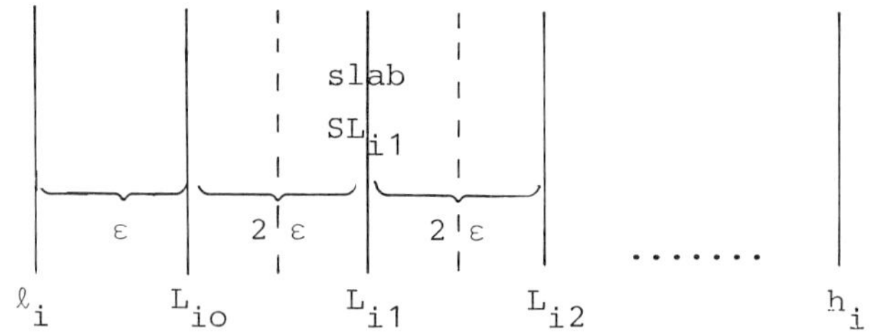

<u>Claim:</u> a) For every i and j: No half-space defined by L_{ij} contains more than 4n/5 points of S.

b) For every i: If $(h_i - \ell_i)/2\varepsilon \geq \sqrt{n/(20c)}$ then there is a j such that $|S \cap SL_{ij}| \leq \sqrt{36cn/5}$.

c) There is an i such that $(h_i - \ell_i)/2\varepsilon \geq \sqrt{n/20c}$.

<u>Proof:</u> a) Since there are n/5 points x of S with $x_i \leq \ell_i$ there are clearly that many points with $x_i \leq \ell_i + (2j+1)\varepsilon$. Also here are less than 4n/5 points $x \in S$ with $x_i < h_i$ and hence less than 4n/5 points $x \in S$ with $x_i \leq \ell_i + (2j+1)\varepsilon < h_i$. This proves a).

b) Slabs $SL_{i,j}$, $j \geq 0$, are pairwise disjoint and contain at most 3n/5 points of S together. If $(h_i - \ell_i)/2\varepsilon \geq \sqrt{(1/20c)n}$ then there must be one j such that $|S \cap SL_{ij}| \leq \sqrt{36cn/5}$.

c) Assume otherwise. Then $(h_i - \ell_i) < \varepsilon\sqrt{n/5c}$ for i = 0,1. Let $R_i = \{y \in \mathbb{R}^2;\ \ell_i \leq y_i \leq h_i\}$ and let $c = R_1 \cap R_2$. Furthermore, let

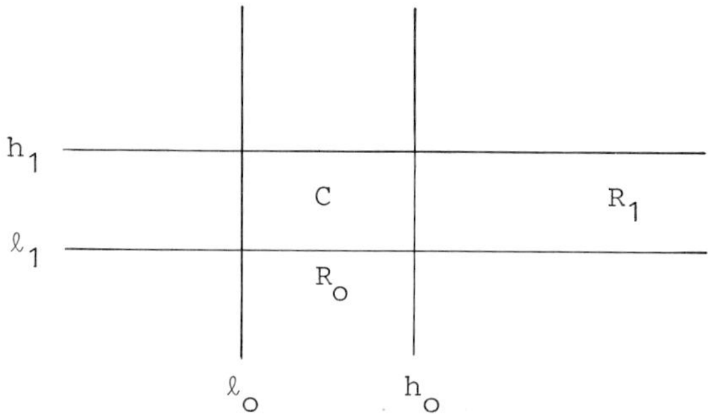

$f = |C \cap S|$ and $n_i = |(R_i - C) \cap S|$. Then $f + n_i \geq 3n/5$ since $|R_i \cap S| \geq 3n/5$ and $n_0 + n_1 + f \leq n$ since sets $R_0 - C$, $R_1 - C$, C are pairwise disjoint. Thus $n \geq n_0 + n_1 + f = (n_0 + f) + (n_1 + f) - f \geq 6n/5 - f$ or

$f > n/5$. C is a rectangle whose sides have length at most $\varepsilon\sqrt{n/5c}$ and is hence easily covered by $n/5c$ circles of radius ε. Since S is (ε,c)-sparse any such circle contains at most c points of S and hence $f < (n/5c)c = n/5$, a contradiction. □

Note that lemma 6 also suggests a linear algorithm for finding a good dividing line. Compute ℓ_o, h_o, ℓ_1, h_1 in linear time using the linear time median algorithm (II.4.). Let us assume w.l.o.g. that $(h_o - \ell_o) \geq \varepsilon\sqrt{n/5c}$. The proof of lemma 6 shows that one of the slabs $SL_{i,j}$, $0 \leq j \leq \sqrt{n/20c}$ contains at most $\sqrt{36cn/5}$ points of S. The number of points in these slabs can be determined in linear time by bucket sort (II.2.2.). Thus a good dividing line can be determined in linear time. We obtain the following recurrence for $T(2,n)$, the time to compute $\varepsilon NN(S)$ for an (ε,c)-sparse set $S \subseteq \mathbb{R}^2$, $|S| = n$.

$$T(2,n) = \max_{n/5 \leq n_1 \leq 4n/5} T(2,n_1) + T(2,n-n_1) + T(1,\sqrt{36cn/5}) + O(n)$$

Since $T(1,n) = O(n \log n)$ we conclude

$$T(2,n) = \max_{n/5 \leq n_1 \leq 4n/5} (T(2,n_1) + T(2,n-n_1)) + O(n)$$

Theorem 9: The good dividing line approach to the fixed radius near neighbours problem leads to an $O(n \log n)$ algorithm in 2-dimensional space.

Proof: In III.5.1. theorem 2a we showed that the recurrence above has solution $T(2,n) = O(n \log n)$. □

Theorem 9 also holds true in higher-dimensional space. In d-space one can always find a dividing hyperplane which splits S into nearly equal parts (1/5 to 4/5 at the worst) and such that the slab around this hyperplan contains at most $O(n^{1-1/d})$ points. This leads directly to an $O(n \log n)$ algorithm in d-space (exercise 26).

VII. 2.3. Lower Bounds

This section is devoted to lower bounds. We cover two approaches. The first approach deals with partial match retrieval in minimum space and shows that rootic search time is the best we can hope for. In particular, we show that dd-trees are an optimal data structure. The second, more general approach deals with a wide class of dynamic multi-dimensional region searching problems. A region searching problem (cf. introduction to VII.2.) over universe U is specified by a class $\Gamma \subseteq 2^U$ of regions. We show that the cost of insert, delete and query operations can be bounded from below by a combinatorial quantity, the spanning bound of class Γ. The spanning bound is readily computed for polygon and orthogonal range queries and can be used to show that polygon trees and range trees are nearly optimal.

VII. 2.3.1 Partial Match Retrieval in Minimum Space

Dd-trees are a solution for the partial match retrieval problem with rootic search time and linear space. In fact, dd-trees are a minimum space solution because dd-trees are easily stored as linear arrays. The following figure shows an ideal dd-tree for (invertible) set $S = \{(1,II),(2,IV),(3,III),(4,V),(5,I)\}$ and its representation as an array. The correspondence between the

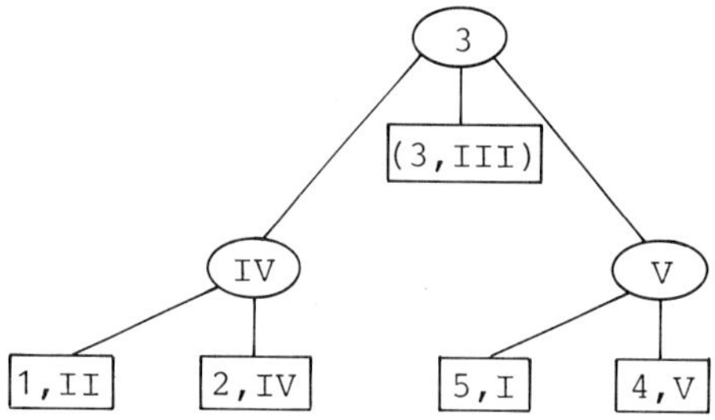

1	II
2	IV
3	III
5	I
4	V

and array is the same as for binary search (cf. III.3.1.).

The aim of this section is to show that dd-trees are an optimum minimum space solution for the partial match retrieval problem; more precisely, we show $\Omega(n^{1-1/d})$ is a lower bound on the time complexity of partial match retrieval in d-dimensional space with one specified component in a decision tree model of computation. The exact model of computation is as follows.

Let S_n be the set of permutations of elements $0,1,\dots,n-1$. For $\Pi_1,\dots,\Pi_{d-1} \in S_n$ let $A(\Pi_1,\dots,\Pi_{d-1}) = \{(i,\Pi_1(i),\dots,\Pi_{d-1}(i));\ 0 \le i \le n\}$ and let

$I_n = \{A(\Pi_1,\ldots,\Pi_{d-1});\ \Pi_1,\ldots,\Pi_{d-1} \in S_n\}$. Then $|I_n| = (n!)^{d-1}$. I_n is the class of invertible d-dimensional sets of cardinality n with components drawn from the range 0,1,...,n-1. We restrict ourselves to this range because in the decision tree model of computation only the relative size of elements is relevant. A decision tree algorithm for the partial match retrieval problem of size n consists of

1) a storage assignment SA which specifies for every $A \in I_n$ the way of storing A in a table M[0...n-1,0...d-1] with n rows and d columns, i.e. SA: $(S_n)^{d-1} \to S_n$ with the following interpretation. For all $\Pi_1,\ldots,\Pi_{d-1} \in S_n$ and $\Pi = SA(\Pi_1,\ldots,\Pi_{d-1})$: Tuple $(i,\Pi_1(i),\ldots,\Pi_{d-1}(i))$ of set $A(\Pi_1,\ldots,\Pi_{d-1})$ is stored in row $\Pi(i)$ of table M, i.e. $M[\Pi(i),j] = \Pi_j(i)$ for $0 \le j \le d-1$, $0 \le i < n$. Here Π_0 is the identity permutation.

2) d decision trees $T_0,\ldots,T_{d-1}$. Trees T_j are ternary trees. The internal nodes of tree T_j are labelled by expressions of the form X? M[i,j] where $0 \le i < n$. The three edges out of a node are labelled <, =, and >. Leaves are labelled yes or no.

A decision tree algorithm is used as follows. Let $A \in I_n$, let $y \in \mathbb{R}$ and let $j \in [0\ldots d-1]$. In order to decide whether there is $x = (x_0,x_1,\ldots,x_{d-1}) \in A$ with $x_j = y$ we store A in table M as specified by SA and then use decision tree T_j to decide the question, i.e. we compare y with elements in the j-th column of M as prescribed by T_j.

<u>Theorem 1:</u> If $SA,T_0,\ldots,T_{d-1}$ solves the partial match retrieval problem of size n in d-space then there is a j such that depth$(T_j) = \Omega(n^{1-1/d})$, i.e. the worst case time complexity of a decision tree algorithm for the partial match retrieval problem is $\Omega(n^{1-1/d})$.

<u>Proof:</u> The proof consists of two parts. In the first part we reformulate the problem as a membership problem and in the second part we actually derive a lower bound.

Consider tree T_j. It decides whether there is an tuple $x = (x_0,\ldots x_{d-1}) \in A$ with $x_j = y$, i.e. it decides membership of y in the projection of A onto the j-th coordinate. It does so by searching in an array, namely the j-th column of table M. The j-th column of table M contains n distinct elements, here integers 0,...n-1. The crucial observation is that these n different elements appear in many different orderings. This observation leads to the following definitions.

For $0 \le j < d$ let OT(j) be the set or order types occuring in the j-th column, i.e.

$$OT(j) = \{\sigma \in S_n;\ \text{there are } \Pi_1,\ldots,\Pi_{d-1} \in S_n \text{ such that}$$
$$\sigma = SA(\Pi_1,\ldots,\Pi_{d-1}) \circ \Pi_j^{-1}\}$$

This definition needs some explanation. Let $\Pi_1,\ldots,\Pi_{d-1} \in S_n$, let $\Pi = SA(\Pi_1,\ldots,\Pi_{d-1})$, and let $A = A(\Pi_1,\ldots,\Pi_{d-1})$. When set A is stored in table M then tuple $(i,\Pi_1(i),\ldots,\Pi_{d-1}(i))$ is stored in row $\Pi(i)$ of table M, i.e. $M[\Pi(i),j] = \Pi_j(i)$. In other words, $M[\Pi(\Pi_j^{-1}(\ell)),j]$ contains integer ℓ, $0 \le \ell < n$, i.e. $\Pi \circ \Pi_j^{-1}$ is one of the order types occuring in the j-th column.

<u>Lemma 1:</u> There is a j such that $|OT(j)| \ge (n!)^{1-1/d}$.

<u>Proof:</u> The discussion following the definition of OT(j) shows that the mapping $(\Pi_1,\ldots,\Pi_{d-1}) \to (\sigma_0,\ldots,\sigma_{d-1})$ where $\sigma_j = SA(\Pi_1,\ldots,\Pi_{d-1}) \circ \Pi_j^{-1}$ is injective. Hence $\prod_{0 \le j \le d-1} |OT(j)| \ge (n!)^{d-1}$. □

Next, we describe precisely the computational power of decision trees T_j. Let $\hat{\Pi} \subseteq S_n$ be a set of permutations. A decision tree T solves problem SST(Π) - <u>s</u>earching <u>s</u>emi-sorted <u>t</u>ables - if for every $B = \{x_0 < x_1 < \ldots < x_{n-1}\}$, every x and every $\sigma \in \hat{\Pi}$: If B is stored in linear array $M[0\ldots n-1]$ according to order type σ, i.e. $M[\sigma(\ell)] = x_\ell$ for $0 \le \ell < n-1$, then T correctly decides $x \in B$.

<u>Lemma 2:</u> T_j solves SST(OT(j)) for $0 \le j \le d-1$.

<u>Proof:</u> Note first that T_j solves SST(OT(j)) for every $B = \{x_0 < x_1 < \ldots < x_{n-1}\}$ if it does so for $B = \{0,1,\ldots n-1\}$. Next let $\sigma \in OT(j)$. Then there must be $\Pi_1,\ldots,\Pi_{d-1}$ such that $\sigma = SA(\Pi_1,\ldots,\Pi_{d-1}) \circ \Pi_j^{-1}$. In particular, if our partial match retrieval algorithm is applied to set $A = A(\Pi_1,\ldots,\Pi_{d-1})$ then A is stored in table $M[0\ldots n-1, 0\ldots d-1]$ such that $M[\sigma(\ell),j] = \ell$ for all ℓ; i.e. $B = \{0,\ldots,n-1\}$ is stored in the j-th column of M according to order type σ. Thus T_j solves SST(OT(j)). □

Lemmas 1 and 2 reduce the partial match retrieval problem to the searching semi-sorted tables problem. Lemma 3 gives a lower bound on the complexity of the latter problem.

Lemma 3: Let $\hat{\Pi} \subseteq S_n$ and let decision tree T solve SST(Π)

a) For every injective mapping σ: $[0...k-1] \to [1...n]$:
$|\{\Pi(k);\ \Pi \in \hat{\Pi} \text{ and } \Pi(i) = \sigma(i) \text{ for } 0 \le i < k\}| \le \text{depth}(T)$.

b) $|\hat{\Pi}| \le \text{depth}(T)^n$.

Proof: b) Is a simple consequence of part a). Namely, let $\hat{\Pi}_k = \{\Pi|_{[0...k-1]};\ \Pi \in \hat{\Pi}\}$. Then $|\hat{\Pi}_0| = 1$ and $|\hat{\Pi}_{k+1}| \le \text{depth}(T)\ |\hat{\Pi}_k|$ by part a). Hence $|\hat{\Pi}| = |\hat{\Pi}_n| \le \text{depth}(T)^n$.

a) Let σ: $[0...k-1] \to [1...n]$ be injective, let $\Pi \in \hat{\Pi}$ and let B = $\{x_0 < x_1 < \dots < x_{n-1}\}$ be stored in table M[0...n-1] according to Π. Consider a search for x, $x_{k-1} < x < x_k$. It defines a path in tree T leading to a leaf which is labelled "no". On this path x is compared with at most depth(T) distinct table positions, say $M[i_1],\dots,M[i_h]$, $h \le \text{depth}(T)$. We claim $\Pi(k) = i_\ell$ for some ℓ, $1 \le \ell \le h$.

Assume otherwise. Then $T[i_\ell] \neq x_k$ for all ℓ. Consider a search for $x = x_k$. It will lead to exactly the same leaf because the outcome of all comparisons is unchanged. Hence T decides that x_k does not belong to B, a contradiction. We have thus shown that $\Pi(k) = i_\ell$ for some ℓ, $1 \le \ell \le h \le \text{depth}(T)$. This proves a). □

Theorem 1 is now an immediate consequence of lemmas 1, 2 and 3. By lemma 1, there is a j with $|OT(j)| \ge (n!)^{1-1/d}$. By lemma 2, T_j solves SST(OT(j)) and hence has depth $|OT(j)|^{1/n}$ by lemma 3. Finally, $|OT(j)|^{1/n} \ge ((n!)^{1-1/d})^{1/n} = ((n!)^{1/n})^{1-1/d} = \Omega(n^{1-1/d})$ since $n! \approx \sqrt{2\pi n}\,(n/e)^n$ by Stirling's approximation. □

It is open whether theorem 1 is also valid for more general models of computation. In particular, it is not known whether the lower bound is valid in a more general decision tree model where comparisons of the form T[i,j]? T[h,j] are also allowed. It is conceivable, that comparisons of this form can speed up searches considerably, because they can be used to infer information about the storage assignment. This point is followed up in exercise 29. We should also emphasize at this point that the restriction to minimum space solutions which is captured in the definition of storage assignment is essential for the argument. After all, range trees provide us with polylogarithmic search time if we are willing to use non-linear space. Exercises 3o - 32 discuss various extensions.

VII. 2.3.2 The Spanning Bound

We introduce the spanning bound and use it to prove lower bounds on the complexity of polygon retrieval and orthogonal range queries.

We will first define the region searching problem in an abstract setting. Let U be the key space, let M be a commutative monoid (i.e. a set M with a commutative, associative operation $+: M \times M \to M$ and an element $0 \in M$ such that $x + 0 = x$ for all $x \in M$) and let $\Gamma \subseteq 2^U$ be a set of regions U. The Γ-region searching problem is to (efficiently) maintain a partial function $S: U \to M$ under the operations

Insert(x,m)	precondition: $x \notin \text{dom } S$, $x \in U$, $m \in M$
	effect: $S \leftarrow S \cup \{(x,m)\}$
Delete(x)	precondition: $x \in \text{dom } S$, $x \in U$
	effect: $\text{dom } S \leftarrow \text{dom } S - \{x\}$
Query(R)	precondition: $R \in \Gamma$
	effect: output $\sum_{x \in R \cap \text{dom} S} S(x)$

This is in complete agreement to our previous discussion of searching problems. U is the key space. The problem is to maintain a set of pairs (x,m), where $x \in U$, $m \in M$; m is the "information" associated with key x. Insert and Delete add and delete pairs and Query sums the information over a region R.

Next we fix the model of computation. There is an infinite supply v_0, $v_1, v_2, \ldots$ of variables which take values in M. Initially, 0 is stored in every variable. The instruction repertoire consists of $v_i \leftarrow v_j + v_k$, $v_i \leftarrow$ INPUT, OUTPUT $\leftarrow v_i$, $i,j,k \geq 0$. Exercise 33 discusses a larger instruction repertoire. A program is given by an (infinite) state space Z, an initial state $z_0 \in Z$ corresponding to the empty function S, and three functions f_I, f_D, f_Q. Here f_I: U x M x Z → Z x INS*, f_D: U x Z → Z x INS*, and f_Q: Γ x Z → Z x INS* where INS* is the set of all sequences of instructions from the repertoire. Function f_I has the following semantics. If the algorithm is in state z ∈ Z, operation Insert(x,m) is to be executed, and $f_I(x,m,z) = (z',\sigma)$ then z' is the new state and sequence σ ∈ INS* is to be executed. The first instruction of σ is of the form v_i ← INPUT and places m into register v_i. The remaining instructions of σ are of the form $v_i \leftarrow v_j + v_k$. The semantics of f_D, and f_Q are defined similary, i.e. after a deletion a sequence of additions is executed and after a query a sequence of additions followed by an output instruction is executed.

A program Z, z_0, f_I, f_D, f_Q is correct if it is correct for all choices of monoid M. It is correct for a particular choice of M if the answers to all queries are computed correctly.

The cost of inserting(x,m) in control state z is the number of instructions in σ, where $(z',\sigma) = f_I(x,m,z)$. The cost of a sequence of operations is the sum of the costs of the operations in the sequence. We use C_n to denote the maximal cost of any sequence of n insertions, deletions and query operations (starting with empty function S).

<u>Example</u> (One-dimensional range trees): Let U = ℝ, M = ($\mathbb{N}_o$,+,0), and let Γ be the set of intervals. The set Z of control states is the set of all BB[α]-trees T for finite subsets of ℝ, z_o is the empty tree. Let T be a BB[α]-tree. With every node of T we associate a variable v which contains the weight (= number of leaves) in the subtree rooted at that node. An insert or delete requires the update of O(log n) variables; the update requires only additions if we start updating at the leaves. Also a query can be answered by summing O(log n) variables. □

The basic idea for the lower bound argument is as follows. It is intuitively clear and will be made precise below that every variable contains the sum of S(x) over some subset of U. A query for region R is then answered by summing some variables, i.e. by assembling R ∩ dom S from smaller pieces. If all queries are "easy" to answer, then set R ∩ dom S can be assembled from only a few pieces for every R ∈ Γ. This implies that we need to store information about some x ∈ dom S in many (the precise number depends on the structure of Γ) different places. If we delete x at this point then a lot of variables become useless and must be recomputed after inserting x with a different monoid value m. This argument suggests that updates are costly if queries are cheap. The lower bound is then obtained by balancing the cost of the two operations. More generally it suggests that there is a trade-off between query and update cost. In the case of range trees we have seen such a trade-off (as an upper bound) in VII.2.2..

Definition: a) Let $X \subseteq U$, X finite and let $R_1, R_2, \ldots, R_\ell$ be all sets of the form $X \cap R$, $R \in \Gamma$. Then $F = \{Y_1, \ldots, Y_m\}$, $\emptyset \neq Y_i \subseteq X$, is a spanning family for X (with respect to Γ) if

1) every R_i is the disjoint union of some Y_j's and
2) every Y_i which is not a singleton is the disjoint union of some Y_j and Y_h.

b) For $F = \{Y_1, \ldots Y_m\}$ a spanning family define

$$t(F) = \max_i \min\{t;\ \text{there is a representation of } R_i \text{ by } t \text{ disjoint } Y_j\text{'s in } F\}$$

and

$$\rho(F) = \max_{x \in X}\{d;\ x \text{ is contained in } d\ Y_j\text{'s}\}$$

c) For $X \subseteq U$, X finite, let

$$B(X) = \min\{\max(t(F), \rho(F));\ F \text{ is a spanning family for } X\}$$

and

$$B_n = \max\{B(X);\ X \subseteq U,\ |X| \le n\}$$ □

We can now state the main theorem of this section:

Theorem 2: For every program Z, z_0, f_I, f_D, f_Q: $C_n \ge \lfloor n/16 \rfloor\, B_n$

Proof: We construct a sequence of operations $Op_1, Op_2, \ldots, Op_n$ of total cost at least $\lfloor n/16 \rfloor\, B_n$. The construction is in three steps. In step one we show that we can restrict attention to normal form programs, in step two we associate the cost of normal form programs with the spanning bound and in step three we finally construct a hard sequence of operations.

Definition: A program Z, z_o, f_I, f_D, f_Q is in normal form if no variable is assigned to twice.

Lemma 4: For every program there is a normal form program of the same cost.

Proof: Lemma 4 states that space can be used intentionally wasteful and we all are experts in that. A formal argument goes as follows. Let the normal form program have variables $v_o', v_1', v_2', \dots$ and control set $Z' = Z \times W$ where W is the set of finite, injective mappings from $V = \{v_o, v_1, \dots\}$ to $V' = \{v_o' v_1', \dots\}$. Any sequence σ of instructions is replaced by a sequence of instructions which assigns to unused variables only. Association $w \in W$ is updated accordingly. □

We open step two by fixing monoid M. Let M be the set of multi-subsets of $U \times \mathbb{N}$ with operation union. We will only consider sequences of operations $Op_1, \dots, Op_n$ where each Insert is of the form Insert(x,(x,t)). In addition, t counts the number of times x was inserted so far. Moreover, x was deleted exactly (t-1)-times before it is inserted for the t-th time. Let v be any variable. Then val(v), the value stored in v, is a multi subset of $U \times \mathbb{N}$. set(v) is the projection of val(v) on U.

Let $Op_1, Op_2, \dots$ be a sequence of Inserts, Deletes and Queries. Let S_h denote function S after execution of $Op_1, \dots Op_h$. Then $S_h(x) = (x,t)$ for some t for every $x \in \text{dom } S_h$. t is the number of insertions Insert(x,) in $Op_1, \dots, Op_h$. We say that variable v is useless at h iff $\text{val}(v) \nsubseteq \text{Range}(S_h)$. If v is not useless at h then v is useful at h.

Lemma 5: a) If v is useless at h then v is useless at h' for all $h' \geq h$.

b) For every h: $F = \{\text{set}(v);\ v \text{ is useful at } h \text{ and } \text{set}(v) \neq \emptyset\}$ is a spanning family for dom S_h.

Proof: a) If v is useless at h then $\text{val}(v) \nsubseteq \text{Range}(S_h)$, i.e. there is a pair $(x,t) \in \text{val}(v) - \text{Range}(S_h)$. Since $(x,t) \in \text{val}(v)$ and val(v) must be a sum of some of the monoid elements assigned to variables after insertions, x was inserted at least t times during $Op_1, \dots Op_h$. Since $(x,t) \notin \text{Range}(S_h)$, it was also deleted at least t times. Hence $(x,t) \notin \text{Range}(S_h)$ for all $h' \geq h$ by our choice of $Op_1, Op_2, \dots$. Since val(v) will never change we infer that v is useless at all $h' \geq h$.

b) We have to verify properties 1) and 2) of a spanning family. Let us verify property 2) first. If v was assigned by $v \leftarrow$ Input, then set(v) is a singleton. Hence if set(v) is not a singleton then v was assigned by $v \leftarrow u + w$ and hence $\text{val}(v) = \text{val}(u) + \text{val}(w)$. Since v is useful at h and hence $\text{val}(v) \subseteq \text{Range}(S_h)$ we conclude that $\text{set}(v) = \text{set}(u) \cup \text{set}(w)$ and that $\text{set}(u) \cap \text{set}(w) = \emptyset$ (For this inference it is important that we take the monoid of multi-subsets and not the monoid of subsets under union). This proves property 2).

Property 1) can be seen as follows. Let $R \in \Gamma$ and suppose (for the moment) that $Op_{h+1} = \text{Query}(R)$. The answer to this query, i.e. $\Sigma\{S(x);\ x \in R \cap \text{dom } S_h\}$ is computed as a sum of some variables. Call the set of these variables A. No variable $v \in A$ can be useless at h since $\text{val}(v) \not\subseteq \text{range}(S_h)$ implies $\Sigma\{\text{val}(v);\ v \in A\} \not\subseteq \text{range}(S_h)$. Also sets set(v), $v \in A$ must be pairwise disjoint by the argument used to prove property 2). □

We are now ready to construct sequence $Op_1,\ldots,Op_n$ of cost at least $\lfloor n/16 \rfloor B_n$. Let $m = \lceil n/2 \rceil$ and let $X = \{x_1,\ldots,x_k\} \subseteq U$, $|X| \le m$ be such that $B(X) = B_m$. The following program defines $Op_1,\ldots,Op_n$.

a) Let $Op_i = \text{Insert}(x_i,(x_i,1)$ for $1 \le i \le k$
b) <u>do</u> $\lfloor n/4 \rfloor$ <u>times</u>
  - - at this point $F = \{\text{set}(v);\ \text{set}(v) \neq \emptyset$ and v useful$\}$
  - - is a spanning family for X and hence $B_m = B(X) \le \max\{\rho(F),\ t(F)\}$

<u>Case 1:</u> $t(F) \ge B_m$: Then there is $R \in \Gamma$ such that at least B_m elements of F are needed to span $R \cap \text{dom } S = R \cap X$. We let the next operation be query(R). Answering this query requires to sum at least B_m variables.

<u>Case 2:</u> $\rho(F) \ge B_m$: Then there is $x \in X$ such that x is contained in at least B_m elements of F. Let the next two operations be Delete(x), Insert(x,(x,t)) for the appropriate t. This will make all variables v with $(x,t-1) \in \text{val}(v)$ and $\text{set}(v) \in F$ useless. There are at least B_m such variables.

It remains to estimate the complexity of sequence $Op_1,Op_2,\ldots,Op_n$ defined above. Let a (b) be the number of times case 1 (2) was executed. Then $a + b \ge \lfloor n/4 \rfloor$. Also the total cost of case 1 is at least aB_m. In case 2 at least bB_m variables are made useless. Hence at least that many variables must be assigned to. Thus

$$C_n \geq \min_{a+b=\lfloor n/4 \rfloor} \max\{aB_m, bB_m\}$$

$$\geq \lfloor n/8 \rfloor B_m \geq \lfloor n/16 \rfloor B_n$$

where the last inequality follows from

Lemma 6: a) $B_m \leq B_n$ for $m \leq n$

b) $B_{m+n} \leq B_m + B_n$ for all m and n.

Proof: a) Immediate from the definition.

b) Let $X \subseteq U$, $|X| = m + n$, be such that $B(X) = B_{m+n}$. Let X_1, X_2 be a partition of X with $|X_1| \leq m$, $|X_2| \leq n$. Then there are spanning families F_1 and F_2 for X_1 and X_2 respectively with $\max(t(F_i), \rho(F_i)) \leq B(X_i)$ for $i = 1,2$. $F = F_1 \cup F_2$ is a spanning family for $X = X_1 \cup X_2$ with $t(F) = t(F_1) + t(F_2)$ and $\rho(F) = \max(\rho(F_1), \rho(F_2))$. Thus $B_{n+m} = B(X) \leq \max(t(F), \rho(F)) \leq B(X_1) + B(X_2) \leq B_n + B_m$. □□

The significance of theorem 2 lies in the fact that it relates the complexity of an algorithm, a quantity which involves time and is therefore difficult to handle, with a purely combinatorial quantity, which is much easier to deal with. Before we apply the spanning bound to orthogonal range queries and polygon retrieval it is helpful to visualize spanning families in terms of graphs.

Let $\Gamma \subseteq 2^U$ be a set of regions and let $X = \{x_1,\ldots,x_n\} \subseteq U$. Let R_1, $R_2,\ldots,R_n$ be all sets of the form $X \cap R$, $R \in \Gamma$ (We may assume w.l.o.g. that the number of sets is equal to the number of points because we can always add either fictious points or regions). Furthermore, let $F = \{Y_1,\ldots,Y_m\}$ be a spanning family. Let us construct a bipartite graph G with node set $\{x_1,\ldots,x_n,R_1,\ldots,R_n\}$ and edge set $E = \{(x_i,R_j);\ x_i \in R_j\}$. For every region R_j let $S_j \subseteq \{1,\ldots,m\}$ be such that R_j is the disjoint union of Y_ℓ, $\ell \in S_j$.

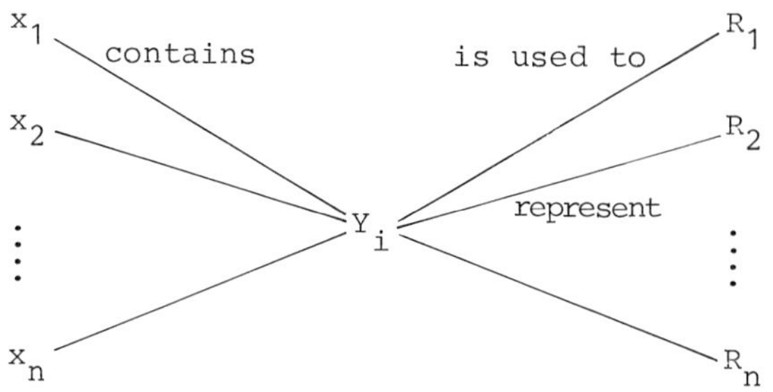

We can now "factor" graph G into disjoint complete bipartite graphs as follows. For every Y_ℓ consider the complete bipartite graph with nodes $\{x_i ; x_i \in Y_\ell\}$ on the X-side and nodes $\{R_j ; \ell \in S_j\}$ on the R-side.

Lemma 7: E is the disjoint union of the sets $\{(x_i,R_j); x_i \in Y_\ell$ and $\ell \in S_j\}$, $1 \le \ell \le m$.

Proof: Let $(x_i,R_j) \in E$, i.e. $x_i \in R_j$. Then there is exactly one ℓ such that $x_i \in Y_\ell$ and $\ell \in S_j$. □

For $x_i (R_j)$ let $\deg(x_i)$ $(\deg(R_j))$ be the degree of $x_i (R_j)$ in the factored graph, i.e. $\deg(x_i) = |\{\ell; x_i \in Y_\ell\}|$ and $\deg(R_j) = |\{\ell; \ell \in S_j\}|$. Then $t(F) = \max_j \deg(R_j)$ and $\rho(F) = \max_i \deg(x_i)$. We want to derive lower bounds on $\max(t(F),\rho(F)) = \max_{i,j}(\deg(R_j),\deg(x_i))$ which is certainly no smaller than

$$[\sum_i \deg(x_i) + \sum_j \deg(R_j)]/2n = [\sum_\ell (\ell\deg(Y_\ell) + r\deg(Y_\ell))]/2n$$

Here $\ell\deg(Y_\ell) = |Y_\ell|$ and $r\deg(Y_\ell) = |\{j; \ell \in S_j\}|$. It thus suffices to prove lower bounds on the total degree of sets Y_ℓ, $1 \le \ell \le m$.

Application 1: Polygon Retrieval

We consider a special case of polygon retrieval: line retrieval. More precisely, we assume $U = \mathbb{R}^2$ and Γ the set of all lines in $\mathbb{R}^2$, i.e. $\Gamma = \{\{(x_o,x_1) \in \mathbb{R}^2; ax_o + bx_1 = c\}; a,b,c \in \mathbb{R}, a \neq 0 \text{ or } b \neq 0\}$.

Lemma 8: Let $S = \{y_1,y_2,\dots,y_n\} \subseteq \mathbb{R}^2$ and let $L_1,\dots,L_n$ be a set of n pairwise distinct lines. Let $r_i = |L_i \cap S|$ be the number of points of S on line L_i and let $F = \{Y_1,\dots,Y_m\}$ be a spanning family for S with respect to Γ. Then

$$\max(t(F),\rho(F)) \geq \sum_{i=1}^{n} r_i/2n$$

Proof: Consider any Y_ℓ. We claim that $\min(\ell deg(Y_\ell), rdeg(Y_\ell)) \leq 1$. Assume $\ell deg(Y_\ell) \geq 2$, i.e. there are points y_j, y_h, $j \neq h$, such that $\{y_j, y_h\} \subseteq Y_\ell$. Since two points determine a line there is at most one line L_k such that $Y_\ell \subseteq L_k$. Thus $rdeg(Y_\ell) \leq 1$.

Next observe that

$$\begin{aligned} |E| &= \sum_\ell \ell deg(Y_\ell)\ rdeg(Y_\ell) && \text{, by lemma 7} \\ &\leq \sum_\ell (\ell deg(Y_\ell) + rdeg(Y_\ell)) && \text{, since } \min(\ell deg(Y_\ell), rdeg(Y_\ell)) \leq 1 \\ &\leq 2n \max(t(F), \ell(F)) && \text{, by discussion following lemma 7.} \end{aligned}$$

Thus $\max(t(F),\rho(F)) \geq |E|/2n = \sum_{i=1}^{n} r_i/2n$. □

We can now prove a lower bound on the complexity of line retrieval by exhibiting a set of lines of large total rank.

Theorem 3: The complexity of line retrieval is $\Omega(n^{4/3})$, i.e. there is a sequence of n insertions, deletions and line retrievals of total cost $\Omega(n^{4/3})$.

Proof: In view of lemma 8 and theorem 2 it suffices to construct a set of n points and n lines such that most lines contain many points.

Let $A = \lfloor\sqrt{n}\rfloor$ and let $S = [1...A] \times [1...A]$. For integers i,j,a,b let $L(i,j,a,b)$ be the line through points (i,j) and $(i+a,j+b)$. We consider the set L of such lines given by $1 \leq a \leq A^{1/3}$, $1 \leq i \leq a$, $1 \leq j \leq A/2$, $1 \leq b \leq a$, $\gcd(a,b) = 1$.

Claim a): If $(i,j,a,b) \neq (i',j',a',b')$ then lines $L(i,j,a,b)$, $L(i',j',a',b')$ are distinct.

b) The number N of lines in L satisfies $A^2 \geq N = \Omega(A^2)$

c) The total number of points from S on lines in L is $\Omega(n^{4/3})$.

Proof: a) Assume that the two lines are identical. Then they must have identical slopes and hence $b/a = b'/a'$. Since $\gcd(a,b) = \gcd(a',b') = 1$ we conclude $a = a'$ and $b = b'$. Next, from $(i,j) \in L(i',j',a,b)$ we conclude $(i,j) = (i',j') + x(a,b)$ for some $x \in \mathbb{R}$. Since $\gcd(a,b) = 1$ we must have $x \in \mathbb{N}$ and hence $i \equiv i' \bmod a$. From $1 \le i,i' \le a$ we infer $i = i'$ and hence $j = j'$.

b) The number N of lines is certainly no larger than $A/2(A^{1/3})^3 = A^2/2$. Also it is at least

$$A/2 \sum_{a=1}^{A^{1/3}} a\cdot|\{b;\ \gcd(a,b) = 1 \text{ and } b \le a\}|$$

$$\ge A^{4/3}/2 \sum_{a=A^{1/3}/2}^{A^{1/3}} |\{b;\ \gcd(a,b) = 1 \text{ and } b \le a\}|$$

$$= \Omega(A^{4/3}(A^{1/3})^2) = \Omega(A^2)$$

since $\sum_{a=1}^{m} |\{b;\ \gcd(a,b) = 1 \text{ and } b \le a\}| = (3/\pi^2)m^2 + O(m \log n)$

(cf. G. Hardy, E. Wright: The Theory of Numbers, Fourth Edition, Oxford University Press, 1965, p. 265).

c) Every line in L contains at least $(A/2)/A^{1/3} = A^{2/3}/2$ points of S. Thus the total number of points from S on lines in L is $\Omega(A^{8/3})$ by part b) which in turn is $\Omega(n^{4/3})$.

We conclude from lemma 8 that the spanning bound for set S is $\Omega(n^{1/3})$ and further from theorem 2 that the complexity of line retrieval is $\Omega(n^{4/3})$.

□

Similar arguments can be used to show lower bounds of the same order for half-space retrieval and circular queries (exercises 34, 35). The best upper bound $n^{0.77}$ on polygon retrieval is by polygon trees. There is still a gap to close.

Application 2: Orthogonal Range Queries

The lower bound for orthogonal range queries is somewhat harder to obtain. However, there is a merit to that. It agrees with the upper bound.

Theorem 4: The complexity of orthogonal range queries in $\mathbb{R}^d$ is $\Omega(n(\log n)^d)$, i.e. for every n there is a sequence of n insertions, deletions and orthogonal range queries of cost at least $\Omega(n(\log n)^d)$.

Proof: We will prove a lower bound of order $(\log n)^d$ on the spanning bound. Let $A = \lfloor n^{1/d} \rfloor$, let $X = [1...A]^d$. Then $|U| = A^d$. Also we consider the following class of A^d "one-sided" range queries. For $y \in X$ let $R_y = \{x \in U;\ x \le y\}$, where $x \le y$ if $x_i \le y_i$ for $0 \le i < d$.

Let $F = \{Y_1,...,Y_m\}$ be a spanning family for X. As above consider the complete bipartite graph associated with Y_ℓ (cf. discussion following proof of theorem 2), i.e. let $In(Y_\ell) = \{x \in X;\ x \in Y_\ell\}$ and let $Out(Y_\ell) = \{R_y;\ Y_\ell$ is used to represent $R_y,\ y \in X\}$. Then Y_ℓ contributes all of $In(Y_\ell) \times Out(Y_\ell)$ to the bipartite graph G with edge set $\{(x,R_y);\ x \le y\}$ associated with the orthogonal range query problem.

The idea for the proof is now as follows. If Y_ℓ contributes many edges to graph G then most edges (x,R_y) contributed by Y_ℓ must have $x \ll y$. This suggests to weight the edges (x,R_y) of G such that the weight is a decreasing function of y - x. We can then hope to bound the weight of the edges covered by any Y_ℓ from above and the weight of all edges from below. This would give the bound. What weight function should we choose? It should be symmetric with respect to the coordinates. About the simplest decreasing function with this property is to assign weight

$$w(x,y) = ((y_0 - x_0 + 1)(y_1 - x_1 + 1) \ldots (y_{d-1} - x_{d-1} + 1))^{-1}$$

to edge (x,R_y) for $x \le y$.

Lemma 9: For every $Y_\ell \in F$:

$$\sum_{\substack{x \in In(Y_\ell) \\ R_y \in Out(Y_\ell)}} w(x,y) \le (2\pi)^d (|In(Y_\ell)| + |Out(Y_\ell)|)$$

Proof: Let $m_i = \max\{x_i;\ (x_0,x_1,\ldots,x_{d-1}) \in In(Y_\ell)\}$ and let $B = \{(m_0 - x_0,\ldots,m_{d-1} - x_{d-1});\ (x_0,\ldots,x_{d-1}) \in In(Y_\ell)\}$, $C = \{(y_0 - m_0,\ldots,y_{d-1} - m_{d-1});\ (y_0,\ldots,y_{d-1}) \in Out(Y_\ell)\}$. Then all elements of B and C are non-negative. This is obvious for B and follows for C from the fact that $x \in In(Y_\ell)$, $R_y \in Out(Y_\ell)$ implies $x \in R_y$ and hence $x \le y$. We have

$$\sum_{\substack{x\in In(Y_\ell)\\ R_y\in Out(Y_\ell)}} w(x,y) = \sum_{\substack{u\in B\\ v\in C}} w(m - u, m + v)$$

$$= \sum_{u\in B, v\in C} ((u_0 + v_0 + 1) \ldots (u_{d-1} + v_{d-1} + 1))^{-1}$$

$$\le \sum_{u\in B\cup C, v\in B\cup C} ((u_0 + v_0 + 1) \ldots (u_{d-1} + v_{d-1} + 1))^{-1}$$

For $i_o \ge 0, i_1 \ge 0,\ldots,i_{d-1} \ge 0$ let

$$a_{i_0 i_1 \ldots i_{d-1}} = \begin{cases} 1 & \text{if } (i_0,i_1,\ldots,i_{d-1}) \in B \cup C \\ 0 & \text{otherwise} \end{cases}$$

Then

$$\sum_{\substack{x\in In(Y_\ell)\\ R_y\in Out(Y_\ell)}} \le \sum_{\substack{i_0\ge 0,\ldots,i_{d-1}\ge 0\\ j_0\ge 0,\ldots,j_{d-1}\ge 0}} \frac{a_{i_0 i_1\ldots i_{d-1}}\, a_{j_0 j_1\ldots j_{d-1}}}{(i_0 + j_0 + 1)\ldots(i_{d-1} + j_{d-1} + 1)}$$

$$\le (2\pi)^d \sum_{i_0,\ldots i_{d-1}\ge 0} a^2_{i_0 i_1\ldots i_{d-1}}$$

$$= (2\pi)^d\, |B \cup C|$$

$$\le (2\pi)^d (|B| \cup |C|) = (2\pi)^d (|In(Y_\ell)| + |Out(Y_\ell)|)$$

Here the next to last inequality follows from the following fact.

Fact: Let $a_{i_0\ldots i_{d-1}}, a_{j_0 j_1\ldots j_{d-1}} \ge 0$, be d-fold subscripted variables. Then

$$\sum_{\substack{i_o,\dots,i_{d-1}\ge o\\ j_o,\dots,j_{d-1}\ge o}} \frac{a_{i_o\dots i_{d-1}}\, a_{j_o\dots j_{d-1}}}{(i_o+j_o+1)\dots(i_{d-1}+j_{d-1}+1)} \le (2\pi)^d \sum_{i_o,\dots i_{d-1}\ge o} a^2_{i_o\dots i_{d-1}}$$

Proof: Case d = 1 is implied by Hilbert's inequality

$$\sum_{i,j\ge o} a_i a_j/(i+j+1) \le \Pi \sum_{i\ge o} a_i^2$$

, cf. G. Hardy, J. Littlewood, G. Polya, Inequalities, Cambridge University Press, 1967, p. 235. The general case can be shown along similar lines. A complete proof can be found in M.L. Fredman, A Lower Bound on the Complexity of Orthogonal Range Queries, JACM 28 (1981), 696-7o5. □□

Lemma 1o: For all $n \ge 1$, $A = \lfloor n^{1/d} \rfloor$

$$\sum_{(1,\dots,1)\le x\le y\le (A,\dots,A)} w(x,y) = \Omega((A \log A)^d) = \Omega(n(\log n)^d)$$

Proof: We have

$$\sum_{(1,\dots,1)\le x\le y\le(A,\dots,A)} w(x,y) \ge \sum_{\substack{(1,\dots,1)\le x\le (A/2)\\ (o,\dots,o)\le y-x\le (A/2,\dots,A/2)}} ((y_o-x_o+1)\dots (y_{d-1}-x_{d-1}+1))^{-1}$$

$$= (A/2)^d \Big(\sum_{o\le y_o-x_o\le A/2} 1/(y_o-x_o+1)\Big)^d$$

$$= \Omega((A \log A)^d) = \Omega(n(\log n)^d$$ □

The proof of theorem 4 is now easily complteted. We have

$$\max(\rho(F),t(F)) \ge (\sum_\ell |In(Y_\ell)|+|Out(Y_\ell)|)/2n$$ by the discussion following lemma 7

$$\ge \sum_\ell \sum_{\substack{x\in In(Y_\ell)\\ R_y\in Out(Y_\ell)}} w(x,y)/((2\pi)^d 2n)$$ by lemma 9

$$= \sum_{(1,\ldots,1)\le x\le y\le (A,\ldots,A)} w(x,y)/((2\pi)^d 2n)$$

$$= \Omega((\log n)^d) \qquad \text{by lemma 1o}$$

We have thus shown an $\Omega((\log n)^d)$ lower bound on the spanning bound of orthogonal range queries. An application of theorem 2 finishes the proof. □

Theorem 4 shows that range trees are optimal. They allow to process n insertions, deletions and queries in time $O(n(\log n)^d)$ and no data structure can do better.

VII. 3. Exercises

1) Show that every integer n can be uniquely written as

$n = \sum_{i=o}^{k} \binom{a_i}{i}$ where $i - 1 \le a_i$ and $a_1 < a_2 < \ldots < a_k$ (Hint: use the identity $\sum_{i=o}^{k} \binom{r+i}{i} = \binom{r+k+1}{k+1}$)). Analyse the k-binomial transformation based on this representation.

2) Let $f : \mathbb{N} \to \mathbb{N}$ be any non-decreasing function with $f(i) \ge 2$ for all i. Let S be any set with n elements. Let $i = \lfloor \log n \rfloor$ and let

$n - 2^i = \sum_{j \ge o} a_j b^j$ where $b = f(i)$ and $a_j \in \mathbb{N}_o$ and $0 \le a_j < b$.

a) Design a dynamization method based on the following representation of set S. S is represented by a large block S_{large} containing 2^i points and structures S_j, $j \ge 0$. S_j contains exactly $a_j b^j$ points of S.

b) Design a dynamization method based on the following representation of S. S is represented by a large block S_{large} containing 2^i points and structures $S_{j,\ell}$, $j \ge 0$, $1 \le \ell \le a_j$. A structure $S_{j,\ell}$ contains exactly b^j points of S.

Determine $Q_D(n)$ and $\bar{I}_D(n)$ in both cases. Reformulate your answers and prove theorem 3.

3) Reconsider weighted trees as investigated in section III.4. Let $\beta_1,\ldots,\beta_n$ be a probability distribution and let rank(i) = $|\{j;\ \beta_j \ge \beta_i\}|$. Is the depth of node i in a weighted tree bounded by O(rank(i))?

4) Work out weighted interpolation search in detail. In particular, state precisely under what assumption the O(loglog n) bound on search time applies to all blocks constructed by weighting.

5) Describe algorithm Demote(y,a) in a weighted dynamic data structure in detail. Analyse its running time.

6) Use weighting to turn sorted arrays + binary search into weighted dictionaries. Do not only support successful but also unsuccesful searches. There are probabilities associated with unsuccessful searches

as well, i.e. start with a distribution $(\alpha_o,\beta_1,\ldots,\beta_n,\alpha_n)$ as in III.4. (Hint: Define distribution $\gamma_1,\ldots,\gamma_n$ by $\gamma_i := \beta_i + (\alpha_{i-1} + \alpha_i)/2$ and use ideas similar to the ones used to prove theorem 7).

7) Do exercise 6) for interpolation search

8) Develop self-organizing (cf. III.7) data structures for monotone decomposable searching problems. (Hint: Use algorithm Promote of theorem 8 to implement a "Move to first group" or "Move up one group" heuristic. Choose the elements which move down carefully (randomly!))

9) Let T be an (a,b)-tree (cf. III.5.2) with n leaves. For a node v let w(v) be the number of leaves in the subtree with root v and let d(v) be the depth of v. Is there a constant $c > 1$ such that $w(v) \le n/c^{d(v)}$ for all v and T? If not, what does this mean for the dynamization of order decomposable problem based on (a,b)-trees. In particular, is the remark following lemma 2 valid?

10) Let VD(S) be the Voronoi diagram (cf. VIII.3) of point set $S \subseteq \mathbb{R}^2$. Show that Voronoi diagrams can be maintained in time O(n) per insertion and deletion (Hint: Use order decomposability).

11) A half-space in $\mathbb{R}^2$ is a set $\{(x,y) \in \mathbb{R}^2,\ ax + by \le c\}$ for some $a,b,c \in \mathbb{R}$. Show that the intersection of n halfspaces can be computed in time O(nlog n) and that the intersection can be maintained under insertions and deletions in time $O((\log n)^2)$ per update. (Hint: The intersection is always a convex polygon. Use order decomposability and the results of section VIII.1)

12) For $(x_1,y_1),(x_2,y_2) \in \mathbb{R}^2$ let $(x_1,y_1) \le (x_2,y_2)$ if $x_1 \le x_2$ and $y_1 \le y_2$. Show that the maximal elements of a set $S \subseteq \mathbb{R}^2$, $|S| = n$, can be computed in time O(nlog n) and that it can be maintained in time $O((\log n)^2)$ per insertion and deletion.

13) Define weight-balanced dd-trees (as outlined in the remarks following VII.2.1, theorem 1). Rebalance a weight-balanced dd-tree after an insertion/deletion by replacing the largest subtree which went out of balance by an ideal dd-tree. Show that the amortized cost of an insertion/deletion is O((d + logn)logn).

14) Are theorems 2,3 and 4 true for weight-balanced dd-trees? (Hint: Consider weight-balanced 2d-trees with $\alpha = 1/4$. Take a tree where every node of even depth has balance 1/4 and every node of odd depth has balance 1/2. Consider a partial mathch query with specified 0-th coordinate. This coordinate is chosen such that the search is always directed into the heavier subtree).

15) Show that the counting version of partial match retrieval has time complexity $O(n^{1-1/(d-s+1)})$ in ideal dd-trees.

16) Compute function f(d,d-s) of theorem 3 explicitely. Can you improve upon the argument used to prove theorem 3 in order to get a better bound on f(d,d-s)?

17) Prove theorem 2.1.4. for arbitrary d.

18) Show that an arbitrary polygon query may have linear running time in an ideal 2d-tree.

19) A j-way subdivision of the plane consists of two infinite parallel lines L_1, L_2 and half-lines $L_3, L_4, \ldots, L_j$ such that the starting point of L_i lies on L_{i-1}, L_i intersects L_1 and is fully to the right of L_{i-1}. A j-way subdivision divides the plane into 2j open regions and j one dimensional regions. Show that for every set $S \subseteq \mathbb{R}$, $|S| = n$, not all points of S collinear, there is a j-way subdivision such that $|S \cap R_i| \le \lceil n/2j \rceil$ for any of the open regions R_i. Discuss polygon trees based on j-way subdivisions and show that they yield $O(sn^{\log(j+1)/\log 2j})$ retrieval time. Here s is the number of sides of the polygon.

20) Design a static data structure for orthogonal range queries which uses space $O(n^{1+\varepsilon})$ for some $\varepsilon > 0$ and has query time $O(d\log n)$. (Hint: Find a hierarchical decomposition of set S into contiguous subsets such that every contiguous subset of S can be found by using only a few pieces).

21) Base range trees on (a,b)-trees (cf. III.5.2). Reprove some or all of lemmas 1-4 in section 2.2.

22) For $x = (x_0, \ldots, x_{d-1})$ and $y = (y_0, \ldots, y_{d-1})$ define $x \le y$ iff

$x_i \le y_i$ for all i. For $S \subseteq U_0 x \ldots x U_{d-1}$ and $x \in S$ let rank(x) = $|\{y \in S;\ y < x\}|$ be the number of points less than x. Rank is also called the empirical cumulative distribution function. Show that rank(x), $x \in S$ can be computed in time $O(n(\log n)^{\max(1,d-1)})$ (Hint: Use range trees).

23) Let $S \subseteq U_0 x \ldots x U_{d-1}$ and let $\subseteq$ be defined as in exercise 22).

Show how to compute the set of maxima of S in time $O(n(\log n)^{\max(1,d-2)})$. (Hint: Use multi-dimensional divide-and-conquer).

24) Design an algorithm for the fixed radius near neighbors problem with respect to the Lp-norm, p > 0. We have $\text{dist}_p(x,y) = (\sum_{0 \le i < d} |x_i - y_i|^p)^{1/p}$. Cases p = 1 and P = ∞ are particularly interesting Here $\text{dist}_\infty(x,y) = \max_i |x_i - y_i|$ is the city-block metric.

25) Complete the proof of Theorem 7 of section VII.2.2.

26) Extend lemma 6 of VII.2.2 to d-space, $d \ge 3$. Use the extension to generalize theorem 9 to d-space.

27) Study the average case complexity of the ε-nearest neighbor problem under the following assumption. S is drawn from $[0,1]^d$ according to the uniform distribution.

28) (Closest Pair). Given $S \subseteq \mathbb{R}^d$, find $x,y \in S$ such that $\text{dist}(x,y) \le \text{dist}(x',y')$ for all $x',y' \in S$, $x' \ne y'$. (Hint: Extend the algorithm for the ε-nearest neighbor problem).

29) (Searching semi-sorted tables): Let $\Pi = \{\pi;$ there is a $j \in [0\ldots n-1]$ such that $\pi(i) = (i + j) \bmod n$ for all $i\}$. Show a <u>linear</u> lower bound for SST(Π) in the decision tree model considered in section VII.2.2.1. Show that O(log n) comparisons suffice if comparisons of the form T[h] ? T[k] are permitted! (Hint: Use the proof technique of lemma 3 to prove the lower bound, use comparisons T[h] ? T[k] to find j for the upper bound).

30) Extend VII.2.3.1, theorem 1 to an average case lower bound.

31) Let $SA, T_0, \ldots, T_{d-1}$ be a solution for the partial match retrieval problem in the sense of section VII.2.3.1. Show $\prod_{0 \le i < d} \text{depth}(T_i) = \Omega(n^{d-1})$, in particular $\text{depth}(T_0)\ \text{depth}(T_1) = \Omega(n)$ for $d = 2$. Modify dd-trees such that a query with specified 0-th coordinate takes time $O(n^{\alpha})$ and a query with specified 1-th coordinate takes time $O(n^{1-\alpha})$. Here $0 < \alpha < 1$.

32) Show that a partial match query with s specified components takes time $\Omega(n^{1-s/d})$ in the worst case in the decision tree model.

33) Show that VII.2.3. Theorem 2 stays truc if additional instructions $v_i \leftarrow cv_k$, <u>if</u> $v_i = v_j$ <u>then</u> ..., $i,j \ge 0$, $c \in \mathbb{N}$ are allowed.

34) Show an $n^{4/3}$ lower bound on the complexity of half-space queries. A half-space in $\mathbb{R}^2$ is of the form $\{(x_0,x_1);\ ax_0 + bx_1 \le c\}$ for some $a,b,c \in \mathbb{R}$.

35) Show an $n^{4/3}$ lower bound on the complexity of circular queries, i.e queries of the form $\{(x_0,x_1);\ (x_0 - a)^2 + (x_1 - b)^2 \le c\}$.

36) Let $\Gamma \subseteq 2^n$ be a set of regions and let $B : \mathbb{N} \to \mathbb{N}$ be the spanning bound with respect to Γ. Show: there is an algorithm in the sense of section VII.2.3.2. with $C_n = O(B_n \log n)$. (Hint: Use VII.1. theorem 5 on deletion decomposable searching problems; show that there is a data structure S which supports deletions in time B_n, i.e. $D_S(n) = B_n$, and which can be built in time nB_n, i.e. $P_S(n) = nB_n$).

VII. 4. Bibliographic Notes

Dynamization was introduced by Bentley (79) and later explored by Bentley/Saxe (80) (theorem 1 and exercise 1), Overmars/v. Leeuwen (81,81) (theorems 2,5 and 6), Mehlhorn/Overmars (81) (theorem 3) and Mehlhorn (81) (theorem 4). The section on weighting follows Frederickson (82) and Alt/Mehlhorn (82). Overmars (82) introduced order decomposable problems.

D-dimensional trees were introduced by Bentley (75) and theorems 1 and 2 of 2.1. are taken from there. Weight-balanced dd-trees were discussed by Overmars/v. Leeuwen (82). The analysis of orthogonal range queries (theorem 4) in dd-trees is taken from Lee/Wong (77). Theorem 3 has not appeared before.

Polygon trees are due to Willard (82). Edelsbrunner/Welzl (83) recently improved the search time to $O(n^{0.695})$.

Range trees with slack parameter 1 are due to Bentley (79), Lueker (78), and Willard (78). The treatment of range trees with general slack parameter seems to be new. A static trade-off between space and query time is established in Bentley/Maurer (80). The treatment of multi-dimensional divide and conquer follows Bentley (80); exercises 22-26 can also be found there. Monier (80) treats recurrences arising in this area.

Section 2.3.1. follows Alt/Mehlhorn/Munro (81); exercises 29-31 can also be found there. Section 2.3.2 is the work of Fredman (81,81,81). Yao (82) proves lower bounds on time/space trade-offs for a similar model of computation.

VIII. Computational Geometry

Computational geometry deals with the algorithmic aspects of geometrical problems. The typical objects of (plane) computational geometry are points, lines and line segments, polygons, planar subdivisions (= straight-line embeddings of planar graphs) and collections of these objects. Typical questions are e.g. intersection (line-polygon, polygon-polygon,...), point location (point-point, point-polygon, point-planar subdivision) and decomposition problems (polygon into simpler polygons). The questions are motivated by the widespread use of geometric objects in computer graphics and computer aided design. In particular, the computational problems arising in two- and three-dimensional computer graphics and in VLSI design shaped the field and generated a common interest for it.

We organize this chapter into six sections:
convex polygons, convex hull, Voronoi Diagrams, the sweep paradigm, orthogonal objects, and geometric transformations. In each section we describe the computational tools and paradigms and give the algorithms for the basic problems. Most of the discussion is restricted to two-dimensional geometry. However, we sometimes also discuss three- or higher- dimensional space or at least cite relevant references in the section on bibliographic remarks.

Throughout the chapter we will use the following notation.
Let p and q be points in $\mathbb{R}^2$. The <u>line segment</u> defined by p and q and denoted L(p,q) is the set of points on the line passing through p and q and lying between p and q. Sometimes, we will use L(p,q) to denote the line through p and q or even the <u>oriented</u> (in the direction from p to q) line through p and q. The ambiguity in the notation will always be resolved from the context.

Let L be an oriented line and let p be a point not on

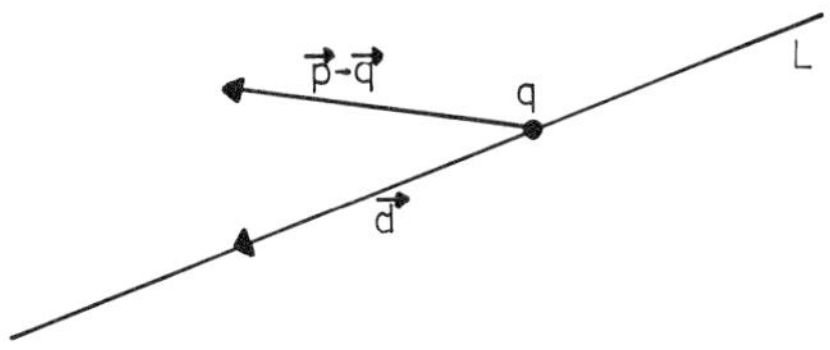

line L. Let $\vec{d}$ be the vector defining the orientation of line L and let q be an arbitrary point of line L. Then point p lies to <u>the right of</u> oriented line L if vector $\vec{p} - \vec{q}$ can be turned into vector $\vec{d}$ by a (counter-clockwise) rotation of less than 180 degrees, in other words, if the third component of the vector product of $\vec{p} - \vec{q}$ and $\vec{d}$ is positive, i.e. $\vec{p} - \vec{q} = (x,y)$, $\vec{d} = (d_x, d_y)$ and $xd_y - yd_x > 0$.
In the diagram above, p lies to the right of L.

The right (left) halfspace defined by oriented line L is the set of all points on or to the right (left) of line L. We always assume lines to be oriented. If no explicite orientation is defined then the default value is "upwards" (to the "right" in case of a horizontal line).

If L and L' are lines or line segments we use $\cap(L,L')$ to denote the intersection of L and L'.

A polygon is a sequence $v_0, v_1, \ldots, v_n$ of points. The v_i's are the <u>vertices</u> of the polygon. A polygon is <u>simple</u> if line segments $L(v_i, v_{i+1})$ and $L(v_j, v_{j+1})$, $0 \le i < j \le n$ (indices are taken mod (n+1)), intersect only if $j = i+1$ or $\{i,j\} = \{0,n\}$ and then intersect in their common endpoint.

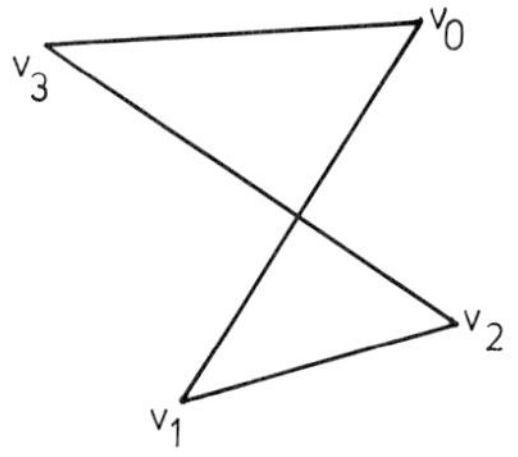

a non-simple polygon

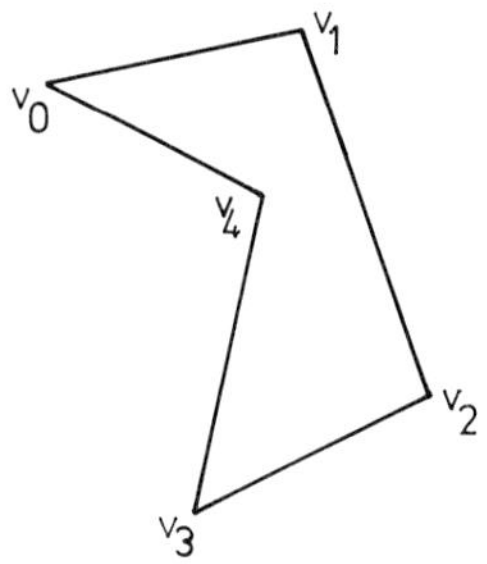

a simple polygon

Let $P = v_0, \ldots, v_n$ be a simple polygon. Removing the polygonal chain of line segments $L(v_0, v_1), \ldots, L(v_{n-1}, v_n)$, $L(v_n, v_0)$ from the plane divides the plane into two regions. The bounded region is called the <u>interior</u> of the polygon, the unbounded region is called the <u>exterior</u> of the polygon. We assume that the vertices of a simple polygon are ordered such that the interior is to the right as we traverse sequence $v_0, v_1, \ldots, v_n, v_0$.

A region $R \subseteq \mathbb{R}^2$ is <u>convex</u> if for all points $p,q \in R$ the entire line segment $L(p,q)$ is contained in R. A simple polygon is convex if its interior is a convex region. Equivalently, a simple polygon is convex if no interior angle exceeds π. A vertex v of a simple polygon is a <u>cusp</u> if the interior angle at v exceeds π. A region is <u>polygonal</u> if its boundary is a simple polygon.

Let $S \subseteq \mathbb{R}^2$ be a set. The <u>convex hull</u> CH(S) is the intersection of all convex sets containing S, i.e. $CH(S) = \cap \{R;\ S \subseteq R \text{ and } R \text{ convex}\}$. Since the intersection of a family of convex sets is convex, the convex hull CH(S) is a convex set. It is the smallest (with respect to set inclusion) convex set containing S. If S is a finite set then the convex hull of S is a convex polygonal region.

We close this introduction with an important application of binary search and more generally binary search trees. Let L,R be two vertical lines, let $p_1,\ldots,p_n$ be a sequence of points on L and let $q_1,\ldots,q_n$ be a sequence of points on R. We assume that both sequences are ordered from top to bottom. Let

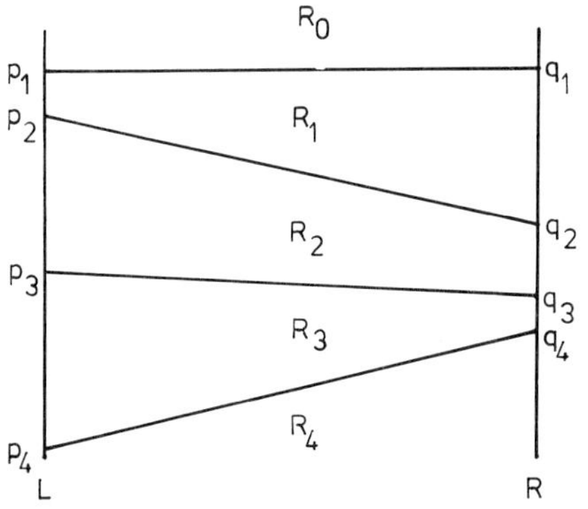

$L_i = L(p_i,q_i)$ be the line segment connecting points p_i and q_i. Then the line segments L_i, $1 \le i \le n$, do not intersect (except maybe in points on line L or R) and divide the vertical strip between lines L and R into n+1 pairwise disjoint regions $R_0,R_1,\ldots,R_n$. The regions are ordered from top to bottom in a natural way and so are the line segments. We can use this ordering to find the region containing a query point p (lying in the strip between L and R) in time O(log n) by binary search. For the following program we assume that p lies below L_1 and above L_n.

```
(1)  top ← 1; bottom ← n; middle ← ⌊(1+n)/2⌋ ;
(2)  while  bottom > top + 1
(3)  do  if p lies above L_middle
(4)        then bottom ←  middle
(5)        else top ←  middle
(6)        fi ;
(7)        middle ←  ⌊(top + bottom)/2⌋ ;
(8)  od
```

After termination, we know that p lies in the region between lines L_{top} and L_{bottom} and bottom = top + 1.

In line (3) we have to determine whether p lies above L_{middle}. If p_i (q_i,p) has cartesian coordinates (a,py_i) $((b,qy_i), (p_x,p_y))$ then the test in line (3) is equivalent to

$p_y \geq py_i + (qy_i - py_i)(p_x-a)/(b-a)$ and hence takes time O(1).

Thus the entire search takes time O(log n).

A similar situation is as follows. Let $L_1,\ldots,L_n,L$ be lines and let $p_i := \cap(L_i,L)$, $1 \leq i \leq n$. Assume that the points p_i, $1 \leq i \leq n$, appear in the

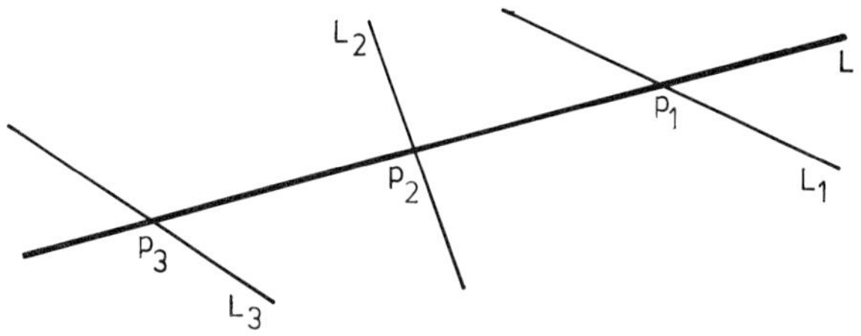

order $p_1,\ldots,p_n$ on line L (cf. the diagram). Let L' be an arbitrary line and let $p := \cap(L',L)$. Then we can determine the position of point p relative to the points p_i by binary search in time O(log n), i.e. we can determine i such that p lies between p_i and p_{i+1} on line L.

The only change required in the program above is to replace line (3) by

(3') <u>if</u> p lies above $\cap(L,L_{middle})$ on L

Note that line (3') takes time O(1) and that it is not necessary to precompute the p_i's. Rather O(log n) p_i's are computed in line (3') during execution of the algorithm.

We will use both applications of binary search and tree search frequently in the sequel. It is important to observe that all methods described in sections III.3 to III.6 work for <u>all</u> ordered universes as long as a comparison takes time O(1). In both examples above the line segments $L_1, L_2, \ldots, L_n$ form an ordered universe for the problem at hand.

Finally, if $v \in \mathbb{R}^2$ then we use x(v) and y(v) to denote the x- and y- coordinate of point v respectively.

VIII. 1. Convex Polygons

Convex polygons are particularly easy to deal with computationally. They are also a preferable kind of polygons in many applications, e.g. graphics and numerical analysis. Therefore we will study the problem of decomposing arbitrary polygons into convex parts, in particular into triangles, in section VIII.4.2.. In this section we describe algorithms for basic questions about convex polygons: deciding whether a point lies inside a polygon, computing the intersection of a line and a polygon, deciding whether two polygons intersect and computing the intersection of two polygons. We will see that convexity permits very efficient solutions, a general fact in computational geometry. The triangulation algorithm of section 4.2. will be another example of the use of convexity for developing fast algorithms. We assume throughout this section that adjacent edges of a polygon are not collinear.

In general, we assume that polygons are given by the sequence of their vertices in clockwise order. For convex polygons a (balanced) hierarchical representation is particularly useful.

Definition: A sequence $P_o, P_1, \ldots, P_k$ of polygons is a balanced hierarchical representation of convex polygon P if

a) P_o has at most four vertices
b) $P_k = P$
c) P_{i-1} can be obtained from P_i by deleting some vertices.

More precisely, out of three consecutive vertices of P_i at least one is deleted and no four consecutive points are deleted. □

The following diagram shows a balanced hierarchical representation of a polygon with 9 vertices. Polygon P_2 consists of all 9 vertices, P_1 consists of vertices 1, 3, 5 and 7 and P_o consists of vertices 1 and 5. A balanced hierarchical representation of a polygon is obtained naturally if we store the sequence of edges in the leaves of a balanced tree, say a (2,4)-tree.

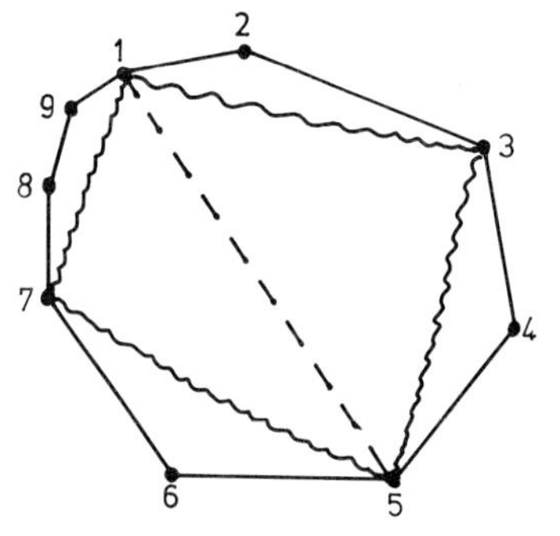

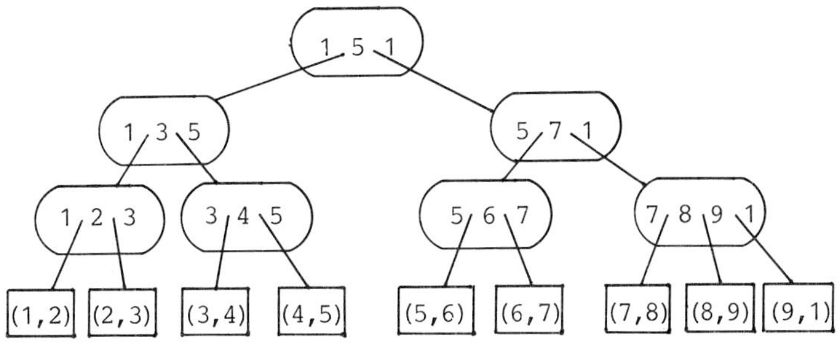

Then every level of the tree corresponds to one of the polygons in the hierarchical representation, i.e. the root node is polygon P_0, the nodes of depth 1 represent polygon P_1, ... In our example polygon P_0 consists of points 1 and 5 only. When we pass to polygon P_1 we replace edge (1,5) of P_0 by the chain (1,3), (3,5), a fact which is reflected in the first son of the root, and we replace edge (5,1) of P_0 by chain (5,7), (7,1), a fact which is reflected in the second son of the root. Similarly, edge (7,1) of polygon P_1 is replaced by chain (7,8), (8,9), (9,1), a fact which is reflected in the right-most grandson of the root.

We can draw two simple, but important consequences from the fact that balanced hierarchical representations of polygons are obtained by storing the edges in a (2,4)-tree.

Lemma 1: a) A hierarchical representation of polygon P can be computed in time O(n) where n is the number of vertices of P.

b) If $P_0, P_1, \ldots, P_k$ is a hierarchical representation of P then $k = O(\log n)$.

Proof: obvious. □

Our first use of the hierarchical representation of convex polygons is a simple algorithm for deciding whether a point lies inside a polygon.

Theorem 1: Given a balanced hierarchical representation of convex polygon P, a point p inside P and an arbitrary point x one can decide whether x lies in P in time O(log n) where n is the number of vertices of P.

Proof: Consider a subdivision of the plane obtained by drawing n semi-infinite straight lines starting at point p and going through the vertices of P. This subdivision splits the plane into n segments which can be ordered in a natural way, namely in clockwise (say) order around p. The idea is then to use binary search on the n segments to determine the segment which contains x and then to decide in one additional step whether x is inside or outside P.

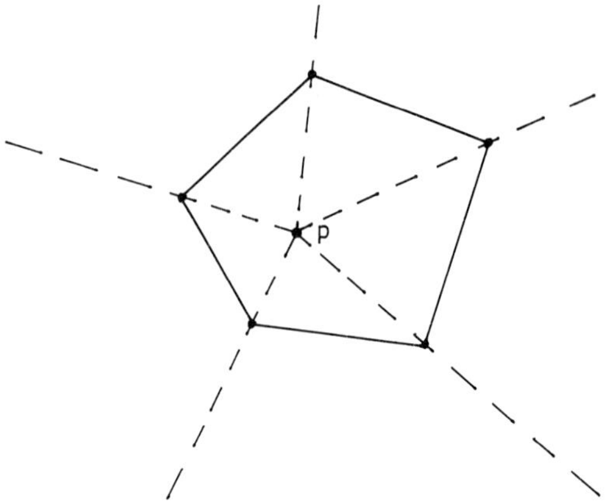

This algorithm is easily implemented as a tree search. Let T be a (2,4)-tree defining the balanced hierarchical representation of P. The vertices stored in the root together with point p define a subdivision into at most 4 segments. The segment containing x can be found in O(1) time. We proceed to the appropriate son of the root thereby refining the segment containing x to at most 4 smaller segments. Again we can identify the segment containing x in O(1) time. Iterating this process O(log n) times finishes the search. □

We will next describe an algorithm for intersecting a straight line and a convex polygon. The basic idea underlying this algorithm is very simple. We start with P_o and determine the vertex v of P_o closest to line L. Then we grow P_o towards L, i.e. we replace the vicinity of vertex v by a part of P_1, and so on. Lemma 2 below states that letting a polygon grow towards a line is an efficient process.

Lemma 2: Let $P_o, P_1, \ldots, P_k$ be a balanced hierarchical representation of polygon P and let d be a direction in the plane. Let $d(P_i)$, $0 \le i \le k$, be the set of vertices of P_i which are maximal in the direction d. Then

a) $|d(P_i)| \le 2$

b) if $p \in d(P_{i+1})$ then there is $q \in d(P_i)$ such that either p = q or p and q are separated by at most two nodes on the vertex list of P_{i+1}.

Proof: a) Since adjacent edges are not collinear.

b) Let $p \in d(P_{i+1}) - d(P_i)$. Draw a tangent to P_i which is perpendicular to direction d. It touches P_i in the vertices in $d(P_i)$ and it divides the plane into two halfspaces one of which completely contains P_i. Consider edges of P_i and their replacements when passing to P_{i+1}. If such a replacement has a vertex in the other halfspace then the corresponding edge of P_i must be incident to a vertex of $d(P_i)$ by convexity. Finally observe, that replacing an edge can introduce at most three new vertices. □

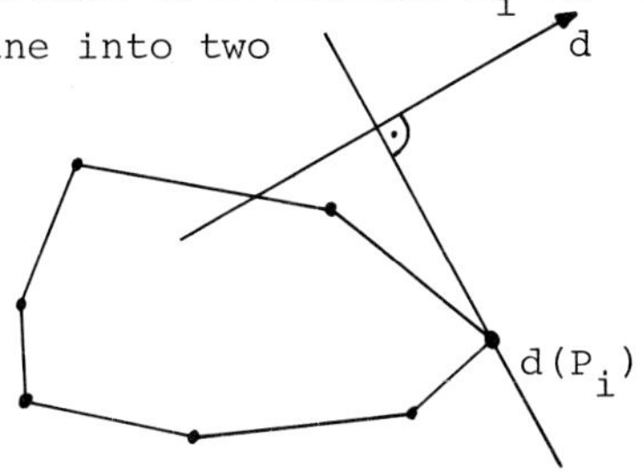

Lemma 2 leads immediately to a logarithmic time algorithm for intersecting straight lines and convex polygons.

<u>Theorem 2:</u> Given a balanced hierarchical representation of a convex n-gon P and a straight line L one can determine the intersection of P and L in time O(log n).

<u>Proof:</u> Assume that L does not intersect P_o, the other case being simpler. Let d be a direction perpendicular to line L. Since P_o has at most four vertices we can determine $d(P_o)$ in time O(1). Next we run through $P_1, P_2, \ldots, P_i, \ldots, P_k$ in turn and compute $d(P_i)$ until either $i = k$ or P_i intersects L. Note that $d(P_i)$ can be computed from $d(P_{i-1})$ in constant time by lemma 2. Also under the assumption that P_{i-1} does not intersect L one can decide in constant time whether P_i intersects L. This follows from the observation that an intersection can only occur in a constant size neighbourhood of $d(P_{i+1})$. We conclude that in time O(log n) we have either found that P_k does not intersect L or we have found the smallest i such that P_i intersects L. In the latter case we have also found the pair $e_1(i)$, $e_2(i)$ of edges of P_i which are intersected by L. We can now replace edges $e_1(i)$, $e_2(i)$ of P_i by the chain of (at most 3) edges of P_{i+1} represented by them and so compute edges $e_1(i+1)$, $e_2(i+1)$ of P_{i+1} intersected by L in constant time. Proceeding in this fashion we compute $P \cap L$ in time O(log n). □

Theorem 2 is readily extended to line segments and as a special case to points. It thus provides us with an alternate proof of theorem 1.

Theorem 3: Given a balanced hierarchical representation of n-gon P and

a) a line segment S one can compute $P \cap S$ in time $O(\log n)$

b) a point p one can decide whether p is inside P in time $O(\log n)$.

Proof: a) Let S be a segment of straight line L. By theorem 2 we can compute $P \cap L$ in time $O(\log n)$. $P \cap L$ is a line segment. From $P \cap L$ we can compute $(P \cap L) \cap S = P \cap S$ in constant time.

b) Immediate from part a) and the observation that a point is a degenerated line segment. □

Our most complex use of balanced hierarchical representations of convex polygons is deciding intersections of convex polygons. We will show that one can decide in logarithmic time whether two convex polygons intersect. (Theorem 4). The actual computation of the intersection is much harder. Note that two convex n-gons may have $\Omega(n)$ points of intersection (cf. figure) and therefore no sublinear algorithm for computing intersections can exist. Theorem 5 describes an $O(n)$ algorithm for computing the intersection of two convex n-gons.

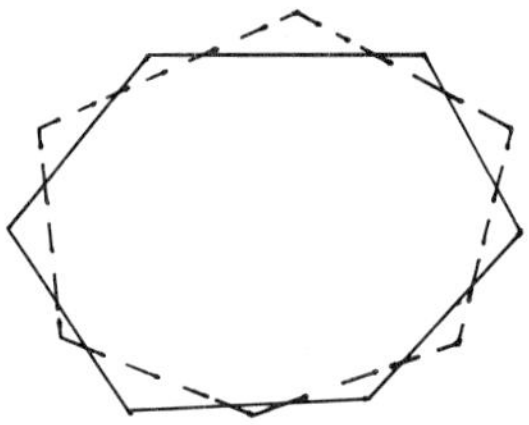

Theorem 4: Given balanced hierarchical representations of n-gon P and m-gon Q one can decide in time $O(\log(n+m))$ whether P and Q intersect.

Proof: The proof is based on a sequence of lemmas. In a first lemma we replace the problem by a simpler one, namely deciding whether two monotone polygonal chains intersect, and in a second step we show how to solve the simplified problem in logarithmic time.

A monotone polygonal chain is a sequence of vertices $v_o, v_1, \ldots, v_k$ with $y(v_i) > y(v_{i+1})$. A monotone polygonal chain defines an (infinite) convex region if we add two semi-infinite horizontal rays, one for

$y = y(v_o)$ and one for $y = y(v_k)$. It is easy to see that given a balanced hierarchical representation of n-gon P one can decompose P into two monotone polygonal chains P_L and P_R in time O(log n). Here P_R (P_L)

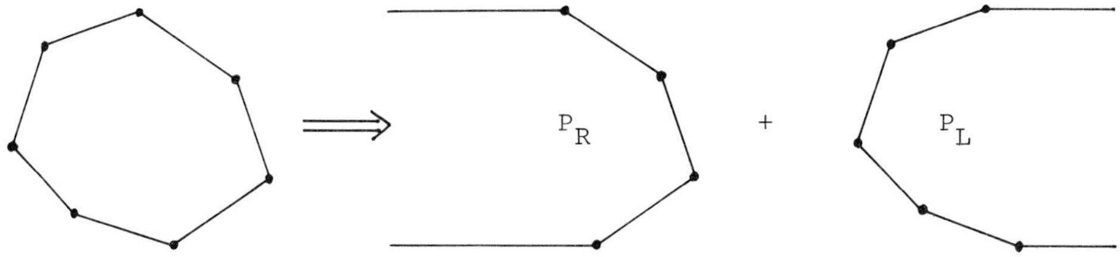

is closed to the right (left). The decomposition can be achieved by computing the vertices of P with maximal and minimal y-coordinate which is easily done by the method outlined in lemma 2 and theorem 2. Also we can compute balanced hierarchical representations for P_R and P_L in logarithmic time by performing a split operation of the (2,4)-tree representing P.

Lemma 3: Let P and Q be convex polygons. Then $P \cap Q \neq \emptyset$ iff $P_L \cap Q_R \neq \emptyset$ and $P_R \cap Q_L \neq \emptyset$.

Proof: Since $P = P_L \cap P_R$ and $Q = Q_L \cap Q_R$ we immediately have that $\emptyset \neq P \cap Q = P_L \cap P_R \cap Q_L \cap Q_R$ implies $P_L \cap Q_R \neq \emptyset$ and $P_R \cap Q_L \neq \emptyset$.

If $P \cap Q = \emptyset$ then there is a straight line L separating P and Q. If L is horizontal then clearly $P_L \cap Q_R = P_R \cap Q_L = \emptyset$. If L is not horizontal then assume w.l.o.g. that P is to the left of L. Then $P_R \cap Q_L = \emptyset$. □

Lemma 3 allows us to concentrate on a simpler problem: deciding whether two monotone polygonal chains intersect. Let R(L) be a monotone polygonal chain which is closed to the right (left) and let $r_1,\dots,r_m$ ($\ell_1,\dots,\ell_n$) be the edges of R(L). Here r_1, r_m, l_1, l_n are infinite rays with r_1 (l_1) above r_m (l_n) and all the other edges are finite. We will use (a variant of) binary search to decide whether R and L intersect. Let $i = \lfloor (m+1)/2 \rfloor$ and $j = \lfloor (n+1)/2 \rfloor$ and let R_i (L_j) be the lines supporting line segments r_i (ℓ_j). We assume that R_i and L_j intersect (otherwise, L_{j+1} will intersect R_i since adjacent edges are assumed not to be collinear). Then lines R_i and L_j divide the plane into four regions. R and L can each exist in two of these regions. Furthermore, they can coexist in one of the regions. Label the four regions LR, L,

R and empty as shown in the diagram below, i.e. chain R can exist in

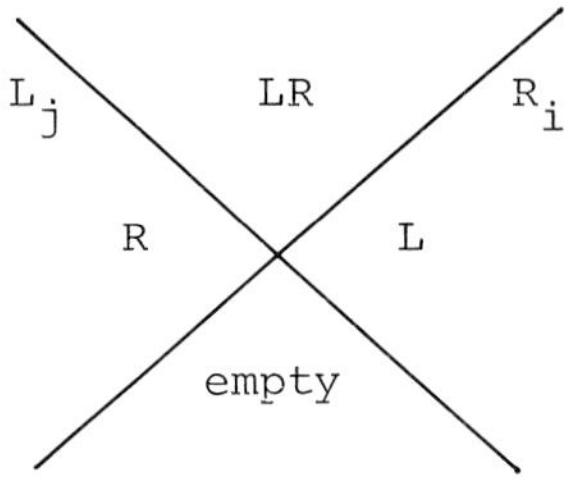

regions R and LR. Define four new monotone chains from R and L as follows. R_{top} consists of edges $r_1,\ldots,r_i$ and a horizontal ray ending in the lower endpoint of r_i. R_{bot} consists of edges r_i, $r_{i+1},\ldots,r_m$ and a horizontal ray ending in the upper endpoint of r_i. L_{top} and L_{bot} are defined similarly. The algorithm relies on the following

Lemma 4: If lines R_i and L_j intersect and segments r_i and ℓ_j do not, and if region LR is above region empty (i.e. seeks $+\infty$ in the y-direction) then

a) if the lower endpoint of r_i does not lie in the LR region then $R \cap L \neq \emptyset$ iff $R_{top} \cap L \neq \emptyset$

b) if the lower endpoint of ℓ_j does not lie in the LR region then $R \cap L \neq \emptyset$ iff $R \cap L_{top} \neq \emptyset$

c) if both endpoints of r_i and ℓ_j lie in the LR region and the lower endpoint of r_i has no larger (no smaller) y-coordinate than the lower endpoint of ℓ_j then $R \cap L \neq \emptyset$ iff $R_{top} \cap L \neq \emptyset$ ($R \cap L_{top} \neq \emptyset$).

Proof: a) If the lower endpoint of r_i does not lie in the LR region then edges $r_{i+1},\ldots,r_m$ of R are completely contained in region R and hence cannot intersect chain L. Also the new edge or R_{top} does not intersect L. Hence $R \cap L \neq \emptyset$ iff $R_{top} \cap L \neq \emptyset$.

b) similar to part a).

c) Suppose that both endpoints of r_i and ℓ_j lie in the LR region and that the lower endpoint of r_i has no larger y-coordinate than the lower endpoint of ℓ_j.

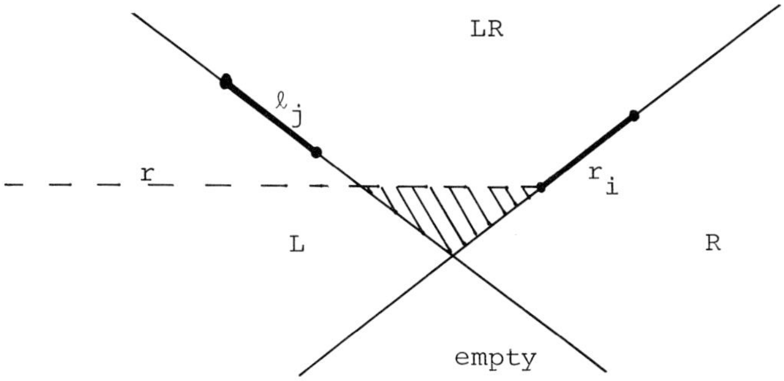

We claim that $R_{top} \cap L \neq \emptyset$ iff $R \cap L \neq \emptyset$. Assume first that $R_{top} \cap L = \emptyset$, but $R \cap L \neq \emptyset$. Then one of the edges $r_{i+1},\ldots,r_m$ must intersect L. Hence chain L must have a point in the dashed region of the diagram above. Hence by convexity chain L must intersect R_{top}, a contradiction. Hence $R_{top} \cap L = \emptyset$ implies $R \cap L = \emptyset$. Assume next that $R_{top} \cap L \neq \emptyset$, but $R \cap L = \emptyset$. Then only the lower horizontal ray of R_{top}, call it r, can intersect L. Ray r cannot intersect the top horizontal ray ℓ_1 of chain L by the relative position of r_i and ℓ_j. Hence if we follow chain L starting at the lower horizontal ray ℓ_n, we find $k > 1$, such that ℓ_k intersects r. Continuing on chain L we move into the convex region defined by chain R. Since chain R seeks $-\infty$ in the x-direction and chain L seeks $+\infty$ in the x-direction there must be an intersection of R and L. Thus $R_{top} \cap L \neq \emptyset$ implies $R \cap L \neq \emptyset$. □

An analogous lemma can be shown for the case when region LR is below region empty. Lemma 4 allows us to reduce in a constant number of steps the number of edges of one of the polygonal chains by half. More precisely, we consider the middle edges r_i and ℓ_j and supporting lines R_i and L_j. If R_i and L_j are collinear and R_i is to the left of L_j then L and R do not intersect. If R_i and L_j are collinear and R_i is to the right of L_j then R_{i+1} (the line supporting edge r_{i+1}) and L_j will intersect. We assume for the remainder of the discussion that R_i and L_j intersect, the other case being similar. If segments r_i and ℓ_j intersect then we found a point of intersection. If segments r_i and ℓ_j do not intersect then we can discard half of one of chains by lemma 4 and thus reduce the size of the problem by a constant fraction.

Thus in $O(\log(n+m))$ steps we will reduce one of the chains to a chain of a bounded number of edges, say at most 1o. For each such edge we can test for intersection with the other chain in logarithmic time by theorem 3a. Thus another $O(\log(n+m))$ steps will finish the test for intersection. □

Theorem 5: Let P and Q be convex n-gons. Then $P \cap Q$ can be computed in time $O(n)$.

Proof: Let $P = p_1, p_2, \ldots, p_n$ and let $Q = q_1, q_2, \ldots, q_m$, $m \le n$ be the vertex lists for P and Q. Let p be a point inside P; e.g. we might take p to be the center of gravity of vertices $p_1, p_2, \ldots, p_n$. Point p can certainly be computed in linear time from the vertex list of P. As in the proof of theorem 1 consider the subdivision of the plane defined by the rays starting at point p and going through the vertices of P.

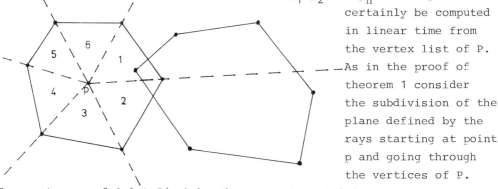

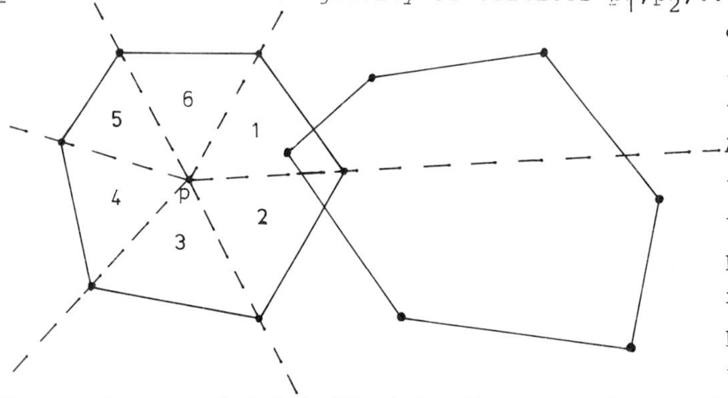

For vertex q_j of Q let $S(q_j)$ be the segment containing q_j.

We show next that we can compute all intersections of edges of Q with edges of P in linear time. Note first that we can certainly compute $S(q_1)$ in time $O(n)$. Next look at line segment $L(q_1,q_2)$. In time $O(1+s_1)$, where s_1 is the number of rays crossed by line segment $L(q_1,q_2)$, we can determine all intersections of edge $L(q_1,q_2)$ with edges of P. This follows from the fact that we only have to look at the rays bounding $S(q_1)$ and the one edge of P going through that segment in order to decide whether $L(q_1,q_2)$ intersects that edge (and if does, where it does intersect) and whether $L(q_1,q_2)$ leaves the segment. If it does not leave the segment we are finished in time $O(1)$, if it does leave the segment we can apply the same argument to the segment entered. Similarly, we can compute all intersections of edge $L(q_2,q_3)$ with the edges of P in time $O(1+s_2)$ where s_2 is the number of rays intersecting $L(q_2,q_3)$. Continuing in this fashion we compute all intersections of edges of Q and edges of P in time $O(m + \sum_i s_i)$. Finally, observe $\sum_i s_i \le 2n$ since every ray can cut at most 2 edges of Q.

The algorithm as it is described above, correctly computes $P \cap Q$ if there are some edges of P and Q which intersect or if Q is completely contained in P. Assume now that all vertices of Q are outside P and there are no edge intersections; note that both facts will be reported by our algorithm. Then P and Q intersect iff P is contained in Q iff p is contained in Q. The latter fact is easily tested in time O(m).

In summary, we have computed the intersection of P and Q in time O(n + m). □

VIII. 2. Convex Hulls

This section is devoted to the convex hull problems. Let $S \subseteq \mathbb{R}^2$ be finite. The convex hull CH(S) is the smallest convex set containing S. The convex hull of S is always a polygon whose vertices are points of S. This is intuitively obvious from the rubber band model. Take a rubber band and stretch it such that it encloses all points of S. If one lets it loose then the rubber band will form the convex hull of set S. It will clearly form a convex polygon whose vertices are points of S. A proof of this fact is left to the reader (exercise 8).

We use BCH(S) to denote the boundary of the convex hull of S. The convex hull problem is then defined as follows: Given $S \subseteq \mathbb{R}^2$ compute the boundary points BCH(S) in clockwise order, i.e. compute the standard representation of convex polygon BCH(S).

We show that BCH(S) can be computed in time O(n log n), n = |S|, even if S is not given at once but is given point by point (theorems 2 and 4). Moreover, this is optimal (theorem 3). A linear time algorithm exists if S is sorted or, more generally, if a simple polygon with S as its vertex set is given (theorem 1). Finally, convex hulls can be maintained under insertions, deletions in time $O((\log n)^2)$ per operation (theorem 5).

Theorem 1: Let $S \subseteq \mathbb{R}^2$ and let P be a simple polygon whose vertices are the points of S. Then BCH(S) can be computed in time O(|S|).

Proof: We will first show that it suffices to solve a somewhat simpler problem, the "upper" convex hull problem. Let p_ℓ (p_r) be a point with minimal (maximal) x-coordinate in S. Then chord $L(p_\ell, p_r)$ divides CH(S) into two convex regions which we call the upper and lower convex hull of S (with respect to chord $L(p_\ell, p_r)$). Apparently, it suffices to compute the upper and lower convex hull of S. We show how to compute the upper convex hull of S.

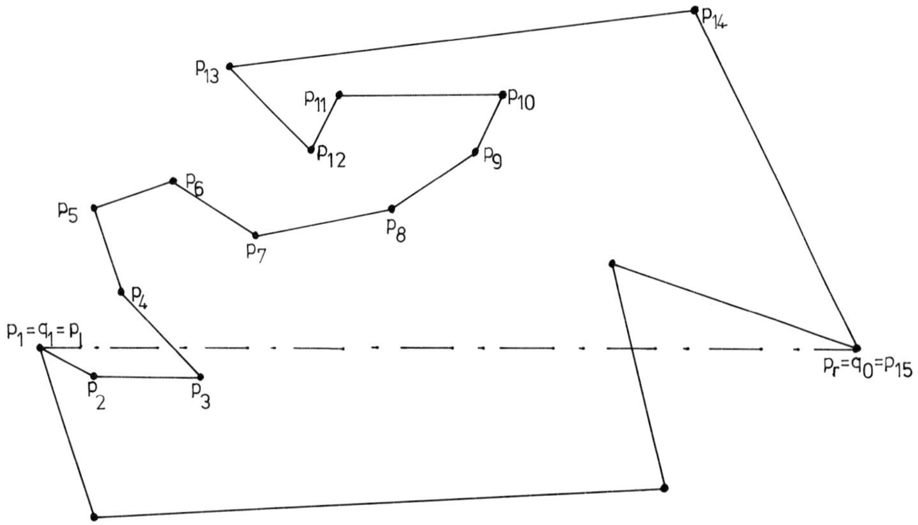

Let $p_1, p_2, \ldots, p_n$ with $p_1 = p_\ell$, $p_n = p_r$ be the upper path from p_ℓ to p_r in polygon P. Our algorithm constructs the upper convex hull by considering points $p_2, \ldots, p_n$ in turn. It uses a stack $q_0, q_1, q_2, \ldots, q_t$ to store the points which might be vertices of the convex hull, q_t is the top of the stack. We initialize the stack with $q_0 = p_r$, $q_1 = p_\ell$ and q_2 the first point on path $p_1, p_2, \ldots$ which is above $L(p_\ell, p_r)$. Vertex q_2 can be found by

```
s ← 2;
while (q_o,q_1,p_s) is a left turn do s ← s + 1 od;
push p_s;
```

Recall that (q_0, q_1, p_s) is a right turn if p_s lies to the right of directed line $L(q_0, q_1)$. In our example, we have $q_2 = p_4$. We will next consider points $p_{s+1}, \ldots, p_n$ in turn and determine the convex hull iteratively.

```
(1)  while s < n
(2)  do -- stack q_o,...,q_t is a subsequence of p_r,p_1,...,p_s
        -- with
        -- a) q_o = p_r, q_1 = p_ℓ = p_1, t ≥ 2, q_t = p_s
```

-- b) $q_0, \dots, q_t, p_r$ is a convex polygon

-- c) the upper convex hull of S is a subsequence

-- of $q_0, q_1, \dots, q_t, p_{s+1}, \dots, p_n$

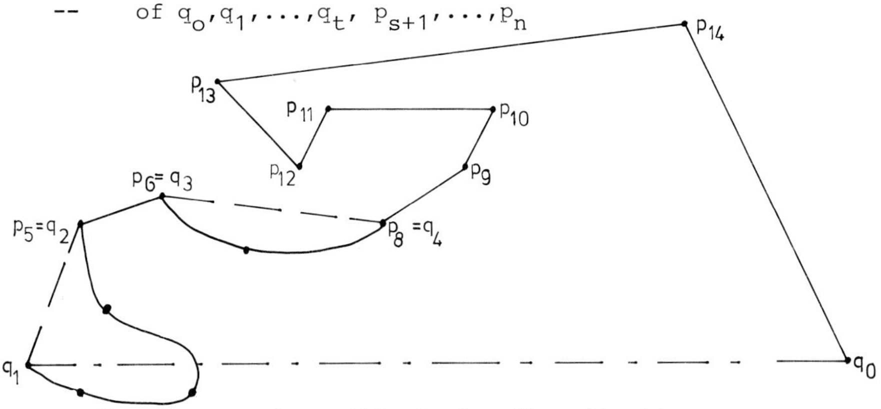

-- the diagram above illustrates the situation

-- with s = 8, t = 4 for our example

(3) <u>repeat</u> $s \leftarrow s + 1$

(4) <u>until</u> p_s is to the left of or on $L(q_t, q_0)$ or
p_s is to the left of $L(q_{t-1}, q_t)$;

(5) <u>while</u> (q_{t-1}, q_t, p_s) is not a right turn

(6) <u>do</u> pop q_t from the stack <u>od</u>;

(7) push p_s

(8) <u>od</u>;

(9) $q_0, \dots, q_t$ is the upper convex hull of S

In our example, we leave loop (3) - (4) with s = 9, then pop $q_4 = p_8$ from the stack and push p_9. In the next iteration p_9 is popped and p_{10} is pushed. Then p_{10} and p_6 are popped and p_{11} is pushed. At this point we have p_r, p_ℓ, p_5, p_{11} in the stack, s = 11 and t = 3. In the next iteration, we advance s to 13 in loop (3) - (4) because p_{12} is neither to the left of $L(p_{11}, p_r)$ nor to the left of $L(p_5, p_{11})$. Then p_{11} is popped and p_{13} is pushed, ...

It remains to show that properties a) to c) are an invariant of the while-loop. Suppose that a) to c) are true before executing the loop body (lines (2) to (7)). We show that a) to c) hold after executing the loop body and that in addition $s \le n$ at this point. Thus the program terminates with s = n and hence correctly computes the upper convex hull by parts b) and c) of the invariant.

The following diagram illustrates the situation before an execution of line (3).

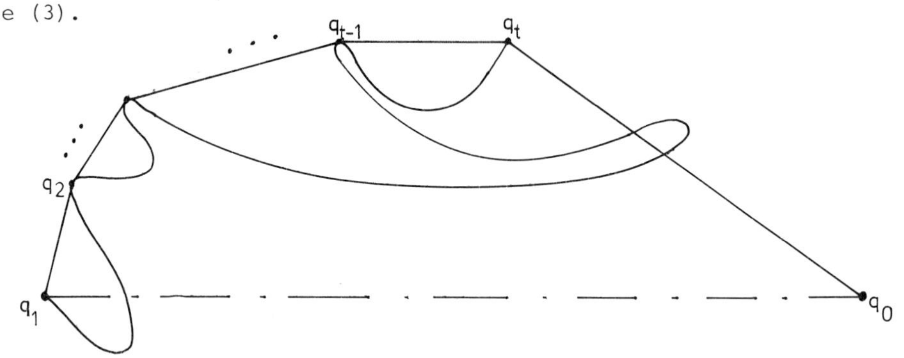

In the repeat-loop (lines 3 and 4) we search for the next input vertex which does not lie in the cone C defined by the rays starting in q_t and going through nodes q_0 and q_{t-1} respectively. We claim that no vertex discarded by the repeat-loop can possibly be a vertex of the convex hull. Assume otherwise and let v be the first such node on P following q_t, i.e. v is discarded by the repeat-loop, v is a vertex of the upper convex hull and none of the vertices between q_t and v is a vertex of the upper convex hull. Then v must lie in the region defined by the chain, call it CH, consisting of edges $L(q_1,q_2),\dots,L(q_{t-2},q_{t-1})$, the vertical line going through q_1 (since q_1 has minimal x-coordinate) and the ray starting in q_{t-1} and extending to $-\infty$ in the direction of line $L(q_t,q_{t-1})$. Let CH' be the chain of polygon edges leading from q_1 to

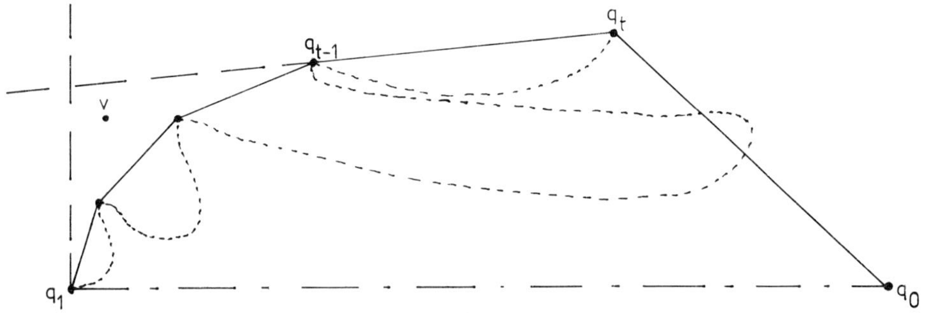

q_{t-1} and let CH" be the chain of polygon edges leading from q_t to v. Then CH" is contained within cone C and hence CH' and CH" intersect, a contradiction to the simplicity of polygon P. This shows that no vertex discarded by the repeat-loop is a vertex of the upper convex hull. Finally, observe that the repeat-loop always terminates with $s \le n$ since p_n $(= q_0)$ lies on $L(q_t,q_0)$.

Thus when control arrives at line (5) we know that the upper convex hull is a subsequence of $q_o,\dots,q_t$, $p_s,\dots,p_n$, that $q_o,\dots,q_t$, p_r is a convex polygon, that $s \le n$, $q_o = q_r$, $q_1 = p_\ell = p_1$, $t \ge 2$ and that p_s lies either to the left or on $L(q_t,q_o)$ or to the left of $L(q_{t-1},q_t)$.

Next we delete some (possibly none) vertices from the stack in the inner while-loop (lines (5) and (6)). More precisely, we delete the top vertex q_t from the stack as long as (q_{t-1},q_t,p_s) is not a right turn. Let $a \le t$ be such that q_{a+1} is deleted from the stack and q_a is not. Then clearly $a \ge 1$ since (q_o,q_1,p_s) is always a right turn. Furthermore,

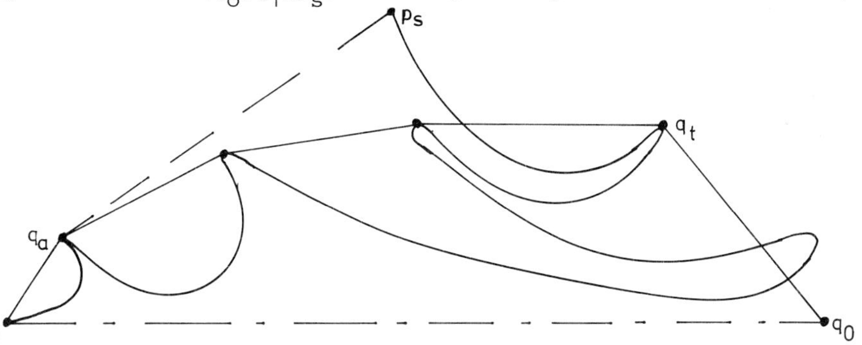

nodes $q_{a+1},\dots,q_t$ lie to the right of line $L(q_a,p_s)$. This follows immediately from the observation that line $L(q_a,p_s)$ is a tangent of chain $L(q_1,q_2),\dots,L(q_{t-1},q_t)$. Thus none of the points $q_{a+1},\dots,q_t$ is a vertex of the upper convex hull, since they all lie in the interior of the polygon formed by edges $L(q_1,q_2),\dots,L(q_{a-1},q_a)$, $L(q_a,p_s)$, $L(p_s,p_{s+1}),\dots,L(p_{n-1},p_n)$. This completes the argument that properties a) to c) are invariants of the major loop. In addition, the body of the major loop is always left with $s \le n$. Thus the algorithm correctly computes the upper convex hull of a simple polygon. □

Although the algorithm described above is fairly short the proof of correctness was quite involved. If the simple polygon is known to be monotone in x-direction, i.e. $x(p_1) \le x(p_2) \le \dots \le x(p_n)$, then a much simpler algorithm can be used to construct the convex hull (exercise 9); in essence, one can shrink the body of the major loop to the while-loop (lines (5) to (6)). A completely different convex hull algorithm for monotone simple polygons, i.e. sets ordered according to x-coordinate, can be derived from the divide and conquer paradigm (exercise 12 and lemma 1).

Theorem 2: Let $S \subseteq \mathbb{R}^2$, $|S| = n$. Then BCH(S) can be computed in time $O(n \log n)$.

Proof: Sort S lexicographically, i.e. $p < q$ if $x(p) < x(q)$ or $x(p) = x(q)$ and $y(p) < y(q)$. Let $p_1,\ldots,p_n$ be the sorted version of S. Then $p_1,\ldots,p_n,p_{n-1},\ldots,p_1$ is a simple polygon through set S from which BCH(S) can be computed in linear time. Thus the total cost of constructing the convex hull is $O(n \log n)$. □

Can we do better than time $O(n \log n)$? The following theorem shows that we cannot hope to do better.

Theorem 3: In the rational decision tree model, it takes time $\Omega(n \log n)$ to compute BCH(S) for a set S of n elements.

Proof: We will reduce the sorting problem to the problem of constructing the convex hull. Let $x_1,x_2,\ldots,x_n$ be an arbitrary sequence of real numbers and let $S = \{(x_i,x_i^2);\ 1 \le i \le n\}$. Then all points of S lie on the parabola $y = x^2$ and hence all points of S are vertices of the convex hull. Moreover, the order of the vertices of the convex hull coincides with the order of x-coordinates. Hence computing BCH(S) is tantamount to sorting sequence $x_1,\ldots,x_n$ and the theorem follows from II.1. theorem 12. □

The proof of theorem 3 relies very heavily on our definition of the convex hull problem: compute the vertices of the boundary in <u>clock-wise order</u>. An apparently simpler problem is to compute the set of vertices in <u>some</u> order. An $\Omega(n \log n)$ lower bound for the simpler problem was shown in section II. 6, theorem 17.

Let us turn to the convex hull problem for dynamic sets next, i.e. sets which grow and shrink by insertions and deletions. If we restrict ourselves to insertions only then the methods of section 1 provide us with an efficient solution.

Theorem 4: Let $S \subseteq \mathbb{R}^2$, $|S| = n$, and $p \in \mathbb{R}^2$. Given a balanced hierarchical representation of BCH(S) a balanced hierarchical representation of BCH(S $\cup$ {p}) can be computed in time $O(\log n)$.

Proof: Determine first whether p lies in the interior of BCH(S). This takes time O(log n) by 1. theorem 1. If so then we are done. If not, then we compute the tangents of p and BCH(S) by binary search as follows. Suppose that we look for the "upper" tangent and let q be a

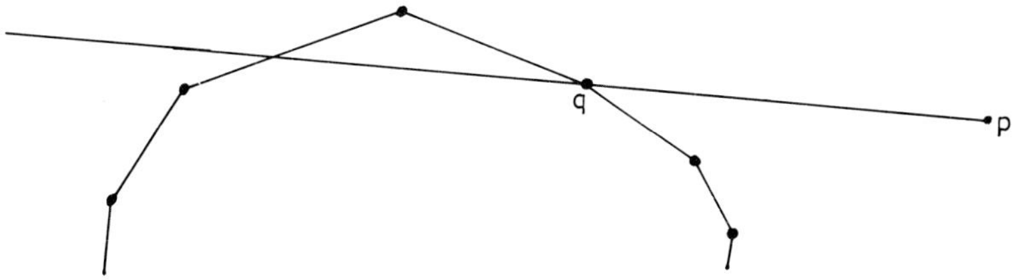

vertex of BCH(S). Consider line L(p,q) and how it intersects the polygon. If q is the only point of intersection then we are done. If not, then L(p,q) either enters the polygon at q or leaves the polygon at q. The three cases are easily distinguished in time O(1) by comparing line L(p,q) with the edges of BCH(S) incident with q. Moreover, the case distinction determines whether to continue the search in the clockwise or counter-clockwise direction. Thus the tangents can be computed in time O(log n). Two split and one concatenate operation on the balanced hierarchical representations finish the construction. □

Intermixed insertions and deletions are harder to deal with. We show an $O((\log n)^2)$ bound by applying the theory of order decomposable problems.

Theorem 5: There is a data structure for convex hulls such that insertions and deletions take time $O((\log n)^2)$ where n is the actual size of the set.

Proof: By section VII.1.3., theorem 1o it suffices to show that the convex hull problem is order decomposable with $C(n) = O(\log n)$.

Let $\le$ be the lexicographic ordering on $\mathbb{R}^2$. Then we have

Lemma 1: Let $p_1 \le p_2 \le \dots \le p_n$, $p_i \in \mathbb{R}^2$, and $1 \le m \le n$. Given balanced hierarchical representations of $BCH(\{p_1,\dots,p_m\})$ and $BCH(\{p_{m+1},\dots,p_n\})$ we can compute the balanced hierarchical representation of $BCH(\{p_1,\dots,p_n\})$ in time $O(\log n)$.

Proof: Let $L = BCH(\{p_1,\ldots,p_m\})$ and $R = BCH(\{p_{m+1},\ldots,p_n\})$. Note that L and R are disjoint. Our main problem is to compute the two tangents of L and R. We show how to compute the upper tangent in time O(log n) by

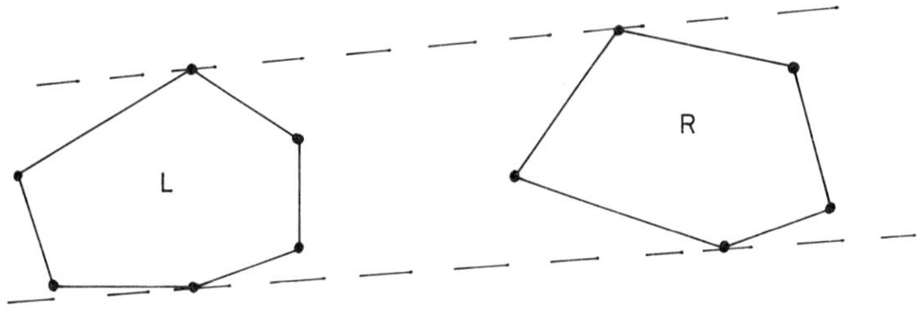

binary search on the upper path from the leftmost point of L (R) to the rightmost point of L (R). Let $r_1,\ldots,r_t$ be that path in L and $q_1,\ldots,q_s$ be that path in R. Points r_1,r_t,q_1,q_t are easily determined in time O(log n). We have to find h, $1 \le h \le t$, and k, $1 \le k \le s$, such that line $L(r_h,q_k)$ does not intersect either L or R. Assume inductively, that we found Llow, Lhigh, Rlow, Rhigh such that $Llow \le h \le Lhigh$ and $Rlow \le k \le Rhigh$. Let $i \leftarrow \lfloor (Llow + Lhigh)/2 \rfloor$ and $j \leftarrow \lfloor (Rlow + Rhigh)/2 \rfloor$. Consider oriented line $L(r_i,q_j)$. This line either touches polygon L in r_i or enters it or leaves it and similarly for polygon Q; cf. the diagram below

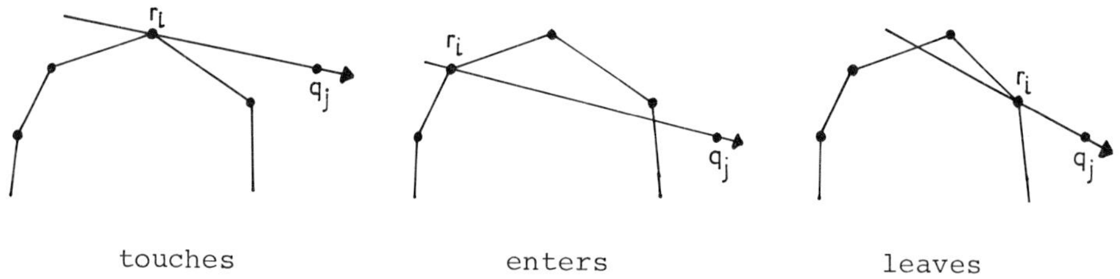

Thus we have to distinguish nine cases.

Case 1: $L(r_i,q_j)$ touches in r_i and q_j. Then we are done and have h = i, k = j.

Case 2: $L(r_i,q_j)$ touches in r_i and enters in q_j. Then r_h certainly does

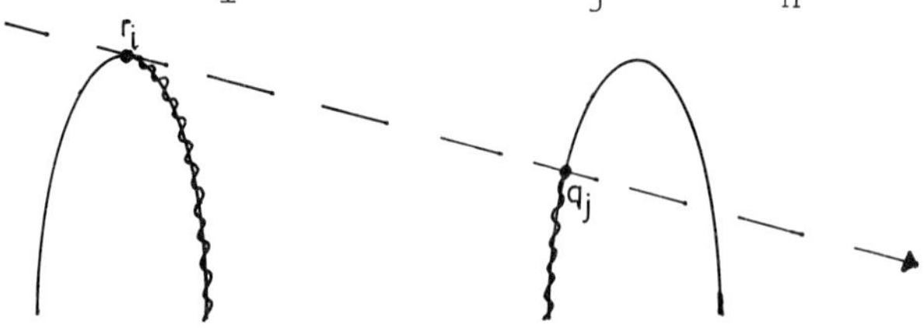

not follow r_i, i.e. $h \leq i$, and q_k does not precede q_j. Hence Lhigh ← i and Rlow ← j reduces the size of the problem and discards a fraction (shown wiggled in the figure above) of both polygonal chains.

Case 3: $L(r_i,q_j)$ touches in r_i and leaves in q_j. Then r_h certainly does

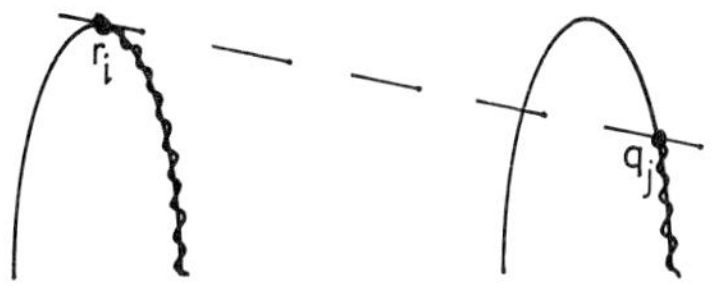

not follow r_i and q_k does not follow q_j. Hence Lhigh ← i and Rhigh ← j reduces the size of the problem.

Case 4: $L(r_i,q_j)$ leaves in r_i and touches in q_j. This case is symmetric to case 2.

Case 5: $L(r_i,q_j)$ enters in r_i and touches in q_j. This case is symmetric to case 3.

Case 6: $L(r_i,q_j)$ leaves in r_i and enters in q_j.

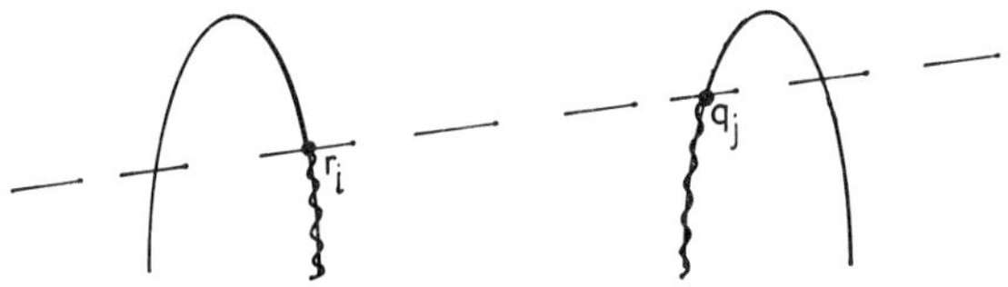

Then certainly r_h does not follow r_i and q_k does not precede q_j. Hence Lhigh ← i and Rlow ← j reduces the size of the problem.

Case 7: $L(r_i,q_j)$ leaves in r_i and leaves in q_j.

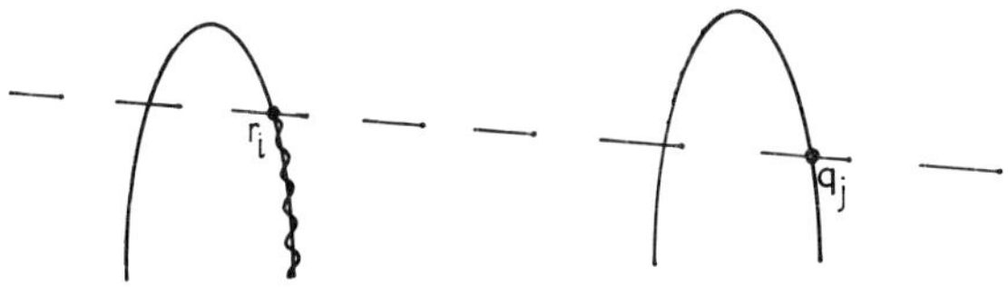

Then certainly r_h does not follow r_i and hence Lhigh ← i reduces the size of the problem.

Case 8: $L(r_i,q_j)$ enters in r_i and enters in q_j. This case is symmetric to case 7.

Case 9: $L(r_i, q_j)$ enters in r_i and leaves in q_j. Let m be a vertical

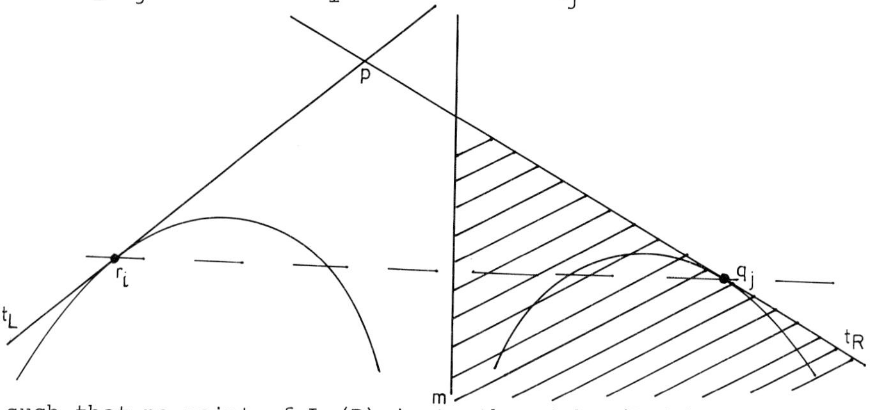

line such that no point of L (R) is to the right (left) of m, and let t_L (t_R) be a tangent to L (R) in point r_i (q_j). Let p be the intersection of t_L and t_R. Assume that p is to the left or on m, the other case being symmetric. Since all of R is to the right or on m and below or on t_R and hence below t_L we conclude that r_h cannot precede r_i. Hence Llow ← i reduces the size of the problem.

In either case, we have shown how to eleminate in time O(1) at least half of one of the paths. Hence after log s + log t steps at least one of the paths is reduced to a single point. After that only cases 1 to 5 can occur and hence another log s + log t steps will finish the computation.

We have thus shown how to compute the tangents of L and R in time O(log n). It is now easy to complete the construction. A few split and concatenate operations suffice.

By lemma 1 we can merge two (disjoint) convex hulls in time O(log n), Thus the convex hull problem is order decomposable with C(n) = O(log n) and the theorem follows. □

VIII. 3. Voronoi Diagrams and Searching Planar Subdivisions

In this section we study closest point problems and related searching problems in the plane. A very versatile data structure for closest point problems are Voronoi diagrams. A Voronoi diagram for a point set S partitions the plane into |S| polygonal regions, one for each node v of S. The (open) Voronoi region of point x consists of all points of $\mathbb{R}^2$ which are closer to x than to any other point of S. We will show that the Voronoi diagram can be constructed in time $O(n \log n)$, where $n = |S|$. Moreover, Voronoi diagrams can be searched efficiently in logarithmic time. More generally, we will show that any planar subdivision, i.e. a partition of the plane into polygonal regions allows for logarithmic search time. In addition, the data structure required for the search takes linear space and can be constructed in time $O(n \log n)$. We close the section with a discussion of several applications of Voronoi diagrams.

VIII.3.1 Voronoi Diagrams

Let $S = \{x_1,\ldots,x_n\} \subseteq \mathbb{R}^2$. For i, $1 \le i \le n$, let $VR(x_i) = \{y;\ dist(x_i,y) \le dist(x_j,y)$ for all $j\}$ be the Voronoi region of point x_i. The example shows a Voronoi diagram for a set of 5 points.

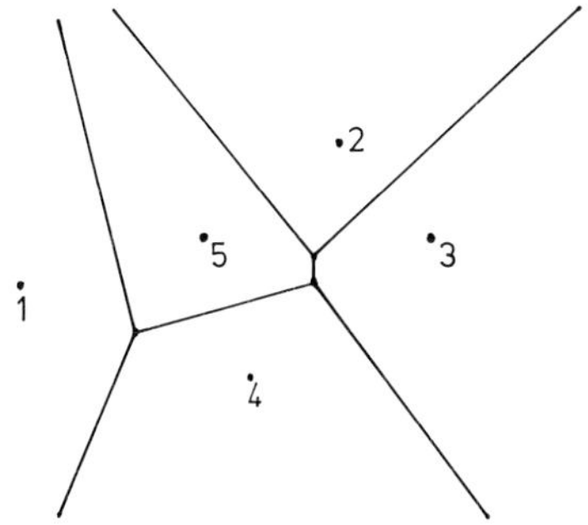

For integers i,j, $1 \le i,j \le n$, let

$$H(i,j) = \{y \in \mathbb{R}^2;\ dist(x_i,y) \le dist(x_j,y)\}.$$

H(i,j) is a half-space defined by the perpendicular bisector of line segment $L(x_i,x_j)$. Clearly, $VR(x_i) = \bigcap_{j \ne i} H(i,j)$.

Thus $VR(x_i)$ is a convex polygonal region. We can now define the Voronoi diagram VD(S) of S as the union of the set of edges and vertices of Voronoi regions $VR(x_i)$, $1 \le i \le n$. The regions of the Voronoi diagram are the Voronoi regions. Clearly, for every vertex x of the Voronoi diagram there are at least three points x_i,x_j,x_k of S such that $dist(x,x_i) = dist(x,x_j) = dist(x,x_k)$. Throughout this section we use point for elements of S and vertex for elements of the Voronoi diagram.

Also, the edges of the Voronoi diagram are (parts of) perpendicular bisectors of line segments $L(x_i,x_j)$, $i \neq j$. A Voronoi region is either bounded or unbounded. The unbounded regions are associated with boundary points of the convex hull.

<u>Lemma 1:</u> $VR(x_i)$ is unbounded iff x_i belongs to BCH(S).

<u>Proof:</u> $\Rightarrow$ (indirect). Assume that $VR(x_i)$ is unbounded but x_i does not belong to BCH(S). Since $VR(x_i)$ is a convex polygonal region there is a semi-infinite ray, say L, starting in x_i and running within $VR(x_i)$. Since x_i does not belong to BCH(S) ray L must intersect some edge, say $L(x_j,x_k)$, of the convex hull. Finally observe, that any point on ray L, which is far enough away from point x_i, is closer to x_j (and x_k) than to x_i, a contradiction.

$\Leftarrow$. Suppose that x_i belongs to BCH(S). Let x_j and x_k be the neighbours of x_i on BCH(S), as shown in the figure. Then every point in the shaded region, i.e. in the cone defined by the rays starting in x_i and being perpendicular to lines $L(x_i,x_k)$ and $L(x_i,x_j)$ respectively, is closer to x_i than to any other point of S. □

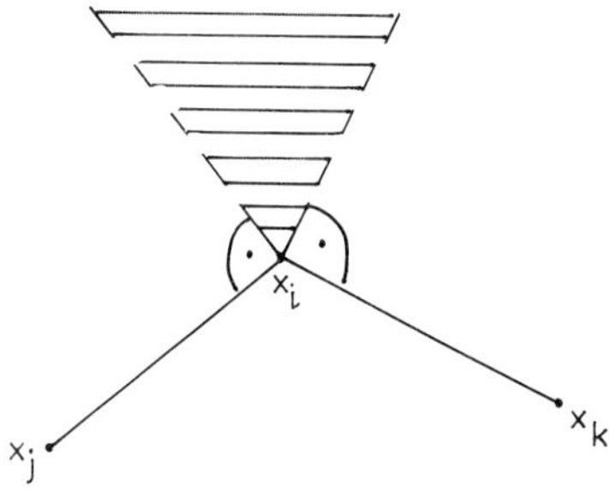

A Voronoi diagram for point set S partitions the plane into n, n = |S|, convex polygonal regions. Thus it is essentially a planar graph. In view of IV.1o., lemma 2, the following lemma is not surprising.

<u>Lemma 2:</u> A Voronoi-diagram for a set of n points has at most 2n-4 vertices and 3n-6 edges.

<u>Proof:</u> We consider a graph D which is dual to the Voronoi diagram. The vertices of D are the regions of the Voronoi-diagram. Thus D has n vertices. Two vertices of D are connected by an edge if the corresponding regions share an edge (In the diagram below dual edges are dashed). Thus D is a planar graph and has therefore at most 3n-6 edges (IV.1o., lemma 2). Since the edges of D are in one-to-one correspondence to the edges of the Voronoi-diagram we infer that the number of edges of the

Voronoi-diagram is at most 3n-6. Finally, since every vertex of the diagram has degree at least three, there are at most 2n-4 vertices.

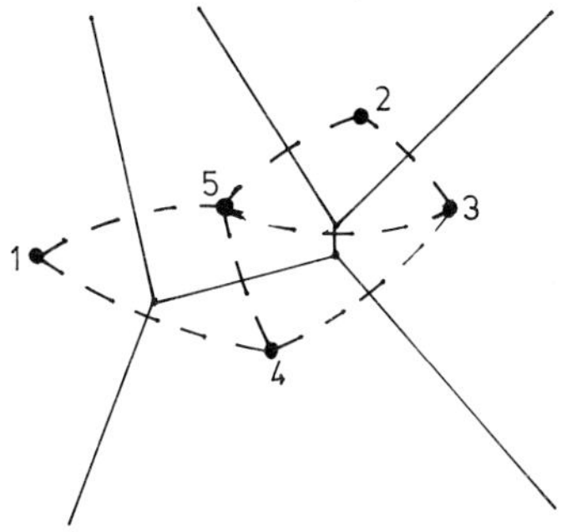

□

We are now ready for the main theorem of his section.

Theorem 1: Let $S \subseteq \mathbb{R}^2$ be given, $n = |S|$. Then the Voronoi diagram of S can be computed in time $O(n \log n)$.

Proof: The algorithm is based on the divide-and-conquer paradigm. Since we aim for an $O(n \log n)$ algorithm we might as well assume that S is sorted lexicographically. Let S_L be the first half of sorted set S, $|S_L| = \lfloor n/2 \rfloor$, and let S_R be the second half of set S. Assume inductively,

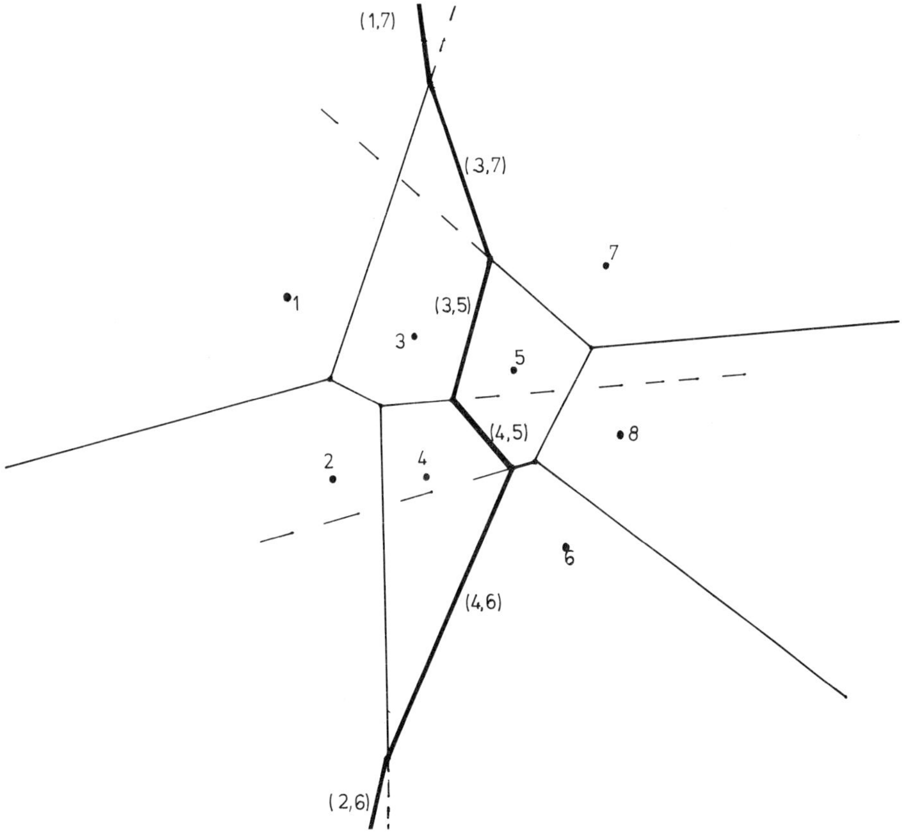

that we constructed the Voronoi diagrams $VD(S_L)$ and $VD(S_R)$ of sets S_L and S_R by applying our algorithm recursively. This will take time $T(\lfloor n/2 \rfloor) + T(\lceil n/2 \rceil)$. Also, $T(1) = O(1)$, since the Voronoi diagram of a singleton set is trivial. The goal is now to construct $VD(S)$ from $VD(S_L)$ and $VD(S_R)$ by "merging". In the example above $VD(S)$ is shown solid, the parts of $VD(S_L)$ and $VD(S_R)$ which do not belong to $VD(S)$ are dashed, and line P which belongs to $VD(S)$ but to neither $VD(S_L)$ nor $VD(S_R)$ is emphasized by a thick line. We have $S_L = \{1,2,3,4\}$ and $S_R = \{5,6,7,8\}$.

Line P is crucial for the merging process. We define it by

$$P := \{y \in \mathbb{R}_2,\ dist\ (y,S_L) = dist(y,S_R)\}$$

where $dist(y,T) = \min\{dist(x,y),\ x \in T\}$ for a point y and a set T. The following lemma shows that P consists of edges of VD(S) and that P is monotone.

Lemma 3: a) $P = \{y;$ y lies on an edge of VD(S) which is a perpendicular bisector of some $x_i \in S_L$ and some $x_j \in S_R\}$. In particular, P consists of two infinite rays and some number of straight line segments.

b) P is monotone, i.e. P can be directed such that no line segment runs downward.

Proof: a) and b) Let P' be the set defined in part a) of the lemma. Then clearly $P' \subseteq P$. It remains to show the contrary. Let $y \in P$ be arbitrary. Then there are $x_i \in S_L$, $x_j \in S_R$ such that $dist(y,x_i) = dist(y,x_j) \le dist(y,x)$ for all $x \in S$. Thus y lies on the edge which separates the Voronoi regions $VR(x_i)$ and $VR(x_j)$ and hence $y \in P'$. This proves $P = P'$.

We conclude, in particular, that P consists of a set of line segments. Every line segment is the perpendicular bisector of some $x_i \in S_L$ and some $x_j \in S_R$. Direct the line segment such that x_i is to the left of the line segment. Then no line segment is directed downward, because this would imply that the x-coordinate of x_i is larger than the x-coordinate of x_j, a contradiction. Since S is lexicographically ordered, we may even conclude that there is at most one horizontal line segment (which then is directed right to left).

Finally, since the curve P is monotone, it cannot be a closed curve. Thus it consists of two infinite rays and some number of (finite) line segments. □

Lemma 3 characterizes line P. The significance of line P is given by

Lemma 4: Let P be as defined above. Direct P in order of increasing y-values and let L(P) be the region of the plane to the left of P. Similarly, let R(P) be the region of the plane to the right of P. Then

$$VD(S) = (VD(S_L) \cap L(P)) \cup P \cup (VD(S_R) \cap R(P))$$

Proof: Let VD be the set defined by the expression on the right hand side. We show $VD(S) \subseteq VD$ and $VD \subseteq VD(S)$.

"$\subseteq$": Let y be an element of VD(S), i.e. y lies on an edge of VD(S). Then there are i,j such that $dist(y,x_i) = dist(y,x_j) \le dist(y,x)$ for all $x \in S$. If $i,j \in S_L$ then $y \in VD(S_L) \cap L(P)$, if $i \in S_L$, $j \in S_R$ or vice versa then $y \in P$ and if $i,j \in S_R$ then $y \in VD(S_R) \cap R(P)$.

"$\supseteq$": Let $y \in VD$. If $y \in P$ then $y \in VD(S)$ by lemma 3. So let us assume that $y \in VD(S_L) \cap L(P)$. Since $x \in L(P)$ we have $dist(y,S_L) < dist(y,S_R)$ and since $y \in VD(S_L)$ there are $i,j \in S_L$ such that $dist(y,S_L) = dist(y,x_i) = dist(y,x_j)$. Thus $y \in VD(S)$. □

We infer from lemma 4 that the construction of line P essentially solves the problem of merging diagrams $VD(S_L)$ and $VD(S_R)$. Lemma 3 characterizes line P. However, it does not give an efficient algorithm for constructing P. Our approach will be to construct P in order of increasing y-values. Thus the first goal must be to construct the (lower) infinite ray L of line P.

Consider the convex hull $BCH(S_L)$ and $BCH(S_R)$. We can obtain BCH(S) from $BCH(S_L)$ and $BCH(S_R)$ by drawing two tangents T_L and T_U. Let T_L be the "lower" tangent. We have shown in section 2, lemma 1 how to construct BCH(S) and T_L in time O(log n) from $BCH(S_L)$ and $BCH(S_R)$. Moreover, we have:

Lemma 5: Let the "lower" tangent T_L of $BCH(S_L)$ and $BCH(S_R)$ connect $x_i \in S_L$ and $x_j \in S_R$. Then L is the perpendicular bisector of line segment $L(x_i,x_j)$, i.e. of tangent T_L.

Proof: By lemma 3 L is the perpendicular bisector of line segment $L(x_i,x_j)$ for some $x_i \in S_L$, $x_j \in S_R$. Moreover, L is an edge of VD(S). Thus regions $VR(x_i)$ and $VD(x_j)$ are unbounded in VD(S) and hence x_i and x_j belong to BCH(S) by lemma 1. Since $x_i \in S_L$, $x_j \in S_R$ we finally conclude that $L(x_i,x_j)$ is a tangent of $BCH(S_L)$ and $BCH(S_R)$. □

Lemma 5 allows us to start the construction of curve P. The idea is now to extend P line segment by line segment. More precisely, let P = $\ell_1,\ell_2,\ldots,\ell_m$ where ℓ_1 and ℓ_m are infinite rays and $\ell_2,\ldots,\ell_{m-1}$ are line segments. Assume inductively, that we constructed $\ell_1,\ldots,\ell_{h-1}$ for some $h \ge 1$ and that we have determined points $x_i \in S_L$, $x_j \in S_R$ such that ℓ_h is part of the perpendicular bisector of x_i and x_j. Lemma 5 is the base of the induction.

Line segment ℓ_h starts at the terminal point of ℓ_{h-1} ($-\infty$ for h = 1). It is part of the perpendicular bisector, call it L, of x_i and x_j for some $x_i \in S_L$, $x_j \in S_R$. Conceptually travel along ray L (in order of increasing y) starting in the terminal point of ℓ_{h-1}. At the beginning of the journey we are within Voronoi regions $VR_L(x_i)$ of x_i with respect to S_L and $VR_R(x_i)$ of x_i with respect to S_R. Ray L will intersect either an edge of $VD(S_L)$ before an edge of $VD(S_R)$ or vice versa, or it intersects neither an edge of $VD(S_L)$ or an edge of $VD(S_R)$. In the latter case, L = ℓ_m and we are done.

In the former case assume w.l.o.g. that L intersects an edge, say e, of $VD(S_L)$ before (or simultaneously with) an edge of $VD(S_R)$. Call the point of intersection z. Point z lies on the boundary of the Voronoi region of x_i with respect to S_L. Thus there is $x_i' \in S_L$ such that $dist(x_i,z) = dist(x_i',z) = dist(x_j,z)$. In other words, z is a vertex of the Voronoi diagram of set S as shown in the diagram next page. In vertex z three edges of VD(S) meet, namely ℓ_h, the perpendicular bisector of x_i and x_j, e, the perpendicular bisector of x_i and x_i', and ℓ_{h+1}. Thus ℓ_{h+1} is the perpendicular bisector of x_i' and x_j. We summarize the discussion in the following algorithm.

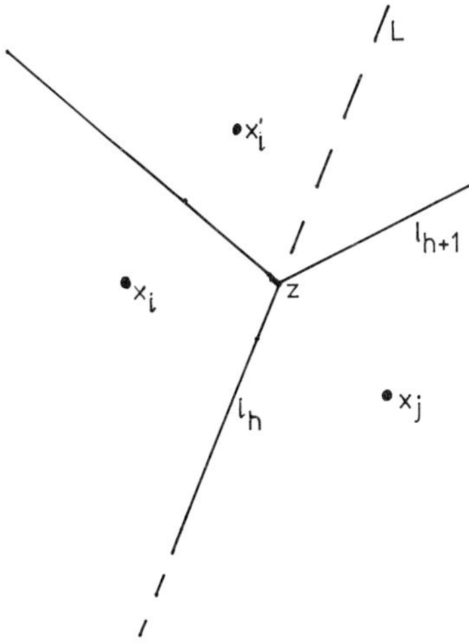

(1) $h \leftarrow 1$;
Let T_L be the "lower" tangent of $BCH(S_L)$ and $BCH(S_R)$, T_L connects $x \in S_L$ and $y \in S_R$, say;
Let L be an infinite ray starting at $-\infty$ and being the perpendicular bisector of x and y. Furthermore, let line segment ℓ_1 on L start in $-\infty$.

(2) <u>while</u> L intersects either $VD(S_L)$ or $VD(S_R)$

(3) <u>do</u> <u>if</u> L intersects an edge, say e, of $VD(S_L)$ not after an edge of $VD(S_R)$

(4) <u>then</u> let z be the point of intersection;

(5) terminate ℓ_h in z;

(6) let e be the perpendicular bisector of $x \in S_L$ and $x' \in S_L$;

(7) $x \leftarrow x'$; $h \leftarrow h + 1$;

(8) let L be the infinite ray, starting in z and being the perpendicular bisector of x and y, and extending towards $+\infty$;

(9) let ℓ_h be a line segment on L starting in z

<u>else</u> ⋮

symmetric to then-case

<u>fi</u>

(1o) <u>od</u>

Before we can analyse the algorithm above we need to be more specific about the representation of the Voronoi diagram. We postulate the following representation:

a) each face of the Voronoi diagram, i.e. each Voronoi region, is given by the doubly-linked list of its boundary edges. Also the point of S to which the region belongs and the representation of the region are linked and the two occurences of every edge are linked.

b) the boundary of the convex hull of S is given by its hierarchical representation.

Part b) of the representation is only needed for the algorithm above, part a) is the genuine representation of the diagram. We have seen in section 2 that the lower tangent T_L, points x and y in statement (1) and the hierarchical representation of BCH(S) can be constructed in time O(log n) from the hierarchical representation of $BCH(S_L)$ and $BCH(S_R)$. Thus line (1) takes time O(log n).

Let us consider while-loop (2) - (1o) next. From the considerations above it is clear that at most n iterations of the loop can occur. The test in line (2) is carried out as follows.

When line (2) is executed we "move" within the Voronoi regions $VR_L(x)$ of point $x \in S_L$ with respect to S_L and $VR_R(y)$ of point $y \in S_R$ with respect to S_R. Region $VR_L(x)$ (and $VR_R(y)$) is represented by a circular list. Find the lowest (smallest y-coordinate) point on that list. This is done at most once for every point and hence takes total time O(n) by lemma 2. Next associate two pointers with the list, one with the

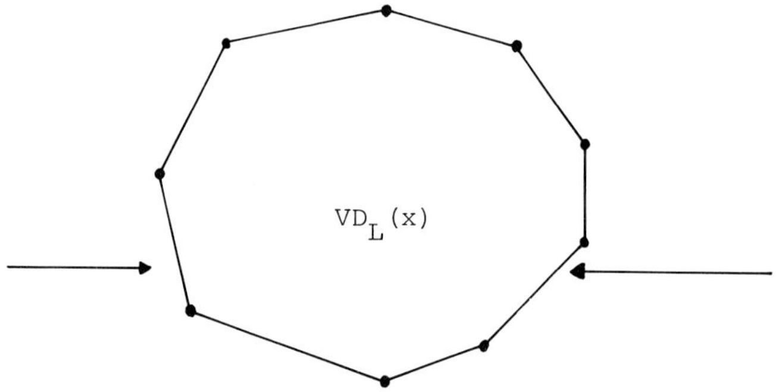

left part and one with the right part (cf. the diagram above). We use these pointers to implement a scan line which scans $VR_L(x)$ and $VR_R(y)$ simultaneously from bottom to top and finds the first (= lowest, since P is monotonic) intersection of L with any edge of $VR_L(x)$ and $VR_R(y)$. This process is very similar to merging four sorted lists. The time required to find an intersection is clearly proportional to the number of edges discarded. Since P is monotone and hence no back-tracking is ever needed every edge is discarded only once. Once we have determined the edge of intersection we only have to follow the pointer to the other copy of the edge in order to find point x' in line 6. The process is then continued with x' instead of x in the next iteration of the loop. We summarize in

Lemma 6: Voronoi diagram VD(S) can be constructed from $VD(S_L)$ and $VD(S_R)$ in time O(n).

Proof: We argued above that the cost of one execution of the loop body is proportional to the number of edges discarded. Also every edge is discarded at most once and the number of iterations of the loop is at most n. Thus line P can be constructed in time O(n) from $VD(S_L)$ and $VD(S_R)$. Once line P is found it is easy to construct VD(S) from $VD(S_L)$ and $VD(S_R)$ in linear time. In fact, the construction is easily incorporated into the program given above. The only change required is to update VR(s) and VR(y) in the loop body by throwing away some of their edges and to add ℓ_h as a new edge. We leave the simple details to the reader. □

It is now easy to complete the proof. By lemma 6 we have the following recurrence for the time T(n) required to construct the Voronoi diagram for a set of n points.

$$T(1) = O(1)$$
$$T(n) = T(\lceil n/2 \rceil) + T(\lfloor n/2 \rfloor) + O(n)$$

Thus T(n) = O(n log n) as claimed. □

How good is our algorithm for constructing Voronoi diagrams? It is even optimal? The following argument shows that constructing Voronoi diagrams is at least as hard as sorting and hence that the algorithm above is optimal with respect to wide range of computational models. Consider $S \subseteq \mathbb{R}^2$ where S consists of n + 1 points, the origin and n points on the unit circle. Then the Voronoi diagram for S is an n-gon containing the origin and n rays emanating from the vertices of the n-gon. The rays sort the n points on the unit circle in an obvious way. Thus sorting n points on the unit circle by angle is no easier than constructing the Voronoi diagram.

We close this section with a brief discussion on updating Voronoi diagrams. Suppose that we have computed the Voronoi diagram VD(S) and we either want to delete $x \in S$ or we want to add a point y to S. In the latter case we also assume that $x \in S$ with $y \in VR(x)$ is given. We will discuss methods for finding y in the next section.

A worst case bound for the complexity of insertions and deletions is given by the theory of order decomposable problems. Let $\le$ be the lexicographical order on $\mathbb{R}^2$. Then the problem of constructing the Voronoi diagram is order-decomposable with respect to ordering $\le$ with merging time $C(n) = O(n)$. Thus insertions and deletions take time $O(n)$ in the worst case by the results of section VII, 1.3.. Since the Voronoi diagram may be changed drastically by an insertion or deletion this bound cannot be improved.

However, on the average one can do much better. Exercises 14 and 15 discuss algorithms for updating Voronoi diagrams whose running time is bounded by $O(s)$ and $O(s \log s)$ respectively where s is the size of the change of the diagram.

VIII. 3.2 Searching Planar Subdivisions

A Voronoi diagram is a partition of the plane into polygonal regions some of which are unbounded. In this section we show how to search Voronoi diagrams in logarithmic time, i.e. we describe two data structures which given $y \in \mathbb{R}^2$ allow to find $x \in S$ with dist(y,x) minimal in logarithmic time. Moreover, the data structures can be constructed in linear time and use linear space.

In searching Voronoi diagrams, the Voronoi regions are the regions of "constant answer", i.e. $\text{dist}(y,x) = \min\{\text{dist}(y,x);\ x \in S\}$ if and only if $y \in VR(x)$. In other words, x is the nearest point to y among all points in S iff $y \in VR(x)$. Thus in some sense the Voronoi diagram is a method of tabulating the answers to all nearest neighbour searches. Of course, we still have to describe how to search the table efficiently. That is the purpose of this section.

More generally, the methods to be described can be used in the following situation. Suppose that $f: \mathbb{R}^2 \to T$ for some set T assumes only finitely many different values and that for each $t \in T$, $f^{-1}(t)$ is a polygonal region $R_t \subseteq \mathbb{R}^2$. Then $\{R_t, t \in T\}$ is a subdivision of $\mathbb{R}^2$. Assume further that the total number of edges of all polygonal regions R_t, $t \in T$, is m. Then the data structures to be described allow us to compute f in time $O(\log m)$. Moreover, the data structures can be constructed in time $O(m \log m)$ and require space $O(m)$. In the Voronoi diagram searching problem we have $T = S$ and $f(y) = x$ where $dist(x,y) = dist(y,S)$. Other examples are $T = S$ and $f(y) = x$ where $dist(x,y) \geq dist(z,y)$ for all $z \in S$ (furthest neighbour) or $T = S \times S$ and $f(y) = (x,x')$ where $dist(x,y) \leq dist(x',y) \leq dist(z,y)$ for all $z \in S$, $z \neq x,x'$ (two nearest neighbours). In both examples, it is clear that the regions of constant answer are convex polygonal regions since these regions can be written as intersection of half-spaces. It is not clear however whether these regions can be computed efficiently. We refer the reader to the exercises.

A planar subdivision is a straight line embedding $\hat{G}$ of a planar graph G. An embedding is straight line if all edges of G are embedded as straight line segments (cf. diagram). In this section we describe three

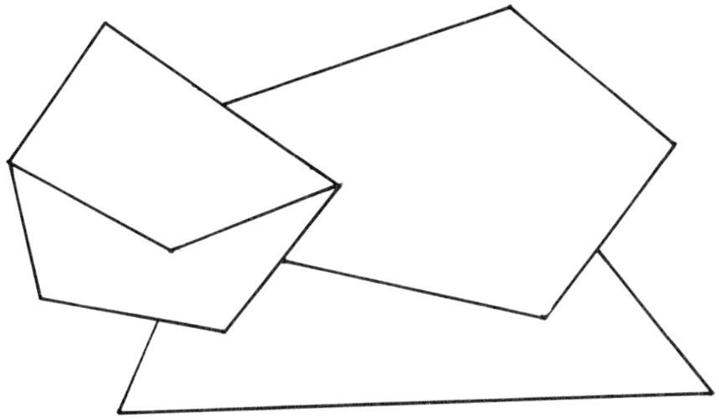

solutions to the planar subdivision searching problem; several other solutions are discussed in the exercises. The first two solutions have logarithmic search time but can deal only with static subdivisions, the third solution has search time $O((\log n)^2)$ but can deal with dynamic subdivisions. We present three solutions because each solution illustrates an important algorithmic paradigm. In the first solution the planar subdivision is successively simplified by the removal of a large independent set of vertices of small degree. The existence of such a set is guaranteed in every planar graph (Lemma 8 below). The method of removing large independent sets of vertices can also be successfully used for obtaining hierarchical representations of (convex) polyhedra, cf. exercise 2 and section 4.3.. The second solution is based on path decompositions of planar subdivisions. It is computationally superior to the first solution in the sense that the constants involved in the O-expressions are much smaller. Path decompositions will be used again in section 5.1.4. on skeleton structures. Finally, the third solution combines the ideas of path decomposition and weight-balanced trees in order to obtain a dynamic solution.

We close this introduction with a short discussion of a more general and of a more restricted searching problem. A planar subdivision is <u>simple</u> if all (including the infinite) faces of $\hat{G}$ are triangles. A <u>generalized</u> planar subdivision is a planar subdivision together with a set of pairwise non-intersecting rays which start at the nodes on the boundary of the infinite face. The diagram below shows a generalized

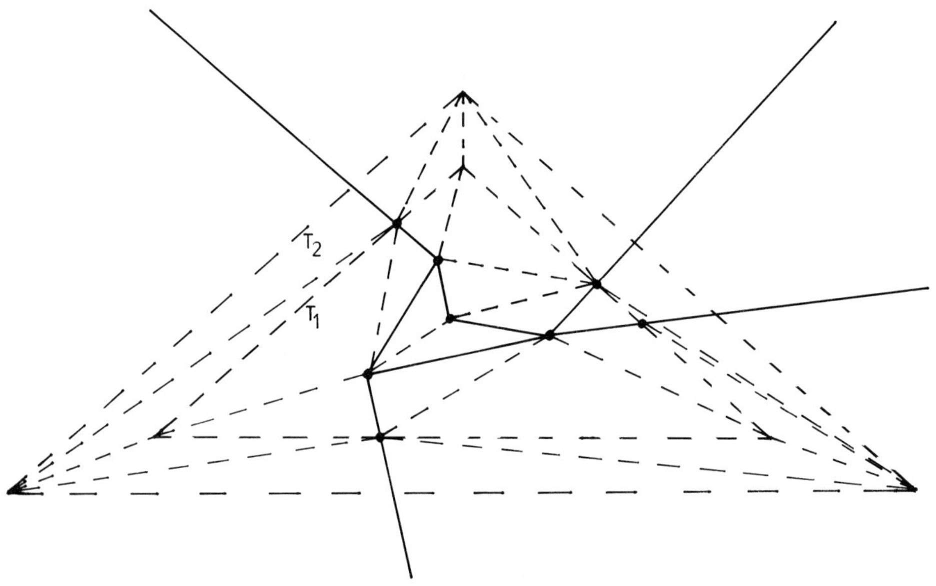

planar subdivision. If the dotted edges are added then we obtain a generalized subdivision with a simple core. The following lemma shows that it suffices to solve simple searching problems.

Lemma 7: If the searching problem for simple planar subdivisions with n edges can be solved with search time O(log n), preprocessing time O(n) and space O(n) then the searching problem for generalized subdivisions with n edges can be solved with search time O(log n), preprocessing time O(n log n) and space O(n). If all faces of the generalized subdivision are convex then preprocessing time O(n) suffices.

Proof: Let $\hat{G}$ be a generalized planar subdivision with n edges and $m \le n$ vertices. We enclose the finite part of $\hat{G}$ in two large component triangles T_1 and T_2 (cf. diagram above) such that T_2 contains T_1. Triangles T_2 and T_1 together with the part of $\hat{G}$ which lies in the interior of T_1 defines a planar subdivision. We turn this subdivision into a simple subdivision $\hat{G}'$ by triangulating all its faces. Note that every infinite ray defines an edge of $\hat{G}'$ which has one vertex on triangle T_1. However, no part of the infinite rays outside T_1 belongs to $\hat{G}'$. Thus triangulation actually produces a subdivision in which the outer face is also a triangle, i.e. $\hat{G}'$ is simple. The simple subdivision $\hat{G}'$ has clearly O(n) edges and can be obtained in time O(n log n) using the methods of section 4.2.. If all faces of $\hat{G}$ are convex then $\hat{G}'$ can be obtained in time O(n).

We can now search for point y in $\hat{G}$ as follows. In time O(1) we decide whether y lies inside or outside T_1. If y lies inside T_1 then we use the efficient solution for simple subdivision $\hat{G}'$which exists by assumption. If y lies outside T_1 then we locate y in logarithmic time by binary search on the infinite rays as follows. We divide the set of rays into two disjoint sets, the right-going and the left-going rays. (A ray is right-going if it extends towards infinity in the direction of the positive x-axis). For the rays in each class, a simple compari-

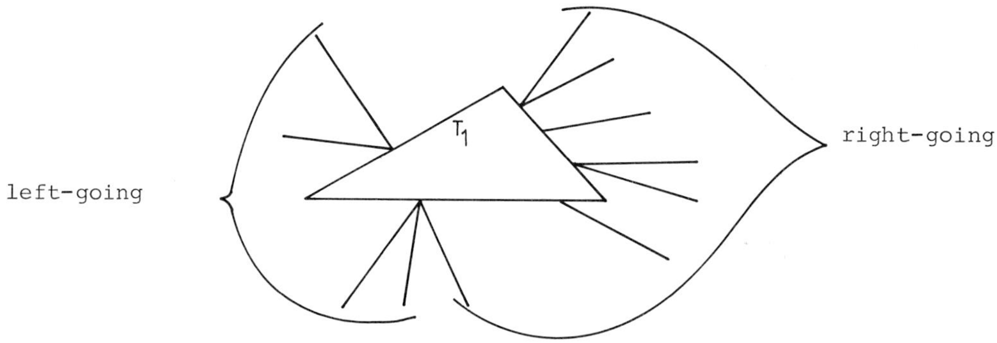

son decides in time O(1) whether y lies above or below the ray and hence binary search locates point y in time O(log n).

Thus in either case (y inside or outside T_1) we can locate y in time O(log n). Furthermore, the space requirement is clearly O(n + space of solution for $\hat{G}'$). Also the preprocessing time is O(n log n + preprocessing time for $\hat{G}'$). □

VIII. 3.2.1 Removal of Large Independent Sets

Our first solution uses divide-and-conquer by the removal of large independent sets. The same technique is applicable to a number of other problems in computational geometry, most notably to problems concerning convex polyhedra, cf. exercise 2 and section 4.3. In these applications one uses the technique of removing large independent sets of nodes in order to obtain "simpler" versions of convex polyhedra.

The idea is as follows. Let $\hat{G}$ be a simple planar subdivision with n vertices and hence 3n-6 edges. Since $\hat{G}$ is a planar graph it has a large (at least size cn for some constant $c > 0$) subset I of vertices which are pairwise independent and have small degree, say at most 9. Two vertices are independent if they are not connected by an edge. Removal of the vertices in I from $\hat{G}$ yields a subdivision $\hat{G}'$ with at most (1-c)n vertices. The faces of $\hat{G}'$ are m-gons with $m \le 9$ and different vertices in I lie in different faces in $\hat{G}'$. We turn $\hat{G}'$ into a simple subdivision $\tilde{G}$ by triangulating all faces of $\hat{G}'$. In the following example (see next page), nodes x,y, and z form an independent set. Removal of {x,y,z} yields $\hat{G}'$; triangulating the three non-triangular faces yields $\tilde{G}$. The newly added edges are drawn dashed. The faces of $\tilde{G}$ which correspond to the same node in I = {x,y,z} are labelled by the same character. Let $\tilde{D}$ be a search structure for $\tilde{G}$ which we assume to exist inductively. We can construct $\tilde{D}$ by applying the technique recursively or by some other means. In our example $\tilde{D}$ has 10 leaves corresponding to the 1o faces of $\tilde{G}$. We obtain a search structure $\hat{D}'$ for $\hat{G}'$ from $\tilde{D}$ by simply combining all the leaves corresponding to the subfaces of a face of $\hat{G}'$ to a single leaf. In our example, we combine faces A_1, A_2, and A_3 to face A. The search structure $\hat{D}'$ is now easily turned into a search structure $\hat{D}$ for $\hat{G}$. Consider a face, say F, of $\hat{G}'$. If there is no vertex in I which lies in F, then F is also a face of $\hat{G}$ and there is nothing to do. In our example, this case arises for the infinite face. If there is a vertex, say x, in I which lies in F, then we observe first that this vertex is unique since I is an independent set of vertices. Vertex x and the edges, say $e_1,\ldots,e_k$ $(k \le 9)$, incident to x subdivide F into faces $F_1,\ldots,F_k$ of $\tilde{G}$. Hence we can obtain $\hat{D}$ from $\hat{D}'$ by replacing the leaf corresponding to F by a program which locates a query point with respect to the "star" defined by vertex x and the edges incident to x. Since x has degree at most 9 this decision takes time O(1) and hence the cost of locating a point in $\hat{G}$ is only a constant more than the cost of locating a point in $\tilde{G}$. Since $\tilde{G}$ has at most (1-c)n vertices we should obtain logarithmic search time in this way. In our example, face A of $\hat{D}'$ has subfaces a,b,c,d of $\hat{G}$. Once we have determined that a query point y lies in A a simple comparison of y with the edges incident to x also determines the face of $\hat{G}$ which contains y.

It remains to fill in the details. We first show that there are always large independent sets of nodes of small degree.

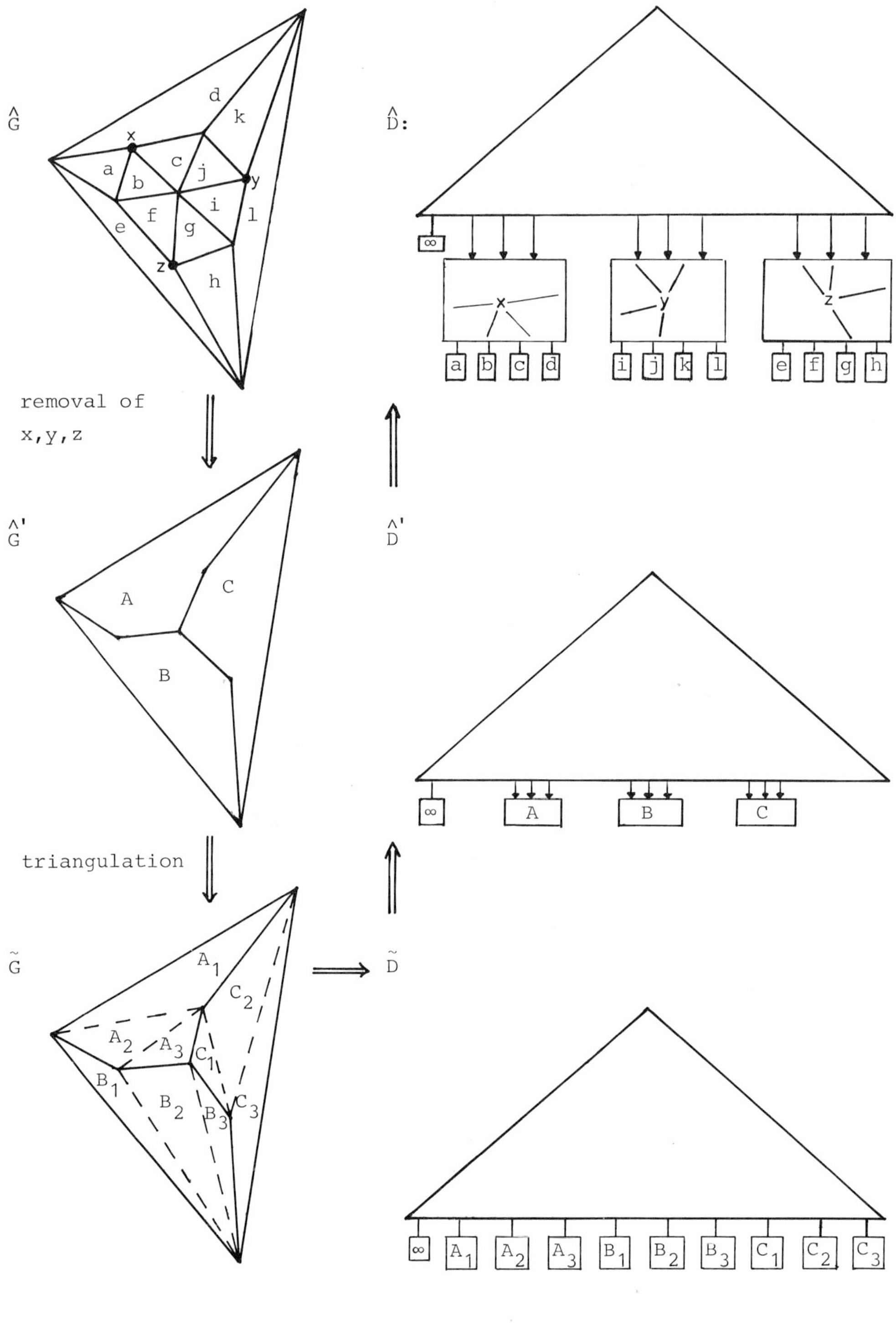

Ĝ
D̂:
a
b
c
d
e
f
g
h
i
j
k
l
x
y
z
∞
removal of
x,y,z
Ĝ'
D̂'
A
B
C
triangulation
G̃
D̃
A1
A2
A3
B1
B2
B3
C1
C2
C3

Lemma 8: Let $G = (V,E)$ be a planar graph with $n = |V|$ nodes, minimum degree 3, and let $V' \subseteq V$. Then there is an independent set $I \subseteq V - V'$ of nodes of degree at most 9 which has size at least $(4n + 12 - 7|V'|)/70$. I is independent if $v,w \in I$ implies $(v,w) \notin E$. Moreover, I can be found in time $O(n)$.

Proof: Let V" be the set of nodes of G which have degree at most 9, and let $x = |V''|$. Since G is planar the number of edges of G is at most $3n - 6$. Also there are exactly $n - x$ nodes of degree 10 or more and every other node has degree at least three. Thus $(3x + 10(n - x))/2 \le 3n - 6$ or $x \ge (4n + 12)/7$.

Consider the subgraph induced by $V'' - V'$. It has $x - |V'|$ nodes and every node has degree at most 9. Thus it can be colored using at most 10 colors such that adjacent nodes are colored differently. Moreover, such a coloring can be found in time $O(n)$ as follows. Assume that we use colors $1,\dots,10$. Consider the nodes in some order. When node v is considered, color it with the lowest numbered color not yet used on a neighbour of v. This algorithm clearly runs in time $O(n)$ and uses at most 10 colors. Finally observe, that there must be one color class containing at least $(x - |V'|)/10 \ge (4n + 12 - 7|V'|)/70$ nodes. □

We are now ready to prove

Theorem 2: Let $\hat{G}$ be a simple planar subdivision with n vertices. Then the searching problem with respect to $\hat{G}$ can be solved with search time $O(\log n)$, space requirement $O(n)$, and preprocessing time $O(n)$.

Proof: We use induction on the number n of vertices in $\hat{G}$. For $n \le 100$ the claims are certainly true by appropriate choice of the constants in the bounds.

Assume now that $n > 100$. Let I be an independent set of nodes none of which has degree 10 or more and none of which lies on the boundary of the infinite face. By lemma 8 (let V' be the vertices on the boundary of the infinite face which is triangle and hence $|V'| = 3$) we can find such a set I with $|I| \ge (4n - 9)/70$ in time $O(n)$.

Removal of set I and the edges incident to vertices in I leaves us with a planar subdivision $\hat{G}'$ with at most $66n/70 + 1 < n$ vertices.

Note that the faces of $\hat{G}'$ are m-gons with $3 \le m \le 9$. Every face of $\hat{G}'$ can be triangulated in time $O(1)$ using $m - 3$ edges. Thus we can turn $\hat{G}'$ into a simple planar subdivision $\tilde{G}$ with at most $66n/70 + 1$ vertices in time $O(n)$.

Applying the method recursively to $\tilde{G}$, we obtain a search structure $\tilde{D}$ for $\tilde{G}$ which we then turn into a search structure $\hat{D}$ for $\hat{G}$ as described above. We can clearly obtain $\hat{D}$ from $\tilde{D}$ in time $O(n)$ using additional space $O(n)$ and increasing the depth by $O(1)$. Thus we obtain the following recurrences for the depth $d(n)$ of the search structure, the construction time $T(n)$, and the space requirement $S(n)$.

$$d(n) = O(1) \qquad \text{for } n \le 100$$
$$d(n) = O(1) + \max\{d(n');\ n' \le 66n/70 + 1\} \quad \text{for } n > 100$$

and

$$T(n) = O(1) \qquad \text{for } n \le 100$$
$$T(n) = \max\{O(n) + T(n');\ n' \le 66n/70 + 1\} \quad \text{for } n > 100$$

and similarly for $S(n)$. Thus $d(n) = O(\log n)$, $T(n) = O(n)$ and $S(n) = O(n)$ as a simple inductive argument shows. □

VIII. 3.2.2 Path Decompositions

We will now present a second solution to the planar subdivision searching problem. It is based on path decompositions of planar subdivisions. We will use path decompositions again in section 5.1.4. where we will show how to greatly extend the power of plane sweep algorithms. The present section is organized as follows. We first introduce path decompositions and derive a suboptimal solution with $O((\log n)^2)$ search time and $O(n^2)$ storage space from it. We will then show how to reduce the space requirement to $O(n)$ by removing redundancy. Finally, we reduce search time to $O(\log n)$ by a clever combination of binary search in x- and y-direction.

Let $\hat{G}$ be a simple planar subdivision. We assume w.l.o.g. that no edge of $\hat{G}$ is horizontal. Let s (t) be the vertex of $\hat{G}$ with maximal (minimal) y-coordinate. An s-t path is a sequence $v_0,\ldots,v_m$ of vertices such that $v_0 = s$, $v_m = t$, and (v_i,v_{i+1}) is an edge of $\hat{G}$ for $0 \le i < m$. A path $v_0, \ldots, v_m$ is <u>y-monotone</u> if $y(v_i) \geq y(v_{i+1})$ for $0 \leq i < m$, where $y(v_i)$ is the y-coordinate of vertex v_i. Throughout this section we will use path to mean y-monotone (s,t)-path.

The significance of y-monotone paths stems from the following simple observation. A y-monotone path divides the strip between the horizontal lines through s and t into two parts. Given a point q in the strip, one can clearly locate the part containing q in time O(log m) by binary search for y(p) in the ordered set $y(v_0), \ldots, y(v_m)$ followed by a comparison of p with a single edge of the path.

A sequence $P_1, \ldots, P_k$ of paths is a path decomposition of simple planar subdivision $\hat{G}$ if

1) every P_i is a y-monotone (s,t)-path
2) every edge of $\hat{G}$ belongs to at least one path
3) if $i < j$ then every horizontal line L intersects P_i to the left or at the same point as P_j.

For the sequel, we will always assume that $k = 2^{d+1} - 1$ for some integer d. This can always be achieved by duplicating path P_k a few times. The following diagram (see top of next page) shows a simple planar subdivision and a path decomposition of it.

A path decomposition $P_1, \ldots, P_k$ of $\hat{G}$ gives rise to an O((log k)(log n)) search algorithm immediately; we show below that $k \leq 4n$ is always

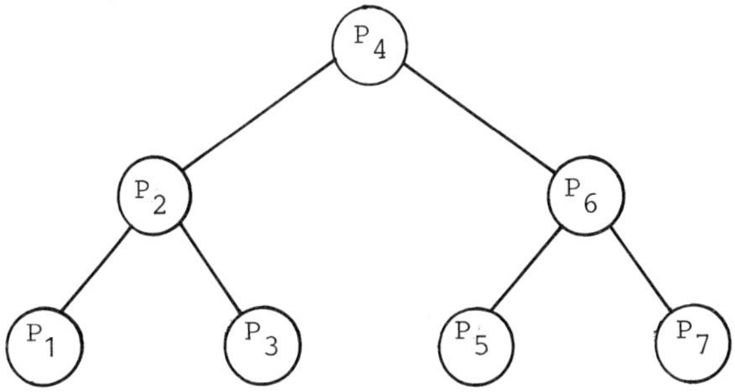

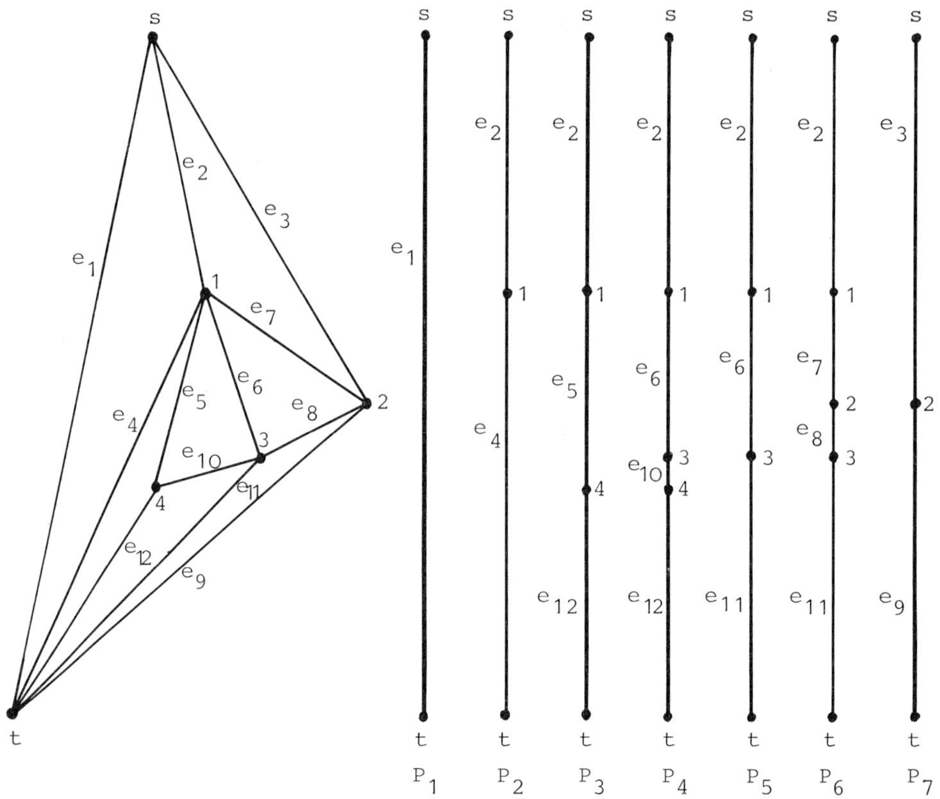

possible. We arrange the paths in a complete binary tree, which we call super-tree (see preceding page), of depth d with $k = 2^{d+1} - 1$ nodes. We number the nodes in inorder such that path P_i is associated with node i. In each node of the super-tree we use the binary search algorithm described above to determine the position of the query point with respect to the path associated with that node. More precisely, we determine also the edge of the path which is intersected by the horizontal line (call it L) through q. In this way, we determine in time $O((\log n)^2)$ an index i and edges e of P_i and e' of P_{i+1} such that q lies between edge e of P_i and e' of P_{i+1}. This pair of edges determines a unique face of $\hat{G}$.

It is interesting to observe that the solution to subdivision searching based on path decomposition is nothing but a twofold application of binary search. Note that a path decomposition decomposes the planar subdivision into regions (between adjacent paths) which are ordered in x-direction in a natural way. We can therefore use binary search in x-direction to locate a query point with respect to these regions. Each step in this binary search process requires us to determine the location of the query point with respect to a path. Since paths are y-monotone we can use binary search in y-direction for that purpose.

The basic algorithm described above has several shortcomings; it does not achieve search time O(log n) and it uses space $O(n^2)$ since it requires to store O(n) paths of length O(n) each. We show how to reduce the storage requirement first.

Let e be an edge of a simple planar subdivision $\hat{G}$ and let $P_1,\ldots,P_k$ be a path decomposition. Then, if e belongs to P_i and P_j, $i < j$, then e also belongs to P_ℓ for all ℓ, $i \le \ell \le j$. This follows immediately from property (3) of path decompositions. We can therefore describe a path decomposition in linear space by listing for each edge e of $\hat{G}$ a pair (L(e), R(e)) of integers such that e belongs to P_j iff $L(e) \le j \le R(e)$. In our example, the values of L(e) and R(e) are given by the following table. The significance of entry Pos(e) is explained below. We

	L	R	Pos
e_1	1	1	1
e_2	2	6	4
e_3	7	7	7
e_4	2	2	2
e_5	3	3	3
e_6	4	5	4
e_7	6	6	6
e_8	6	6	6
e_9	7	7	7
e_{10}	4	4	4
e_{11}	5	6	6
e_{12}	3	4	4

call this representation of a path decomposition its implicite representation.

<u>Lemma 9:</u> The implicite representation of a path decomposition can be constructed in linear time.

<u>Proof:</u> We construct the paths from left to right. Suppose that we constructed (the implicite representation of) path P and also all positions on P where we can "move" the path to the right. We call these positions the <u>candidates</u> of path P. Let $P = v_o, \ldots, v_m$. An edge (v_i, v_{i+1}) is a candidate of P and edges (v_i, p), (p, v_{i+1}) are its <u>substitutes</u> if v_i, p, v_{i+1} is a face of $\hat{G}$, p is to the right of P and $y(v_i) > y(p) > y(v_{i+1})$. A pair (v_i, v_{i+1}), (v_{i+1}, v_{i+2}) of consecutive edges of P is a candidate and edge (v_i, v_{i+2}) is its substitute if v_i, v_{i+1}, v_{i+2} is a face of $\hat{G}$ which lies to the right of P. The following figure illustrates both notions.

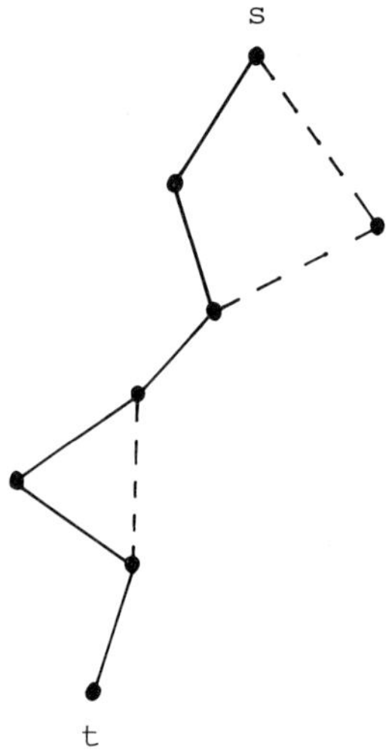

an edge and its substitute

a pair of edges and its substitute

We are now ready for the algorithm

```
(1)  P ← leftmost (s,t)-path; count ← 1;
(2)  for all edges e of P do L(e) ← 1 od;
(3)  while P has a non-empty set of candidates
(4)  do for all edges e in the set of candidates
(5)     do R(e) ← count;
(6)        replace e by its substitute(s) e' (and e");
(7)        L(e) ← (L(e") ←) count + 1
(8)     od;
(9)     count ← count + 1
(1o) od
(11) for all edges e of P do R(e) ← count od
```

For the correctness of this algorithm it suffices to show that every path P different from the rightmost path has a non-empty set of candidates. Assume otherwise. Then every face to the right of P has at most one edge in common with P. Let $P = v_o, \dots, v_m$ and let i be minimal such that $y(p) > y(v_{i+1})$ where p is the third vertex of the face which has edge (v_i, v_{i+1}) on its boundary and is to the right of P. The existence of index i can be seen as follows. Let $k > o$ be minimal such that v_k lies on the rightmost path and v_{k-1} does not. Then edge (v_{k-1}, v_k) has the property stated above since the rightmost path is y-monotone. We claim that $y(v_i) > y(p)$ and hence edge (v_i, v_{i+1}) is a candidate. Assume otherwise, i.e. $y(v_i) < y(p)$. Then $i > 0$ since $s = v_o$ is the vertex with maximal y-coordinate. Also, we must have $y(v_i) < y(p')$ where p' is the third vertex of the face (to the right of P) determined by

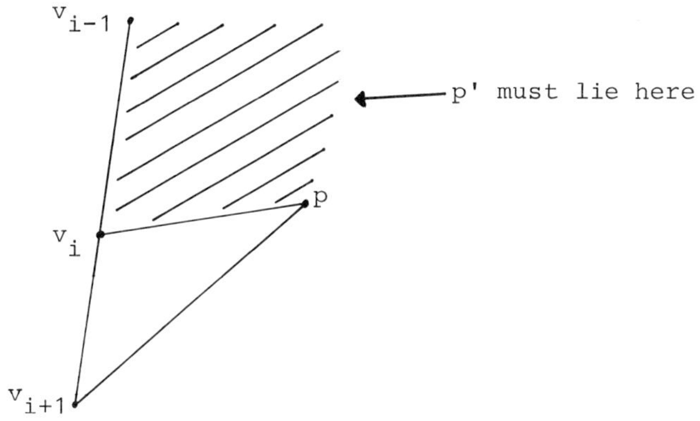

edge (v_{i-1}, v_i). This contradicts the choice of i and hence establishes correctness.

It remains to estimate running time. Path P is represented as a doubly linked list. Also, the set of candidates of P is represented as a linked list. It is then easy to execute lines (5) - (8) in time O(1) and also to check whether one of the substitutes is a candidate for the new path. Note that every candidate of the new path must contain an edge added in line (6). Thus one execution of lines (4) - (1o) takes time proportional to the number of edges for which R(e) is defined during that execution. Since R(e) is defined only once for each edge the time bound follows.

We have now established that the implicite representation of some path decomposition $P_1,\ldots,P_k$, $k = 2^{d+1} - 1 \le 4n$ (recall that we replicate P_k in order to bring k into that special form) of a simple planar subdivision can be constructed in linear time. We will next use this fact to reduce the storage requirement of the search structure to O(n) by storing every edge of $\hat{G}$ only once. More precisely, we store edge e of $\hat{G}$ only in the highest node of the super tree whose associated path contains e. Using functions L(e) and R(e) if is easy to define that node, call it Pos(e). Node Pos(e) is the lowest common ancestor of nodes L(e) and R(e) of the super-tree. Then path $P_{Pos(e)}$ contains e (since $L(e) \le Pos(e) \le R(e)$) and no path associated with an ancestor of Pos(e) contains e. Another way of characterizing Pos(e) is as follows. If L(e) = R(e) then clearly Pos(e) = L(e). If L(e) < R(e) then let $\ldots\, \alpha_2\, \alpha_1\, \alpha_0$ $(\ldots\, \beta_2\, \beta_1\, \beta_0)$ be the binary representation of L(e) (R(e)) and let j be maximal such that $\alpha_j \ne \beta_j$. Then $\alpha_j = 0$, $\beta_j = 1$ and $\ldots\, \alpha_{j+2}\, \alpha_{j+1}\, \gamma\, 0\ldots 0$ is the binary representation of Pos(e) where $\gamma = 0$ if $\alpha_j = \alpha_{j-1} \ldots = \alpha_0 = 0$ and $\gamma = 1$ otherwise.

We are now ready for the definition of the <u>reduced search structure</u>. In the reduced search structure node i contains a balanced search tree T_i for the y-coordinates of the endpoints of all edges e with Pos(e) = i. Also, the node of T_i corresponding to the lower endpoint of edge e contains a pointer to edge e. In our example we have

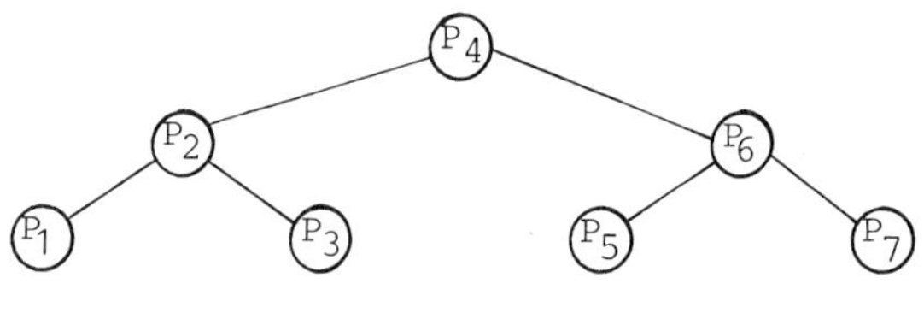

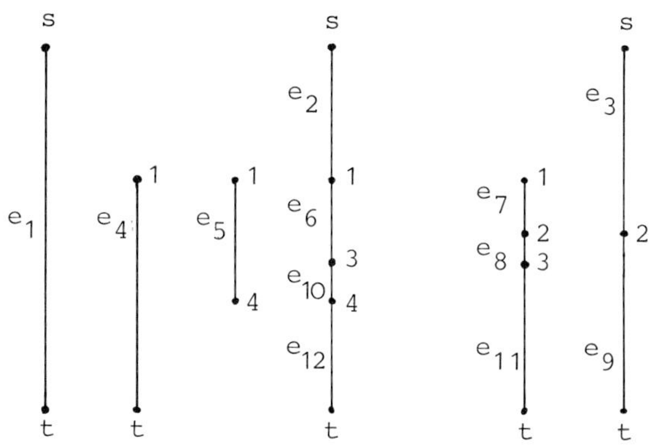

Lemma 1o: a) The search time in the reduced search structure is $O((\log n)^2)$.

b) The reduced search structure requires storage space $O(n)$ and can be constructed in time $O(n)$.

Proof: a) For the following algorithm we assume $P_o = P_1$, $P_{k+1} = P_k$ and $k = 2^{d+1}-1$ for some d. Furthermore, we assume that query point q lies between P_o and P_{k+1}, a fact which is easily checked in time $O(1)$. Recall that P_o and P_{k+1} are the boundary of the infinite face which is a triangle. Finally, L is a horizontal line through q.

```
(1)   ℓ ← 0; r ← k + 1;
(2)   e_ℓ (e_r) ← edge of P_ℓ (P_r) intersected by L;
(3)   while r > ℓ + 1
(4)   do -- point q lies between P_ℓ and P_r and line
         -- L intersects edge e_ℓ (e_r) of P_ℓ (P_r);
(5)      m ← ⌈(ℓ + r)/2⌉;
(6)      if R(e_ℓ) ≥ m
(7)      then ℓ ← m
(8)      else if L(e_r) ≤ m
(9)           then r ← m
(1o)          else find the edge of P_m intersected by L by binary
                   search and redefine ℓ,r,e_ℓ, and e_r appropriately
(11)          fi
```

```
(12)      fi
(13   od
```

The correctness of this algorithm is almost immediate. If either edge e_ℓ or edge e_r belongs to P_m then the step in the binary search is trivial. If neither e_ℓ nor e_r belongs to P_m then let e be the edge of P which is intersected by L. We must have Pos(e) = m since P_m runs between P_ℓ and P_r, $e \neq e_\ell$, and $e \neq e_r$. Thus the correct decision is made in line (1o). This proves part a).

b) The space bound is obvious because every edge of $\hat{G}$ is stored exactly once. It remains to argue the O(n) bound on preprocessing time. We show an O(n log n) bound first (which is probably good enough for practical purposes) and then sketch the linear time solution.

Observe first that Pos(e) can be computed in time O(log n) by the following simple algorithm, for every edge e.

```
if L(e) = R(e)
then Pos(e) ← L(e)
else count ← - 1; ℓ ← L(e); r ← R(e); flag ← true;
     while ℓ ≠ r
     do count ← count + 1;
        if ℓ is odd then flag ← false fi;
        ℓ ← ⌊ℓ/2⌋; r ← ⌊r/2⌋
     od;
     if flag then Pos(e) ← L(e) else Pos(e) ← (ℓ·2+1)2^count fi
fi
```

We conclude that array Pos(e), e ∈ E, can be computed in time O(n log n). Using bucket sort (Pos(e) is the bucket to which edge e is sent; cf. section II.2.1.) we can compute the set of edges associated with any node of the super tree. However, we want this set sorted according to y-coordinate. The O(n log n) cost of sorting can be overcome as follows. Turn $\hat{G}$ into directed graph by directing all edges downwards, i.e. direct edge (v,w) from v to w iff y(v) > y(w). This takes time O(n). Then sort $\hat{G}$ topologically (cf. section IV.2.) in time O(n); let Num(e) be the number of edge e. Associate pair (Pos(e), Num(e)) with edge e and sort these pairs lexicographically by bucket sort in time O(n). In this way, we obtain the edges associated with any node of the super-tree in sorted order according to the y-coordinates of their endpoints. Finally, we have to build a balanced search tree for each node of the super-tree. This clearly takes linear time. In summary, we have shown how to construct the reduced search structure in time $O(n \log n)$.

In order to prove an $O(n)$ bound on the preprocessing time it suffices to compute the array $Pos(e)$, $e \in E$, in time $O(n)$. A more abstract view of the problem is as follows. Given the complete binary tree T with $k = 2^{d+1} - 1$ nodes and pairs (x_i, y_i), $1 \le i \le 4n$, of nodes compute for each pair its lowest common ancestor $a_i = Lca(x_i, y_i)$. We have $x_i = L(e)$, $y_i = R(e)$ and $a_i = Pos(e)$ for some edge e in the problem of computing array Pos.

We solve the lowest common ancestor problem as follows. In a first step we compute several auxiliary functions on tree T by an ordinary tree traversal (cf. section I. 5), namely

$$Rthread(v) = \begin{cases} \text{rightmost leaf, which is a descendant of } v & \text{if } v \text{ is not a leaf} \\ \text{successor of } v \text{ in the inorder traversal of } T & \text{if } v \text{ is a leaf} \end{cases}$$

$Rmost(v) =$ __if__ v is a leaf __then__ v __else__ $Rthread(v)$

and

$Lra(v) = Rthread(Rmost(v))$

Function Lra yields for every node v the lowest ancestor which follows v in the inorder traversal. The symmetric functions Lthread, Lmost and Lla are defined similarly. We leave it to the reader to show that all these functions can be computed in time $O(n)$. Using functions Rmost and Lmost one can decide in time $O(1)$ whether node x is an ancestor of node y; namely x is an ancestor of y iff $Lmost(x) \le Lmost(y) \le Rmost(y) \le Rmost(x)$. Thus in time $O(n)$ we can compute a_i for all pairs (x_i, y_i) where x_i is an ancestor of y_i or vice versa. If neither x_i is an ancestor of y_i nor y_i is an ancestor of x_i then $Lca(x_i, y_i) = Lca(Rmost(x_i), Rmost(y_i))$. We may therefore assume w.l.o.g. that the x_i's and y_i's are leaves of T.

Let $d_i = y_i - x_i + 1$ and $ld_i = \lfloor \log(y_i - x_i + 1) \rfloor$. We can compute ld_i,

$1 \le i \le 4n$, in time $O(n)$ by first tabulating function $m \to \lfloor \log m \rfloor$, $1 \le m \le k$, and then using table-lookup. Let C_h be the nodes of height $h-1$ of T and let $Q_h = \{(x_i,y_i);\ ld_i = h\}$ for $h \ge 1$. We can compute sets Q_h ordered in increasing order of the x_i's by creating triples (ld_i, x_i, i) and sorting them into lexicographic order by bucket sort. In a next step we compute app_i (approximate lowest common ancestor) where $app_i \in C_{ld_i}$ and app_i is an ancestor of x_i for all i. We can compute app_i for all $(x_i,y_i) \in Q_h$ by "merging" Q_h with C_h in time $O(|Q_h| + |C_h|)$. Since C_h, $h \ge 0$ is a partition of the node set of T and since Q_h, $h \ge 0$ is a partition of the set $\{(x_i,y_i),\ 1 \le i \le 4n\}$ the total time needed to compute app_i for all i is $O(n)$.

We claim that $a_i \in \{Lra(app_i), Lra(Lra(app_i))\}$. Let $w = Lra(Lra(app_i))$. Since x_i is descendant of app_i and hence of $Lra(app_i)$ and w, it suffices to show that y_i is not a descendant of app_i, but y_i is a descendant of w. Let $h = ld_i$.

(1) y_i is not a descendant of app_i.
Node app_i is a node of height $h-1$ and hence has $2^h - 1$ descendants. Leaf x_i is a descendant of app_i and $d_i \ge 2^h - 1$. Hence y_i is not a descendant of app_i.

(2) y_i is a descendant of $w = Lra(Lra(app_i))$.
Let z be the right son of w. Then node z has height at least h. If y_i is not a descendant of w then all descendants of z lie between x_i and y_i. Hence $y_i - x_i - 1 \ge 2^{h+1} - 1$ or $ld_i \ge h+1$, a contradiction.

We have thus shown that array Pos(e), $e \in E$, can be computed in time $O(n)$. Hence the time to construct the reduced search structure is $O(n)$. This proves part b). □

For the remainder of this section we show how to improve the search time to $O(\log n)$. The search time in the reduced structure is $O((\log n)^2)$ because we spend time $O(\log n)$ in each node on the search path in the super-tree. Time $O(\log n)$ per super-node is required because we need to do a binary search (in y-direction) on a path of length $O(n)$. No attempt is made to use the information gained about the y-coordinate of query point q in order to speed up later searches in y-direction. One possible usage were a locality principle, i.e.

having determined the position of query point with respect to path P_i we can restrict attention to a small subsegment of the paths stored in the sons of node i. Realization of a locality principle requires that we "align" the paths stored in adjacent nodes of the super-tree so as to provide for a smooth transition between them. How can we align the path stored in node v with the paths stored in the sons, say x and y, of node v? One possible way of achieving alignment is to include a suitable subset of the vertices of the paths associated with nodes x and y into the path stored in node v. The subset has to be dense within the paths in nodes x and y in order to enforce locality and it should be not too dense in order to keep the storage space linear. A reasonable compromise is to include every other node. The details are as follows.

Let P_i^{red} be the sequence (ordered according to y-coordinate) of vertices stored in node i of the reduced search structure. We use Q_i to denote the sequence (ordered according to y-coordinate) stored in node i of the improved search structure. We define

$$Q_i = \begin{cases} P_i^{red} \cup \{s\} & \text{if } i \text{ is a leaf of the super-tree} \\ P_i^{red} \cup \mathrm{Half}(Q_{lson(i)}) \cup \mathrm{Half}(Q_{rson(i)}) & \text{if } i \text{ is not a leaf} \end{cases}$$

where operator Half extracts the odd elements of a sequence, i.e. $\mathrm{Half}(v_1,v_2,v_3,v_4,\ldots) = v_1,v_3,v_5,\ldots$. In our example we obtain

Super-Node	P_i^{red}	Q_i
1	s,t	s,t
2	1,t	s,1,4,t
3	1,4	s,1,4
4	s,1,3,4,t	s,1,2,3,4,t
5	$\emptyset$	s
6	1,2,3,t	s,1,2,3,t
7	s,2,t	s,2,t

The sequences Q_i are stored as ordered linear lists except for Q_{root} which is organized as a balanced search tree. The balanced search tree is organized according to the y-coordinates of the elements of Q_{root}.

With every interval between adjacent elements of Q_i we associate a pointer (the edge-pointer) to an edge of $\hat{Q}$. The pointer is stored in the upper endpoint of the interval and points to edge e if e is stored in P^{red} and if the interval is contained in the interval (of y-coordinates) covered by edge e. If there is no such edge then the pointer is undefined. In our example, sequences Q_4 and Q_6 have the following structure.

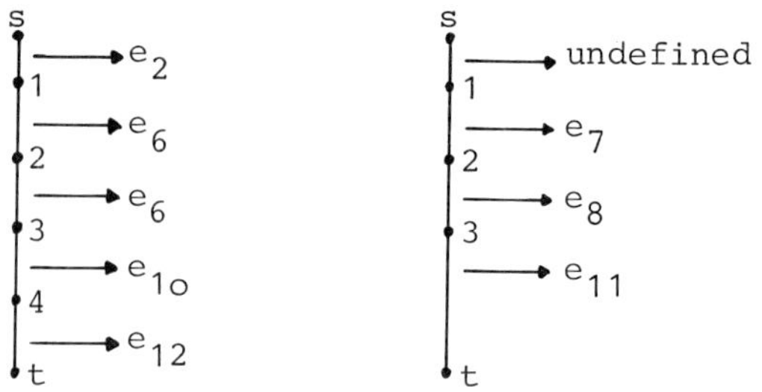

Q_4 Q_6

Note that in Q_4 there are two intervals pointing to edge e_6 and that in Q_6 the edge pointer of interval (s,1) is undefined.

Finally, we have to make the alignment between the sequences explicite. We do so by associating two pointers (Ralign and Lalign) with every element of Q_i; if v is an element of Q_i and i is not a leaf of the super-tree then Ralign(v) points to node w on $Q_{rson(i)}$ where w is such that $y(w) \geq y(v) > y(suc(w))$ and suc(w) is the successor of w in $Q_{rson(i)}$. If i is a leaf of the super-tree then Ralign(v) points to v itself. Pointer Lalign(v) is defined symmetrically. In our example, we obtain the diagram next page. In this diagram the Q_i's are drawn vertically, the alignment pointers are drawn horizontally, and the values of the edge-pointers are shown directly on the sequences.

<u>Lemma 11:</u> a) The search time in the improved search structure is O(log n).

b) The improved search structure requires storage space O(n) and can be constructed in time O(n) from the reduced search structure.

<u>Proof:</u> a) We will modify the search algorithm described in lemma 1oa

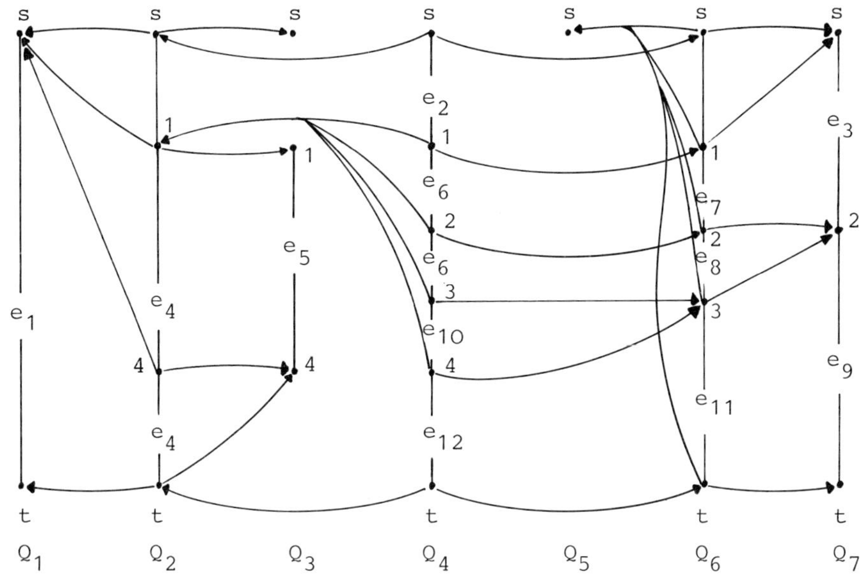

such that O(log n) time is spent in the root node of the super-tree and O(1) time in every other super-node on the search path. Clearly, we obtain O(log n) search time in this way.

As in lemma 1o we assume $P_0 = P_1$, $P_{k+1} = P_k$ and $k = 2^{d+1} - 1$ for some d, that query point q lies between P_0 and P_{k+1} and that L is a horizontal line through q. We assume furthermore that each element of a sequence Q_i is a record with fields y (the y-coordinate of the element), suc (a pointer to the successor on Q_i), Edge-pointer, Ralign, and Lalign. Fields Edge-pointer, Ralign, and Lalign are as defined above.

(1) $\ell \leftarrow 0$; $r \leftarrow k+1$; $m \leftarrow \lceil(\ell+r)/2\rceil$;
(2) e_ℓ (e_r) ← edge on P_ℓ (P_r) intersected by L;
(3) let v be a pointer to the node on Q_m such that
  v↑.y ≥ y(q) > v↑.suc↑.y
(4) <u>while</u> r > ℓ + 1
(5) <u>do</u> -- v is a pointer to a node on Q_m, $m = \lceil(\ell+r)/2\rceil$,
  -- with v↑.y ≥ y(q) > v↑.suc↑.y. Also, point q lies between
  -- P_ℓ and P_r and line L intersects edge e_ℓ (e_r) of P_ℓ (P_r);
(6) <u>if</u> $L(e_r) \le m$ or $L(e_r) > m$ and q lies to the left of edge
  v↑.Edgepointer
(7) <u>then</u> m ← r; v ← v↑.Lalign; redefine e_r
(8) <u>else</u> ℓ ← m; v ← v↑.Ralign; redefine e_ℓ

```
(9)      fi;
(1o)     m ← ⌈(ℓ+r)/2⌉;
(11)     if q(y) ≤ v↑.suc↑.y
(12)     then v ← v↑.suc
(13)     fi
(14) od
```

The running time of this algorithm is clearly O(log n) since we need time O(log n) to find node v in line (3) by binary search on the balanced tree Q_{root} and because each execution of the loop body takes time O(1). It remains to argue correctness. Note first that the position of query point q with respect to path P_m is decided correctly in lines (6) - (9); point q lies to the left of P_m iff either edge e_r belongs to P_m or e_r does not belong to P_m and q lies to the left of the edge associated with interval v↑.y to v↑.suc↑.y.

Let u be the node of Q_m which is pointed to by v and let w be the node on the new Q_m which is aligned with u, i.e. v points to w before execution of line (11). By definition of pointers Ralign and Lalign we have $y(w) \ge y(u)$. Also since every other element of the new Q_m is also an element of the old Q_m and hence either suc(w) or suc(suc(w)) (successor with respect to the new Q_m) is an element of the old Q_m we have $y(suc(u)) \ge y(suc(suc(w)))$ where suc(u) is taken with respect to the old Q_m. Thus we correctly establish invariant $v\uparrow.y \ge y(q) \ge v\uparrow.suc\uparrow.y$ in lines (11) - (13). This proves correctness.

b) In order to prove the linear bound on the storage requirement it suffices to prove that the total length of the sequences Q_i is O(n). We have

$$|Q_i| \le \begin{cases} 1 + |P_i^{red}| & \text{if i is a leaf} \\ |P_i^{red}| + (|Q_{\ell son(i)}| + |Q_{rson(i)}|)/2 & \text{if i is not a leaf} \end{cases}$$

and hence

$$\sum_{i=1}^{k} |Q_i| \le \sum_{i=1}^{k} (1 + |P_i^{red}|)(1 + 1/2 + 1/4 + 1/8 + \ldots)$$

$$= 2(n + \sum_{i=1}^{k} P_i^{red}) = O(n)$$

The first inequality follows from the observation that all nodes of P_i^{red} contribute to Q_i, one half of them contributes to $Q_{father(i)}$, one fourth of them contributes to $Q_{father(father(i))}$, ...

It remains to show that we can obtain the improved search structure in time O(n) from the reduced search structure. We can clearly construct Q_i from P_i^{red}, $Q_{\ell son(i)}$, and $Q_{rson(i)}$ by merging in time $O(|P_i^{red}| + |Q_{\ell son(i)}| + |Q_{rson(i)}|)$. Furthermore, it is easy to set-up the pointers Edge-pointer, Lalign and Ralign during the construction without increasing the cost by more than a constant factor. Hence the improved search structure can be constructed in time $O(\sum_i |Q_i|) = O(n)$. □

We summarize the discussion of this section in

Theorem 3: Based on path decomposition the searching problem for simple planar subdivisions can be solved with search time O(log n), storage space O(n), and preprocessing time O(n).

We have travelled quite a distance in this section. We started out with the basic concept of path decompositions and obtained very quickly a data structure with $O((\log n)^2)$ search time and $O(n^2)$ storage requirement. We then refined the data structure and first reduced storage space and preprocessing time to O(n) and then search time to O(log n). We will see path decompositions again in section 5.1.4..

3.2.3 Searching Dynamic Planar Subdivisions

In the preceding section we described two optimal solutions to the searching problem for planar subdivisions. Several other solutions are discussed in the exercises. All these solutions have a common weakness. They only apply to static subdivisions and do not seem to adopt easily to changes in the underlying planar subdivision.

Consider the following szenario which captures a simple form of dynamic behavior ; a solution to more general forms of dynamic behavior is not within sight at the day of this writing. At any point of time we can

either query the planar subdivision with respect to a query point $q \in \mathbb{R}^2$ or subdivide one of the finite faces of the subdivision by a straight line thus adding one additional edge and up to two additional vertices. The initial subdivision is a triangle. Note that all vertices constructed by adding new edges have degree at least three.
Our goal for this section is to prove the following

Theorem 4: There is a solution to the dynamic planar subdivision searching problem with query and update time $O((\log n)^2)$. The bound on query time is worst case and the bound on update time is amortized.

Proof: Our approach is similar to the one used in section 3.2.2, i.e. we will again use binary search on a path decomposition. However, there are some major differences. First, we cannot assume that our planar subdivison is triangulated and hence we cannot insist on a path decomposition into monotone paths. Rather, we have to use arbitrary (s,t)-paths in the decomposition. Second, the super-tree is not static anymore but needs to be adapted as the subdivision changes. In order to keep the cost of updating the super-tree low we organize the super-tree as a weight-balanced tree.

Let $\hat{G}$ be the (current) planar subdivision and let s(t) be the vertex of $\hat{G}$ with maximal (minimal) y-coordinate. Note that s and t do not depend on time since only finite faces can be refined. As before, an (s,t)-path is a sequence $v_0, v_1, \ldots, v_m$ of vertices with $v_0 = s$, $v_m = t$, (v_i, v_{i+1}) an edge of $\hat{G}$ for $0 \le i < m$, and $(v_i, v_{i+1}) \neq (v_j, v_{j+1})$ for $i \neq j$.
An (s,t)-path P divides $\hat{G}$ into two parts which we call the left and right part of $\hat{G}$ with respect to P.

A sequence $P_1, \ldots, P_N$ of paths is a complete path decomposition of $\hat{G}$ if

1) every P_i, $1 \le i \le N$, is an (s,t)-path and every edge of $\hat{G}$ belongs to at least one P_i.
2) P_1 is the leftmost (s,t)-path, P_N is the rightmost (s,t)-path and P_{i+1} is to the right of P_i, $1 \le i < N$, i.e. no horizontal line intersects P_i to the right of P_{i+1}.
3) for every i, $0 \le i < N-1$, there is exactly one face of $\hat{G}$, say F, such that all edges belonging to either P_i or P_{i+1} but not to both border the same face of $\hat{G}$. We will say that pair (P_i, P_{i+1}) moves across face F in this case.

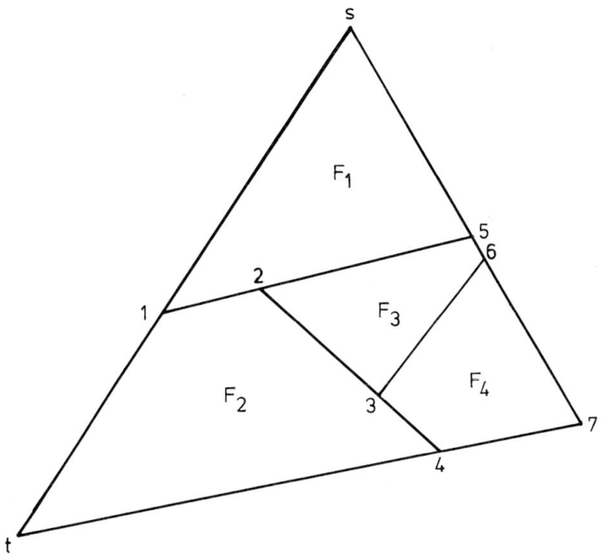

In our example, there are four faces and hence a complete path decomposition consists of five paths P_1,P_2,P_3,P_4 and P_5.
We might have P_1 = s,1,t, P_2 = s,1,2,3,4,t, P_3 = s,1,2,5,6,3,4,t, P_4 = s,5,6,3,4,t, and P_5 = s,5,6,7,4,t. Then pair (P_1,P_2) moves across face F_2 and pair (P_2,P_3) moves across face F_3.

We can now describe the search structure for subdivision $\hat{G}$ in more detail. Let $P_1,\ldots,P_N$ be a complete path decomposition of $\hat{G}$. Then the super-tree is a BB[α]-tree, say α = 0.28, with N nodes; cf. section III.5.1. for a discussion of BB[α]-trees. Node i corresponds to path P_i. Node i contains a data structure which allows us to decide the position of query point q with respect to path P_i in time O(log n). Since the super tree has depth O(log n) a total query cost of $O((\log n)^2)$ results.

As before, this basic solution suffers from its huge storage requirement which now also implies huge update cost. We proceed as in the preceding section, and store in node v of the super tree only those edges of path P_v which do not belong to a path P_w for w an ancestor of v. We denote this set of edges as P_v^{red}.
In our example, we might use the following super tree in BB[1/4]

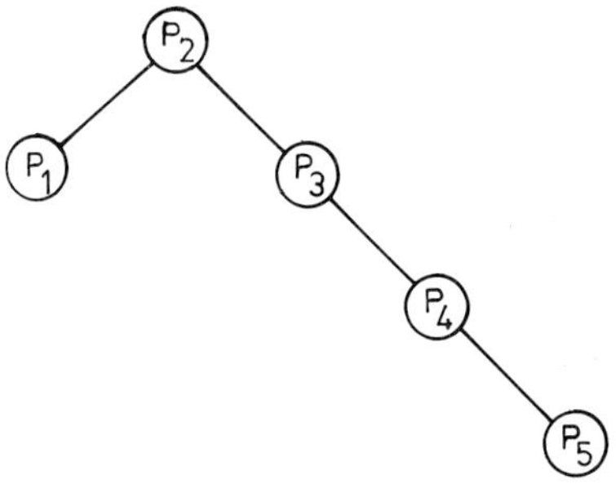

Then $P_3^{red} = \{(2,5),(5,6)\}$ and $P_5^{red} = \{(6,7),(7,4)\}$

For edge e, let L[e] (R[e]) be the minimal (maximal) i such that e belongs to path P_i. We will describe below how integers L(e) and R(e) are maintained such that computation of L(e) and R(e) take time O(log n) each. For the description of the query algorithm we assume the existence of algorithms for computing L(e) and R(e). Also we assume that the data structure associated with node i has the following property (called property (*)):

given point $q \in \mathbb{R}^2$ and a horizontal line L through find edges e and e' in P_i^{red} (if they exist) such that L intersects e and e', q lies between e and e' and no other edge in P_i^{red} intersects L between the intersections with e and e'.

<u>Lemma 9:</u> Let $m = |P_i^{red}|$. Then a search structure for P_i^{red} with property (*) and query time O(log m) can be constructed in time O(mlog m).

<u>Proof:</u> The set P_i^{red} is a set of pairwise non-intersecting edges (except at common endpoints). Draw horizontal lines through all endpoints of edges in P_i^{red} and extend them to the closest edge in P_i^{red}.

In our example, we have $P_3^{red} = \{(2,5),(5,6)\}$ and hence we obtain the following planar subdivision by this process.

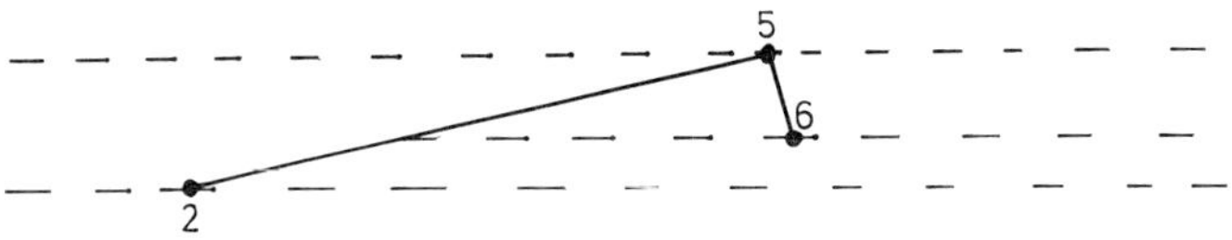

In general, we obtain a planar subdivision with O(m) vertices all of whose faces are convex. Moreover, we can obtain this subdivision in time O(mlog m) by plane sweep. We can now use either one of the methods of the two preceding sections to obtain a search structure with property (*) of depth O(log m) in time O(mlog m) □

The bound on the query time is easily derived at this point.

Lemma 10: Given query point $q \in \mathbb{R}^2$ one can determine the face of $\hat{G}$ containing q in time $O((\log n)^2)$ where n is the number of vertices of $\hat{G}$.

Proof: We use a tree search on the super tree. In each node of the super tree we spend time O(log n). Let L be a horizontal line through q. Assume inductively that the search has reached node i of the super tree and that we determined paths P_j and P_k and edges e_L on P_j and e_R on P_k such that q lies between e_L and e_R, i.e. L intersects e_L and e_R. Also, nodes j and k are ancestors of node i. Note that either j or k or both may not exist. The following diagram illustrates the situation. In this diagram paths P_j and P_k are shown dashed (--) and path P_i is shown solid (—). Furthermore, edges e_L, e_R, e, and e' are indicated.

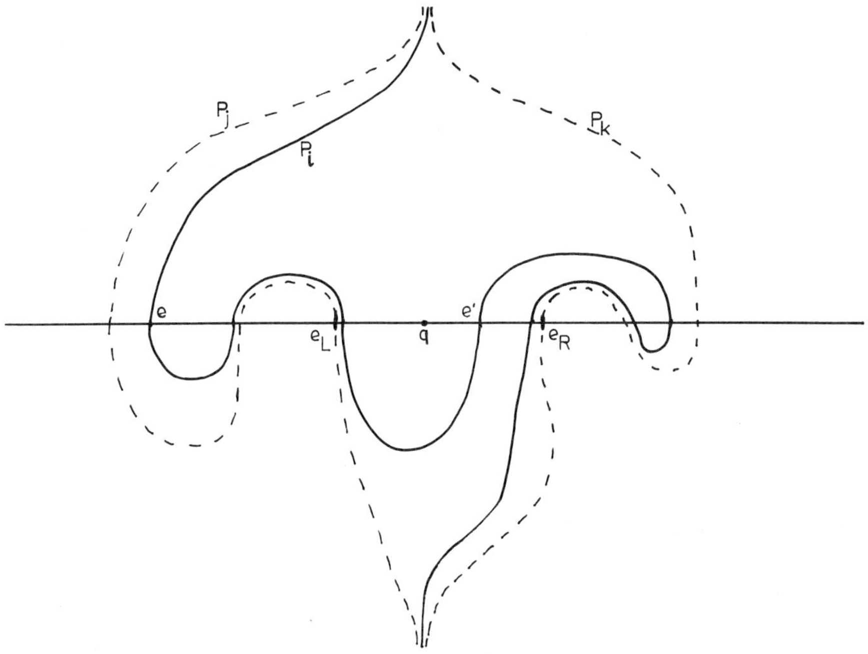

We can now use the data structure (with property *) for P_i^{red} to determine a pair of edges e and e' of P_i^{red} such that q lies between e and e'. Also, we can determine whether edges e_L and e_R belong to P_i by looking up their L- and R- values. Using this knowledge it is then easy to decide on which side of path P_i the query point q lies. Thus time O(log n) suffices to determine the position of pont q with respect to P_i and hence total search time is $O((\log n)^2)$.

We turn to the insertion of new edges next. An additional edge splits a face, say F, into F_1 and F_2. If (P_i, P_{i+1}) is the pair of paths which moves across F then $P_1, \ldots, P_i, P, P_{i+1}, \ldots, P_N$ is a complete path decomposition of the new planar subdivision where path P runs between paths P_i and P_{i+1} and uses edge e. More precisely, if e = (x,y), then P consists of the initial segment of P_i (P_{i+1}) from s to x if x lies on the left (right) boundary of F, followed by edge e, followed by a terminal segment of P_i (P_{i+1}) from y to t if y lies on the left (right) boundary of F.

In our example, we can split face F_4 by adding an edge from vertex 6 to vertex 4. Then $P_1, P_2, P_3, P_4, P, P_5$ is a complete path decomposition of the new planar subdivision where P = s,5,6,4,t. We obtain a super tree for the new path decomposition by adding a node P between P_4 and P_5. The new super tree does not belong to class BB[0.28]since

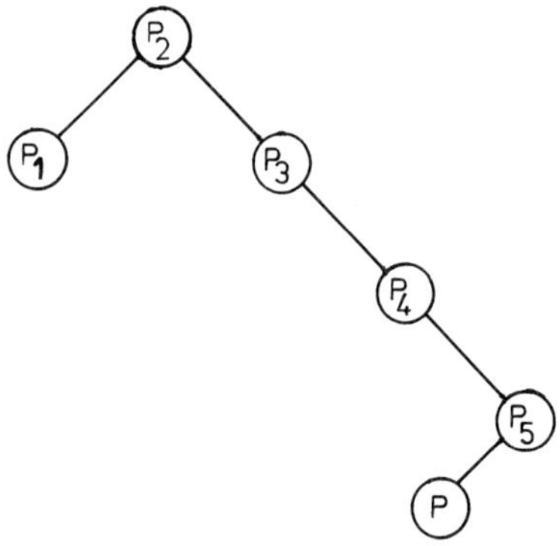

the balance of node P_3 is $1/4 \notin [0.28, 0.72]$.
Therefore, we need to rebalance the super tree at node P_3.

In general, we add a node for P as either a right son of node i (if i is a descendant of i+1) or as a left son of node i+1 (if node i+1 is a descendant of node i).

Also, P^{red} consists exactly of the new edge e since all other edges of P also belong to ancestors of the new node. It is therefore trivial to construct a data structure (with property (*)) for P^{red}.

Of course, the super tree can go out of balance, i.e. leave class $BB[\alpha]$, by adding the new node corresponding to path P and hence rebalancing is necessary. Before we can describe the rebalancing algorithm we need to discuss in detail how arrays L and R are maintained. We store them implicitely as follows. Note first that we can partition the edges on the boundary of every face into two blocks in a natural way. Let F be a face and let pair (P_i, P_{i+1}) be the pair of paths which moves across F. Then the left boundary LB(F) of F consists of all edges of P_i which do not belong to P_{i+1}. The right boundary RB(F) is defined symmetrically. Next observe, that if edge e belongs to LB(F) then R(e) = i and if edge e' belongs to RB(F) then L(e) = i+1 where pair (P_i, P_{i+1}) moves across face F. Finally, observe that every edge belongs to the boundary of exactly two faces. More precisely, it belongs to the left boundary of some and to the right boundary of some other face.

These observations suggest the following method for storing arrays L and R implicitely. For every face F we store the edges in LB(F) (RB(F)) in a balanced tree. The edges are ordered clockwise. In the root of the tree for LB(F) (RB(F)) we store a pointer to node i (i+1) of the super tree where i (i+1) is the common value of R[e] (L[e]) for the edges in LB(F) (RB(F)). With every edge e we associate two pointers. Pointer LP(e) (RP(e)) points to the copy of edge e in a left (right) boundary list LB(F) (RB(F)) of some face F. Using these data structures we can compute R[e] as follows; the computation of L[e] is symmetric.
We follow pointer LB(e) to the (unique) copy of edge e on a left boundary list, say LB(F), then we inspect the root of the tree representation of LB(F) and obtain a pointer to node R[e] of the super tree. Note that a knowledge of a pointer to node R(e) suffices for the query algorithm; the numerical value R[e] is not required. The representation described above clearly allows us to compute L[e] and R[e] in time O(log n).

We now return to the discussion of the insertion algorithm. Adding a new edge e splits a face, say F, into two faces, say F_1 and F_2. Also a new path P is added to the path decompostion. The tree representation of $LB(F_1)$, $LB(F_2)$, $RB(F_1)$, $RB(F_2)$ can be obtained from LB(F) and RB(F) in time O(log n) by a few split and concatenate operations (cf. section III.5.3.1). This shows that we can add a new edge in time O(log n) excluding the time required for rebalancing the super tree.

Let i be the highest node of the super tree which is out of balance after adding edge e. Let $I = [\ell \ldots r]$ be the set of descendants of i (including i) and let $E = \bigcup_{j \in I} P_j^{red}$ be the set of edges stored in the descendants of i. Finally, let $m = |E|$ and $k = |I|$. We rebalance the tree by replacing the subtree rooted at i by a perfectly balanced tree with node set I. This takes time O(k). We then go through all edges in E, compute their L- and R-values as described above and decide in what node of the new subtree each edge has to be stored. This takes time O(mlog n) since each L- and R-value can be computed in time O(log n). In this way we compute for each node j, $\ell \le j \le r$, the set $\tilde{P}_j^{red}$ of edges which has to be stored in node j of the new subtree.
Let $m_j = |\tilde{P}_j^{red}|$. Then it takes time $O(m_j \cdot \log m_j)$ to construct the data structure with property (*) for node j and hence time $\sum_{j \in I} O(m_j \cdot \log m_j)$ $= \sum_{j \in I} O(m_j \log n) = O(|I| + \sum_{j \in I} m_j \log n) = O(k + m\log n)$ to construct these data structures for all nodes in I. This finishes the description of the rebalancing algorithm. Note that the L- and R-values of all edges remain unchanged since the path decomposition is not changed; only its arrangement in the super tree is changed. Thus no action is required for the L- and R- values. We summarize the discussion in

<u>Lemma 11:</u> Rebalancing at a node i with k descendants takes time $O(k \cdot \log n)$

<u>Proof:</u> We have shown above that rebalancing takes time O(k + mlog m). It therefore suffices to prove that m = O(k). This can be seen as follows. Note first that k+1 is the number of faces of $\hat{G}$ between paths $P_{\ell-1}$ and P_{r+1} of the decomposition. Next consider the following planar graph with k+1 nodes. Its nodes are the faces between $P_{\ell-1}$ and P_{r+1} and its edges are the duals of the edges in E, i.e. edges connect adjacent faces. This planar graph has m edges and <u>no</u> parallel edges since any two finite faces of the planar subdivision can share at most one edge. This fact can easily be seen by induction on the number of edges added to the planar subdivision. Thus m = O(k) by lemma 1 of section IV.10 □

We are now ready to derive a bound on the amortized insertion cost.

Lemma 12: The amortized cost of an insertion is $O((\log n)^2)$.

Proof : We infer from lemma 11 that the cost of rebalancing at a node with k descendants is O(klog n). Hence the total cost of all rebalancing operations required to process n insertions is

$$O(n \sum_{i=1}^{\log n} (1-\alpha)^{-i} \log n (1-\alpha)^{i}) = O(n(\log n)^2)$$

by (a variant of) theorem 5 of section III.6.3. Thus amortized rebalancing cost is $O((\log n)^2)$. Finally, observe that the cost of changing the path decomposition after adding an edge is O(log n). This proves lemma 12. □

Lemmas 10 and 12 together imply theorem 4. □

Theorem 4 deals only with very limited versions of dynamic behaviour. In particular, deletions, replacement of edges by pairs of edges, and non-connected subdivisions cannot be handled. A treatment of the more general forms of dynamic behaviour would be of great help in the usage of the sweep paradigm in three-dimensional space as we will see in section 4.3.

3.3 Applications

In this section we discuss several applications of Voronoi diagrams: the all pair nearest neighbor problem, the Euclidian Spanning tree problem and the Euclidian traveling salesman problem. Let $S \subseteq \mathbb{R}^2$.
In the all pair nearest neighbor problem we want to find for each $x \in S$ an element $y \in S$ such that $dist(x,y) = dist(x,S-\{x\})$, i.e. the element closest to x.
For the two other problems we consider the complete network $N = (S, S\times S, c)$ with vertex set S and edge costs as given by the Euclidian distance, i.e. $c(x,y) = dist(x,y)$. Other applications can be found in the exercises. For the three applications discussed here the following lemma is crucial.

Lemma 13: Let $S \subseteq \mathbb{R}^2$, let $x,y \in S$, $x \neq y$. If $VR(x) \cap VR(y) = \emptyset$ or $VR(x) \cap VR(y)$ is a singleton set then there is $z \in S$ such that $dist(x,z) \leq dist(x,y)$ and $dist(y,z) < dist(x,y)$ and VR(x) and VR(z) have a non-trivial line segment in common.

Proof: Let $x,y \in S$, $x \neq y$ and assume that VR(x) and VR(y) do not share a non-trivial line segment. Consider the straight line segment L connecting x and y. Let p be the point of intersection of L and the boundary of VR(x) and let z be such that p lies on an edge common to VR(x) and VR(z). It is conceivable that p is an endpoint of this edge. We show $dist(x,z) \leq dist(x,y)$ and $dist(y,z) < dist(x,y)$.

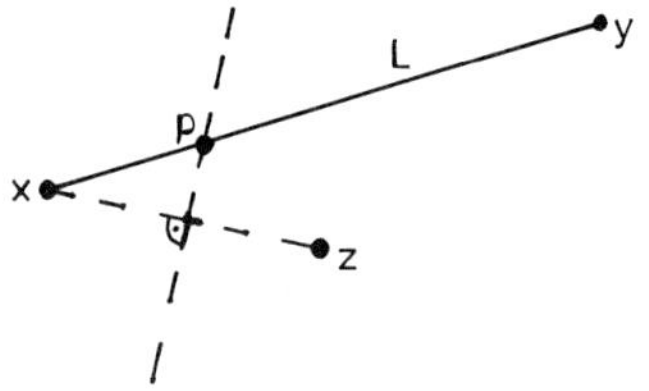

$dist(y,z) < dist(x,y)$: Note first that $dist(y,z) \leq dist(x,y)$ since y and z lie on the same side of the perpendicular bisector of x and z. If $dist(y,z) = dist(x,y)$ then y lies on the perpendicular bisector of x and z and hence $y = p$. Thus y, a point of S, lies on the boundary of VR(x), a contradiction. We conclude $dist(y,z) \neq dist(x,y)$ and hence $dist(y,z) < dist(x,y)$.

$dist(x,z) \leq dist(x,y)$: We observe that $dist(x,z) \leq 2\ dist(x,p)$, $dist(x,p) \leq dist(p,y)$ since $p \in VR(x)$ and $dist(x,y) \leq dist(x,p) + dist(p,y)$. Thus $dist(x,z) \leq 2dist(x,y) \leq dist(x,p) + dist(p,y) = dist(x,y)$. □

We are now ready for the applications.

Theorem 5: Let $S \subseteq \mathbb{R}^2$, $|S| = n$. Given the Voronoi diagram of S one can solve the all pair nearest neighbor in time $O(n)$.

Proof: Let $x \in S$ be arbitrary. We infer from lemma 13 that x has a nearest neighbor y such that VR(x) and VR(y) have a non-trivial line segment in common. Thus we can find the nearest neighbor of x by inspecting all y such that VR(x) and VR(y) have an edge in common; this takes time $O(m(x))$ where $m(x)$ is the number of edges on the boundary of VR(x).

We conclude that total running time is $O(\sum_{x \in S} m(x)) = O(n)$ by lemma 2. □

Theorem 6: Let $S \subseteq \mathbb{R}^2$, $|S| = n$. Then a minimum cost Euclidian spanning tree of S can be computed in time $O(n\log n)$

Proof: We want to compute a minimum cost spanning tree of the network $N = (S, S \times S, c)$ with $c(x,y) = dist(x,y)$. Let $E = \{(x,y);\ x,y \in S,\ x \neq y$ and $VR(x)$ and $VR(y)$ share a non-trivial line segment$\}$. We show that the edges of a minimum cost spanning tree can be taken from set E.

Claim: There is a minimum cost spanning tree T of network N such that all edges of T belong to E.

Proof: Let T be a minimum cost spanning tree of network N such that T has a maximal number of edges in E. If all edges of T belong to E then we are done. So let us assume otherwise. Then there must be an edge (x,y) of T with $(x,y) \notin T$. Thus $VR(x)$ and $VR(y)$ do not have a non-trivial line segment in common and hence by lemma 13 there is $z \in S$ such that $VR(x)$ and $VR(z)$ share a non-trivial line segment, $dist(x,z) \leq dist(x,y)$ and $dist(y,z) < dist(x,z)$. Also, either $T_1 = (T - \{(x,y)\}) \cup \{(x,z)\}$ or $T_2 = (T - \{(x,y)\}) \cup \{(y,z)\}$ is a spanning tree of N. However, T_1 has more edges in E than T and the same cost as T and T_2 has smaller cost than T. Thus in either case we have a contradiction to the fact that T uses edges outside E and has minimum cost. □

We conclude from the claim above that it suffices to determine a minimum spanning tree of the network (S,E,c). Set E can be determined in time $O(n\log n)$ by constructing the Voronoi diagram of S. Also $|E| = O(n)$ by lemma 2 and hence a minimum cost spanning tree of (S,E,c) can be determined in time $O(n\log n)$ by IV.8.theorem 2. Actually, in view of IV.8.theorem 4, time $O(n)$ suffices for the final step since (S,E) is a planar graph. □

From theorem 6 we obtain a good approximation algorithm for Euclidian traveling salesman tours.

Theorem 7: Let $S \subseteq \mathbb{R}^2$, $|S| = n$, and let L_{opt} be the length of an optimal Euclidian traveling salesman tour of S. Then a tour of length at most $2L_{opt}$ can be found in time $O(n\log n)$.

Proof: By theorem 6 we can find a minimum cost Euclidian spanning tree in time O(nlog n). In section VI.7.1 we have shown that the "once around the tree" tour has length at most $2L_{opt}$. The result follows.

□

VIII. 4. The Sweep Paradigm

The sweeping approach is a very powerful paradigm for solving two-dimensional and some higher dimensional geometric problems. It has been mostly used for intersection problems but has also been useful for other problems, e.g. triangulation and order problems. The underlying idea is quite simple. Suppose we have to solve a problem concerning a set of geometric objects in the plane. A concrete example is the intersection problem of line segments. Plane sweep approaches this problem by sweeping a vertical line from left to right across the plane. It uses a data structure, called the y-structure, to record the status of the sweep at the current position of the sweep line. The status of the sweep is all information about the problem to the left of the sweep line which is relevant to solving the problem to the right of the sweep line. In all our applications this information encompasses at least the intersections of the sweep line at its current position with the geometric objects at hand. Moreover, we will always have these intersections sorted by their y-coordinate. Additional information depending on the particular problem to be solved is also associated with the y-structure.

The sweep line gradually moves from left to right. Often, there are only a few positions of the sweep line which can cause a change of the status of the sweep. In our example of intersecting line segments this will be the endpoints of line segments and the points of intersection of line segments. The positions where the status of the sweep changes are stored in the x-structure. Usually, some number of points of the x-structure are already known initially (the endpoints of line segments in our example) and some are computed during the sweep (the points of intersection in our example). Thus the sweep advances from point to point of the x-structure. In each point, the y-structure is updated, some output is computed and some additional points are inserted into the x-structure. Of course, the points to be inserted into the x-structure must lie to the right of the sweep line for plane sweep to work.

The paradigm of plane sweep is captured in the following algorithm.

(1) initialize x-structure and y-structure;

(2) <u>while</u> x-structure $\neq \emptyset$

```
(3)  do p ← Min(x-structure);
(4)      Transition(p)
(5)  od
```

In line (3) the point with minimal x-coordinate is selected in the x-struture and deleted from it. Then in line (4) the sweep line is advanced beyond that point. Of course, the details of procedure Transition depend on the specific problem to be solved. In this chapter we study three applications of the sweep paradigm: intersection problems in the plane, triangulation problems in the plane, and intersection problems in three-dimensional space.

The success of the sweep paradigm in these situations results from the fact that it reduces the dimension of the problem to be solved. More precisely, it solves a static problem in the plane by solving a dynamic problem on the (sweep) line. The latter problem is essentially one-dimensional and therefore simpler and better understood.

VIII. 4.1 Intersection Line Segments and Other Intersection Problems in the Plane

In this section we will solve a number of intersection problems in the plane. We start with intersecting line segments and then extend the basic algorithm to various other situations: decomposing a nonsimple polygon into simple parts, intersecting sets of polygons, translating sets of line segments, ... Some of these applications are treated in the exercises.

Let $L_1, L_2, \ldots, L_n$ be a set of n line segments in the plane. We want to compute all their pairwise intersections, say there are s of them. A first approach is to check all pairs L_i, L_j with $1 \le i < j \le n$ for intersection. It runs in time $O(n^2)$. Of course, this algorithm is optimal if $s = \Omega(n^2)$ since s is the size of the output. However, if $s \ll n^2$ then a much better algorithm exists. We will show how to compute all s intersections in time $O((n+s)\log n)$.

<u>Theorem 1:</u> Let $L_1, \ldots, L_n$ be a set of n line segments in the plane. Then the set of all s pairwise intersections can be computed in time $O((n+s)\log n)$ and space $O(n)$.

<u>Proof:</u> We use plane sweep, i.e. we sweep a vertical line from left to right across the plane. At any point of the sweep we divide the set of line segments into three pairwise disjoint groups: dead, active, and dormant. A line segment is dead (active, dormant) if exactly two (one, zero) of its endpoints are to the left of the sweep line. Thus the active line segments are those which currently intersect the sweep line and the dormant line segments have not been encountered yet by the sweep. For the description of the algorithm we assume that no line segment is vertical and that no two endpoints or intersection points have the same x-coordinate. Both assumptions are made to simplify the exposition. The reader should have no difficulty to modify the algorithm such that it works without these assumptions.

The y-structure stores the active line segments ordered according to the y-coordinate of their intersection with the sweep line. More precisely, the y-structure is a balanced search tree for the set of active line segments. In our example, line segments $L_1, L_2, \ldots, L_6$ are

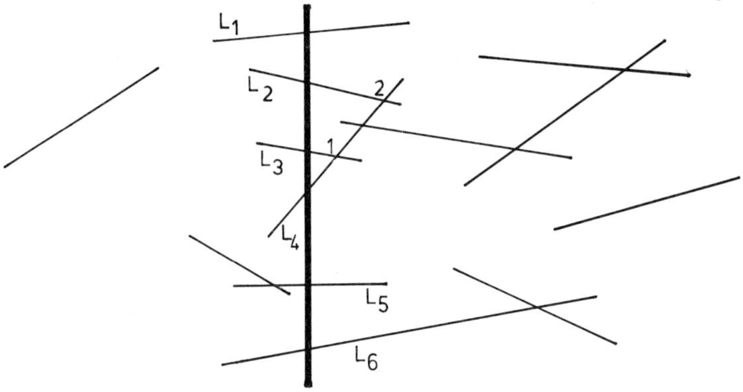

active. They are stored in that order in the y-structure as described in the introduction of this chapter, i.e. the y-structure is a dictionary for the set of active line segments. Any kind of balanced tree can be used for the dictionary. It supports (at least) the following operations in logarithmic time.

Find(p)	given point p on the sweep line, find the interval (on the sweep line) containing p
Insert(L)	insert line segment L into the y-structure
Delete(L)	delete line segment L from the y-structure

Pred(L), Succ(L)	find the immediate predecessor (successor) of line segment L in the y-structure
Interchange(L,L')	interchange adjacent line segments L and L' in the y-structure.

It is worthwhile to observe that the cost of operations Pred, Succ and Interchange can be reduced to O(1) under the following assumptions. First, the procedures are given a pointer to the leaves representing line segment L as an argument and second, the tree structure is augmented by additional pointers. For the Pred and Succ operations we need pointers to the adjacent leaves and for the Interchange operation we need a pointer to the least common ancestor of leaves L and L'. Note that the least common ancestor of leaves L and L' contains the information which discriminates between L and L' in the tree search. We leave it to the reader to convince himself that the additional pointers do not increase the running time of Inserts or Deletes.

We describe the x-structure next. It contains all endpoints of line segments (dormant or active) which are to the right of the sweep line. Furthermore, it contains <u>some</u> of the intersections of line segments to the right of the sweep line. Note that it cannot contain all of them because the sweep has not even seen dormant line segments yet. The points in the x-structure are sorted according to their x-coordinate, i.e. the x-structure is a heap. For the correctness of the algorithm it is important that the x-structure always contains the point of intersection of active line segments which is closest to the sweep line. We achieve this goal by maintaining the following invariant.

If L_i and L_j are active line segments, are adjacent in the y-structure, and intersect to the right of the sweep line then their intersection is contained in the x-structure.

In our example, point 1 must be in the x-structure and point 2 may be in the x-structure. In the space-efficient version of the algorithm below point 2 is not in the x-structure. We have the following consequence of the invariant above.

<u>Lemma 1:</u> Let p be the intersection of active line segments L_i and L_j. If there is no endpoint of a line segment and no other point of inter-

section in the vertical strip defined by the sweep line and p then p is stored in the x-structure.

<u>Proof:</u> If p is not stored in the x-structure then L_i and L_j are not adjacent in the y-structure. Hence there must be active line segment L which is between L_i and L_j in the y-structure. Since L's right endpoint is not to the left of p either $\cap(L,L_i)$ or $\cap(L,L_j)$ is to the left of p, a contradiction.

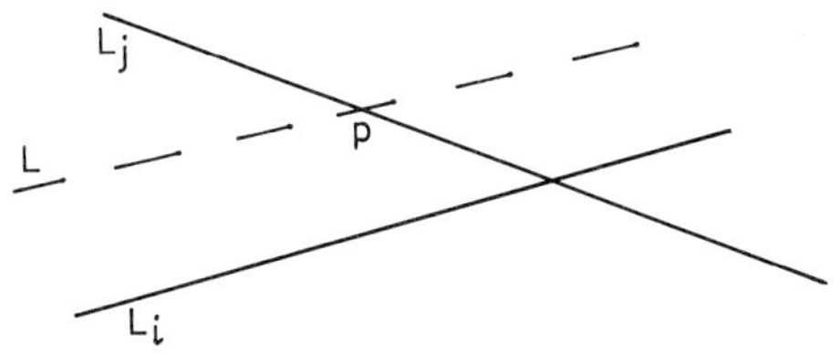

□

Finally, we maintain the following invariant about the output. All intersections of line segments which are to the left of the sweep line have been reported.

We are now in a position to give the details of the algorithm.

```
(1)   y-structure ← ∅;
(2)   x-structure ← the 2n endpoints of the line segments sorted by
                    x-coordinate;
(3)   while x-structure ≠ ∅
(4)   do let p be a point with minimal x-coordinate in the x-structure;
(5)      delete p from the x-structure;
(6)      if p is a left endpoint of some segment L_j
         then
(7)           search for p in the y-structure and insert L_j into the
              y-structure;
(8)           let L_i,L_k be the two neighbours of L_j in the y-structure;
              insert ∩(L_i,L_j) and ∩(L_j,L_k) into the x-structure, if
              they exist;
(9)           [delete ∩(L_i,L_k) from the x-structure]
(1o)     fi;
(11)     if p is a right endpoint of some segment L_j
(12)     then let L_i and L_k be the two neighbours of L_j in the
              y-structure;
(13)          delete L_j from the y-structure;
```

```
(14)            insert ∩(L_i,L_k) into the x-structure if the intersection
                is to the right of the sweep line
(15)        fi;
(16)        if p is ∩(L_i,L_j)
            then -- L_i,L_j are necessarily adjacent in the y-structure
(17)            interchange L_i,L_j in the y-structure;
(18)            let L_h,L_k be the two neighbours of L_i,L_j in the
                y-structure;
(19)            insert ∩(L_h,L_j) and ∩(L_i,L_k) into the x-structure, if
                they are to the right of the sweep line;
(2o)            [delete ∩(L_h,L_i) and ∩(L_j,L_k) from the x-structure;]
(21)            output p
(22)        fi
(23)    od
```

In the algorithm above the statements in square brackets are not essential for correctness. Inclusion of these statements does not increase asymptotic running time, however it improves space complexity from O(n+s) to O(n) as we will see below.

The following example illustrates the algorithm.

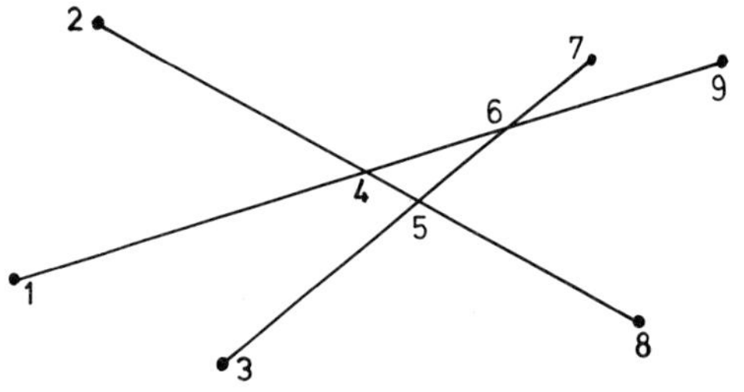

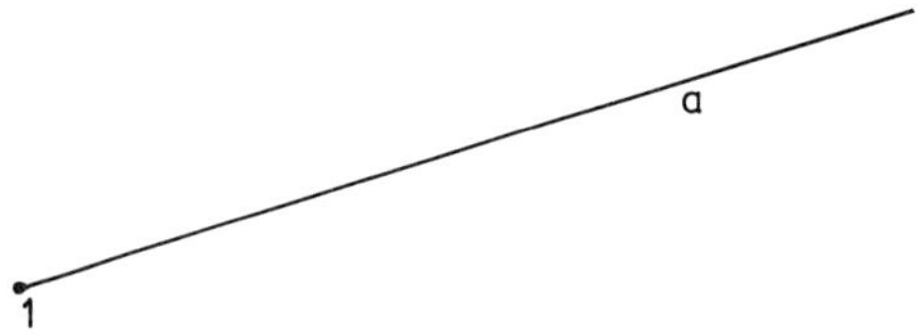

x-structure: 2,3,7,8,9
y-structure: a
sweep line: between 1 and 2

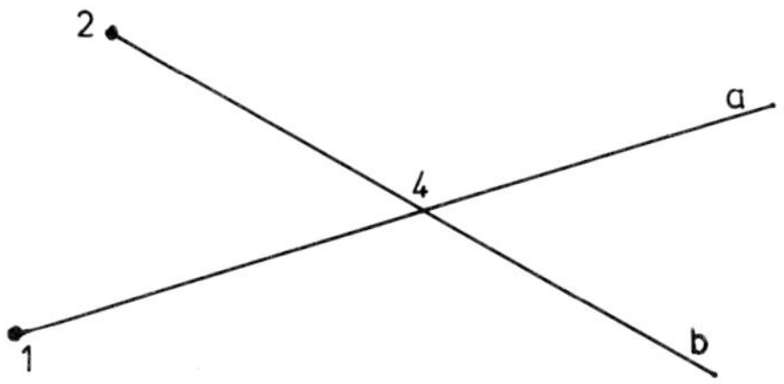

x-structure: 3,4,7,8,9
y-structure: a,b
sweep line: between 2 and 3

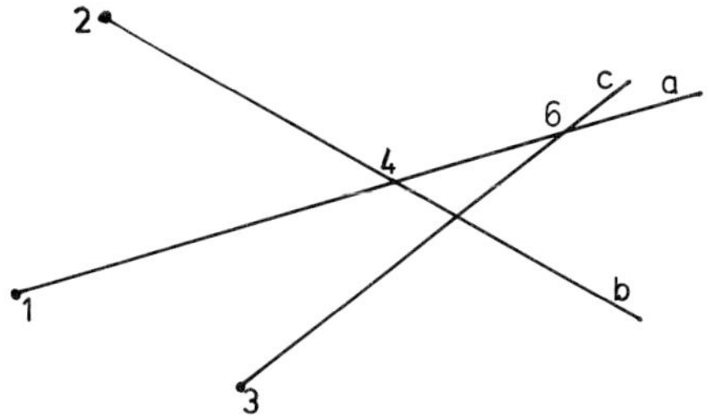

x-structure: 4,6,7,8,9
y-structure: c,a,b
sweep line: between 3 and 4

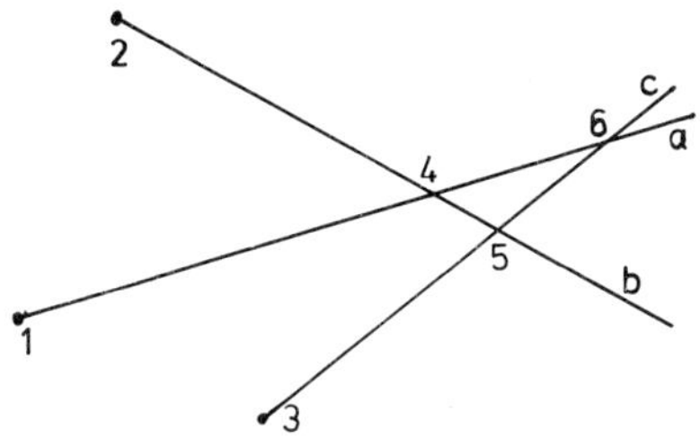

x-structure: 5, [6] ,7,8,9
y-structure: c,b,a
sweep line: between 4 and 5

Remark: In the space-efficient version node 6 is deleted from the x-structure and then reinserted by the transition at point 5.

It remains to prove correctness and to analyse the run time. For correctness it suffices to show that the invariants hold true. Call a point critical if it is either the endpoint of a line segment or an intersection of two line segments. Then the invariant about the x-structure and lemma 1 ensures that the point p selected in line (4) is the critical point which is closest to and ahead of the sweep line. Thus every critical point is selected exactly once in line (4) and hence all intersections are output in line (21). Furthermore, lines (7), (13), and (17) ensure that the y-structure always contains exactly the active line segments in sorted order and lines (8), (14), and (19) guarantee the invariant about the x-structure. In lines (9) and (2o) we delete points from the x-structure whose presence is not required anymore by the invariant about the x-structure. This finishes the proof of correctness.

The analysis of the run time is quite simple. Note first that the loop body is executed exactly 2n + s times, once for each endpoint and once for each intersection. Also a single execution deletes an element from a heap (time $O(\log n+s)) = O(\log n)$ since $s \le n^2$) and performs some simple operations on a balanced tree of size n(time $O(\log n)$). Thus run time is $O((n+s)\log n)$.

The space requirement is clearly O(n) for the y-structure and O(n+s) for the x-structure. If we include lines (9) and (2o) then the space requirement of the x-structure reduces to O(n) since only intersections of active line segments which are adjacent in the y-structure are stored in the x-structure with this modification. Thus space requirement is O(n). □

The algorithm above works for segments more general than straight line segments, e.g. for circular segments (exercise 24). If all line segments are vertical or horizontal then the run time can be improved to O(s + n log n), exercise 23.

Our next goal is to extend the algorithm above such that it solves more complicated tasks. More specifically, we show how to decompose a polygon into simple parts. Let $x_o,\ldots,x_{n-1}$ be a sequence of points in the plane. Then line segments $L_i := L(x_i,x_{i+1})$, $0 \le i \le n-1$, define a closed curve in the plane. Removal of this curve from the plane divides the plane into r + 1 polygonal regions $R_o,R_1,\ldots,R_r$ one of which is unbounded; say R_o. Each R_i, $1 \le i \le r$, is a polygonal region.

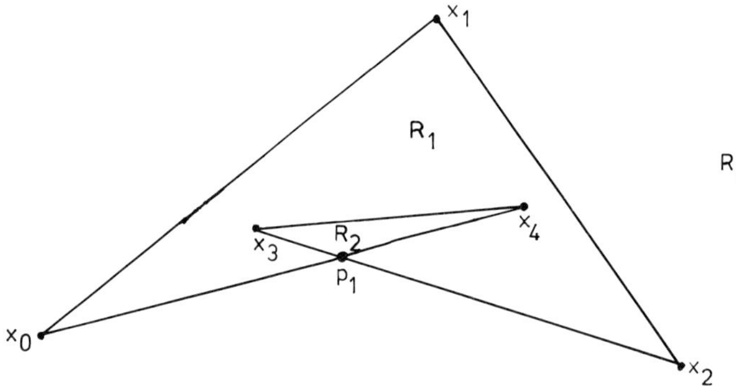

The boundary of R_i is a simple polygon whose vertices are either among the x_i or among the points of intersections of the line segments L_i. Let $p_1,\ldots,p_s$ be the intersections of the line segments L_i. Then the goal is to compute for each region R_i the boundary vertices in cyclic order. In our example, the output is R_0: x_0,p_1,x_2,x_1, R_1: $x_1,x_0,p_1,x_3,$ x_4,p_1,x_2, and R_2: x_3,p_1,x_4.

We have chosen the problem of polygon decomposition for expository purposes. It is a simple intersection problem. Nevertheless, the ideas required to solve it are applicable to a wide variety of problems, e.g. the intersection of a set of polygons. We know already how to compute the points $p_1,\ldots,p_s$ by plane sweep. We will show now how to extend the y-structure such that the more complicated decomposition problem can be solved. Consider our example and suppose that the sweep line is positioned between x_1 and x_4. At this point we have line segments

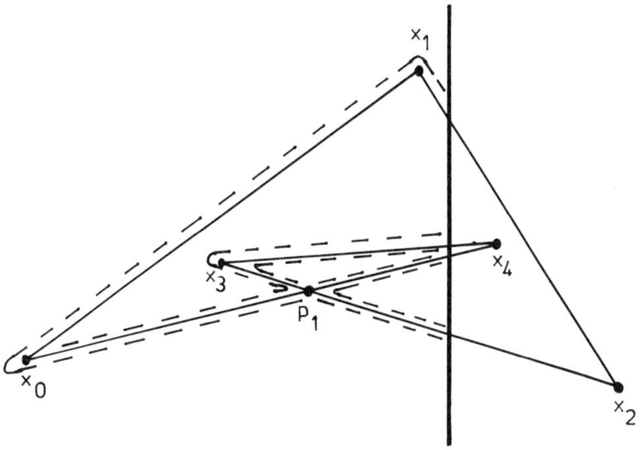

sweep line

$L(p_1,x_2)$, $L(p_1,x_4)$, $L(x_3,x_4)$, $L(x_1,x_2)$ in the y-structure. Note that there is always an even number of line segments in the y-structure since we sweep a closed curve. The four line segments split the sweep line into five intervals, two of which are infinite. For each interval we conceptually record the tentative name of the regions to which the interval belongs (cf. the figure next page), i.e. these names are used to illustrate the algorithm but are not actually stored in the augmented y-structure. Two intervals carry the same name if they belong to the same region and this region is connected to the left of the sweep line. Thus the two infinite intervals always carry the same name. Also, in our example the intervals between $L(x_1,x_2)$ and $L(x_3,x_4)$ and between $L(p_1,x_4)$ and $L(p_1,x_2)$ have different names. Finally, we record

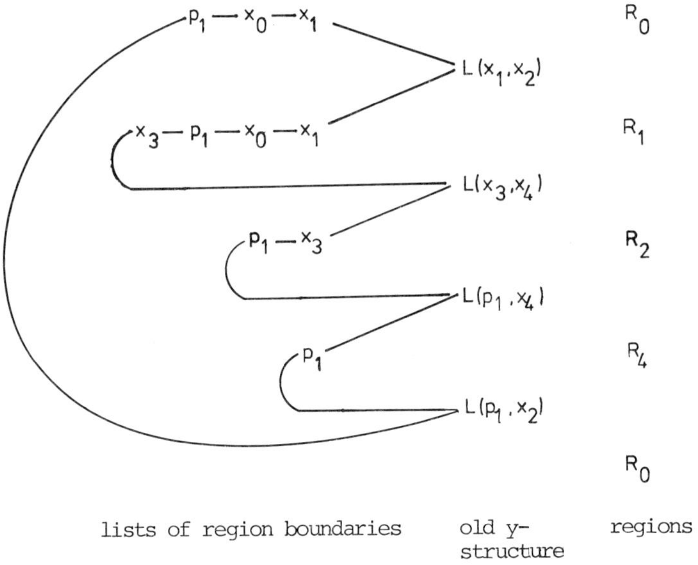

for each region its boundary in doubly linked lists. In our example, the boundary of region R_1 consists of vertices x_1,x_0,p_1,x_3, the line segments between them, and parts of the line segments $L(x_1,x_2)$ and $L(x_3,x_4)$. More generally, the region boundaries are stored as follows. With every entry of the old y-structure we associate two doubly linked lists, one for each of the two regions which have the entry (which is a line segment) on its boundary. Each doubly linked list connects two entries of the old y-structure and stores a polygonal chain. This polygonal chain is part of the boundary of one of the regions. More precisely, assume that there is a region R such that k intervals are known to belong to region R. Then the 2k endpoints $y_1,y_2,\ldots,y_{2k}$ are connected as $y_2-y_3,y_4-y_5,\ldots,y_{2k}-y_1$, in order to reflect the fact that the boundary of region R consists of k polygonal chains, running from y_{2i} to y_{2i+1}, $1 \le i < k$, and from y_{2k} to y_1. The diagram next page illustrates the case $k = 4$; region R is hatched.

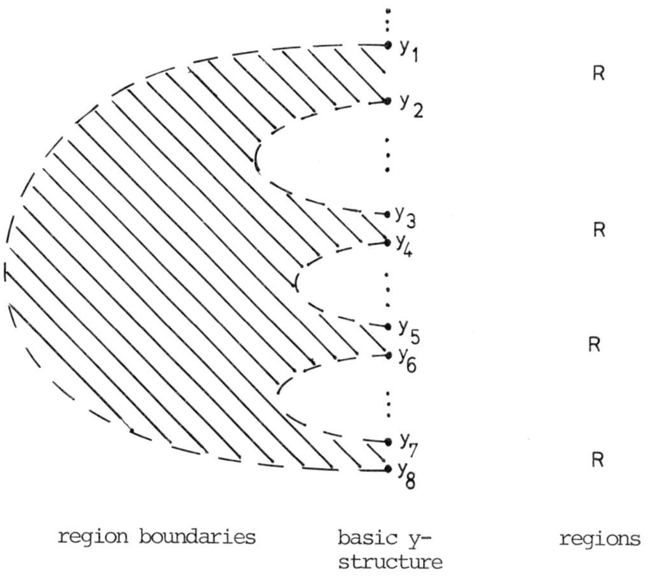

In our running example, we have the following y-structure for a position of the sweep line between x_3 and p_1. Thus the boundary of region

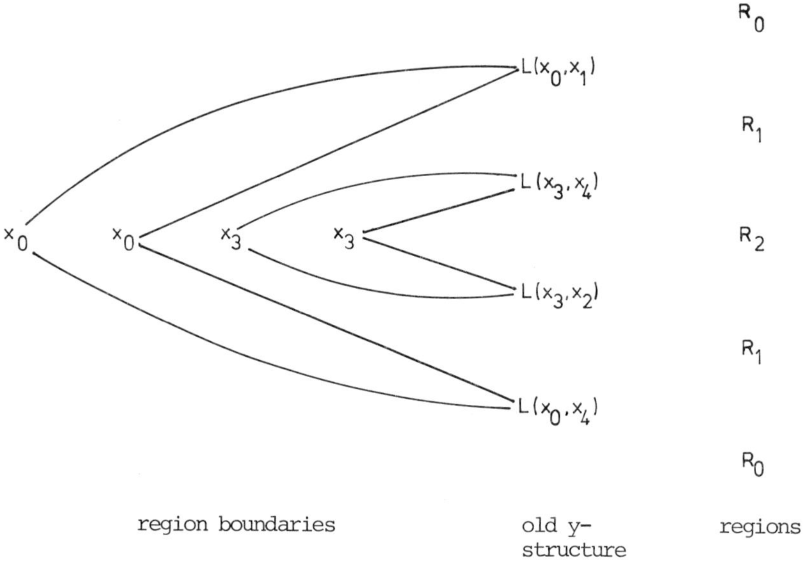

R_1 consists of the interval between $L(x_0,x_1)$ and $L(x_3,x_4)$ followed by the part of line segment $L(x_3,x_4)$ which extends from the sweep line to vertex x_3, followed by a part of line segment $L(x_3,x_2)$ which extends from vertex x_3 to the sweep line, followed by the interval between $L(x_3,x_2)$ and $L(x_0,x_4)$, followed ... .

This completes the description of the augmented y-structure. It remains to describe the transitions in the plane sweep. Since we sweep a closed curve there are exactly four types of transitions, as illustrated below. Either we scan the common left endpoint of two line segment, the common right endpoint of two line segments, the right endpoint of one line segment and the left endpoint of another or a point of intersection. We refer to the four types as start point, endpoint, bend, and intersection. For each of the four types we will now

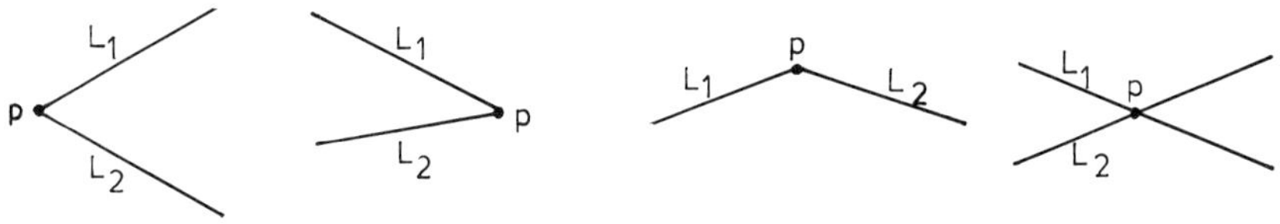

describe the additional actions required. We assume without saying that the actions taken in the basic algorithm are carried out.

<u>Case 1.</u> Two starting line segments (start point): Let line segments L_1 and L_2 share left endpoint p. We insert line segments L_1 and L_2 into the y-structure and associate a new region with the interval between them. Let L and L' be the two line segments adjacent to p in the

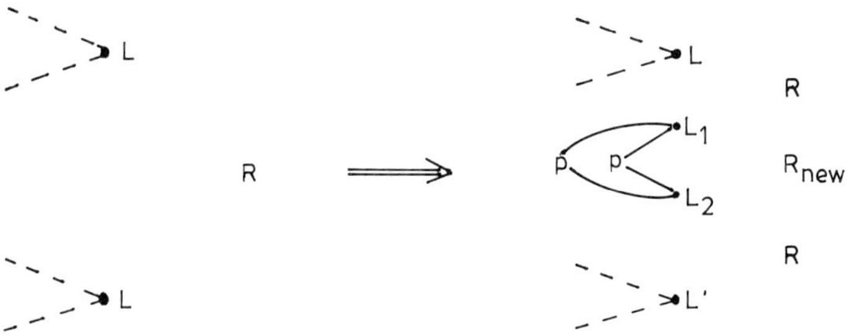

y-structure. Then the interval between them is split into two parts both associated with the same region. Furthermore, we record the fact that the part of L_1 extending from the sweep line to p followed by the part of L_2 extending from p to the sweep line belongs to the boundary of R and R_{new} as illustrated in the diagram above.

<u>Case 2.</u> Two terminating line segments (endpoint): Let line segments L_1

and L_2 share right endpoint p. Let $BLTOP_i$, $BLBOT_i$, i = 1,2 be the boundary

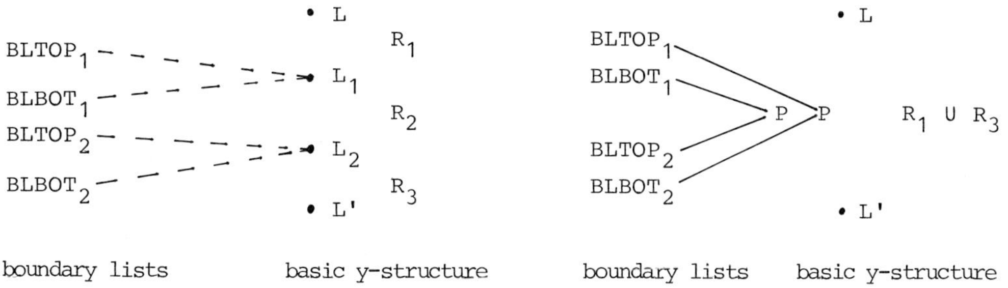

list associated with the interval above (below) L_i at entry L_i of the y-structure. Also let R_1, R_2, R_3 be the regions associated with the intervals between L and L_1, L_1 and L_2, and L_2 and L' respectively. Consider region R_2 first. Lists $BLBOT_1$ and $BLTOP_2$ describe part of the boundary of region R_2. We concatenate $BLBOT_1$, point p, $BLTOP_2$ in order to record the fact that the two partial boundaries meet in vertex p. If lists $BLBOT_1$ and $BLTOP_2$ are not identical (a fact which is easily tested in time O(1) by providing direct links between the two endpoints of each boundary list) then no further action with respect to region R_1 is required. If $BLBOT_1$ and $BLTOP_2$ are identical then p is the rightmost point of region R_1 and the scan of region R_1 is completed. We can thus output its boundary.

Let us turn to regions R_1 and R_3 next; $R_1 = R_3$ is possible. Regions R_1 and R_3 merge in point p and we can join their boundaries by concatenating $BLTOP_1$, vertex p, $BLBOT_2$.

Finally, we delete line segments L_1 and L_2 from the y-structure.

Case 3. One ending, one starting line segment (bend): Let line segment L_1 end in vertex p and let line segment L_2 start in p. Let BLTOP (BLBOT) be the boundary list associated with the region above (below)

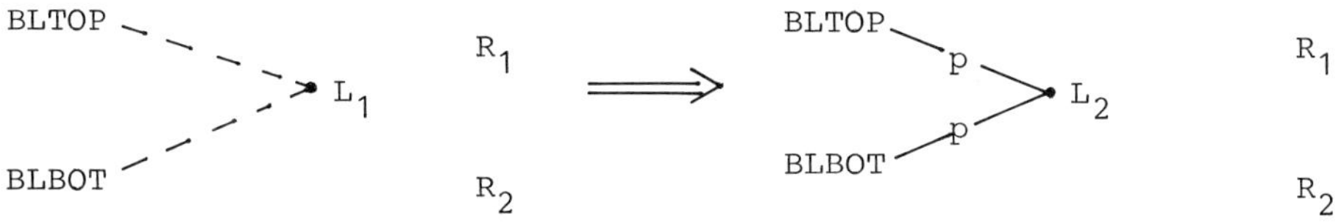

L_1 at entry L_1 of the y-structure. The only action required is to replace L_1 by L_2 in the y-structure and to add point p to lists BLTOP and BLBOT.

Case 4. Point of intersection: Let line segments L_1 and L_2 intersect in vertex p. Conceptually, divide L_1 and L_2 into parts L_1', L_1'' and L_2', L_2'' such that L_1', L_2' end in p and L_1'', L_2'' start in p. This shows that case 4 reduces to case 1 followed by case 2.

We have now arrived at a complete description of the algorithm. The analysis is straightforward. At every transition point, we spend time O(1) in addition to the time spent in the basic algorithm in order to manipulate a few linked lists. Thus running time is still O((n+s)log n) where s is the number of intersections of line segments. We summarize in

Theorem 2: Let $x_0, x_1, \ldots, x_{n-1}$ be a sequence of points in the plane. Then the simple regions defined by the line segments $L_i = L(x_i, x_{i+1})$, $0 \le i \le n-1$, can be determined in time $O((n+s)\log n)$ and space $O(n)$ where s is the number of pairwise intersections of segments L_i.

Theorem 2 can be refined and varied in many ways, cf. exercises 25 to 28. For example, we might start with many instead of one closed curve or we might want to compute a function different from intersection, e.g. symmetric difference. The latter variant of the problem comes up frequently in the design of integrated circuits.

VIII 4.2 Triangulation and its Applications

In this section we study the problem of triangulating a simple polygon and, more generally, of decomposing a simple polygon into convex parts. A decomposition into convex parts or triangles is desirable within computational geometry because convex polygons are much easier to handle than general polygons. It is also desirable in other areas, e.g. numerical analysis, although additional restrictions are often imposed in particular applications as to the shape of the convex parts or triangles. For example, one might want to avoid either small or large angles. Besides being of interest in its own right, the triangulation problem also allows us to illustrate techniques for speeding up plane sweep.

Let P be a simple polygon with vertex set $x_0, x_1, \ldots, x_{n-1}$ in clockwise order. A triangulation of vertex set $\{x_0, \ldots, x_{n-1}\}$ is a maximal set of non-intersecting straightline segments between points in this set. A triangulation of polygon P is a triangulation of its vertex set such that all edges of the polygon are edges of the triangulation. An <u>inner</u> triangulation of P consists of all triangles of a triangulation which are inside P.

In the following diagram polygon edges are shown solid and triangulation edges are shown dashed.

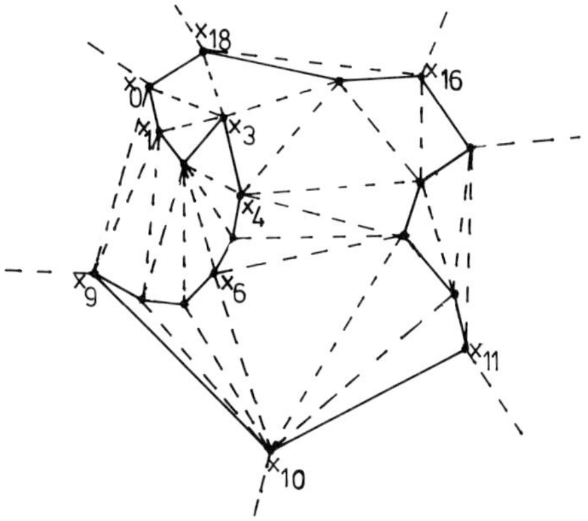

Throughout this section we use n to denote the number of vertices of polygon P and c to denote the number of cusps (concave angles), i.e. $c = |\{i, \measuredangle(x_{i-1}, x_i, x_{i+1}) > \pi\}|$. In our example, we have c = 9. We will present an O(n log n) triangulation algorithm which we later refine to an O(n + c log c) algorithm.

<u>Theorem 3:</u> Let P be a simple polygon. Then an (inner) triangulation of P can be constructed in time O(n log n).

<u>Proof:</u> We will first show how to construct an inner triangulation; a simple modification of the algorithm will then yield a triangulation. We use plane sweep.

The x-structure contains all vertices of the polygon sorted according to x-coordinate. As in the decomposition algorithm above we classify vertices in three groups: start vertices, end vertices and bends. The transition at point p depends on the type of the vertex.

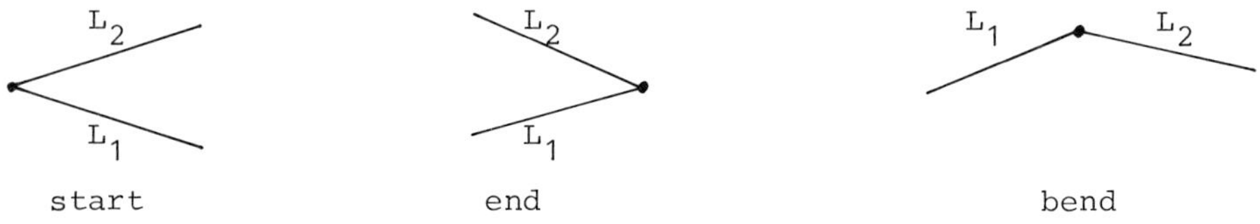

As always, the y-structure contains the active line segments. Since we sweep a closed curve the number of active line segments is always even. The active line segments dissect the sweep line into an odd number of intervals which we label out and in alternately. The two infinite intervals are labelled out. The in-intervals (out-intervals) correspond to regions inside (outside) the polygon. The following diagram shows the y-structure after processing point x_{18}.

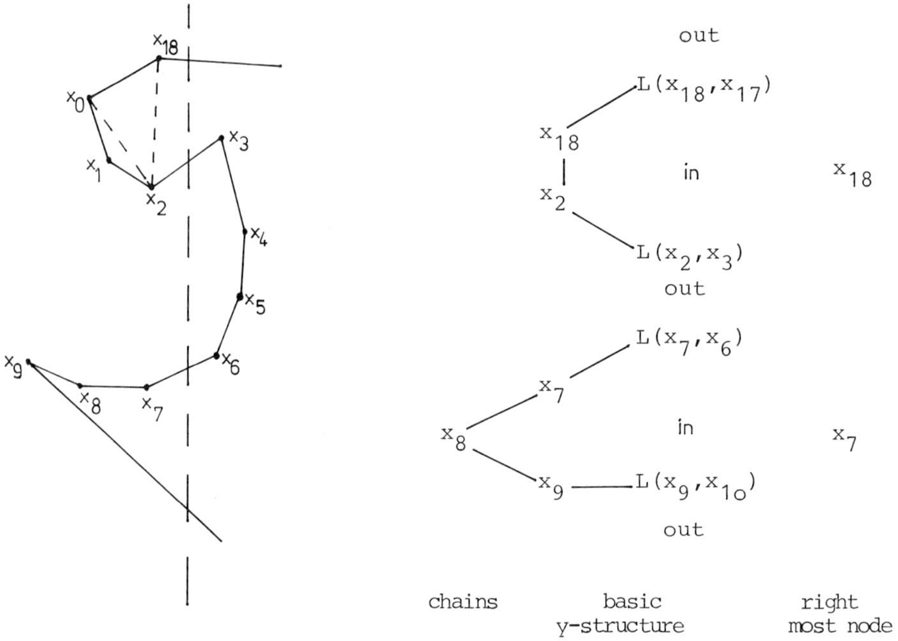

With every in-interval we associate a polygonal chain, say $v_1,\ldots,v_k$, of polygon vertices. Then v_1 and v_k are endpoints of active line segments, and $L(v_i,v_{i+1})$, $1 \le i < k$, is a triangulation edge, i.e. either an edge of the polygon P or an edge constructed in the triangulation process. Furthermore, we maintain the invariant that $\measuredangle(x_i,x_{i+1},x_{i+2}) \ge \pi$

for $1 \le i \le k-2$, i.e. the triangulation of chain $v_1, \ldots, v_k$ cannot be extended locally. Finally, for each in-interval, we provide a pointer to the rightmost node on the chain associated with that interval. Note that the x-coordinates of the nodes on a chain decrease as we follow the chain starting at the rightmost node and proceed towards one of its ends. This follows immediately from the fact that all nodes on a chain (except the two endpoints) are cusps.

We are now ready to give the details of procedure Transition. Let p be the point selected from the x-structure.

Case 1. p is a start point: Let L and L' be the active line segments immediately above and below point p.

Case 1.1. p lies in an out-interval: This case is particularly simple. We split the out-interval between L and L' into three intervals of types out, in, out and associate a chain consisting of node p only with the in-interval. Also,

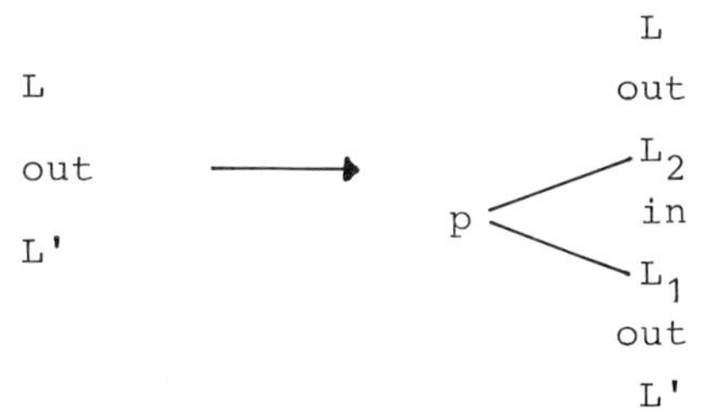

p is the rightmost node of that chain.

Case 1.2. p lies in an in-interval: Let $v_1, \ldots, v_k$ be the chain associated with the in-interval and let v_ℓ be its rightmost node. We can certainly add edge $L(v_\ell, p)$ to the triangulation. Also, we follow the chain starting at v_ℓ in both directions and add edges to the triangulation as long as possible, i.e. until we reach points v_i (preceding v_ℓ on the chain) (and v_j (following v_ℓ)) such that $L(v_i, p)$ can be added to the triangulation but $L(v_{i-1}, p)$ cannot, i.e. until either $i = 1$ or $\measuredangle(v_{i-1}, v_i, p) \ge \pi$. Then we split the in-interval into three intervals of in, out, in and associate chain $v_1, \ldots, v_i, p$ with the upper in-interval and chain $p, v_j, \ldots, v_k$ with the lower in-interval. Also p is the rightmost point of both intervals. The diagrams below illustrate the

transition

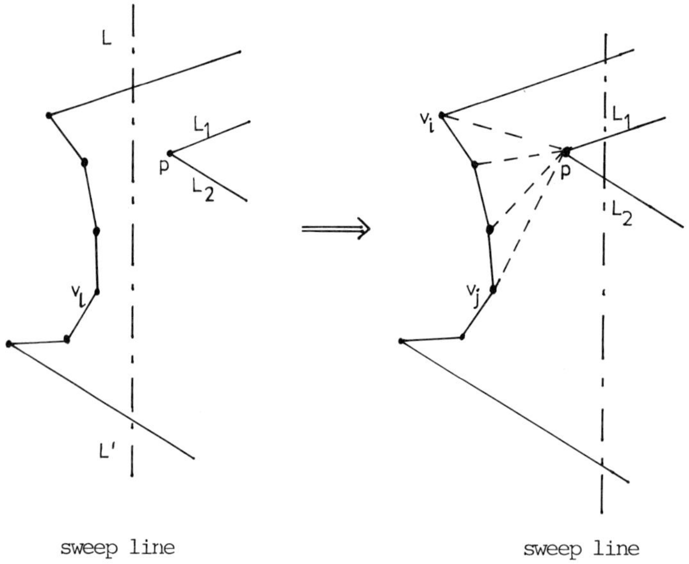

and the effect of the transition on the y-structure

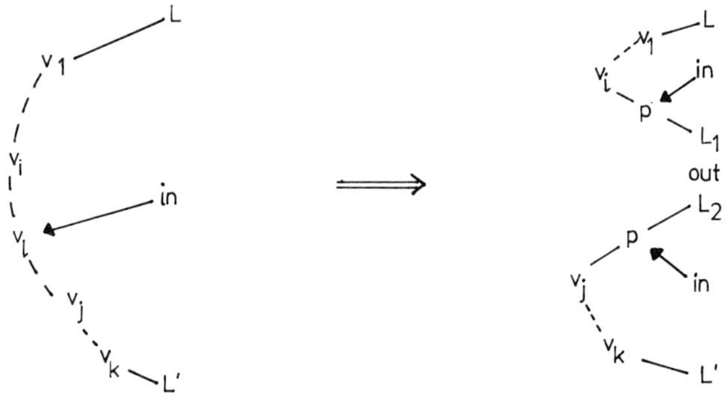

The rightmost element on each chain is indicated by an arrow. The time complexity of this transition is O(log n + number of triangulation edges added).

Case 2. p is a bend: Let L_1 be the edge ending in p and let L_2 be the edge starting in L_2. Then L_1 is on the boundary of an in-interval. Let $v_1,\ldots,v_k$ be the chain associated with that in-interval, where v_1 is the other endpoint of line segment L_1. We add triangulation edges

$L(p,v_2),\ldots,L(p,v_i)$ until $\measuredangle(p,v_i,v_{i+1}) \geq \pi$ and change the chain associated with the in-interval into $p,v_i,v_{i+1},\ldots,v_k$. Also p is the new rightmost node of the chain. The cost of this transition is

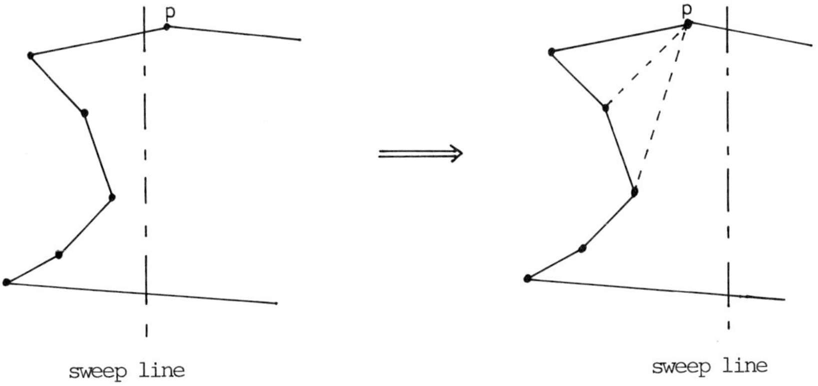

O(1 + number of edges added to triangulation). Note that line segment L_1 can be accessed directly given point p.

Case 3. p is an end node: Let L_1 and L_2 be the two line segments ending in p and let L and L' be the line segment adjacent to L_1 and L_2.

Case 3.1. The interval between L_1 and L_2 is an in-interval: Let $v_1,\ldots,v_k$

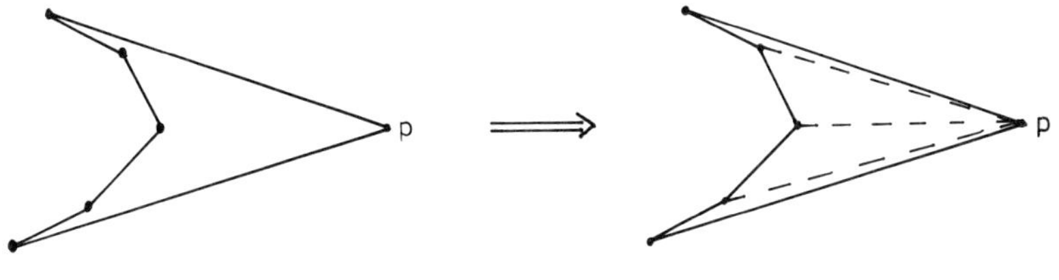

be the chain associated with the in-interval. We add edges $L(p,v_i)$, $2 \leq i \leq k-1$, to the triangulation and delete line segments L_1 and L_2 from the y-structure. The cost of this transition is clearly O(log n + number of edges added to triangulation).

It remains to argue correctness of this transition, i.e. we have to show that the edges of the chain and the newly constructed edges are pairwise non-intersecting. This follows from the fact that $p,v_1,\ldots,v_k,p$ is a simple polygon and that $\measuredangle(v_{i-1},v_i,v_{i+1}) \geq \pi$ for $2 \leq i \leq k-1$.

<u>Case 3.2.</u> The interval between L_1 and L_2 is an out-interval: Let

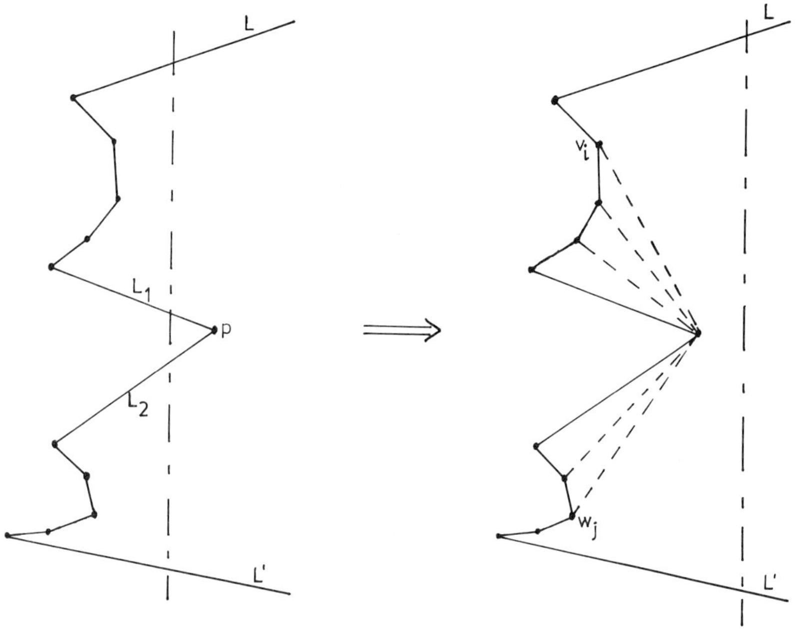

$v_1, \ldots, v_k$ be the chain associated with the in-interval between L and L_1, and $w_1, \ldots, w_h$ be the chain associated with the in-interval between L_2 and L'. Vertex p can be interpreted as a bend for both chains, i.e. we can add triangulation edges $L(p,v_{k-1}), \ldots, L(p,v_i)$ until $\measuredangle(p,v_i,v_{i-1}) \geq \pi$ and edges $L(p,w_2), \ldots, L(p,w_j)$ until $\measuredangle(p,w_j,w_{j+1}) \geq \pi$. Then we merge both in-intervals by deleting edges L_1, L_2 from the y-structure. Also we associate chain $v_1, v_2, \ldots, v_i, p, w_j, w_{j+1}, \ldots, w_k$ with rightmost point p with the new in-interval. The cost of this transition is clearly O(log n + number of edges added to the triangulation).

In summary, we infer that the cost of every transition is bounded by O(log n + number of edges added to the triangulation). Since there are only n transitions and since the number of edges in the triangulation is at most 3n (the triangulation is a planar graph) we infer that total cost is O(n log n). This includes the cost for sorting the n entries of the x-structure. Thus an inner triangulation of a simple polygon P can be constructed in time O(n log n).

We will now extend the algorithm such that it constructs a triangulation. In a preprocessing step we determine the convex hull of polygon P.

This takes time O(n) by section 2, theorem 1. Next we modify the y-structure and associate chains with in-intervals and out-intervals. The chains associated with the out-intervals describe partial triangulations of the outside of P. Finally, we associate hull edges with the two infinite out-intervals; namely the upper and the lower hull edge which are intersected by the sweep line (cf. the diagram below). It is

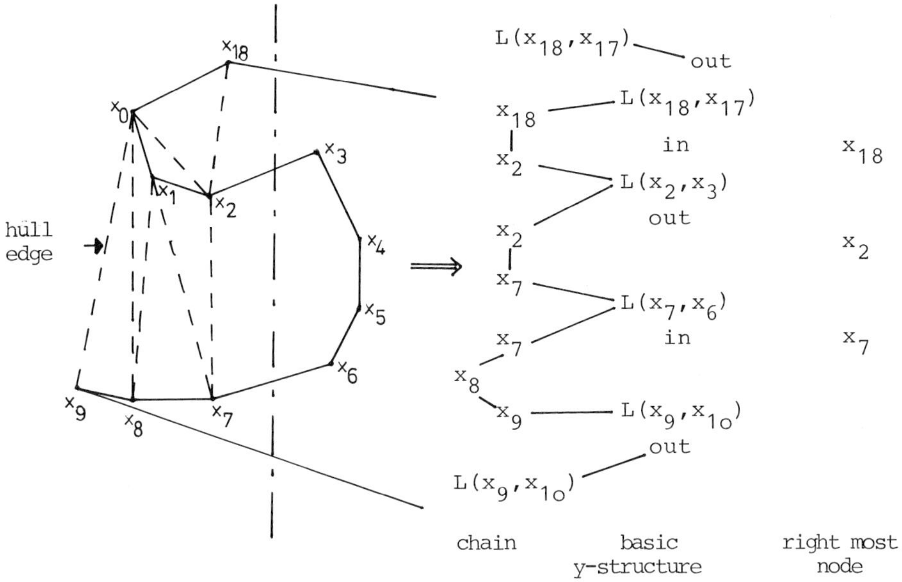

now easy to modify the transitions described above such that a triangulation is constructed. Basically, we only have to treat cases 1.1 and 1.2 and 3.1 and 3.2 symmetrically. We leave the details to the reader.

□

We will next describe an improvement of the triangulation algorithm. The O(n log n) running time of the algorithm stems from two sources; it takes time O(n log n) to sort the vertices of the polygon and it takes time O(n log n) to sweep the plane. The latter statement has to be taken with a grain of salt. Only transitions at end and start points have cost O(log n + ...), the transitions at bends have cost O(1 + ...). Thus the cost of the sweep is O(n + s log s) where s is the number of start and endpoints. The next lemma shows that s = O(c) where c is the number of cusps.

Lemma 2: $s \leq 2 + 2c$

Proof: Let P be a simple polygon and let s_1 be the number of start points. Then $s_1 \leq 1 + c$ since any two start points must be separated by a cusp. A similar argument shows that the number of endpoints is bounded by $1 + c$. Thus $s \leq 2 + 2c$. □

We could reduce the total cost of the algorithm if we could advance the sweep line through the set of start and endpoints only. Then the cost of initializing the x-structure would drop to $O(s \log s)$ and hopefully total running time drops to $O(n + s \log s)$.

Theorem 4: Let P be a simple polygon with n vertices, s start and endpoints, and c cusps. Then P can be triangulated in time $O(n + s \log s) = O(n + c \log c)$.

Proof: The main idea is to only store start and endpoints in the x-structure and to give up the strict regimen of the y-structure. Rather, we allow the y-structure to lag behind the sweep line. As before the y-structure stores an ordered set of line segments which define a set of intervals. For each interval we have its own local sweep line, some of which might lag behind the global sweep line. The global sweep line refers to the sweep line of our basic algorithm. With each interval we associate a chain and a pointer to the rightmost node on the chain as before. Also, the angles at the vertices of the chain are concave as before.

We require two additional invariants. Consider two adjacent intervals in the y-structure. Then the local sweep lines associated with the two intervals must touch a common edge, namely the edge separating the two intervals in the y-structure. The second invariant refers to the ordering of line segments in the y-structure. Conceptually follow the polygon P starting from each of the line segments stored in the y-structure until the global sweep line is reached. In this way we associate a point on the sweep line with every line segment in the y-structure. We require that the ordering of the line segments in the y-structure coincides with the ordering of the associated points on the global sweep line.

The diagram next page illustrates these definitions. Line segments $L_1, \ldots, L_6$ are stored in the y-structure.

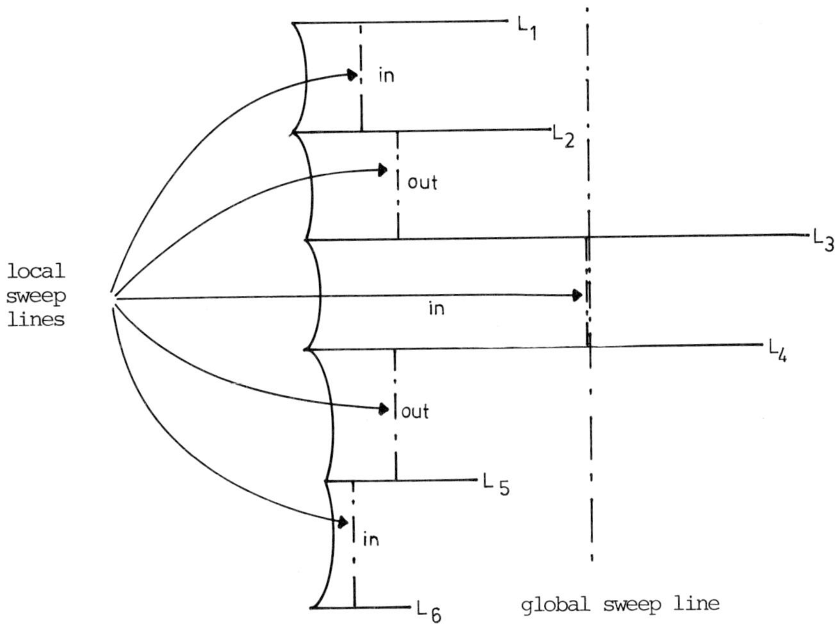

The x-structure stores the s start and endpoints in increasing order of x-coordinate. Thus it takes time O(s log s) to build up the x-structure. Suppose now that we select vertex p from the x-structure and that we want to locate p in the y-structure. Recall that the y-structure is basically a balanced search tree for an ordered set of line segments. When we search for p in the y-structure we compare p with line segments in order to locate p relative to intervals. Since the line segments stored in the y-structure do not necessarily intersect the sweep line such a comparison is potentially meaningless. We proceed as follows.

Suppose that we have to compare p with line segment L which is stored in the y-structure. Then L borders two intervals I_1 and I_2 with associated chains CH_1 and CH_2. Our immediate goal is to close the gap between the local sweep lines for intervals I_1 and I_2 and the global sweep line. We illustrate this process for interval I_1. We extend the chain on both ends all the way up to the sweep line. Note that only bends are encountered in this process. We handle them exactly in the same way as we did in the proof of theorem 3. This strategy is correct because the transition at bends was completely local and since the ordering of intervals is the same as at the corresponding state of the previous algorithm. Suppose now that we extended chain CH_1 all the way to the global sweep line. Then we also might have to extend the chain above CH_1 in order to ensure that the local sweep lines of adjacent intervals touch the same edge, ... It is important to observe that no structural changes in the tree structure underlying the y-structure are necessary. This follows from the invariant about the ordering of line segment in the y-structure. Thus the process of determining the position of p relative to an interval takes time O(1 + number of edges constructed) and hence the search for p in the y-struture takes time O(log s + number of triangulation edges constructed). Note that the number of intervals in the y-structure is at most 2s since intervals only split at start points.

When we have finally determined the position of point p in the y-structure we have also closed the gap between a number of local sweep lines and the global sweep line. In particular, the interval containing p and the two adjacent intervals are processed all the way up to the global sweep line. We can therefore process (start or endpoint) p exactly as we did above.

In summary, there are s transitions. Each transition has cost O(log s + number of triangulation edges drawn). Since only O(n) triangulation edges are drawn altogether, total running time is O(n + s log s) = O(n + c log c) by lemma 2. □

We will now turn to applications of triangulation. Our first application is an extension of our linear time algorithm for intersecting convex polygons (section 1, theorem 5).

<u>Theorem 5:</u> Let P be a simple n-gon and let Q be a convex m-gon. Assume that a triangulation of P is available. Then P ∩ Q can be computed in time O(m + n).

<u>Proof:</u> Let T be a triangulation of P. We first extend T to a planar subdivision T' by adding a set of non-intersecting rays starting at the vertices of the convex hull of P, i.e. we also divide the infinite face into triangles. T' can clearly be obtained from T in time O(n). Also T' has only O(n) edges. Since every edge of T' intersects Q at most twice the

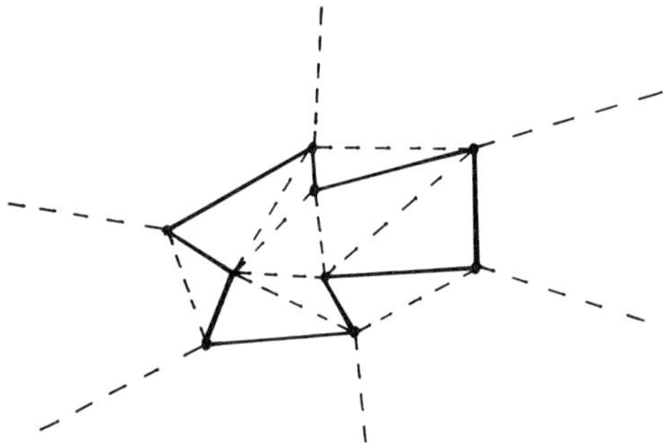

number of intersections of edges of T' and edges of Q iw O(n).

Let $v_1,\ldots,v_m$ be the vertices of Q. We can certainly find the triangle containing v_1 in time O(n). Also knowing the triangle containing v_i, we can find all intersections between T' and line segment $L(v_i,v_{i+1})$ in time $O(1 + s_i)$ where s_i is the number of such intersections. We refer the reader to section 1, theorem 5 for details. Hence the total time needed to find all points of intersection is $O(m + \Sigma s_i) = O(m + n)$, by the argument above. □

Another application is the decomposition of a simple polygon into a nearly minimum number of convex parts. Let P be a simple polygon and let D be a subset of the set of line segments defined by the vertices of P. D is a decomposition into convex parts if the line segments in D are pairwise non-intersecting, are all in the interior of P, and if all the regions defined by P ∪ D are convex. The diagram below shows a decomposition into convex parts; the edges of D are dashed. A decomposition into a minimal number of convex parts can be computed by dynamic programming (exercise 31) in time $O(n^2c^2)$. Here, c is the number of cusps.

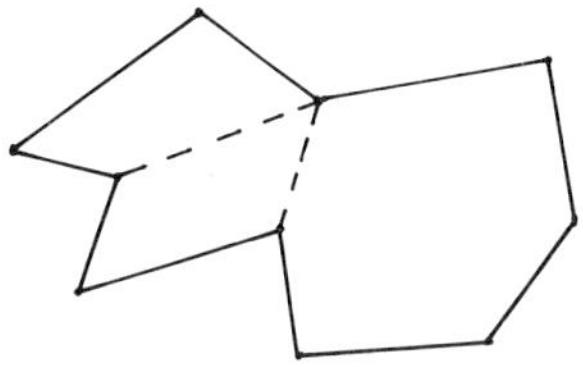

<u>Theorem 6:</u> Let P be a simple n-gon, let T be an interior triangulation of P. Let OPT be the minimal number of parts in any convex decomposition of P. Then a decomposition with at most 4 OPT-3 parts can be constructed in time O(n).

<u>Proof:</u> Observe first that $OPT \geq 1 + \lceil c/2 \rceil$ since at least one partitioning edge is necessary for each cusp. We will partition P into at most $2c + 1 \leq 4\,OPT-3$ parts as follows.

Go through the edges in T in an arbitrary order. Delete an edge of T if its deletion does not create a concave angle in any part of the decomposition. We claim that the decomposition obtained in this way has at most 2c + 1 parts.

This can be seen as follows. Consider any of the remaining edges. Assign any such edge to one of its endpoints. Edge e may be assigned to endpoint p if removal of e creates a concave angle at p. Of course, p is a cusp of the original polygon. Assume for a contradiction that three edges are assigned to any cusp p. Let $e_1, e_2, \ldots, e_5$ be the polygon edges and the three assigned edges in cyclic order. Then $\measuredangle(e_1, e_3) > \pi$ and $\measuredangle(e_3, e_5) > \pi$ and hence $\measuredangle(e_1, e_5) > 2\pi$, a contradiction. Hence at most two edges are assigned to any cusp and thus we have constructed a decomposition with at most $2c + 1$ parts. □

Another application of triangulation is to visibility problems. Let P be a simple polygon and let m be a point in the interior of P. Let Vis be the set of points visible from m, i.e. Vis = {v; L(m,v) does not intersect P}. Then Vis is clearly a simple polygon. The goal is to compute the vertices of Vis in clockwise order. This task is easily solved in linear time given a triangulation of P as follows. Consider the following graph G. Its vertices are the triangles of the triangulation; two triangles (= nodes) are connected by an edge if they share a non-trivial edge in the triangulation. We claim that G is a tree. This can be seen as follows. Let t_1, t_2 be triangles. Since the vertices of t_1 are vertices of P removal of t_1 splits P into exactly three disjoint parts. Exactly one of these parts contains t_2. Hence the first edge on a simple path from t_1 to t_2 in G is uniquely defined and hence (by induction) there is a unique simple path in G from t_1 to t_2. Thus G is a tree.

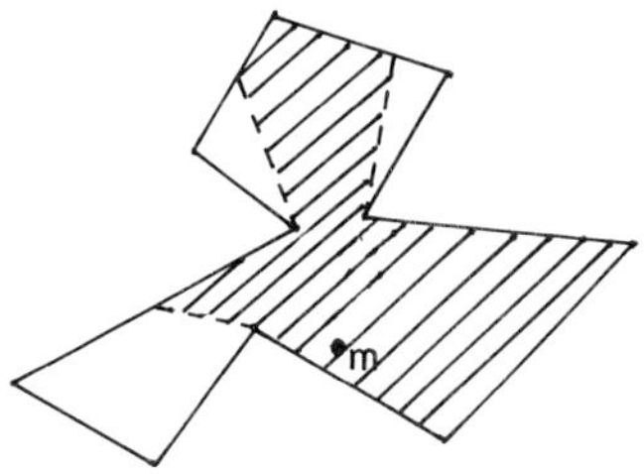

Let t be the triangle containing m. Make t the root of G and compute visibility top-down. More precisely, let e be an edge of some triangle t'. If e is an edge of t then all of e is visible. If e is not an edge of t then let e' be the immediate predecessor of e on the path to the root. Knowing the visible part of e' it is trivial to compute the visible part of e' in time O(1). Thus all visible parts can be computed in time O(n). We summarize in

Theorem 7: Let P be a simple n-gon and let m be a point in the interior of P. Given an inner triangulation of P one can compute the visibility polygon with respect to m in linear time O(n).

VIII. 4.3 Space Sweep

In this section we want to illustrate that the sweep paradigm can also be used to solve three-dimensional problems. More precisely, we will show how to compute the intersection of two convex polyhedra P_0 and P_1 in time $O((n_0+n_1)\log(n_0+n_1))$ where $n_0(n_1)$ is the number of vertices of $P_0(P_1)$. An alternative algorithm with the same time bound is discussed in exercise 2 . The success of plane sweep in two dimensions stems from the fact that it turns a two-dimensional problem into a one-dimensional problem. In other words, the y-structure is linearly ordered in a natural way and hence balanced search trees can be used successfully to maintain it. In three-dimensional space the situation is more complicated in general. The intersection of the sweep plane with the geometric objects is an arbitrary planar subdivision which changes dynamically as the sweep plane advances. Unfortunately, the techniques developed in section 3.2. for maintaining dynamic planar subdivisions are not strong enough to handle the sweep of general three-dimensional objects. However, there is one special case which we can handle: the sweep of convex polyhedra. The intersection of the sweep plane with a convex polydron is essentially a convex polygon, and convex polygons behave very nicely as we saw in section 1.

W.l.o.g. let no two vertices of one of the two polyhedra have equal x-coordinates. We assume throughout this section that all faces of polyhedra P_i, $i = 0,1$, are triangles. To achieve this, all polygonal faces are partitioned into co-planar triangles by drawing <u>improper edges</u> from their respective point of minimal x-coordinate. Also, we assume the following representation of polyhedra. For each vertex we have the list of incident edges in clockwise order, for each edge we have pointers to the endpoints and to the adjacent faces and for each face we have the list of edges in clockwise order.

<u>Theorem 8:</u> Let P_0 and P_1 be convex polyhedra with n_1 and n_2 vertices respectively, let $n = n_1 + n_2$. Then convex polyhedron $P_0 \cap P_1$ can be computed in time $O(n \log n)$.

<u>Proof:</u> $P_0 \cap P_1$ is a convex polyhedron. We divide the set E of edges of $P_0 \cap P_1$ into two disjoint classes E_1 and E_2. E_1 consists of all edges of $P_0 \cap P_1$ which lie on the surface of P_0 and P_1 and E_2 is the remaining set of edges of $P_0 \cap P_1$. Each edge in E_2 is (part of) an edge of

P_0 or P_1. Each edge in E_1 is the intersection of a face of P_0 and a face of P_1. Note however, that edges in E_1 can also be part of <u>edges</u> of P_0 or P_1.

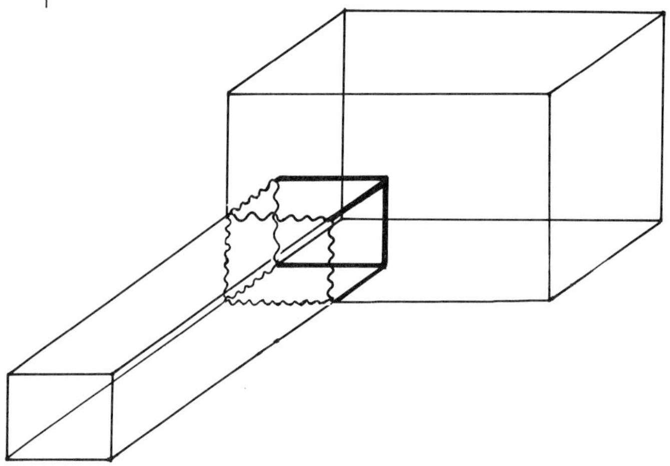

In the example above the edges in E_1 (E_2) are shown as wiggled (heavy) lines. The edges in E_1 are naturally grouped into connected components (if two edges share an endpoint then they belong to the same component). In our example there is only one component. We compute $P_0 \cap P_1$ in a two step process. In the first step we will compute at least one point (on an edge) of each component by space sweep and in the second step we will use these points as starting points for a systematic exploration of $P_0 \cap P_1$. We denote the problem of computing at least one point of each component by ICP'. We assume that each point in the solution set to ICP' is given as the intersection of an edge of P_i with a face of P_{1-i}, $i = 0$ or $i = 1$.

<u>Lemma 3:</u> Given a solution to ICP' one can compute $P_0 \cap P_1$ in time $O(n)$.

<u>Proof:</u> The basic idea is to explore $P_0 \cap P_1$ starting from the solution set to ICP' by any of the systematic methods for exploring graphs. More precisely, we proceed as follows. Let S be the solution set to ICP'. We step through the points in S in turn. For every $x \in S$ we construct the set of edges in $E_1 \cup E_2$ incident to x and put them into queues Q_1 and Q_2 respectively. Edges in E_1 are given as the intersection of a face of P_0 and a face of P_1. These faces are not co-planar. Edges in E_2 are part of an edge of P_0 or P_1. We represent them by a pointer to an edge of P_0 or P_1 and the set of their endpoints which

are already constructed. Note that an edge in E_2 shares either two or one or zero endpoints with edges in E_1. The other endpoints are vertices of P_o or P_1. Having processed the points in S we construct E_1 by looking at the edges in Q_1 in turn. For every edge removed from Q_1 we construct all edges in $E_1 \cup E_2$ incident to its endpoints and add them to Q_1 and Q_2 respectively (if they were not added before). In this way all edges in E_1 are found. Furthermore Q_2 contains all edges in E_2 which share at least one endpoint with an edge in E_1. We now construct all edges in E_2 by looking at the edges in Q_2 in turn. For every edge removed from Q_2 we have processed either one or two of its endpoints. If only one endpoint has been processed then we add all edges incident to the other endpoint (which is a vertex of P_o or P_1) to Q_2 (if they were not added before). Note that all endpoints of edges in E_2 which are not vertices of P_o or P_1 where constructed when processing S or computing E_1.

We have to describe next how to construct all edges in $E_1 \cup E_2$ incident to a node x. Special care has to be taken when x lies on co-planar faces D_o of P_o and D_1 of P_1. We therefore treat this case first. Let F_o (F_1) be the convex polygon formed by the union of all faces of P_o (P_1) which are co-planar to D_o (D_1). We intersect F_o and F_1 in time $O(deg_o(F_o) + deg_1(F_1))$ using the methods of section 1 and process all vertices of the intersection as described in one of the cases below. Also, all the edges of the intersection are added to E_1; they do not have to be added to Q_1. In the sequel, all points of S which belong to either F_o or F_1 can be ignored. We achieve this by marking all faces comprising F_o and F_1 as done. The special treatment of co-planar faces is required for the following reason. If co-planar faces were treated as other faces are it is conceivable that a large number of intersections were discovered which are in the interior of a face of $P_o \cap P_1$ as illustrated in the diagram below. The diagram (top of next page) shows co-planar faces of P_o (—) and P_1 (--) and their unessential intersections.

This finishes the description of the treatment of co-planar faces. We return now to the discussion of how to construct all edges in $E_1 \cup E_2$ incident to a point x. Let x be given as the intersection of an edge e bordering faces F' and F" of P_i and face F of P_{1-i}. We have to distinguish several cases.

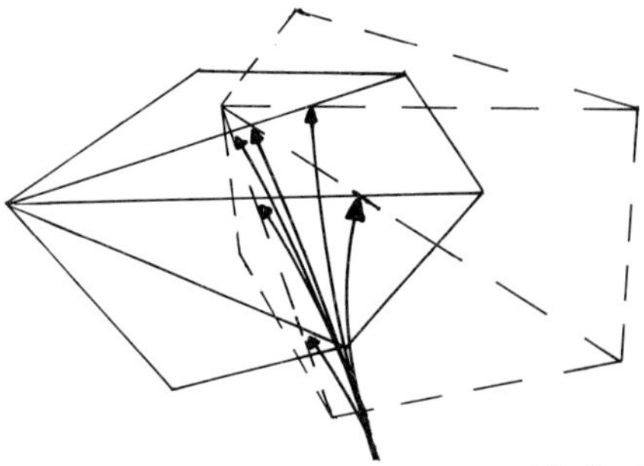

Assume first that x is a vertex of either P_0 or P_1, say a vertex of P_j. Then x lies either in the interior of a face of P_{1-j} or on an edge of P_{1-j} or is a vertex of P_{1-j}. If x lies in the interior of a face, say D, we first check whether D is co-planar with one of the faces of P_j. If so, and if the faces concerned are not "done", we use the method described above. In addition (otherwise, respectively) we can certainly compute all edges in $E_1 \cup E_2$ incident to x in time $O(deg_j(x))$ by intersecting D with all the faces of P_j incident to x. We use $deg_j(v)$ to denote the degree of x in polyhedron P_j. In general, there will be two edges in E_1 incident to x and some number of edges in E_2 as

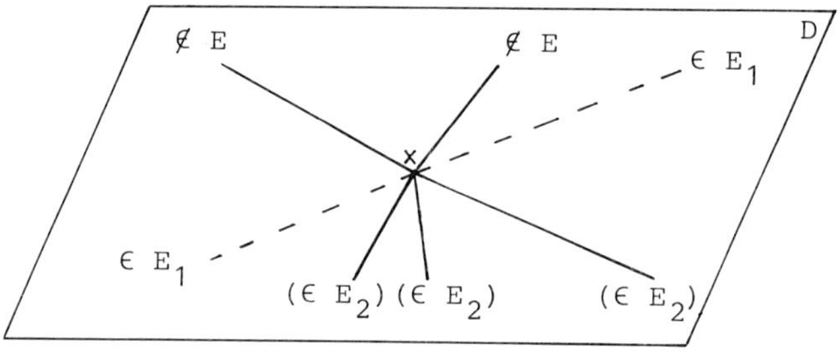

indicated in the diagram. If x lies on an edge of P_{1-j} but is not a vertex of P_{1-j} then x lies on the boundary of exactly two faces of P_{1-j}. We basically only have to intersect both of them with the faces of P_j incident to x. Again, time $O(deg_j(v))$ suffices. So let us finally assume that x is a vertex of both polyhedra. Let r be a ray extending from x into the interior of P_0, and let D be a plane perpendicular to r and intersecting r in a point different from x. Let $e_1, \ldots, e_m$ be the edges of P_0 incident to x in clockwise order, extended to rays. Convexity implies that all these rays intersect D; the points of intersection define a convex polygon C_o. Also extend the edges of P_1 incident to x to rays; two adjacent rays bound an infinite "triangular" face. Intersecting these faces with plane D yields a convex polygon C_1, or an open convex polygonal segment C_1 as shown below, or the empty set.

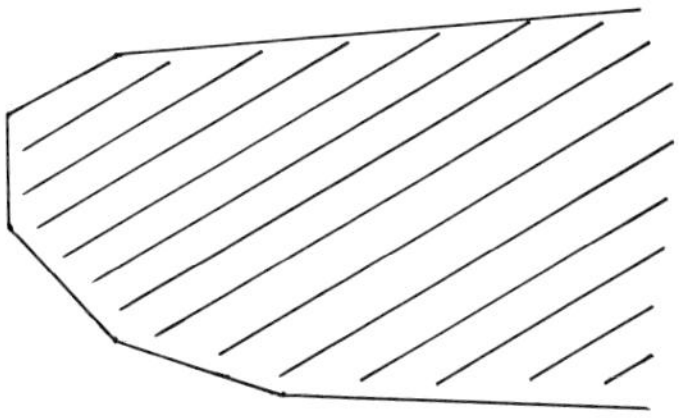

Using the methods of section 1, we can compute the intersection of C_o and C_1 in time $O(deg_o(x) + deg_1(x))$. Having determined the intersection of C_o and C_1 it is simple to determine all edges of E_1 (E_2) incident to x.

Again, it is possible to detect co-planar faces in this process. They are treated as before. Additional time O(sum of degrees of newly intersected co-planar polygons) is sufficient.

In all the three cases we mark vertex x in the appropriate polyhedron/ polyhedra. This completes the discussion of the case that x is a vertex of P_o or P_1.

Assume next that x lies on the boundary of F, i.e. x lies on an edge d of P_{1-i}. Let F''' be the other face of P_{1-i} which has d on its boundary. If none of F or F''' is co-planar to F' or F" then the structure of $P_o \cap P_1$ in the vicinity of x is readily computed in time O(1) by intersecting the four faces F, F', F", and F'''. Otherwise we proceed as described above.

Let us finally assume that x lies in the interior of face F. Then x has to be a proper intersection, and F cannot be co-planar with either F' or F". $F \cap F'$ and $F \cap F''$ belong to E_1, and the part of e which is directed to the inside of F belongs to E_2.

This finishes the description of the construction of all edges in E_1 and E_2 which are incident to a node in the solution set to ICP'. The construction of all such edges clearly takes time O(n). Handling co-planar faces can also be done in total time O(n) since each such face is explored only once.

We use these edges as the basis for the exploration of $P_0 \cap P_1$. First we completely explore E_1.

```
(1)  for i ∈ {0,1}
(2)  do Q_i ← subset of edges of E_i determined by processing the solu-
           tion set to ICP' as described above
(3)  od;
(4)  while Q_1 ≠ ∅
(5)  do remove an arbitrary edge e form Q_1; e is given as the inter-
        section of a face F_o of P_o and a face F_1 of P_1;
(6)     let x,y be the two endpoints of e;
(7)     for z ∈ {x,y}
(8)     do if z was not visited before
(9)        then find all edges in E_1 and E_2 incident to z as described
                above and add them to Q_1 and Q_2 respectively
(10)       fi
(11)    od
(12) od
```

We claim that the program above explores all remaining edges in E_1 in time O(n). Note first that Q_1 is initialized with at least one edge of every component of E_1. Hence all remaining edges in E_1 are explored and every edge is explored at most twice, once from either side. We turn to the time bound next. We infer from the preceding discussion that the total time spent in line (9) is O(n). Furthermore each execution of lines (5) and (6) takes time O(1) since faces are triangles. It remains to consider line (8). Point z is either a vertex of P_0 or P_1 or it lies on an edge of P_0 or P_1. Also, at most two vertices of $P_0 \cap P_1$ can lie on any edge of P_0 or P_1. Hence, if we mark visited vertices of P_0 or P_1 and associate other vertices of $P_0 \cap P_1$ with the edge of P_0 or P_1 on which the vertex lies, then the test in line (8) takes time O(1). Since the number of edges in $P_0 \cap P_1$ is O(n) the time bound follows.

It remains to explore the edges in E_2. Recall that every edge in E_2 is part of an edge of either P_0 or P_1. Also note that all endpoints of edges in E_2 which are not vertices of P_0 or P_1 have been determined at this point. Furthermore, all edges in E_2 which have such endpoint belong to Q_2 at this moment. It is now easy to find the remaining edges in E_2 in time $O(n)$. We leave the details to the reader. □

We will now show how to solve ICP' by space sweep. As before, we have two structures. The x-structure contains all vertices of P_0 and P_1 in order of increasing x-coordinate. The yz-structure, which replaces the y-structure, stores the status of the sweep. It stores for each of the two polyhedra a crown which represents the intersection of the polyhedron and the sweep plane.

Let P_i, $i = 0,1$, be one of the polyhedra. Let e_j, $0 \le j < n_i$, be the edges of P_i which are intersected by the sweep plane in cyclic order. Here, two edges are adjacent if they bound the same face. A prong is the portion of a face bounded by two consecutive edges e_j and $e_{j+1 (\mathrm{mod}\ n_i)}$ and, to the left, by the sweep plane. The set of all prongs is called the crown. We also call edges e_j, $0 \le j < n_i$, the forward edges of the crown, the edges connecting the intersections of the e_j's with the sweep plane the base edges and the remaining edges the prong edges. Prong edges connect tips of prongs.

The following figure illustrates these definitions. The different types of edges are indicated by characters b, f and p.

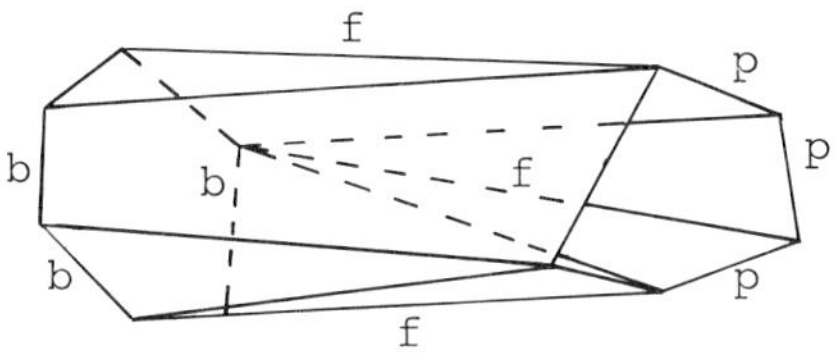

We store a crown in a balanced tree as follows. For polyhedron P_i we select an axis line L_i ; for instance the line connecting the vertices of P_i with minimal and maximal x-coordinate, respectively. Let $p \in \mathbb{R}^3$. The cylindrical coordinates (x, alfa, radius) of p with respect to L_i are defined as follows. First, x is the x-coordinate of point p. Second, pair (alfa, radius) forms the polar coordinates in the plane, say E, which goes through p and is parallel to the yz-plane. The origin of the polar system is the intersection of E and L_i and the angle is measured against a fixed direction in that plane; say, the y-direction. A forward edge of the crown C_i of P_i is represented by the cylindrical coordinates of its endpoints with respect to L_i, $i = 0,1$, i.e. by a six-tuple (x_o, $alfa_o$, r_o, x_1, $alfa_1$, r_1). If p is a point of this forward edge with x-coordinate x, $x_o \le x \le x_1$, then the pair (alfa,r) corresponding to p can be computed in time O(1). Next observe, that although alfas and radii change with x, the cyclic ordering of forward crown edges remains invariant between transitions. Hence we can store forward edges in a balanced tree, organized with respect to the alfas. For concreteness, we assume a (2,4)-tree. The following diagram illustrates the radial representation of the crown.

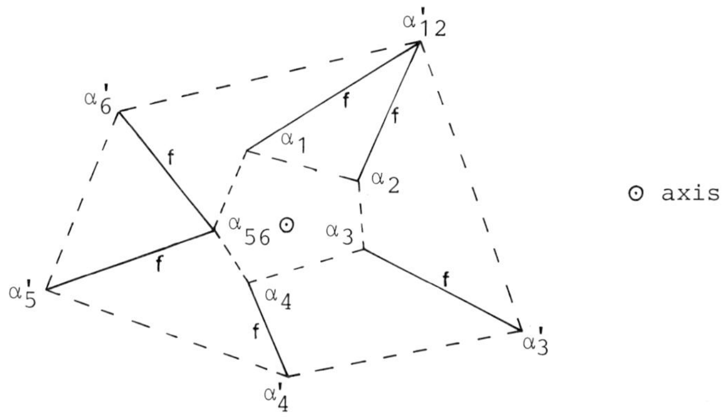

We are now ready for the space sweep algorithm. The global structure of the algorithm is as given in the introduction of section 4. A transition at vertex p of polyhedron P_i is performed as follows.

(1) <u>procedure</u> Transition(p,i):
(2)   update crown C_i of P_i;
(3)   <u>for</u> every face F of P_i having a starting edge at p
(4)   <u>do</u> intersect the starting edges of F with the crown C_{1-i} of polyhedron P_{1-i} and report all intersections;
(5)   <u>if</u> no intersection is found
(6)   <u>then</u> choose one forward edge of C_{1-i} and intersect with all faces of P_i which are co-planar with F, report intersections if any
(7)   <u>fi</u>

(8) <u>od</u>

(9) <u>end</u>

Before we analyse the running time of the algorithm we show its correctness.

<u>Lemma 4:</u> The algorithm above correctly solves ICP'.

<u>Proof:</u> It is clear that a set of intersections is computed. Thus we only need to show that at least one point of each component will be reported.

Let S be any component, and let v be a vertex of S with minimal x-coordinate. Clearly y is the intersection of an edge e of polyhedron P_i with a face of polyhedron P_{1-i}. If v is not reported then e must start before F (in the sweep order). Consider the state of the sweep just after the start vertex p of F was encountered. At this point edge e is a forward edge of the crown C_i of P_i.

Trace (conceptually) component S in the polygon F_p containing face F and crown C_i starting at point v. Two cases may arise:

<u>Case 1.</u> We are not able to trace S completely in polygon F_p and crown C_i. Then we either hit a bounding edge of F_p before a base or prong edge of C_i or vice versa. In the former case there is a bounding edge, say e', of F_p which intersects a prong, say PR, of C_i. The intersection of e' and PR was either detected when processing p (if p is the starting edge of e') or will be detected when processing the starting point of e'. Note that PR is still a prong of C_i at this point. In the latter case, we must hit a prong edge, say e", of C_i. This follows from the fact that v is in front of the sweep plane and has minimal x-coordinate among all points in S. When the sweep advances to the starting point of e" polygon F_p is still part of the crown of P_{1-i}. Hence we will pick up the intersection of e" and F at that point. □

<u>Case 2:</u> We are able to trace S completely in F_p and crown C_i. Since F_p is part of a plane, and since the prongs of C_i are parts of planes S must be a closed curve and therefore runs through all forward edges of C_i. Hence <u>all</u> forward edges of C_i intersect F_p, and a point of S is found in line (6) of Transition. □

Let us now examine the time required for different actions of Transition.

Lemma 5: The updating of crowns P and Q can be done in total time $O(n + m)$.

Proof: Consider updating C_i at a transition vertex v. Let c_1 edges end at vertex v and let c_2 edges start at vertex v. It is easy to provide direct access to these edges. Also since we assumed that edges incident to a node are given in cyclic order we know in which order the c_2 edges starting at v have to appear in the crown. Hence we only have to delete c_1 edges (at known positions) from the tree and to insert c_2 edges (at known positions) into the tree. Thus the amortized cost of the insertions and deletions at point v is $O(c_1 + c_2)$ by section III.5.3.2.. Hence the total time required to update the crowns is $O(n + m)$. □

Lemma 6: Let C be a crown with c forward edges and let L be a line which does not intersect the base of C. Then $C \cap L$ can be computed in time $O(\log c)$.

Proof: The algorithm is a variant of the algorithm used to prove theorem 2 in section 1. We view the balanced tree representation of the crown as a hierarchical representation of the crown. Let $v_1,\ldots,v_c$ be the intersections of the forward edges with the base plane of the crown in cyclic order and let $w_1,\ldots,w_c$ be the forward endpoints of the forward edges in cyclic order. Note that $v_j = v_{j+1}$ $(= v_{j+2} = \ldots)$ or $w_j = w_{j+1}$ $(= w_{j+2} = \ldots)$ is possible. Let t be the forward endpoint of the axis, i.e. t is the vertex with maximal x-coordinate of the polygon to which crown C belongs. Consider the convex hull of point set $\{v_1,\ldots,v_c,w_1,\ldots,w_c,t\}$. The faces of the convex hull are the prongs, and the triangles w_j,w_{j+1},t (with $w_{c+1} := w_1$); $1 \le j \le c$. A balanced tree defines a hierarchical representation of this polyhedron as follows. Let D^i be the forward edges which are stored in the i-th level of the tree, $1 \le i \le k = O(\log c)$. Then the convex hull of the endpoints of the edges in D^i and point t is the approximation C^i of the crown C. We have $C^k = C$. Also note, that if $e = (v_j,w_j)$ and $e' = (v_h,w_h)$ are adjacent edges in D^i then they determine one or two faces of the approximation C^i, namely either the triangle $v_j,w_j = w_h,v_h$ or

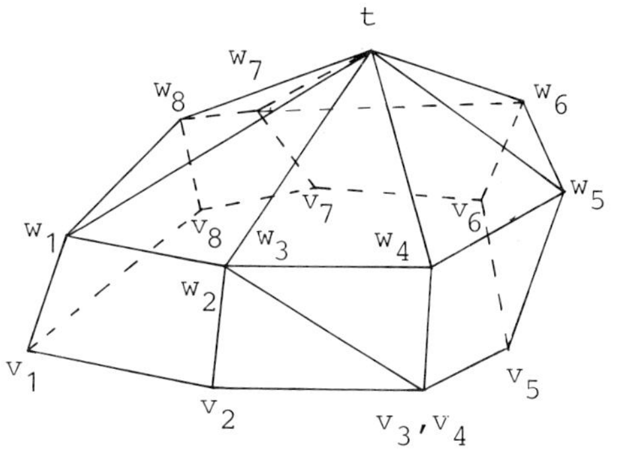

the triangle w_j, w_h, t and the quadrilateral v_j, w_j, w_h, v_h which collapses to a triangle if $v_j = v_h$. We can now use essentially the algorithm of section 1, theorem 2 to compute $C \cap L$.

We use the following notation. If x is a point of a C^i then a face F of C^{i+1} is <u>in the vicinity of</u> x if F and the face of C^i containing x have an edge in D^i in common. A point y of C^{i+1} is in the vicinity of x if a face of C^{i+1} to which y belongs is in the vicinity of x. Finally, if x does not intersect C^i then we use p_i to denote the point of C^i which has smallest distance from line L. Note that p_i is not necessarily a vertex of C^i. However, we may assume w.l.o.g. that p_i lies on an edge of C^i. The following lemma captures the heart of the algorithm.

<u>Lemma 7:</u> a) If L intersects P^{i+1} but does not intersect P^i then the faces of P^{i+1} which are intersected by L are in the vicinity of p_i.

b) If L does not intersect P^{i+1} then p_{i+1} is in the vicinity of p_i.

c) If L intersects P^i then the intersections of L and P^{i+1} are in the vicinity of the intersections of L and P^i.

d) If L is a line and e is a line segment then the point $y \in e$ closest to L can be computed in time O(1).

<u>Proof:</u> a) and b): Let E be a plane parallel to L and supporting C^i in point p_i. Then plane E divides the space into two half-spaces one of which contains L and one of which contains C^i. Call the former half-space H. If L intersects P^{i+1} then $H \cap P^{i+1}$ must be non-empty. By

convexity of C^{i+1} only faces in the vicinity of x can possibly intersect H. This proves parts a) and b).

c) Obvious.

d) Let L' be a line containing line segment e. Let L (L') be given by point a (a') and direction $\vec{b}$ ($\vec{b}'$). If L and L' are parallel then the solution is trivial. Otherwise, consider the plane E determined by a and directions $\vec{b}$ and $\vec{b}'$. It contains line L and is parallel to L'. Let $\vec{c}$ be the direction normal to the plane, let a" be the intersection of E and the line of direction $\vec{c}$ through a', and let L" be the line through a" parallel to L'. Let x be the intersection of L and L" and let y be the projection of x onto L' in the direction $\vec{c}$. Then points x,y realize the minimum distance between L and L'. If y is a point of e then we are done. If y does not belong to e then the endpoint of e closest to y realizes the minimum distance. □

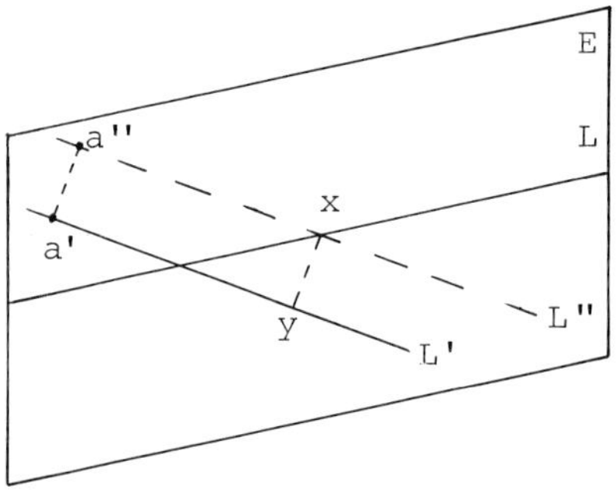

We infer from the lemma above that L ∩ C can be found by following at most two paths in a balanced tree. In each node of the tree O(1) work is required. □

Combining lemmata 3 to 7, we obtain:

<u>Lemma 8:</u> ICP' can be solved in time $O(n_o \log n_1 + n_1 \log n_o)$.

<u>Proof:</u> The total cost of updating the crowns is $O(n_o + n_1)$ by lemma 6. Also, the total cost of line (4) of procedure Transition is $O(n_o \log n_1 + n_1 \log n_o)$ by lemma 7. The remaining lines of Transition have cost $O(n_o + n_1)$. □□

The goal of this section was to illustrate the use of the sweep paradigm in three-dimensional space and also to provide an algorithm for a basic problem in algorithmic geometry. The alternative algorithm discussed in exercise 2 is conceptually simpler; in fact the proof of lemma 7 was inspired by a solution to that exercise. On the other hand, the algorithm given above only needs to store a cross section of the polyhedron and hence uses less space. Also, it is more efficient since the hierarchical representations obtained in a solution to exercise 2 have depth c log n for a fairly large constant c. We refer the reader to the related problem discussed in section 3.2., lemma 8 .

VIII. 5. The Realm of Orthogonal Objects

In this section we explore the geometry of orthogonal or iso-oriented objects, i.e. objects all of whose edges are parallel to a coordinate axis. Thus in two-dimensional space, we have to deal with points, horizontal and vertical line segments, and rectangles whose sides are axis-parallel. More generally, an iso-oriented object in $\mathbb{R}^d$ is the cartesian product of d real intervals one for each coordinate, i.e. it has the form $\prod_{x=1}^{d} [\ell_i, r_i]$ where $\ell_i \le r_i$ for all i.

As above, we will mostly concentrate on two-dimensional problems. The two major algorithmic paradigms which have been used in this area are plane-sweep and divide-and-conquer. There are many problems which can be solved using either paradigm; the elegance of the solution may however differ drastically as we will see. We devote section 5.1 to plane-sweep and section 5.2 to divide-and-conquer algorithms. In the section on plane-sweep we will introduce three new data structures (interval, priority search, and segment trees) which can handle special types of planar range queries more efficiently than range trees (cf. VII.2.2); we will also see that some of the algorithms generalize to non-orthogonal objects (sections 5.1.4) and higher dimensions (section 5.3).

5.1 Plane Sweep for Iso-Oriented Objects

Plane sweep is a very powerful technique for solving two-dimensional problems on iso-oriented objects. Recall that iso-oriented objects are points, horizontal and verticall line segments, and axis-parallel rectangles. Typically, the transition points are the points, the endpoints of the line segments and the vertices of the rectangles.

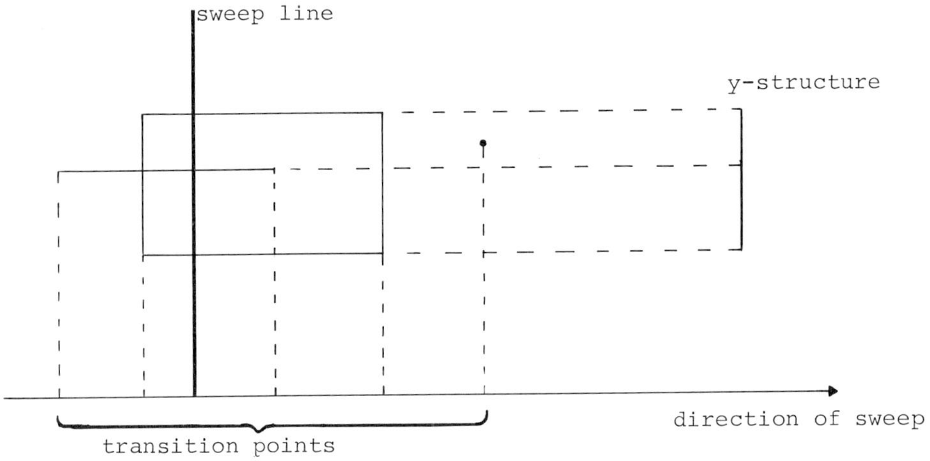

Also, the y-structure typically contains information about the horizontal line segments and the rectangles which are intersected by the sweep line in its current position. Horizontal line segments correspond to points and rectangles correspond to intervals.

Throuhout this section we use the following <u>notation for intervals</u> on the real line. Let $x,y \in \mathbb{R}$, $x \leq y$. Then $[x,y]$ denotes the closed, (x,y) the open interval, and $[x,y)$ and $(x,y]$ denote the half-open intervals with endpoints x and y, i.e.

$$[x,y] = \{z;\ x \leq z \leq y\}$$
$$(x,y) = \{z;\ x < z < y\}$$
$$[x,y) = \{z;\ x \leq z < y\}$$
$$(x,y] = \{z;\ x < z \leq y\}$$

Note that a closed interval $[x,x]$ with identical endpoints corresponds to a point.

In the course of a plane sweep algorithm for iso-oriented objects one has to maintain dynamic sets of intervals. Whenever the sweep reaches a left (right) side of a rectangle or horizontal line segment one has to insert (delete) an interval into (from) the y-structure. Also, one typically has to query the y-structure at transition points.

Intervals are often conveniently represented as points in two-dimensional space. Then queries about intervals can often be phrased as (special types of) range queries. We illustrate this observation by a few examples. Let $S = \{[x_i,y_i];\ 1 \le i \le n\}$ be a set of closed intervals and let $I = [x_o,y_o]$ be a query interval. We can view S as a set A(S) of points $p_i = (x_i,y_i)$, $1 \le i \le n$, in $\mathbb{R}^2$.

<u>Fact 1:</u> Intervals $[x_o,y_o]$ and $[x,y]$ intersect iff $x \le y_o$ and $y \ge x_o$

Hence we can find all intervals in S intersecting the query interval $I = [x_o,y_o]$ by finding all points (x,y) in the associated set A(S) with $x \le y_o$ and $y \ge x_o$. This corresponds to a range query (cf. chapter VII) in $\mathbb{R}^2$ with right boundary $x = y_o$

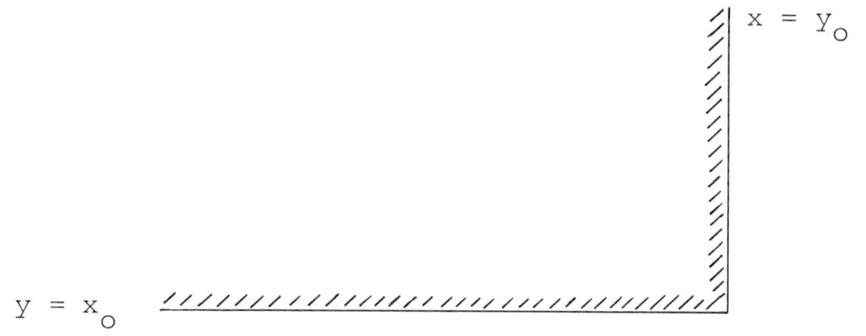

and bottom boundary $y = x_o$ (cf. diagram). Of course, we could use range trees (cf. VII.1.2) to store set A(S) but more elegant data structures exist. For the query above we will discuss interval trees in section 5.1.1.

<u>Fact 2:</u> Interval [x,y] is contained in query interval $[x_o,y_o]$ if $x_o \le x \le y \le y_o$.

Hence we can find all intervals contained in the query interval $I = [x_o,y_o]$ by finding all points (x,y) in the associated set A(S) with left boundary $x = x_o$ and right boundary $y = y_o$ (cf. diagram). Priority search trees(section 5.1.2) are a good data structure for this type (and more general types) of range query.

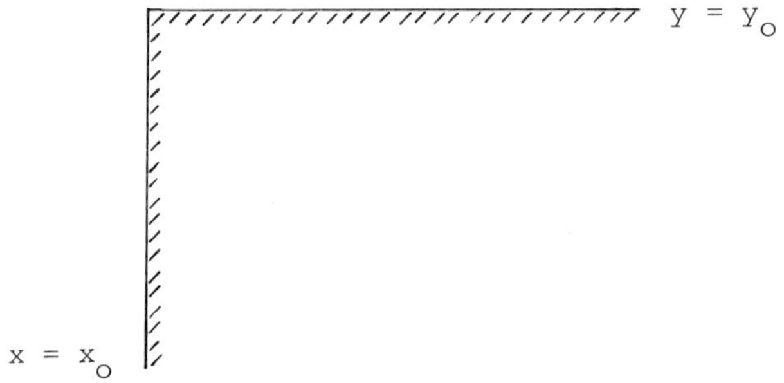

Remark: Note that all points $(x,y) \in A(S)$ satisfy $y \geq x$. Hence the containment query searches really a bounded region and the intersection query searches an unbounded region. This shows that the two types of queries are different and cannot be transformed into one another by reflection.
A third data structure are segment trees (section 5.1.3). They are particularly useful when we want to store additional information about intervals. We will use them to solve the measure problem (compute the area covered by the union of a set of rectangles) and a three-dimensional hidden line elimination problem. In the latter problem we will associate with each rectangle (interval in y-structure) its height (= z-coordinate) in order to decide visibility.

All these tree structures are easily explained in the static case. They can all be made dynamic; but at least in the case of interval and segment trees the details of the dynamic version are tedious and the programs become very long. Fortunately, a semi-dynamic version suffices for all plane - sweep algorithms. In the semi-dynamic version we consider trees over a fixed universe (usually the y-coordinates of the vertices) and handle only intervals whose endpoints are drawn from the universe. We can then handle insertions and deletions; however, the cost of the operations is dictated by the size of the universe and not by the size of the set which is actually stored.

For all three tree structures we use the following common terminology. Let $U \subseteq \mathbb{R}$ be a finite set, called the universe.
More generally, U might be any finite ordered set. All trees which we

are going to consider are based on leaf-oriented binary search trees for U, i.e. on binary trees with |U| leaves. The leaves correspond to the elements of ordered set U from left to right (cf. section III.5.2). An interior node has at least three fields: pointers to the left and right son and a split field, which is a real number. Thus

```
    type node = record ....
                        case stat: status of
                         leaf: (.....)
                         nonleaf: (split: real;
                                   lson,rson: ↑ node,
                                   ...)
                  end
```

where type status = (leaf, nonleaf) and the dots indicate additional fields. As usual, the split fields direct the search, i.e. the split field of node v is at least as large as all leaves in the left subtree and smaller than all leaves in the right subtree.

For every node v of the tree we define its xrange xrange(v) as follows. The xrange of the root is the half-open real line, i.e. xrange (root) = $(-\infty,+\infty]$, and if v is the left (right) son of node w then xrange(v) = xrange(w) $\cap$ $(-\infty$, split(w)] (xrange(v) = xrange(w) $\cap$ (split(w), $+\infty$]. Note that a search for $x \in \mathbb{R}$ goes through node v iff $x \in$ xrange(v).

Remark: In the section on segment trees we will slightly deviate from these definitions. There, the split field will be pair consisting of a real number denoted split(v) and in indicator ind(v) $\in \{<,\leq\}$. If ind(w) = $\leq$ then xrange(v), v a son of w, is defined as above. If ind(w) = < then a search for x proceeds to the left son of w only if $x <$ split(w) and xrange(v) = xrange(w) $\cap$ $(-\infty$, split(w)) (xrange(v) = xrange(w) $\cap$ [split(w), $+\infty$]) for v being the left (right) son of w.

For the description and analysis of the query algorithms in interval, priority search, and segment trees we need some additional notation. Let I = $[x_o,y_o]$ be a query interval. We define node sets P, C, and C_{max} with respect to query interval I.

$$P = \{v;\ xrange(v) \cap [x_o,y_o] \neq \phi \text{ and } xrange(v) \not\subseteq [x_o,y_o]\}$$

$$C = \{v;\ xrange(v) \subseteq [x_o,y_o]\}$$

$$C_{max} = \{v;\ v \in C \text{ and } father(v) \notin C\}$$

Lemma 1: Let T be a search tree of height h and let $[x_o,y_o]$ be a query interval. Then

a) $|P| \leq 2h$

b) $|C_{max}| \leq 2h$

c) $|C| \leq 2 \cdot$ (number of leaves v with $xrange(v) \subseteq [x_o,y_o]$)

Proof:

a) Note first that $v \in P$ implies $father(v) \in P$ since $xrange(v) \subseteq xrange(father(v))$. Thus P consists of a set of paths in tree T; this explains the use of letter P.
Note next that $v \in P$ and hence $xrange(v) \cap [x_o,y_o] \neq \phi$ and $xrange(v) \not\subseteq [x_o,y_o]$ implies $x_o \in xrange(v)$ or $y_o \in xrange(v)$; here we also used the fact that xrange(v) is an interval.
Thus $v \in P$ implies that v lies on either the path from the root to the leaf v_o with $x_o \in xrange(v_o)$ or on the path to the leaf w_o with $y_o \in xrange(w_o)$. Also, P consists of an initial segment of these paths. This proves $|P| \leq 2h$.

b) The bound on the size of C_{max} is derived as follows. First, if $v \in C_{max}$ then v's brother does not belong to C_{max}. Also, if $v \in C_{max}$ and hence $v \in C$ and $father(v) \notin C$, then $xrange(father(v)) \not\subseteq [x_o,y_o]$ and $xrange(v) \subseteq [x_o,y_o]$ and hence $xrange(father(v)) \cap [x_o,y_o] \neq \phi$.
This shows that $v \in C_{max}$ implies $father(v) \in P$ and hence $|C_{max}| \leq |P| \leq 2h$.

c) Since $v \in C$ implies that both sons of v also belong to C we conclude that the nodes in C form a forest of subtrees of T. Since in a binary tree the number of nodes is at most twice the number of leaves the bound follows. □

The following pictorial definition of sets P,C and C_{max} may help the reader's intuition. The set P consists of the

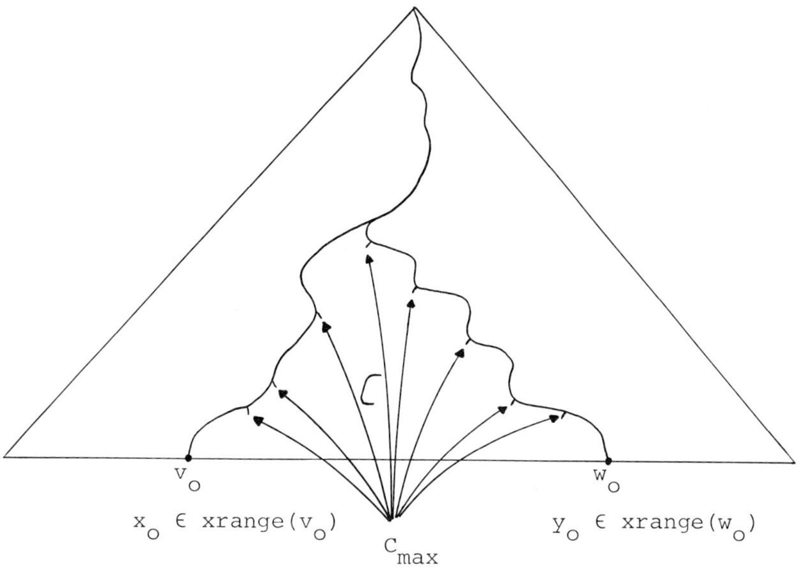

paths to leaves v_0 and w_0 with $x_0 \in \text{xrange}(v_0)$ and $y_0 \in \text{xrange}(w_0)$. The set C is the set of nodes between the two paths and the set C_{max} consists of the maximal nodes in C.

VIII. 5.1.1 The Interval Tree and its Applications

This section is devoted to the interval tree. It will allow us to store a set of n intervals in linear space such that intersection queries can be answered in logarithmic time.

Let $U \subseteq \mathbb{R}$ be a finite set and let $S = \{[x_i, y_i];\ x_i \in U,\ y_i \in \mathbb{R},\ 1 \le i \le n\}$ be a set of n closed intervals on the real line. An interval tree T for S (with respect to universe U) is a leaf-oriented search tree for set U where each node of the tree is augmented by additional information. There are three pieces of information associated with each node v.

a) The node list NL(v) of node v is the set of intervals in S containing the split value of v but of no ancestor of v, i.e.

$$NL(v) = \{[x,y] \in S;\ split(v) \in [x,y] \subseteq xrange(v)\}.$$

We store the node list of node v as two sorted sequences: the ordered list of left endpoints and the ordered list of right endpoints. Both sequences are stored in balanced trees; furthermore, we provide for pointers to the maximal (minimal) element of the sequence of right (left) endpoints.

b) A mark bit stating whether the node list of v or any descendant of v is nonempty.

c) For every node v with nonempty node list a pointer to the next larger (smaller) node in inorder with nonempty node list.

The following figure shows an interval tree for set S = {[1,8], [2,5], [3,7], [4,5], [6,8], [1,3], [2,3], [1,2]} with respect to universe U = {1,2,3,4,5,6,7}. The split fields are shown inside the nodes and leaves, and the node lists are shown besides the nodes. The mark bits are shown as stars on the top of the nodes. Finally, the doubly linked list of nodes with nonempty node list is indicated by dashed lines.

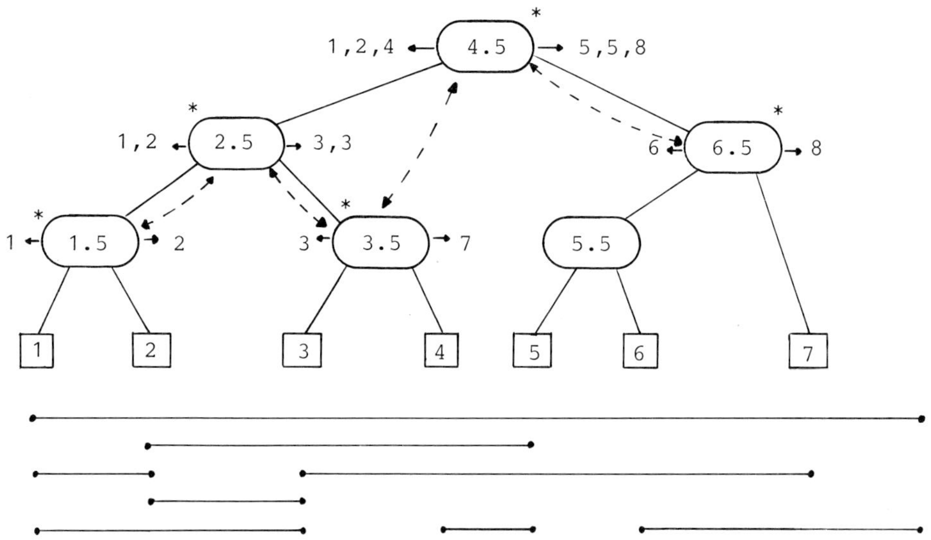

The main power of interval trees stems from the node lists. The mark bits and the doubly linked list of nodes with nonempty node lists are needed to cope with large universes. If U contains only endpoints of intervals in S then the mark bits and the doubly linked list is not needed.

The following lemma shows that interval trees use linear space, can be constructed efficiently, and support insertions and deletions of intervals (with left endpoint in U) efficiently.

Lemma 2: Let $U \subseteq \mathbb{R}$ be an ordered finite set, $N = |U|$, and let S be a set of n intervals with left endpoints in U.

a) An interval tree for S uses space $O(n+N)$.

b) An interval tree for S of depth $O(\log N)$ can be constructed in time $O(N + n \log Nn)$.

c) Intervals (with left endpoint in U) can be inserted into an interval tree of depth $O(\log N)$ in time $O(\log n + \log N)$. The same holds true for deletion.

Proof: a) The search tree for U clearly uses space $O(N)$. Furthermore, the total space required for the node lists is $O(n)$ since every interval in S is stored in exactly one list. This follows immediately from the definition of node list.

b) Let T be a complete binary search tree for the set U. Tree T can clearly be built in time O(N) and has depth O(log N). It remains to construct the node lists. We show how to construct the left part of all node lists in time O(n log n + n log N), the symmetric algorithm can be used to construct the right parts. Sort the intervals in S in increasing order of their left endpoint and propagate the sorted list of intervals down the tree. More precisely, if list L of intervals arrives at node v then split L into L_1, L_2 and L_3 where L_1 (L_3) is moved to the left (right) son of v and L_2 is the node list at v. This can clearly be done in time $O(|L|)$ by comparing every interval in L with split(v). Also, if L is sorted according to left endpoint then so are L_1, L_2, L_3. If we assign the cost of processing list L to its members, then cost O(log N) is assigned to each interval. Hence the total cost of constructing all node lists is O(n log n + n log N) where the O(n log n) accounts for the sorting step. Finally, it is easy to set the mark bits and to construct the doubly linked list of nodes with nonempty node list in time O(N).

c) Let [x,y] be an interval to be inserted into S. Our first task is to find the node v into whose node list interval [x,y] has to be inserted. Node v can be found by a simple tree search. If split(root) $\in$ [x,y] then v is the root of the tree. If split(root) $\notin$ [x,y] then either x > split(root) and the search proceeds to the right subtree or y < split(root) and the search proceeds to the left subtree. Thus v can be determined in time O(log N). Next we insert x and y into the node list of v. This takes time O(log n). If the node list of v was nonempty before the insertion then we are done. Otherwise, we find the largest node w with nonempty node list preceding v in inorder using the mark bits. This takes time O(log N). Finally, we insert v into the doubly linked list of nodes with nonempty node list. In summary, insertions take time O(log N + log n). We leave the corresponding claim for deletion to the reader. □

We can now turn to the main property of interval trees: the efficient support of intersection queries.

Lemma 3: Let S be a set of intervals and let $I = [x_o, y_o]$ be a query interval. Let $A = \{[x,y] \in S;\ [x,y] \cap [x_o,y_o] \neq \emptyset\}$ be the set of intervals in S intersecting I. Then, given an interval tree of height h for S, one can compute A in time $O(h + |A|)$.

Proof: Let P and C be defined as in the introduction of section 5.1., i.e. $P = \{v;\ v$ is a node of T and $xrange(v) \cap I \neq \emptyset,\ xrange(v) \not\subseteq I\}$ and $C = \{v;\ v$ is a node of T and $xrange(v) \subseteq I\}$. Then

$$A = \bigcup_{v \in C} NL(v) \cup \bigcup_{v \in P} \{[x,y] \in NL(v);\ [x,y] \cap I \neq \emptyset\}$$

, since $[x,y] \in NL[v]$ and $[x,y] \cap I \neq \emptyset$ implies $xrange(v) \cap I \neq \emptyset$. Also $v \in C$ clearly implies $NL(v) \subseteq A$. Consider $v \in P$ next. Recall that we organized NL(v) as two ordered lists, the list of left endpoints and the list of right endpoints. Let $x_1 \le x_2 \le \ldots \le x_k$ be the former list and let $y_1 \le \ldots \le y_k$ be the latter list. We have to discuss three cases, two of which are symmetric. Suppose first that split(v) $\in I$. Then $NL(v) \subseteq A$ since $split(v) \in [x,y]$ for all $[x,y] \in NL(v)$. Suppose next, that $split(v) \notin I$, say $split(v) \le x$, the other case being symmetric. Then interval $[x_i, y_j] \in NL(v)$ intersects I iff $x \le y_j$. We can thus find all such intervals by inspecting $y_k, y_{k-1}, \ldots$ in turn as long as they are at least as large as x. Hence we can determine $NL(v) \cap A$ in time proportional to $|NL(v) \cap A|$.

The node sets P and C are easily determined. P consists of the nodes on the search paths to x and y and C is the set of nodes between those paths. Thus the time required to compute A is $O(|P| + |C| + |A|)$. We will now complete the proof by two different arguments, one for the case of a "small" universe U and one for the general case.

Assume first that U contains only endpoints of intervals in S. Then $|C| = O(|A|)$ since all leaves in C are endpoints of intervals in A. Also $|P| \le 2h$ and the time bound follows. Note that we have not used the mark bits and the doubly linked list in this case.

We will now turn to the general case. Clearly, we only need to visit the nodes in C with nonempty node list. Note that there are at most $|A|$ such nodes. We can find one of them using the mark bits in time $O(h)$ and then find all the others by following the doubly linked list since the nodes in $P \cup C$ occur as a contiguous segment in the doubly linked list. Thus we also have the time bound in the general case. □

This finishes the discussion of static or radix interval trees. Dynamic interval trees are based on D-trees; cf. section III.6.2.. The change required with respect to the preceding discussion is minor. We now require that the underlying binary tree is a D-tree for the set of left endpoints of intervals in S, where the weight of a point x is the number of intervals with left endpoint x. Then the total weight (the thickness of the root of the D-tree) is $n = |S|$ and hence the depth of the D-tree is $O(\log n)$. Thus intersection queries can be answered in time $O(\log n + s)$ where s is the size of the answer by lemma 3.

It remains to discuss insertions and deletions. Let $I = [x,y]$ be an interval and suppose that we want to insert I into (delete I from) S. Clearly, we can add (delete) I from the appropriate node list and change the weight of the left endpoint x of I by one in time $O(\log n)$. Next, we have to rebalance the interval tree by rotations and double rotations. Since a double rotation can be realized by two rotations, it suffices to discuss rotations. The underlying D-tree is reorganized as described in section III.6.2.. It remains to discuss the maintenance of the node lists in rotations.

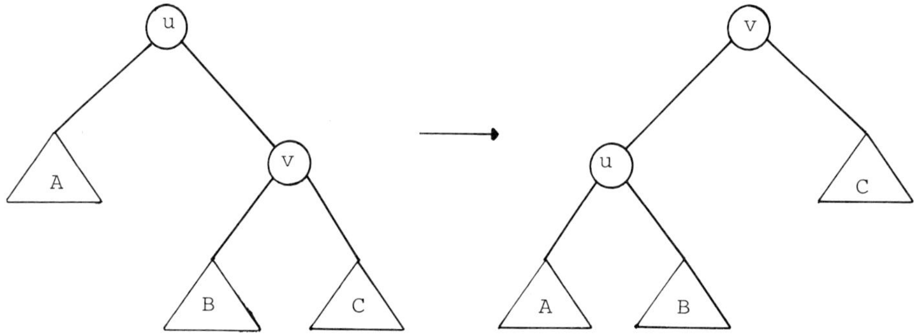

Note first that the node lists of nodes in subtrees A,B, and C are unchanged. This can be seen as follows. Since split(u) and split(v) are not changed by the rotation, the xranges of nodes in subtrees A,B, and C remain unchanged. Hence quantities split(z) and xrange(z) do not change for a node z in these subtrees and thus NL(z) remains the same. The x ranges of nodes u and v change. We have xrange'(v) = xrange(u)

and xrange'(u) = xrange(u) ∩ $(-\infty, split(v)]$ where the prime is used to denote the situation after the rotation. Let NL = NL(u) ∪ NL(v) be the union of the node lists of nodes u and v. Then NL'(v) = $\{[x,y] \in NL;$ $split(v) \in [x,y]\}$ and NL'(u) = NL − NL'(v). It is easy to see that the sorted representations of node lists NL'(v) and NL'(u) can be computed from the sorted representations of NL(u) and NL(v) in time $O(|NL|)$. Thus a rotation at node v has cost $O(|NL|)$ where NL = NL(u) ∪ NL(v).

Lemma 4: Let v be a node of a dynamic interval tree. Then $|NL(v)| = O(th(v))$ where th(v) is the number of leaves in the subtree with root v in the BB[α]-tree (underlying the D-tree underlying the interval tree); cf. section III.6.2..

Proof: If $[x,y] \in NL(v)$ then $[x,y] \subseteq range(v)$. Hence a search for x, the left endpoint of interval [x,y] goes through node v and hence the active x-node is a descendant of v. Thus a fraction of at least $\alpha/2$ of all leaves labelled x in the underlying BB[α]-tree are descendants of v. Thus $|NL(v)| \le 2/\alpha\ th(v)$. □

Lemma 4 together with theorem 5 of section III.6.2. allows us to bound the amortized rebalancing cost of dynamic interval trees.

Lemma 5: The total cost of n insertions and deletions into an initially empty interval tree is $O(n \log n)$.

Proof: The cost of inserting (deleting) the n intervals into (from) the appropriate node lists and the weight changes for the left endpoints is clearly $O(n \log n)$. It remains to discuss the total cost of the rotations and double rotations.

By lemma 4 and the preceding discussion the cost of rotating at a node v of th(v) is $O(th(v))$. Thus the total cost of rotations and double rotations is $O(n \log n)$ by III.6.2., theorem 5 with $f(N) = O(N)$. □

We summarize our discussion of interval trees in

Theorem 1: Let S be a set of n intervals.

a) Let U be a universe containing the left endpoints of intervals in S.

A static interval tree of depth $O(\log N)$, $N = |U|$, for S with respect to U can be constructed in time $O(n \log nN)$. It uses space $O(N + n)$ and allows us to compute the set A of intervals in S intersecting a query interval I in time $O(\log N + |A|)$. In addition, insertions and deletions take time $O(\log n + \log N)$.

b) In dynamic interval trees we have $N \leq n$. However, the time bounds for insertions and deletions are amortized.

Proof: Immediate from lemmas 2 to 5. □

We will now turn to an application of interval trees: reporting insertions of rectangles.

Theorem 2: Let R be a set of n iso-oriented rectangles in the plane. Then the set A of pairs of intersecting rectangles in R can be computed in time $O(n \log n + |A|)$.

Proof: We use the following notation. For $r \in R$ we denote the projection of r into the x-axis (y-axis) by $I_x(r)$ $(I_y(r))$. Our algorithm for computing A is based on plane sweep.

The x-structure contains exactly the left and right endpoints of projections $I_x(r)$, $r \in R$. The y-structure is an interval tree for the set of intervals $I_y(r)$ of rectangles r which are intersected by the sweep line. The transition at point x of the x-structure is as follows.

(1) Let In be the set of rectangles $r \in R$ which have x as the left endpoint of projection $I_x(r)$;

(2) Insert $I_y(r)$ into the y-structure for all $r \in$ In;

(3) For every $r \in$ In, enumerate all rectangles r' which are stored in the y-structure and which intersect the y-projection of r, i.e. $I_y(r) \cap I_y(r') \neq \emptyset$;

(4) Delete all rectangles r from the y-structure which have x as the right endpoint of projection $I_x(r)$.

The algorithm above clearly enumerates only intersecting pairs of rectangles. It remains to argue that it enumerates all intersecting pairs.

Let $r,r' \in R$ with $r \cap r' \neq \emptyset$. Let $I_x(r) = [x_1,x_2]$ and $I_x(r') = [x_1',x_2']$. We assume w.l.o.g. that $x_1' \leq x_1$. Consider the transition at $x = x_1$. When line (3) is reached rectangle r' belongs to the y-structure. Also $I_y(r) \cap I_y(r') \neq \emptyset$ and hence r' is enumerated in line (3) when this line is executed for rectangle r. This proves correctness.

The time bound is also easily established. We may either use dynamic interval trees or static interval trees with U being the set of (bottom) endpoints of intervals $I_y(r)$. Then $|U| \leq n$. Hence we spend time $O(\log n)$ per rectangle $r \in R$ in lines (2) and (4). Also, the cost of line (3) is $O(\log n + |A(r)|)$ where $A(r) = \{r' \in R;\ r \cap r' \neq \emptyset\}$. Thus total running time is $O(n \log n + |A|)$. □

III. 5.1.2 The Priority Search Tree and its Applications

Priority search trees are a blend of search trees and priority queues (heaps). They support 1 1/2-dimensional range queries with logarithmic running time and linear space. Recall that range trees, cf. section VII.2., required space $O(n \log n)$ and time $O((\log n)^2)$. A 1 1/2-dimensional range query is given by a rectangle whose bottom side is missing, i.e. it asks for all points (x,y) in a semi-infinite strip $x_0 \leq x \leq x_1$, $y \leq y_1$. Priority search trees can be used instead of interval trees in reporting intersections of rectangles. Other applications are e.g. containment queries or maintaining buddy systems.

Throughout this section we assume $S = \{(x_i,y_i);\ 1 \leq i \leq n\}$ to be a set of points in the plane. We assume for simplicity that $x_i \neq x_j$ for $i \neq j$, although the theory of priority search tree can also be developed without that assumption. We will indicate the required changes in the discussion below. In many applications this assumption can be achieved by replacing point (x,y) by ((x,y),y), by ordering the first component lexicographically, and by taking some care in formulating queries and interpreting their answers. We leave the details to the reader.

Let U be a set containing at least the x-coordinates of all points in S. A priority search tree for S with respect to universe U consists of a leaf-oriented search tree for set U. As always, we use a field split(v) in each node v to direct the searches. In addition, each node v has a priority field prio(v) which holds an element of S (or nothing). Each element of S is stored in the priority field of exactly one node and this node must lie on the path of search to the x-coordinate of the element, i.e. if prio(v) = (x,y) then $x \in$ xrange(v). The priority fields implement a priority queue on the y-coordinates of the elements of S, i.e. if prio(v) = (x,y) then prio(father(v)) is defined and $y \geq y'$ where prio(father(v)) = (x',y').

The following figure shows a priority search tree for set S = {(1,4), (2,1),(3,7),(4,2),(5,1),(6,3)} with respect to universe U = {1,2,3,4, 5,6}. In nodes the split (priority) field is given above (below) the horizontal line.

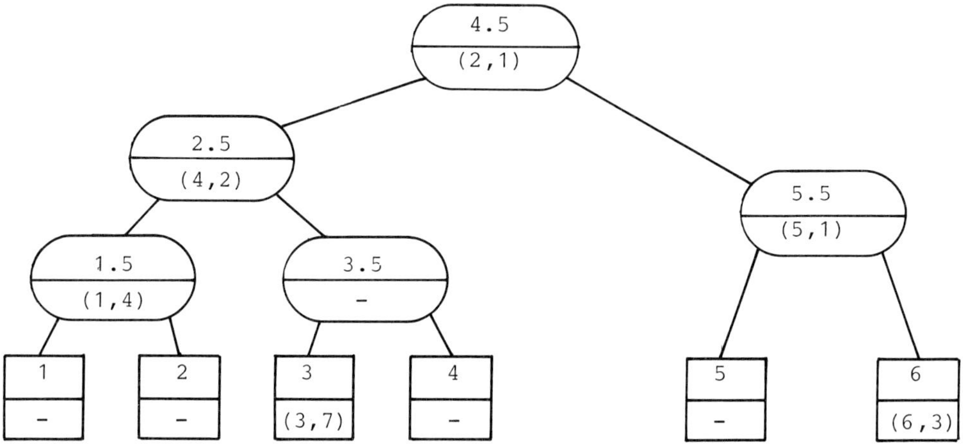

If set S contains points with identical x-coordinate then the following change is required. With each leaf of the tree we associate a sorted sequence which contains some of the elements having the (value associated with the) leaf as x-coordinate. Thus if (3,1o) would also belong to S then the sorted sequence associated with leaf 3 would contain elements (3,7) and (3,1o) in that order. We implement the sorted sequence as an ordinary priority queue. All algorithms below become slightly more involved with that change. We leave the details to the reader.

The algorithms for priority search trees are subtle. We therefore give (almost) complete programs based on the following declarations.

```
type pair   = record x,y: real end;
type status = (leaf, nonleaf);
```

```
type node   = record prio: pair;
                     split: real;
                     case stat: status of
                     leaf:  ;
                     nonleaf: (lson, rson: ↑node)
              end
```

Nodes and leaves are of type node. If the priority field of a node v is undefined then we store (split(v), infinity) in it.

Lemma 6: If S is sorted according to x-coordinate then a priority search tree for S of depth O(log N) can be built in time O(n + N).

Proof: We can clearly build a search tree (based on the complete binary tree with N leaves) for U in time O(N). It remains to fill the priority fields. We do so by playing a knockout tournament on the elements of S. We initialize the tournament by writing element (x,y) of S into the leaf corresponding to x. If no element of S corresponds to a leaf v then the priority field is initialized to (split(v),∞). Next consider a node v such that the priority fields of v's sons are already defined. We move the priority field of the left son of v to v if it has the smaller y-coordinate and we move the priority field of the right son otherwise. This empties the priority field of one of the sons of v which we then fill in exactly the same way. Continuing in this way we finally empty the priority field of a leaf w which we then refill with (split(w),∞). Thus we can compute prio(v) in time proportional to the height of v. Since the number of nodes of height h is $N/2^h$ we need time $O(\sum_{h=1}^{\log N} (N/2^h)\cdot h) = O(N)$ to fill all priority fields. □

We can use priority search trees for the following queries:

$\text{MinXinRectangle}(x_0,x_1,y_1) = \min\{x;\exists y: x_0 \le x \le x_1 \text{ and } y \le y_1 \text{ and } (x,y) \in S\}$

$\text{MaxXinRectangle}(x_0,x_1,y_1) = \max\{x;\exists y: x_0 \le x \le x_1 \text{ and } y \le y_1 \text{ and } (x,y) \in S\}$

$\text{MinYinXRange}(x_0,x_1) = \min\{y;\exists x: x_0 \le x \le x_1 \text{ and } (x,y) \in S\}$

$\text{EnumerateRectangle}(x_0,x_1,y_1) = \{(x,y) \in S: x_0 \le x \le x_1 \text{ and } y \le y_1\}$

Query EnumerateRectangle (x_0,x_1,y_1) enumerates all points of S which lie in the semi-infinite strip $x_0 \le x \le x_1$ and $y \le y_1$. MinXinRectangle (MaxXinRectangle) compute the minimal (maximal) x-coordinate of any point in that strip. Finally, MinYinXrange computes the minimal y-coordinate of any point in the vertical strip determined by x_0 and x_1.

For the lemmas below we recall the definitions of sets P,C and C_{max} of nodes of a search tree T with respect to query interval $[x_{left}, x_{right}]$.

$P = \{v;\ xrange(v) \cap [x_{left}, x_{right}] \neq \emptyset$ and $xrange(v) \nsubseteq [x_{left}, x_{right}]\}$.

$C = \{v;\ xrange(v) \subseteq [x_{left}, x_{right}]\}$

$C_{max} = \{v;\ v \in C$ and $father(v) \notin C\ \}$

Lemma 7: Let T be a priority search tree (for set S with respect to universe U) of height h. Then operation MinYinXRange takes time O(h).

Proof: Consider operation MinYinXRange(x_{left}, x_{right}). If the output of MinYinXRange is undefined then $C = \emptyset$ and hence the searches for x_{left} or x_{right} end in the same or in adjacent leaves. If the output is defined, say $(x^*, y^*) \in S$ with y^* = MinYinXRange(x_{left}, x_{right}), then let w be the leaf whose associated value of U is x^*. Leaf w belongs to $P \cup C$. If $w \in P$ then there is clearly a node $v \in P$ such that prio(v) = (x^*, y^*). If $w \notin P$, i.e. $w \in C$, then consider $z \in C_{max}$ such that z is an ancestor of w. Since y^* in the minimal y-value of any point in the query interval and since the priority fields implement a priority queue on the y-values we conclude that there is an ancestor v of z with prio(v) = (x^*, y^*). In partiular, $v \in P \cup C_{max}$. Thus in either case there must be a node $v \in P \cup C_{max}$ such that prio(v) = (x^*, y^*) and hence MinYinXRange can be answered by inspecting all nodes in $P \cup C_{max}$. Finally, since $|P \cup C_{max}| \le 4h$ since $v \in C_{max}$ implies $father(v) \in P$, and since every $v \in P$ lies on the search path for either x_{left} or x_{right} the nodes in $P \cup C_{max}$ can clearly be inspected in time O(h). The details are given in the following program. In this program we use the additional type

```
type condpair = record p: pair; valid: bool end
```

```
(1)  function MinYinXrange(t : ↑node, x_left, x_right: real): condpair;
(2)      var cand1, cand2: condpair;
(3)      begin cand1.valid ← cand2.valid ← false;
(4)            if x_left ≤ t↑.prio.x ≤ x_right
(5)            then cand1.p ← t↑.prio;
(6)                 cand1.valid ← true
(7)            else if t↑.stat = nonleaf
(8)                 then if x_left ≤ t↑.split
(9)                      then cand1 ← MinYinXrange(t↑.lson, x_left, x_right)
(1o)                     fi;
(11)                     if t↑.split < x_right
(12)                     then cand2 ← MinYinXrange(t↑.rson, x_left, x_right)
(13)                     fi;
(14)                     if (¬cand1.valid) or (cand2.valid and
(15)                         cand2.p.y < cand1.p.y)
(16)                     then cand1 ← cand2
(17)                     fi;
(18)                fi
(19)            fi;
(2o)            MinYinXrange ← cand1
(21)     end
```

There are several remarks in order about that program. Note first that only nodes in $P \cup C$ are visited. Also, if t points to a node $v \in C_{max}$ then the test in line (4) returns true and hence no further recursive calls are initiated. Thus only nodes in $P \cup C_{max}$ are visited and the time bound follows. However, not all nodes in $P \cup C_{max}$ are necessarily visited and hence correctness requires a little argument. Let $v \in P \cup C_{max}$ be such that $prio(v) = (x^*,y^*)$ and let z be any proper ancestor of v. Then $prio(z) = (x,y)$ is defined and $y \le y^*$. If $y < y^*$ then $x \notin [x_{left}, x_{right}]$ by definition of y^* and hence the test in line (4) returns false. Thus appropriate recursive calls are initiated in lines (9) and/or (11). □

Lemma 8: Let T be a priority search tree (for set S with respect to universe U) of height h. Then operation EnumerateRectangle takes time $O(h + s)$ where s is the size of the answer.

Proof: Consider operation EnumerateRectangle $(x_{left}, x_{right}, y_{top})$. Let

$R = \{(x,y); x_{left} \le x \le x_{right}, y \le y_{top}\}$ be the query rectangle. Clearly, all pairs $(x,y) \in R \cap S$ are stored in the priority fields of nodes in $P \cup C$. The crucial observation is now that $v \in C - C_{max}$ and prio(v) $\in R$ implies prio(father(v)) $\in R$. This can be seen as follows. Let prio(v) = (x,y) and let prio(father(v)) = (x',y'). Then $y' \le y \le y_{top}$ and $x_{left} \le x' \le x_{right}$ since father(v) $\in C$. Thus $(x',y') \in R$.

The observation above suggests the following algorithm. Visit all nodes in $P \cup C_{max}$ and inspect their priority fields. For every $v \in C_{max}$ explore the subtree rooted at v top-down. If descendant w of v is visited and prio(w) $\in R$ then also visit both sons of w. If prio(w) $\notin R$ then visit no son of w. The correctness of this algorithm follows immediately from the observation above.

The bound on the running time follows from the fact that if a node v is visited then either prio(v) $\in R$ or father(v) $\in P \cup C_{max}$ or prio(father(v)) $\in R$. Thus at most $3s + 2|P \cup C_{max}| \le 3s + 2h$ nodes are visited and hence running time is $O(h + s)$. □

<u>Lemma 9:</u> Let T be a priority search tree for set S of height h. Then operations MinXinRectangle and MaxXinRectangle take time O(h).

<u>Proof:</u> Operations MinXinRectangle and MaxXinRectangle are symmetric. We therefore only have to consider operation MinXinRectangle(x_{left}, x_{right}, y_{top}). Let $R = \{(x,y);\ x_{left} \le x \le x_{right},\ y \le y_{top}\}$ be the query rectangle and let $(\tilde{x},\tilde{y}) \in R \cap S$ be such that prio(v) = $(\tilde{x},\tilde{y})$ for some $v \in P \cup C_{max}$ and $\tilde{x} \le x$ whenever (x,y) = prio(w) $\in R$ for some node $w \in P \cup C_{max}$. Thus $(\tilde{x},\tilde{y})$ is the "best" answer to the query which is stored in the priority field of a node in $P \cup C_{max}$.

It follows from the proof of lemma 6 (operation MinYinXrange) that $(\tilde{x},\tilde{y})$ is defined iff $R \cap S \ne \emptyset$. Thus we can test in time O(h) whether operation MinXinRectangle is defined.

Assume next that MinXinRectangle is defined. Let $(x^*,y^*) \in S$ be such that x^* = MinXinRectangle(x_{left}, x_{right}, y_{top}). If $x^* = \tilde{x}$ then we can find (x^*,y^*) by visiting the nodes in $P \cup C_{max}$. So let us assume that $x^* < \tilde{x}$. Then pair (x^*,y^*) is stored in the priority field of a node w in $C - C_{max}$ and hence there is a node $v \in C_{max}$ which is an ancestor of

w. Let prio(v) = (x',y'). Then $y' \le y^* \le y_{top}$ since the priority fields implement a priority queue and $x_{left} \le x' \le x_{right}$ since $v \in C$. Thus $(x',y') \in R$ and hence $\tilde{x} \le x'$ by definition of $(\tilde{x},\tilde{y})$. In particular, we have $x^* \le \tilde{x} \le x'$ and hence $\tilde{x} \in$ xrange(v). We conclude that either $(\tilde{x},\tilde{y}) = (x^*,y^*)$ or (x^*,y^*) = prio(w) where w is a descendant of the unique $v \in C_{max}$ with $\tilde{x} \in$ xrange(v). It remains to describe how to find w in the latter case. Note first that if z is a node on the path from v to w then prio(z) $\in R$. Also, z is the right son of its father if and only if $y'' > y_{top}$ where (x'',y'') is the priority field of the left brother of z. Thus we can find w by a simple tree search starting in w. If the search reaches node z and $y'' \le y_{top}$ where (x'',y'') is the priority field of the left son of z then we proceed to the left son, otherwise we proceed to the right son. In this way we are guaranteed to find node w.

In summary, query MinXinRectangle can be answered by visiting the nodes in $P \cup C_{max}$ and by following a single path down the tree starting in a uniquely defined node of C_{max}. Thus time O(h) suffices. An elegant realization is given by:

```
function MinXinRectangle(t: ↑node,x_left,x_right,y_top: real):condpair
    var c: condpair;
    begin c.valid ← false;
          if y_top ≥ t↑.p.y
          then if t↑.stat = nonleaf
               then if x_left ≤ v↑.split
                    then c ← MinXinRectangle(t↑.lson,x_left,x_right,y_top)
                    fi;
                    if ¬c.valid and t↑.split < x_right
                    then c ← MinXinRectangle(t↑.rson,x_left,x_right,y_top)
                    fi
               fi;
               if x_left ≤ t↑.p.x ≤ x_right and t↑.p.y ≤ y_top
                  and (¬c.valid or t↑.p.x < c.p.x)
               then c ← t↑.p; c.valid ← true
               fi
          fi;
    MinXinRectangle ← c
end
```

There are several remarks in order about that program. Note first that only nodes in $C \cup P$ are visited. Next consider a node $v \in C$. If prio(v) $\notin R$ and hence the test in line (4) returns false then no son of v is visited. If prio(v) $\in R$ then the left son of v is always visited. If prio(lson(v)) $\in R$ then the recursive call made in line (7) returns a valid pair and hence no recursive call is made in line (1o). If prio(lson(v)) $\notin R$ then the recursive call made in line (7) aborts immediately because the test in line (4) is negative and hence has cost O(1). Thus at most one recursive call with nonconstant cost is made by a node $v \in C$ and hence only O(h) nodes are visited below each node $v \in C_{max}$. It remains to show that at most one node $v \in C_{max}$ initiates recursive calls at all. Let $v \in C_{max}$ be the first node in C_{max} which initiates recursive calls and let $w \in C_{max}$ be to the right of v. Also let z be the least common ancestor of v and w. Since v(w) is in the left (right) subtree of z the recursive call initiated in line (7) of the procedure when applied to node z returns a valid pair and hence the call in line (1o) is not made. Thus w is never visited, and hence only O(h) nodes are visited altogether.

It remains to argue correctness. Let $v \in C \cup P$ be such that prio(v) = (x^*,y^*) and let $w_0,w_1,\ldots,w_k$ be the path from the root of T to $v = w_k$. Then prio(w_i).y $\le y^* \le y_{top}$ for all i. Hence if w_i is visited and w_{i+1} is the left son of w_i then w_{i+1} is also visited. Assume next that w_{i+1} is the right son of w_i. Let z be the left son of w_i. Then clearly prio(z).x $\le$ split(w_i) $< x^*$ and hence prio(z).y $> y_{top}$ by definition of (x^*,y^*). Thus, if w_i is visited then the visit of node z fails in line (4) and hence no valid pair is returned in line (7). We therefore visit node w_{i+1} in line (1o). This shows that node v is visited by the search and hence x^* is computed correctly. □

Lemmata 7 to 9 show that priority search trees support a number of query operations in logarithmic time. We will now turn to insertions and deletions. As in the case of interval trees we treat the radix priority search trees first.

<u>Lemma 1o:</u> Let T be a priority search tree for set S with respect to universe U and let h be the height of T.

a) Let $(x,y) \notin S$ be such that $x \in U$ and such that there is no $(x',y') \in S$ with $x = x'$. Then we can add (x,y) to S in time O(h).

b) Let (x,y) ∈ S. Then we can delete (x,y) from S in time O(h).

<u>Proof:</u> a) The insertion algorithm is quite simple. It uses variables t: ↑ node and p: pair.

```
t ← ↑root; p ← (x,y);
while t↑.stat = nonleaf
do if p.y < t↑.prio.y
   then exchange p and t↑.prio
   fi ;
   if p.x ≤ t↑.split then t ← t↑.lson else t ← t↑.rson fi
od ;
t↑.prio ← p
```

The insertion algorithm follows a path down the tree. The path is determined by the x-value of p. Whenever p's y-value is smaller than the y-value of the priority field of the current node we store p in that node, pick up the priority field of the node and continue to insert it. This shows correctness and also the bound on the running time.

b) Deletion of (x,y) from S is also quite simple. An ordinary tree search allows us to find node v with prio(v) = (x,y). We delete point (x,y) from the priority field of node v and then refill it by the smaller (with respect to y-value) priority field of the sons of v, which we then in turn refill ... . Thus the deletion algorithm is identical to the algorithm used to fill priority fields when building a tree from scratch and hence it runs in time O(h). □

We summarize our discussion of radix priority search trees in

<u>Theorem 3:</u> Let $U \subseteq \mathbb{R}$, $N = |U|$ and let $S \subseteq U \times \mathbb{R}$, $n = |S|$. Then a priority search tree for S with respect to U can be built in time $O(N + n \log n)$. It supports insertions of points in $U \times \mathbb{R}$, deletions, and queries MinXinRectangle, MaxXinRectangle, MinYinXRange in time $O(\log N)$. Furthermore, operation EnumerateRectangle takes time $O(\log N + s)$ where s is the size of the answer.

We next turn to dynamic priority search trees. For $S \subseteq \mathbb{R} \times \mathbb{R}$ let U(S) be the projection of S onto the first coordinate, i.e. the set of x-coordinates of points in S. In a dynamic priority search tree we use a balanced search tree of set U(S) as the underlying search tree structure. Such a tree has depth O(log n), n = |S|. For the following discussion we assume that the underlying search trees are rebalanced by rotations and double rotations, i.e. we may use BB[α]-trees (cf. chapter III.5.1.), (2,4)-trees realized as red-black trees (cf. chapter III, exercise 27), AVL-trees (cf. chapter III, exercise 25) or half-balanced trees (cf. chapter III, exercise 26). Consider an insertion or deletion. We proceed as described in Lemma 10 except for the following change. An insertion adds an additional leaf to the tree and a deletion deletes some leaf from the tree. In this way we obtain a legal priority search tree except for the possible defect that the underlying search tree is unbalanced. We use rotations and double rotations to rebalance the tree. Since double rotations can be realized by two rotations we only need to discuss rotations.

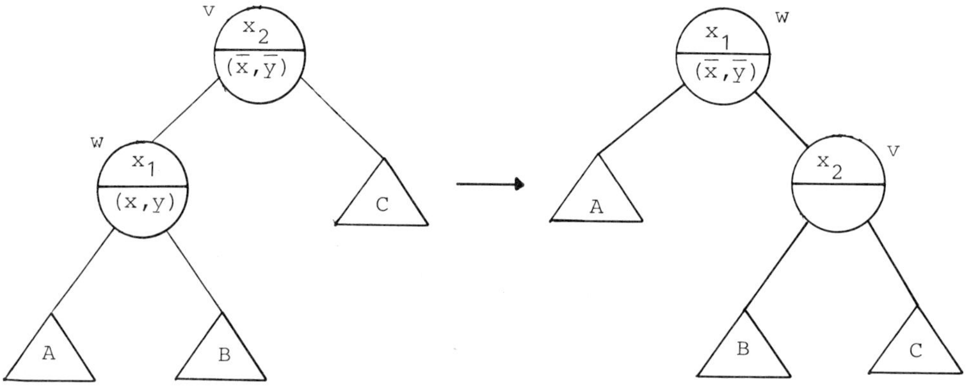

Suppose that we perform a rotation at node v with left son w and let $prio(v) = (\bar{x},\bar{y})$ and $prio(w) = (x,y)$. Then point (x,y) has the smallest y-value of all priority fields in the subtree rooted at v and hence $prio'(w) = (\bar{x},\bar{y})$. We use primes to denote the situation after the rotation. Also, the split fields of nodes v and w are easy to maintain. However, priority fields prio(w) and prio'(v) cause difficulties. We proceed as follows. We first insert point (x,y) into either tree A (if $x \le x_1$) or B (if $x > x_1$). It is important to observe that this insertion does <u>not</u> require a structural change of the underlying search tree. Rather, it updates the priority fields along a path down the tree as described in Lemma 1oa, and hence takes time O(h(v)) where h(v) is the height of node v. Priority field prio'(v) is filled as described in Lemma 1ob, i.e. we move the priority field of either the root of B or C to node v and then continue in this way along a simple path down the tree. Thus filling the priority field of node v after the insertion takes time O(h(v)). We can summarize the discussion in

Lemma 11: A rotation or double rotation at a node v of height h(v) takes time O(h(v)).

Proof: By the discussion above. □

Lemma 11 leads directly to

Theorem 4: Let $S \subseteq \mathbb{R} \times \mathbb{R}$, $n = |S|$. Dynamic priority search trees based on XYZ-search trees (XYZ ∈ {AVL, BB[α], red-black, half-balanced}) support queries MinXinRectangle, MaxXinRectangle, MinYinXrange in time O(log n) and query EnumerateRectangle in time O(log n + s) where s is the size of the answer. Moreover, insertions and deletions take time

$O((\log n)^2)$ in the worst case	if XYZ = AVL
$O((\log n)^2)$ in the worst case and O(log n) in the amortized case	if XYZ = BB[α] or XYZ = red-black
O(log n) in the worst case	if XYZ = half-balanced

Proof: The time bounds for the queries follow immediately from Lemmas 7 - 9. The worst case time bounds for AVL-trees, BB[α]-trees and red-black trees follow from the observation that at most O(log n) rotations and double rotations of cost O(log n) each are required to rebalance such a tree. Since O(1) such operations suffice for half-balanced trees we also have the O(log n) worst case time bound for these trees. It remains to prove the bound on the amortized cost for BB[α] and red-black trees. For both classes of trees we have shown that the total number of rotations and double rotations caused by nodes of height h in a sequence of n insertions and deletions is $O(n/c^h)$ for some c > 1. This is shown in section III.5.1. theorem 4 for BB[α]-trees and in section III.5.3.2. theorem 1o for red-black trees implementing (2,4) - trees. Since the cost of a rotation at a node of height h is O(h) the total cost of all rotations is

$\sum_{h \geq 1} O(n/c^h \cdot h) = O(n)$ and hence O(1) per insertion or deletion. Since the cost of an insertion or deletion outside the rebalancing operations is O(log n) the bound on the amortized cost follows. □

Applications of priority search trees are numerous. We first show how to maintain a dynamic set of intervals on the real line.

Theorem 5: Let S be a set of intervals on the real line, $n = |S|$. Using priority search trees we can insert intervals into S and delete intervals from S in time O(log n). Also, given a query interval $[x_0,y_0]$ we can enumerate

a) all s intervals $[x,y] \in S$ with $[x,y] \cap [x_0,y_0] \neq \emptyset$ in time $O(s + \log n)$

b) all s intervals $[x,y] \in S$ containing the query interval in time $O(s + \log n)$

c) all s intervals $[x,y] \in S$ contained in the query interval in time $O(s + \log n)$.

Proof: For parts a) and b) we represent interval [x,y] by point $(y,x) \in \mathbb{R}^2$ and store the associated set of points in a priority search tree. Then all intervals intersecting the query interval $[x_0,y_0]$ are listed by EnumerateRectangle(x_0,infinity,y_0), i.e. we list all rectangles $[x,y] \in S$ with $x_0 \leq y \leq$ infinity and $x \leq y_0$. Similarly, all intervals $[x,y] \in S$ containing the query interval $[x_0,y_0]$, i.e. $x \leq x_0 \leq y_0 \leq y$, can be listed by EnumerateRectangle(y_0,infinity,x_0).

For part c) we associate point (x,y) with interval [x,y] and store the set of associated points in a priority search tree. Then all intervals $[x,y] \in S$ contained in the query interval $[x_0,y_0]$, i.e. $x_0 \leq x \leq y \leq y_0$, can be listed by EnumerateRectangle(x_0,y_0,y_0). □

Theorem 5a provides us with an alternative proof of theorem 2. We may replace interval trees by priority search trees for computing the set of s pairs of intersecting rectangles in a set of n iso-oriented rectangles in time O(n log n + s).

Another class of applications concerns visibility and containment problems. Let S be a set of points in $\mathbb{R}^2$; each $(x,y) \in S$ defines a vertical semi-infinite ray with lower endpoint (x,y). We can think of the line segments as being either translucent or opaque. Given a query point $(x_o,y_o) \in S$ we want to find all line segment visible along a horizontal line of increasing x. We store the points (x,y) in a priority search tree.

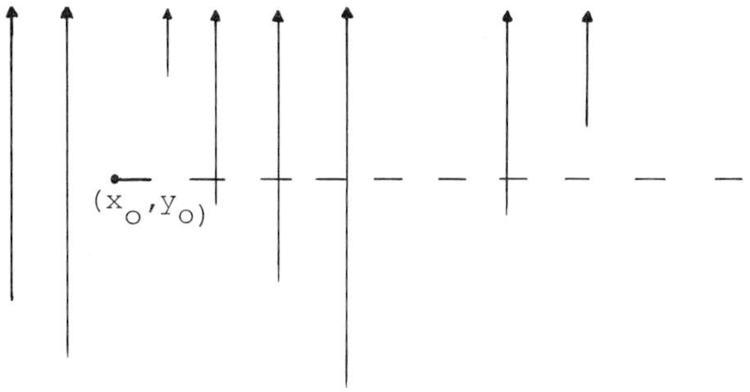

If the line segments are translucent then the segments visible from $(x_o y_o)$ are given by $x_o \le x$, $y \le y_o$, i.e. by EnumerateRectangle(x_o, infinity,y_o). In the opaque case, the solution is given by MinXinRectangle(x_o,infinity,y_o). Note also, that in either case we could restrict the horizontal line segment starting in (x_o,y_o) to some finite length without changing complexity.

The problem becomes harder when we allow the vertical line segments to be finite. In this case we can obtain an $O((\log n)^2)$ method by a combination of interval trees and priority search trees. We represent the set of vertical line segments as an interval tree T. More precisely, let $\hat{S}$ be the set of projections of the vertical line segments onto the y-axis. Then T is an interval tree for set $\hat{S}$. Let v be a node of T and let $[y_{bottom},y_{top}]$ be an interval in its node list. Then $y_{bottom}(y_{top})$ is stored in the left (right) part of v's node list. Next note, that we can view the left (right) part as a set of "semiinfinite" rays extending from (x,y_{bottom}) to (x,split(v)) where x is the x-coordinate of interval $[y_{bottom},y_{top}]$. Thus we can organize both node lists as priority search trees and hence find the visible line segments in v's node list in time $O(\log n + s)$ in the translucent case and $O(\log n)$ in the opaque case. Since the depth of the interval tree is $O(\log n)$ we obtain a total cost of $O((\log n)^2 + s)$ in the translucent case and $O(\log n)^2)$ in the opaque case.

The translucent visibility problem discussed above is an intersection problem. We discuss more general intersection problems in section 5.1.4.. Further applications of priority search trees are discussed in the exercises.

VIII. 5.1.3 Segment Trees

Segment trees are yet another method for storing sets of intervals. They are particularly useful in situations where additional information has to be stored with the intervals. We describe several applications of segment trees in the text and in the exercises, most notably the hidden line elimination problem for three-dimensional scenes (in section 5.1.4.) and the measure problem for a set of polygons.

Let $U \subseteq \mathbb{R}$, $U = \{x_1 < \ldots < x_N\}$, and let S be a set of intervals which have both endpoints in U. A segment tree for S with respect to universe U consists of a search tree with 2N + 1 leaves and some additional information. The leaves correspond to the atomic segments $(-\infty,x_1),[x_1,x_1]$, $(x_1,x_2),[x_2,x_2]$, (x_2,x_3), $[x_3,x_3]$, ... , (x_{N-1},x_N), $[x_N,x_N]$, $(x_N,+\infty)$ defined by U in increasing order from left to right. Here, (x_i,x_{i+1}) denotes the open interval from x_i to x_{i+1} and $[x_i,x_i]$ denotes the closed interval from x_i to x_i, i.e. point x_i. The split fields of the internal nodes are defined such that a search for $x \in \mathbb{R}$ is directed to the atomic segment containing x, i.e. if (x_i,x_{i+1}) $([x_{i+1},x_{i+1}])$ is the rightmost leaf in the left subtree of node v then we follow the pointer to the left subtree if $x < x_{i+1}$ $(x \le x_{i+1})$. Thus we need to store an additional bit distinguishing between the two cases in addition to storing the split field split(v) = x_{i+1}.

The xrange of a node of a segment tree is defined as in the introduction of section 5.1.. Note that the xrange(v) of node v is the union of the atomic segments associated with the leaf descendants of v. We also associate (and store) with each node v its node list NL(v). The node list of v contains (pointers to) all intervals of S which cover v's xrange but do not cover the xrange of v's father, i.e.

$$NL(v) = \{I \in S;\ xrange(v) \subseteq I \text{ and } xrange(father(v)) \not\subseteq I\}$$

The following example illustrates the definitions. We have

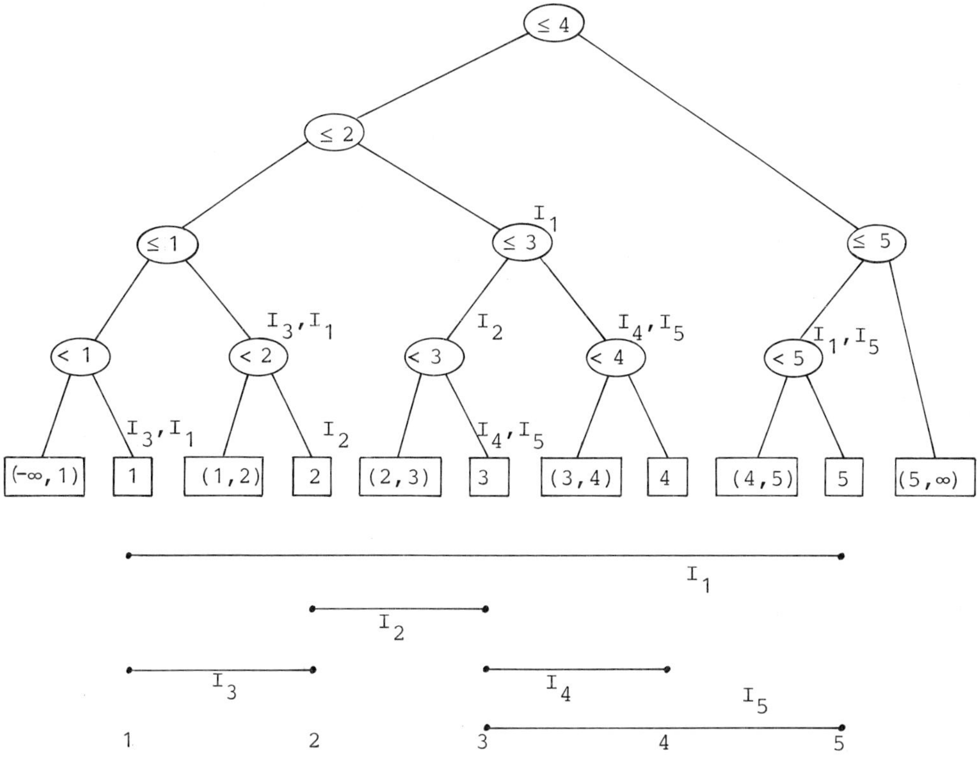

U = {1,2,3,4,5} and S = {[1,5],[2,3],[1,2],[3,4],[3,5]}. The split fields and the condition for following the pointer to the left son are indicated inside internal nodes. The node lists associated with the various nodes are indicated on the top of the nodes.

In a segment tree an interval may be stored in several node lists. Lemma 12 shows that it is stored in at most 2h node lists, where h is the height of the tree.

Lemma 12: Let T be a segment tree of height h for S and let I ∈ S. Then I belongs to at most 2h node lists. Furthermore, I is the disjoint union of the sets xrange(v) where the union is over all nodes v such that I ∈ NL(v).

Proof: Let C = {v; xrange(v) ⊆ I} and let C_{max} = {v; v ∈ C and father(v) ∉ C}. Then I belongs to NL(v) if and only if v ∈ C_{max}. In lemma 2 it was shown that $|C_{max}| \le 2h$. Also, if $v,w \in C_{max}$ then $xrange(v) \cap xrange(w) = \emptyset$. Finally, if $x \in I$ then there is clearly a node $v \in C_{max}$ such that $x \in xrange(v)$. Thus $I = \cup\{xrange(v);\ I \in NL(v)\}$ and the union is over disjoint sets. □

We can draw several consequences from the lemma above. The first observation is that an interval I is stored in a segment tree as a set of disjoint pieces, the piece xrange(v) is stored in NL(v). Also, a node v represents the identical piece, namely xrange(v), of all intervals I with $I \in NL(v)$. Thus we are free to organize the node lists according to secondary criteria. This explains the flexibility of segment trees. The second consequence is that balanced segment trees require space $O(n \log N)$ and can be constructed in time $O(n \log N)$. Finally, given interval I, one can find all nodes v with $I \in NL(v)$ in time $O(\log N)$. Hence insertions and deletions are efficient operations in segment trees. The exact time bounds depend on the structure chosen for the node lists.

<u>Theorem 6:</u> Let $U \subseteq \mathbb{R}$, $|U| = N$, and let S be a set of n intervals with both endpoints in U.

a) A segment tree for S of depth $O(\log N)$ can be constructed in time $O(n \log N)$. It requires space $O(n \log N)$.

b) If time g(m) is required to insert an interval into or delete an interval from a node list of size m and g is nondecreasing then an interval can be inserted into or deleted from a segment tree in time $O(g(n) \log N)$.

<u>Proof:</u> a) Let T be a complete binary tree with 2N + 1 leaves. It is easy to organize the split fields in time O(N) such that T is the skeleton of a segment tree for S. Next observe that for every $I \in S$ we can find the set of nodes v with $xrange(v) \subseteq I$ and $xrange(father(v)) \not\subseteq I$ in time $O(\log N)$. This follows from the fact that the nodes in C_{max} are sons of the nodes in P which in turn are the nodes on the search paths to the two endpoints of interval I. The space bound follows from the observation that every interval is stored in at most $2h = O(\log N)$ node lists.

b) Let I be an interval and suppose that we want to delete I from S.

The case of an insertion is symmetric and left to the reader. By part a) we can find the set $A = \{v;\ I \in NL(v)\}$ in time $O(\log N)$. We have to delete I from NL(v) for every $v \in A$. Since the node list of any node can certainly contain at most n intervals, since g is non-decreasing and since $|A| = O(\log N)$, the total cost of deleting I is certainly $O(g(n) \log N)$. □

In many applications of segment trees we have $g(n) = O((\log n)^k)$ for some small k. Then insertions and deletions take time $O((\log n)^k \log N)$. We are now ready for the first application of segment trees, the <u>measure problem of iso-oriented rectangles</u>. Let $R_1,\ldots,R_m$ be a set of iso-oriented rectangles. We want to compute the measure (area) of $R_1 \cup R_2 \cup \ldots \cup R_m$. We solve this problem by plane sweep. Let U be the set of y-coordinates of the corners of the rectangles R_i, $1 \le i \le m$. Then $|U| \le 2m$. For every position of the sweep line let S be the set of rectangles intersected by the sweep line. We store the (projections onto the y-axis of the) rectangles in S in a segment tree with respect to universe U. In the diagram the sweep line intersects rectangles R_1,

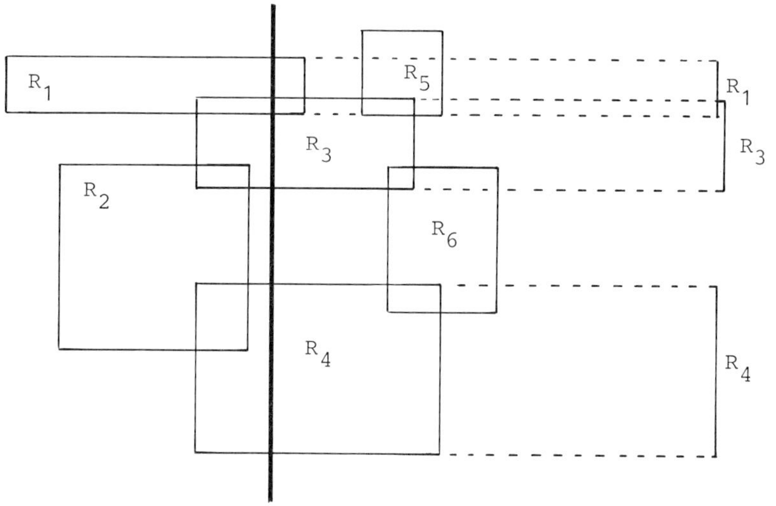

R_3 and R_4. Their projections (shown in the right half of the diagram) are stored in the segment tree. The node lists are organized in an extremely simple way. We only store the <u>cardinality</u> of each node list instead of the complete node lists. Thus the space requirement of each node list is $O(1)$. We also store in each node v a quantity TL(v) which is defined as follows. For an interval I let length(I) be the length of I. Then

$$TL(v) = \begin{cases} \text{length(xrange}(v)) & \text{if } NL(v) \neq \emptyset \\ 0 & \text{if } NL(v) = \emptyset \text{ and } v \text{ is a leaf} \\ TL(\ell son(v)) + TL(rson(v)) & \text{if } NL(v) = \emptyset \text{ and } v \text{ is not a leaf} \end{cases}$$

Then TL(v) is the total length of all atomic segments (in the subtree with root v) which are covered by intervals which belong to a node list of v or a descendant of v. In particular, TL(root) is the length of the union of the intervals stored in S.

The x-structure contains the x-coordinates of the corners of the rectangles R_i, $1 \le i \le m$, in sorted order. The structure of the plane sweep algorithm is as follows. Suppose that we advance the sweep line to transition point x. Let x_{old} be the previous transition point. Then $TL(root)(x-x_{old})$ is the area covered by the rectangles in the vertical strip given by the scan line positions x_{old} and x. We add this quantity to variable A which sums the total covered area to the left of the scan line. Next we delete all rectangles R_j from the tree whose right side is at x and insert all rectangles R_j into the tree whose left side is at x. We claim that insertions and deletions take time O(log m) per rectangle. This can be seen as follows.

We treat the case of a deletion. By theorem 6 we can find the set $A = \{v; I \in NL(v)\}$ in time O(log m). For all nodes $v \in A$ we have to decrease the counter holding the cardinality of the node list by one. If the counter stays positive then no further action is required for that node. If the counter becomes zero then we need to recompute TL(v) as given by the formula above. Also we need to propagate the change to the ancestors of v. Since the ancestors of the nodes in A form two paths in the tree the TL-fields of all ancestors of nodes in A can be updated in time O(log m).

For the sake of completeness we include a detailed program. We assume for this program that an interval with endpoints x and y is stored as half-open interval (x,y]. We also assume that atomic segments (x_i,x_{i+1}) and $[x_{i+1},x_{i+1}]$ are combined to $(x_i,x_{i+1}]$ for all $x_i \in U$. Note that with this convention every interval is still a union of atomic segments. Also, the split field of node v directs a search for x to the left iff $x \le split(v)$. In the program we maintain the invariant that $xrange(v) = (a,b]$, $I = (x,y]$, $xrange(v) \cap I \neq \emptyset$ and $xrange(father(v)) \not\subseteq I$

```
(1)  procedure Delete(x,y,v,a,b);
(2)  begin if x ≤ a and b ≤ y                              --  xrange(v) ⊆ I
(3)        then v↑.count ← v↑.count - 1 fi;
(4)        if v↑.count = 0
(5)        then if v↑.stat = leaf
(6)             then v↑.TL ← 0
(7)             else v↑.TL ← v↑.ℓson↑.TL + v↑.rson↑.TL
(8)             fi
(9)        else if x ≤ v↑.split
(10)            then Delete(x,y,v↑.ℓson,a,v↑.split)
(11)            fi;
(12)            if y ≥ v↑.split
(13)            then Delete(x,y,v↑.rson,v↑.split,b)
(14)            fi;
(15)            v↑.TL ← v↑.ℓson↑.TL + v↑.rson↑.TL
(16)       fi
(17) end
```

The O(log m) time bound for procedure Delete is readily established from the program text. Only nodes v with $xrange(v) \cap I \neq \emptyset$ and $xrange(v) \not\subseteq I$ generate recursive calls. By lemma 2 there are at most 2 log m such nodes. This establishes the time bound.

Procedure Insert is a minor variant of procedure Delete. We only have to replace lines (3) to (8) by

```
then v↑.count ← v↑.count + 1;
     v↑.TL ← b - a
```

We have now shown that insertions and deletions take time O(log m) per rectangle. Since a total of m rectangles has to be handled the cost of the sweep is O(m log m). The cost of sorting the corners of the rectangles according to x- and y-coordinate is also O(m log m). The former sort is required for setting up the x-structure and the latter sort is needed for computing U. We summarize our discussion in

Theorem 7: The measure problem for a set of m iso-oriented rectangles can be solved in time $O(m \log m)$ and space $O(m)$.

Proof: The time bound is immediate from the discussion above. The space bound follows from the fact that only $O(1)$ words are needed per node of the segment tree. □

Further applications of segment trees can be found in sections 5.1.4. and 5.3. and in the exercises. In particular, we will show how to solve the measure problem for arbitrary polygons and how to do hidden line elimination in section 5.1.4.. In section 5.3. we will use segment trees for solving intersection problems of iso-oriented objects in three- and higher-dimensional space.

We close this section with a discussion of dynamic segment trees. Let S be a set of intervals on the real line and let U be the set of left and right endpoints of the intervals in S. Let $n = |S|$ and $N = |U| \le 2n$. A dynamic segment tree for S is based on a D-tree (cf. III.6.2.) with $2N + 1$ leaves, one for each atomic segment. As before, we have atomic segments $(-\infty, x_1)$, $[x_1, x_1]$, (x_1, x_2), ..., (x_{N-1}, x_N), $[x_N, x_N]$, $(x_N, +\infty)$, where $U = \{x_1 < x_2 < \ldots < x_N\}$. The weights of the atomic segments are defined as follows. Segment (x_i, x_{i+1}) has weight 1, $0 \le i \le N$, and the weight of segment $[x_i, x_i]$ is equal to the number of intervals in S which have x_i as an endpoint. As in the case of interval trees we have

Lemma 13: Let v be a node of a dynamic segment tree based on a D-tree. Then $|NL(v)| = O(th(v))$ where $th(v)$ is the number of leaves below v in the $BB[\alpha]$-tree underlying the D-tree (underlying the dynamic segment tree).

Proof: Let v be a node of a dynamic segment tree. If $I \in NL(v)$ then $xrange(v) \subseteq I$ and $xrange(father(v)) \not\subseteq I$. Hence at least one endpoint of I is contained in xrange(father(v)). We can therefore write $NL(v) = N_1 \cup N_2$ where $N_i = \{I \in NL(v);$ exactly i endpoints of I are contained in xrange(father(v))}, i = 1,2. A bound on $|N_1|$ is easily derived. We have

$$|N_1| \le \Sigma\{\text{weight}([x_j,x_j]);\quad \text{the active } [x_j,x_j]\text{-node is a descendant of } v\}$$

$$\le ((1-\alpha)/\alpha)\ \ \text{th}(\text{father}(v)) \le ((1-\alpha)/\alpha^2)\text{th}(v)$$

since the fraction $\alpha/(1-\alpha)$ of all $[x_j,x_j]$-leaves are descendants of the active $[x_j,x_j]$-node. Let us turn to N_2 next. If $I \in N_2$ then $I \subseteq$ xrange(father(v)) and hence xrange(v) $\subseteq I$ implies that xrange(father(v)) and I have a common endpoint. Hence

$$|N_2| \le 2\cdot((1-\alpha)/\alpha)\ \text{th}(\text{father}(v)) \le 2((1-\alpha)/\alpha^2)\text{th}(v)$$ □

by an argument similar to the one above.

We are now in a position to discuss insertions and deletions into dynamic segment trees. We separate two issues. The first issue is to insert or delete an interval without changing the underlying tree structure and the second issue is to rebalance the underlying D-tree by rotations and double rotations.

The total weight of all atomic segments is at most 3n + 1 and hence the depth of a dynamic segment tree is O(log n). Thus time O(log n) suffices to locate the set of nodes whose node lists are affected by the insertion. Let us assume that the cost of inserting an interval into or deleting an interval from a node list of size m is g(m) where g is non-decreasing. Then the total cost of updating the node lists is $\sum_{v\in A} g(|NL(v)|) \le \sum_{v\in A} g(c\ \text{th}(v))$ where A is the set of affected nodes and c is a (small) constant. The set of affected nodes form (essentially) two paths in the tree and hence for every integer i there are at most d nodes in A with $(1-\alpha)^{-i} < \text{th}(v) \le (1-\alpha)^{-i-1}$ for some (small) constant d. Thus the cost of updating the node lists is $C_1 := \sum_{i=0}^{e \log n} d\ g((1-\alpha)^{-i})$ where $e = -1/\log(1-\alpha)$. In particular, we have $C_1 = O((\log n)^{k+1})$ if $g(m) = O((\log m)^k)$ for some $k \ge 0$ and $C_1 = O(n^\alpha)$ if $g(m) = m^\alpha$ for some $\alpha > 0$.

It remains to discuss the cost of rebalancing the underlying D-tree by rotations and double rotations. Since a double rotation is two rotations it suffices to discuss single rotations.

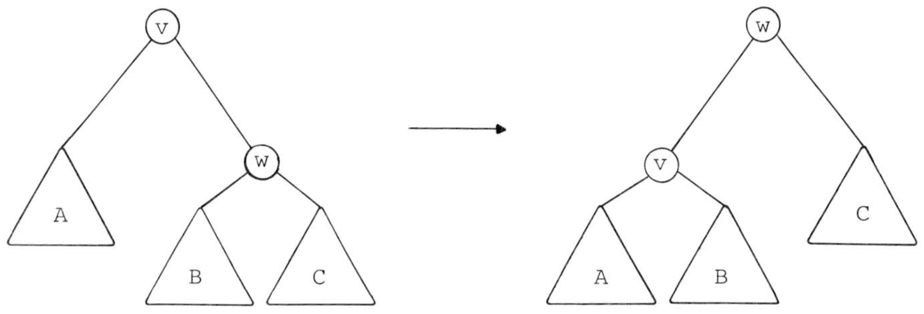

We have (primes denote the situation after the rotation):

$NL'(w) \leftarrow NL(v)$

$NL'(v) \leftarrow NL(root(A)) \cap NL(root(B))$

$NL'(root(A)) \leftarrow NL(root(A)) - NL'(v)$

$NL'(root(B)) \leftarrow (NL(root(B)) - NL'(v)) \cup NL(w)$

$NL'(root(C)) \leftarrow NL(root(C)) \cup NL(w)$

The correctness of these formulae is easily established. For example, we have $I \in NL'(v)$ iff I covers A and B but does not cover C, i.e. $NL'(v) = NL(root(A)) \cap NL(root(B))$. The node lists of all other nodes remain unchanged. This follows from the fact that the node list NL(z) of a node z is determined by xrange(z) and xrange(father(z)) and that only the xranges of nodes v and w change.

The total size of the node lists NL(v), NL(w), NL(root(A)), NL(root(B)), and NL(root(C)) is O(th(v)) by lemma 13. We will therefore assume that the cost of a single rotation at node v is O(f(th(v))) for some non-decreasing function f. Hence the total cost of all rebalancing operations is $C_2 := O(n \sum_{i=0}^{e \log n} f((1-\alpha)^{-i})(1-\alpha)^{i})$ where $e = -1/\log(1-\alpha)$ by theorem 5 of section III.6.2. In particular, if $f(m) = O(m(\log m)^k)$ for some $k \geq 0$ then $C_2 = O(n(\log n)^{k+1})$, i.e. the amortized cost per insertion and deletion is $O((\log n)^{k+1})$. We summarize in:

Theorem 8: Let S be a set of n intervals. Then the amortized insertion and deletion cost into a dynamic segment tree for S is

$$O(\log n + \sum_{i=0}^{e \log n} (g((1-\alpha)^{-i}) + f((1-\alpha)^{-i})(1-\alpha)^{i}))$$ where g and f are defined as above. In particular, g(m) is the cost of inserting (deleting) an interval into (from) a node list of size m and f(m) is the cost of a rotation at a node of thickness m. In particular, if $g(m) = (\log m)^k$ and $f(m) = m(\log m)^k$ for some $k \geq o$ then the amortized cost is $O((\log m)^{k+1})$.

Proof: Immediate from the discussion above. □

VIII. 5.1.4 Path Decomposition and Plane Sweep for Non-Iso-Oriented Objects

In the preceding sections 5.1.1. to 5.1.3. we developed special data structures for plane sweep algorithms on iso-oriented objects, namely interval, segment, and priority search trees. In this section we want to show that many of the plane sweep algorithms generalize to more general objects, in particular to collections of polygons.
The main idea is to turn the collection of polygons into a planar subdivision by adding additional vertices at edge intersections and then to decompose the triangulated subdivisions into paths as described in section 3.1.2. The path decomposition splits the plane into an ordered set of strips (of varying width) which we can use as the atomic segments in a segment tree.

In this section we treat two problems: the measure problem for a union of simple polygons and the hidden line elimination problem. In the first problem we discuss at length how path decompositions allow us to transfer an algorithm from the iso-oriented to the general case.
In the second problem we take this transfer for granted and treat the general problem directly.

Let $Q_1,\ldots,Q_m$ be a set of simple polygons with a total of n vertices. Our goal is to compute the area covered by the union $Q_1 \cup \ldots \cup Q_m$ of the polygons.
Our approach is to extend the algorithm of section 5.1.3 to this more general situation. There are at least two ways to proceed. A first attempt is to use dynamic segment trees instead of static segment trees.

More precisely, consider an arbitrary position of the sweep line. It intersects some of the edges of polygons $Q_1,\dots,Q_m$. Take the ordered set of intersected line segments as the universe of the segment tree. In this way, every leaf of the segment tree corresponds to a (half-open) interval between adjacent active line segments. We invite the reader to carry out the fairly complicated details of this approach. It will allow him/her to appreciate the elegance of the second solution more highly.

For the second approach we first turn the set of polygons into a planar subdivision by adding new vertices at intersections of edges, then triangulate the subdivision and decompose the planar subdivision into an ordered set of strips such that every interval arising in the plane sweep is a union of strips, and finally base the plane sweep on a static segment tree for the set of strips.
The details are as follows.

Let $Q_1,\dots Q_m$ be a set of polygons with a total of n edges.
Assume w.l.o.g. that no edge of any polygon is vertical and that there is a total of k intersections of edges. We can find the k points of intersection in time $O((n+k)\log n)$ by theorem 1 of section 4.1. We add the k points of intersection as additional vertices and call the resulting set of vertices V. Then $|V| = n + k$ and edges intersect only at common endpoints, i.e. we have a planar subdivision with vertex set V. Next, we add the edges of the convex hull of set V and then triangulate all finite faces of the planar subdivision. Call the resulting subdivision $\hat{G}$. We can construct $\hat{G}$ in time $O((n+k)\log(n+k))$ by theorem 2 of section 2 and theorem 3 of section 4.2.

Let s,t be the vertices of minimal and maximal x-coordinate and let $P_1,\dots,P_p$ be a path decomposition of planar subdivision $\hat{G}$ in the sense of section 3.2.2, i.e.

1) each P_i is an x-monotone (in section 3.2.2. we required the path to be y-monotone) path from s to t

2) each edge of P_i belongs to at least one path

3) if vertical line L intersects P_i and P_j and $i < j$ then $L \cap P_i$ is not below $L \cap P_j$.

We have seen in section 3.2.2. that the implicite representation of a complete path decomposition can be computed in time $O(n+k)$, i.e. we compute integer arrays L and R such that edge e belongs to P_i iff

$L(e) \le i \le R(e)$.

Moreover, $p \le n + k$.

A path decomposition of $\hat{G}$ divides the vertical strip defined by vertices s and t into an ordered set of "horizontal" strips in a natural way. The i-th strip is the region between paths P_i and P_{i+1}. We use these strips as the atomic segments of the segment tree. More precisely, we use a static segment tree with universe [1...p] where integer i corresponds to path P_i. We can now proceed in almost complete analogy to section 5.1.3. where we treated the measure problem for iso-oriented objects.

We maintain the following data structures. Consider a fixed position of the sweep line. For each polygon Q_i we maintain the set of edges of the polygon intersected by the sweep line in a balanced tree sorted according to the y-coordinate of the intersections. Actually, it suffices to keep the indices of the paths of the composition containing the edges in a balanced tree. The sweep line intersects polygon Q_i in some number of intervals. For each interval, which then extends between two paths of the decomposition, say P_a and P_b, we store the interval (a...b] in the segment tree. As before, actual node lists are not maintained, only their cardinality has to be stored. In addition to CNL(v) the cardinality of v's node list, we store two other fields in every node of the segment tree: LE(v), the length of v's xrange as a function of the position of the sweep line, and TL(v), the total length of the atomic segments below v which are covered. Field TL(v) is also a function of the position of the sweep line. Field LE(v) is defined as follows. If xrange(v) = (i...j] then LE(v) is the linear function a + bx where a + bx is the vertical distance of paths P_i and P_j at x-coordinate x. Note that LE(v) = LE(lson(v)) + LE(rson(v)) if v is not a leaf. Field LE(v) was a constant in the iso-oriented case; the major task in generalizing the plane sweep algorithm from the iso-oriented case is to maintain the fields LE(v) of the nodes of the segment tree. Finally, fields TL(v) are defined exactly as in the iso-oriented case, i.e.

$$TL(v) = \begin{cases} LE(v) & \text{if } NL(v) \ne \emptyset \\ 0 & \text{if } NL(v) = \emptyset \text{ and } v \text{ is a leaf} \\ TL(lson(v)) + TL(rson(v)) & \text{if } NL(v) = \emptyset \text{ and if } v \text{ is not a leaf.} \end{cases}$$

Note that TL(v) is a linear function for every node v of the segment tree and that TL(root) is the linear function which yields the total length of the union of the intervals stored in the tree.

The X-structure of the plane sweep contains the vertex set V of planar subdivision $\hat{G}$ in increasing order of x-coordinate. Suppose now that we advance the sweep line from transition point z_{old} with x-coordinate x_{old} to transition point z with x-coordinate x. The following three actions are required:

1) compute the area covered by the union of the rectangles in the vertical strip between x_{old} and x
2) update the LE-fields of some of the nodes of the segment tree
3) update the intervals stored in the segment tree for every polygon Q_i having v as a vertex.

Action 1) is very simple. If TL(root) = a + bx is the linear function stored in the TL-field of the root, then $a(x-x_{old}) + b(x^2-x_{old}^2)/2$ is the area covered by the union of the polygons in the vertical strip between x_{old} and x.

Action 2) requires some care; it has no counterpart in the algorithm for iso-oriented objects. Assume that edges $e_1,\ldots,e_\ell$ end in vertex z and that edges $e_1',\ldots e_r'$ start in vertex z.
Assume also that ending and starting edges are ordered from top to bottom.

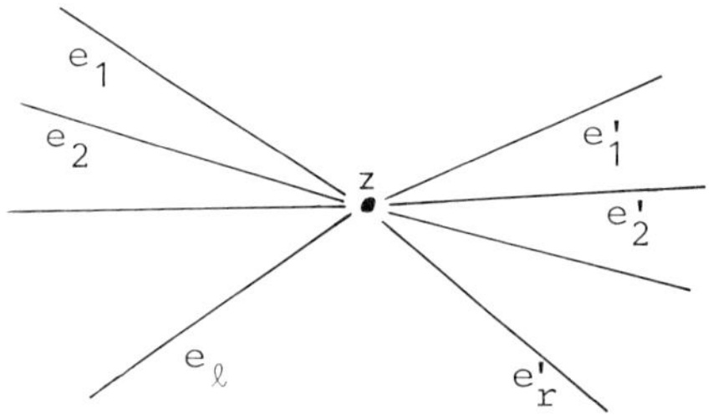

We know that paths $P_a,\ldots,P_b$ where $a = L[e_1]$ and $b = R[e_\ell]$ run through vertex z. Also, paths $P_{L[e_i]},\ldots,P_{R[e_i]}$ use edge e_i, $1 \le i \le \ell$, and paths $P_{L[e_j']},\ldots,P_{R[e_j']}$ use edge e_j' $1 \le j \le r$. It is useful to model the transition through vertex z in two steps. We first move from the left into node z and then leave node z to the right. The first step shrinks the paths between paths $P_{R[e_i]}$ and $P_{L[e_{i+1}]}$ (note that $R[e_i]+1 = L[e_{i+1}]$), $1 \le i < \ell$, to empty sets and the second step expands the strip between paths $P_{R[e'_j]}$ and $P_{L[e'_{j+1}]}$, $1 \le j < r$, to non-trivial intervals. Therefore, the following code suffices to make required changes of the LE-fields and the induced changes of the TL-fields.

(1) <u>for</u> i <u>from</u> 1 <u>to</u> ℓ-1

(2) <u>do</u> LE(leaf corresponding to atomic segment $(R[e_i], R[e_i]+1)$) $\leftarrow$ 0;

(3) propagate change in LE-field and induced change in TL-fields towards the root

(4) <u>od</u>;

(5) <u>for</u> j from 1 to r-1

(6) <u>do</u> LE(leaf corresponding to atomic segment $(R[e'_j], R[e'_j]+1)$) $\leftarrow a_j + b_j x$

(7) propagate change in LE-field and induced change in TL-fields towards the root

(8) <u>od</u>;

(9) LE(leaf corresponding to atomic segment$(L[e'_1]-1, L[e'_1]]$ $\leftarrow a_0 + b_0 x$;

(10) LE(leaf corresponding to atomic segment$(R[e'_r], R[e'_r]+1]$ $\leftarrow a_r + b_r x$;

(11) propagate both changes and the induced changes towards the root.

A small remark is required about lines (2), (6), (9) and (10). In line (2) we store the function which is constant zero in the LE-field. In line (6) (similarly in lines (9) and (10)) we store the linear function which yields the distance between edge e'_j and e'_{j+1} as a function of the x-coordinate in the LE-field. In lines (9) and (10) we update LE-fields corresponding to the strip between P_{a-1} and P_a, $a = L[e_1]$, and P_b and P_{b+1}, $b = R[e_\ell]$.

The cost of action two is $O((\ell+r)\log(n+k))$ since every execution of lines (3), (7) and (11) takes time $O(\log(n+k))$. Since every edge is handled twice in action two during the entire sweep the total cost of of action two is $O((n+k)\log(n+k))$.

Action three is very similar to what we know already from the iso-oriented case. Suppose that z is a vertex of polygon Q_i. In general, z is a vertex of several polygons. Then z is either a start, bend or end vertex of Q_i.

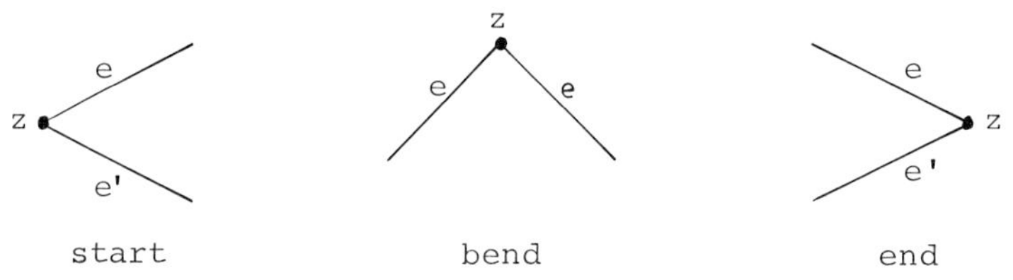

Let e and e' be the two edges of Q_i which are incident to z. Using the tree representation of the set of active edges of polygon Q_i we can easily find the immediate predecessor e_T of e and e' and the immediate successor e_B of e and e' in the top to bottom order of active edges and also insert or delete e and e' whatever is appropriate. Note that e_T and e_B do not necessarily exist. We can also determine whether the region below e belongs to Q_i or not by inspecting the order in which edges e and e' appear on the boundary of Q_i. All of this takes time $O(\log n)$.

We can now finish the transition by a few insertions and deletions into the segment tree. For example, if z is a start vertex and the region between e and e' does not belong to Q_i then we first delete interval $(L[e_T], R[e_B]]$ from the segment tree and then insert intervals $(L[e_T], R[e]]$ and $(L[e'], R[e_B]$. All other cases are similar. The precise code for the insertions and deletions is identical to the code given in section 5.1.3. Thus processing a vertex z takes time $O(m(z)\log n)$ where $m(z)$ is the number of polygons having z as a vertex. Since $\sum_{z \in V} m(z) = O(n+k)$ we conclude that the total cost of action three is $O((n+k)\log n)$. We summarize in

<u>Theorem 9:</u> Let $Q_1,\ldots,Q_m$ be a set of simple polygons with n edges and k intersections of edges. Then the area of the union of polygons can be computed in time $O((n+k)\log n)$.

Proof: We infer a bound of $O((n+k)\log(n+k))$ from the preceding discussion. Since $k \leq n^2$ the bound follows. □

Our second application of path decomposition to plane sweep algorithms is a hidden line elimination algorithm. Let $Q_1,\ldots,Q_m$ be a set of simple plane polygons in $\mathbb{R}^3$ with a total of n edges. (A polygon Q in $\mathbb{R}^3$ is plane if there is a plane containing all vertices of Q). We assume that polygons Q_i and Q_j, $1 \leq i < j \leq m$, do not intersect except at points at their common boundary. We want to compute the visible parts under orthogonal projection into the xy-plane (from $+\infty$ in the z-direction). A similar algorithm works for perspective projections.

Let Q_i' be the projection of Q_i into the xy-plane, $1 \leq i \leq m$, and let k be the number of intersections of edges of the projected polygons Q_i'. As before we obtain a planar subdivision $\hat{G}$ with vertex set V, $|V| = n + k$, by adding the intersections as additional vertices, by adding the edges of the convex hull, and by triangulation all finite faces. Also, as before, we construct a path decomposition $P_1,\ldots,P_p$ of the subdivision $\hat{G}$.

We will now show how to solve the hidden line elimination problem by space sweep. More precisely, we sweep a plane, which is parallel to the yz-plane, from $-\infty$ to $+\infty$ in x-direction. Consider a fixed position of the sweep plane PL. It intersects some of the polygons Q_i. Each intersection is a set of straight line segments (note that the Q_i's are not necessarily convex). Let $L_1,\ldots,L_N$ be the set of straight line segments which can be obtained as an intersection of the sweep plane PL and the polygons Q_i, $1 \leq i \leq m$. Note that line segments $L_1,\ldots,L_N$ do not intersect except at common endpoints. Furthermore, let L_i' be the projection of L_i into the xy-plane. The idea of the algorithm is to maintain the projections L_i' in a segment tree as follows. We use a static segment tree with universe $[1\ldots p]$. Element j of the universe corresponds to path P_j of the path decomposition, $1 \leq j \leq p$. Consider an arbitrary L_i'. It extends between paths P_a and P_b, say, of the decomposition. We therefore store interval $(a,b]$ in the segment tree. Finally, we have to discuss the organization of the node lists. Let v be a node of the segment tree with $xrange(v) = (c,d]$. Then node v represents the strip between paths P_c and P_d of the decomposition. Then node list $NL(v)$ of node v is a set of projected intervals; node v represents the sub-interval between paths P_c and P_d. Since the line segments $L_1,\ldots,L_N$ do not intersect except at common endpoints we can order the node list NL(v) according to z-coordinate. We therefore postulate that NL(v) is maintained as a balanced tree with its elements ordered according to z-coordiate.

In the following example, we have four line segments L_1, L_2, L_3, L_4 and use a segment tree with universe [1...4]. The ordered node lists are shown in the vicinity

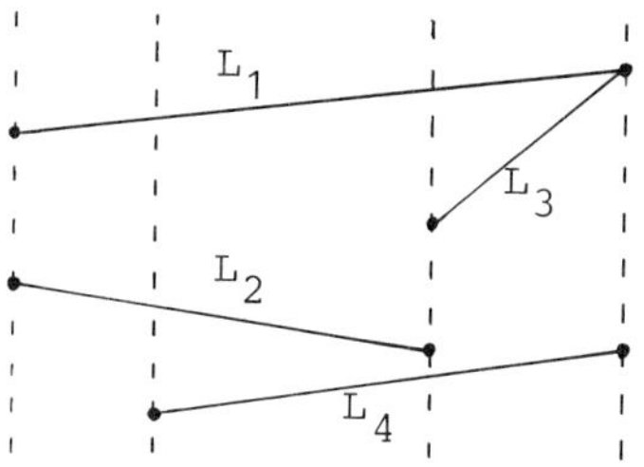

a view of the sweep plane

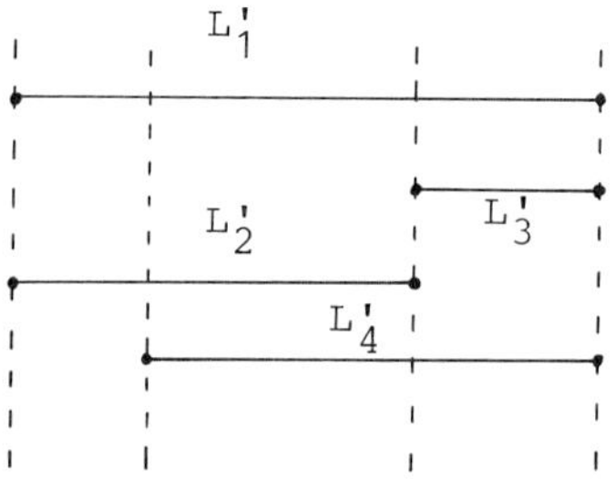

a view of the projected line segments

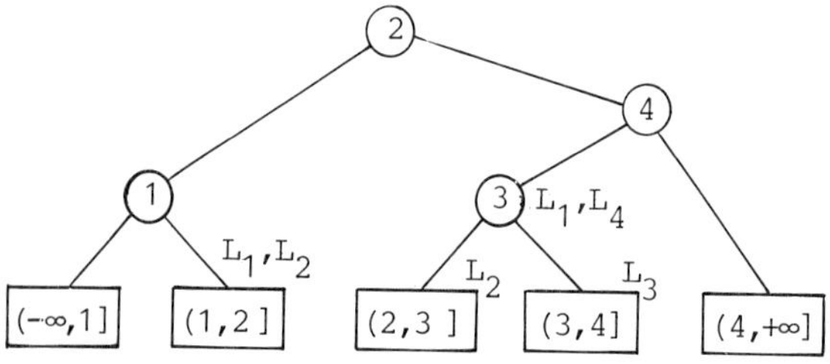

the segment tree

of the nodes; e.g. the node list of node 3 is L_1, L_4 in that order.

We can now give the details of the sweep. The transition points are the vertices V in increasing order of x-coordinate . Suppose that the sweep reaches vertex z. In general, z is a vertex of several polygons Q_i. Two actions are required

1) Update the state of the sweep
2) Check for visibility

The first action is very similar to the third action of the previous algorithm. If z is a vertex of polygon Q_i then it is either a start, bend or end vertex. In all three cases a few insertions or deletions update the segment. For example, if z is an end vertex, i.e. two edges, say e and e', of Q_i terminate in z and the region between e and e' does not belong to Q_i, then let e_T and e_B be the immediate successor and predecessor edges in the tree representation (cf. the previous algorithm) of active edges of polygon Q_i. We have to delete intervals $(L[e_T],R[e]]$ and $(L[e'],R[e_B])$ from the segment tree and we have to insert interval $(L[e_T],R[e_B]]$ into the segment tree. When intervals are inserted into the tree we have to insert the interval into O(log n) node lists. In each node list we have to insert the interval at the appropriate position according to its height for a cost of O(log n) each. Thus inserting or deleting an interval has cost $O((\log n)^2)$ and hence the total cost of actions one is $O(n+k)(\log n)^2)$.

Action two is a check for visibility. It is performed at every transition point after all insertions and deletions required by action one are performed. Let A be the set of edges starting in vertex z. For each edge $e \in A$ we can check its visibility in time $O(\log n)^2)$ as follows. Let $a = L[e]$ and $b = R[e]$, i.e. paths $P_a,\ldots,P_b$ use edge e. Let v be any node of the segment tree which lies on the path from either atomic segment $(b-1,b]$ or atomic segment $(a,a+1]$ to the root. We can clearly check in time O(log n) whether v's node list contains an interval which covers e by comparing the highest interval in v's node list with edge e and hence we can check in time $O((\log n)^2)$ whether any of these nodes contains an interval which covers e. We claim that if none of these nodes contains an interval which covers e then e is visible. Assume otherwise. Then there is a polygon which covers e. Let I be the intersection of that polygon with the sweep plane and let I' be the projection of I. Then I extends between active edges e' and e" where $L[e'] \le L[e]$ and $R[e''] \ge R[e]$. Since I is stored as interval $(L[e'],R[e'']]$ in the segment tree the claim follows.

Visibility of a single edge can thus be checked in time $O((\log n)^2)$ and hence the total time needed for all visibility checks is $O((n+k)(\log n)^2)$. We summarize in

<u>Theorem 10:</u> Let $Q_1,\ldots,Q_m$ be a set of simple plane polygons in $\mathbb{R}^3$ with a total of n edges. Assume further, that polygons Q_i and Q_j,

$1 \leq i < j \leq m$, do not intersect except at common boundary points and that there are k intersection of edges in the orthogonal projection of the polygons into the xy-plane. Then the hidden line elimination problem can be solved in time $O((n+k)(\log n)^2)$ and space $O(n+k)$.

Proof: by the discussion above.

□

Two alternative algorithms for hidden line elimination are discussed in the exercises both of which improve upon the algorithm described above. The first alternative has the same basic structure but uses zig-zag decompositions instead of complete path decompositions. This reduces the space requirement to $O(n)$. Since k might be as large as $\Omega(n^2)$ this is a significant improvement. Unfortunately, it does not seem to be always possible to use zig-zag decompositions instead of complete path decompositions; e.g. it is not clear how to use them for the measure problem. The second alternative keeps the space requirement at $O(n+k)$ but reduces running time to $O((n+k)(\log n))$. It constructs a planar subdivision by introducing new vertices at edge intersections, then computes local visibility in the vicinity of vertices and finally determines global visibility by a sweep in z-direction.

VIII. 5.2 Divide and Conquer on Iso-Oriented Objects

In this section we will show how the divide-and-conquer paradigm can be applied to solving problems on sets of iso-oriented objects. In particular it can be used to report intersections of line segments, to report containment of points in rectangles, to report rectangle intersections and to compute the measure and contour of a set of rectangles. In all these cases the divide-and-conquer paradigm yields algorithms which match the performance of the best plane sweep algorithms.
In some cases, e.g. the contour problem, the algorithm based on the divide-and-conquer paradigm is conceptually simpler and computationally superior. The section is organized as follows. In 5.2.1. we illustrate the paradigm using the line segment intersection problem and in 5.2.2. we apply it to the measure and contour problem.

VIII. 5.2.1 The Line Segment Intersection Problem

Let S be a set of n horizontal and vertical line segments $L_1,\dots,L_n$.

The line segment intersection problem asks for the computation of all pairs of intersecting line segments. We have seen in section 4.1. (cf. exercise 23) that the set of s pairs of intersection can be computed in time O(n log n + s). We will now describe an alternative solution based on the divide-and-conquer paradigm.

Theorem 11: Let S be a set of n horizontal and vertical line segments. Then the s pairs of intersection can be computed in time O(n log n + s).

Proof: Let $S_H(S_V)$ be the set of horizontal (vertical) line segments in S. A horizontal line segment L is given as a triple $(x_1(L), x_2(L), y(L))$, a vertical line segment is given as $(x(L), y_1(L), y_2(L))$.

In order to simplify the exposition and to describe the basic idea more clearly we assume first that all x- and y-coordinates are distinct We will come back to the general problem at the end of the proof.

We apply the divide-and-conquer paradigm as follows. The divide step divides the plane (and more generally a vertical strip defined by two vertical lines) into two parts by means of a vertical dividing line. In the conquer step we deal with both subproblems and in the merge step we combine the answers. The speed of the method comes from the clever treatment of horizontal line segments. They are only handled in subproblems which "contain" exactly one endpoint of the line segment, and hence are handled at most O(log n) times if we divide the problem about equally at every step. Similarly, vertical line segments are only handled in those subproblems which contain it.

A frame $F = (f_1, f_2)$ is the region between vertical lines $x = f_1$ and $x = f_2$ with $f_1 < f_2$. Frames define subproblems of our intersection problem. The recursive algorithm INTERSECT (to be described) applied to a frame F does two things.

1) it reports all intersections between vertical line segments contained in the frame and horizontal line segments having at least one endpoint in the frame. Note however that if both endpoints are in the frame then the intersection is actually reported by a recursive call

2) it computes the sets VERT(F), LEFT(F) and RIGHT(F) to be used at higher levels of the calling hierarchy.

The set VERT(F) is a set of intervals. It contains the projections of all vertical line segments contained in F onto the y-axis. The sets LEFT(F) and RIGHT(F) are sets of points. The set LEFT(F) is the set of intersections of horizontal line segments having one endpoint in frame F with the left boundary of the frame. The set RIGHT(F) is defined symmetrically.

We are now ready to give a (very high level) description of procedure INTERSECT. In this description we use the word object to refer to either vertical line segments or a left or right endpoint of a horizontal line segment.
Procedure INTERSECT is called in the main program with a frame containing all objects.

```
(1)   Procedure INTERSECT (F,VERT,LEFT,RIGHT)
      -- F is input parameter and VERT,LEFT,RIGHT are
      -- output parameters.
(2)   if exactly one object is contained in frame F
(3)   then if the object is a vertical line segment L = (x,y1,y2)
(4)        then VERT ← {[y1,y2]}, LEFT ← RIGHT ← ∅
(5)        else VERT ← ∅ ;
(6)             if the object is a left endpoint of a horizontal
                   line segment L = (x1,x2,y)
(7)             then LEFT ← ∅ ; RIGHT ← {y}
(8)             else RIGHT ← ∅ ; LEFT ← {y}
(9)             fi
(10)       fi
(11)  else choose a vertical line x = f such that about half of the
           objects contained in frame F = (f1,f2) lie to the left of
           the line, let F1 = (f1,f) and F2 = (f,f2);
(12)       INTERSECT ((f1,f),VERT1,LEFT1,RIGHT1);
(13)       INTERSECT ((f,f2),VERT2,LEFT2,RIGHT2);
(14)       LR ← RIGHT1 ∩ LEFT2;
(15)       LEFT ← LEFT1 ∪ (LEFT2 - LR);
(16)       RIGHT ← (RIGHT1 - LR) ∪ RIGHT2 ;
(17)       VERT ← VERT1 ∪ VERT2 ;
(18)       report all intersections induced by RIGHT1 - LR and VERT2
           and by LEFT2 - LR and VERT1
(19)  fi
(20)  end
```

The correctness of this procedure is readily established. Note first that sets LEFT, RIGHT and VERT are computed correctly in all cases. This is clear for lines (3)-(10) and is easy to establish for lines (12)-(17). In line (14) we determine the set of horizontal line segments having one endpoint each in the two subframes of frame F. In lines (15) and (16) the sets LEFT and RIGHT are computed. Note that a horizontal line segment has one endpoint in F and intersects the left boundary of F if it either has one endpoint in F_1 and intersects the left boundary of F_1 or has one endpoint in F_2, intersects the left boundary of F_2 and does not have the other endpoint in F_1. Finally, the set VERT is certainly computed correctly in line (17).

It remains to argue that all intersections are reported correctly in line (18). We need to explain line (18) in more detail first. The set $RIGHT_1$-LR is the set of y-coordinates of left endpoints of horizontal line segments which have one endpoint in frame F_1 and intersect the right boundary of frame F. Thus these line segments extend completely through frame F_2 and therefore we can report an intersection with every vertical line segment in frame F_2 whose associated interval in $VERT_2$ contains the y-coordinate of the horizontal line segment. The intersections induced by RIGHT-LR and $VERT_2$ are hence all pairs (H,V) of horizontal line segment H and vertical line segment V such that the y-coordinate y(H) of H is contained in $RIGHT_1$-LR, the projection I(V) of V onto the y-axis is contained in $VERT_2$, and $y(H) \in I(V)$. The insertions induced by $LEFT_2$-LR and $VERT_1$ are defined similarly.

It is now clear that only actual intersections are reported in line (18). We will next show that all intersections are reported exactly once. Let H(V) be a horizontal (vertical) line segment and assume that H and V intersect. Consider a lowest node, say v, in the tree of recursive calls such that the frame, say F, associated with that recursive call contains V and exactly one endpoint of H. Then $L \cap H$ is not reported in any proper ancestor of v because the frames associated with the ancestors of v contain both endpoints of H. Also $L \cap H$ is not reported in any proper descendant of v because the frames associated with the descendants either do not contain v or contain no endpoint of H. Thus $L \cap H$ is reported at most once. Finally, $L \cap H$ is reported in node v because one of the subframes of F contains V, H extends completely through that subframe, and the other subframe contains an endpoint of H. This finishes the proof of correctness.

Let us turn to the analysis next. In order to support the divide step we sort the objects by x-coordinate and store the sorted sequence in an array. Then line (11) and the tests in lines (2), (3), and (6) take time O(1). The sets LEFT and RIGHT are realized as ordered (according to y-coordinate) linked lists and set VERT is also realized as a linked list. It contains the intervals in sorted order according to the bottom endpoint. It is now easy to see that lines (14)-(17) take time $O(\bar{n})$ where $\bar{n}$ is the number of objects to be handled. Also line (18) takes time $O(\bar{n} + \bar{s})$ where $\bar{s}$ is the number of intersections reported. In all four lines a simple list travesal algorithm (cf. section II.1.4) suffices. We conclude that the cost of a call of INTERSECT is $O(\bar{n} + \bar{s})$ where $\bar{n}$ is the number of objects in the frame and $\bar{s}$ is the number of intersections reported in line (18). Since every intersection is reported exactly once the sum of the $O(\bar{s})$-terms is O(s).
For the $O(\bar{n})$-terms we obtain the recursion

$$T(n) = 2T(n/2) + O(n)$$

which has solution T(n) = O(n log n). This proves the theorem for the case that all x- and y-coordinates are unique.

Multiple x-coordiantes are treated as follows. We again sort the objects according to x-coordinate. Also, for each x-coordinate we precompute the sets VERT,LEFT and RIGHT for the frame consisting of the degenerated rectangle defined by the x-coordinate. It is easy to see that all of this takes time O(n log n) by sorting.
The test in line (2) is changed to
(2') if all objects contained in the frame have the same x-coordinate.
Then lines (3) to (10) can be replaced by a look-up in the set of precomputed solutions. Line (11) is changed to
(11') Choose vertical line x = f where f is the median of the multi-set of x-coordinates of the objects contained in frame F
We then split the objects into three parts: the objects to the left of (on, to the right of) the dividing line. To the objects to the left (right) of the dividing line we apply the algorithm recursively, the objects on the dividing line are handled by a look-up in the set of precomputed solutions. It is now easy to modify lines (14)-(18) to the new situation such that they still operate in time $O(\bar{n} + \bar{s})$.
Thus we still have the same recursion for the running time and hence the running time is O(n log n + s).

The extension to multiple y-coordinates is now very simple. We only have to treat sets LEFT,RIGHT, and VERT as multisets. More precisely, with every element of set LEFT (the other two sets are treated similarly) we associate an ordered list of all objects with that y-coordinate. The ordering is arbitrary, but must be uniform (e.g. we might order horizontal line segments according to some arbitrary but fixed linear ordering of S_H). Then the intersection process in line (14) is still a simple merging process and takes time $O(\bar{n})$. This shows that multiple y-coordinates can also be handled within the O(n log n + s) bound and finishes the proof.

□

A simple variant of the algorithm above can also be used to solve the inclusion problem of points in rectangles and of the intersection problem for set of rectangles (cf. exercise 41 and 42).

VIII. 5.2.2 The Measure and Contour Problems

Let $R_1,\ldots,R_n$ be a list of n iso-oriented rectangles in $\mathbb{R}^2$. The measure problem is the task of computing the area of the union $R_1 \cup \ldots \cup R_n$ of the rectangles. We developed an O(n log n) plane sweep algorithm for this problem in section 5.1.3. The contour problem is also a property of the union of the rectangles. It asks for the computation of the contour, i.e. the boundary between covered and uncovered area, of $R_1 \cup \ldots \cup R_n$. The following example shows a set of rectangles and its contour.

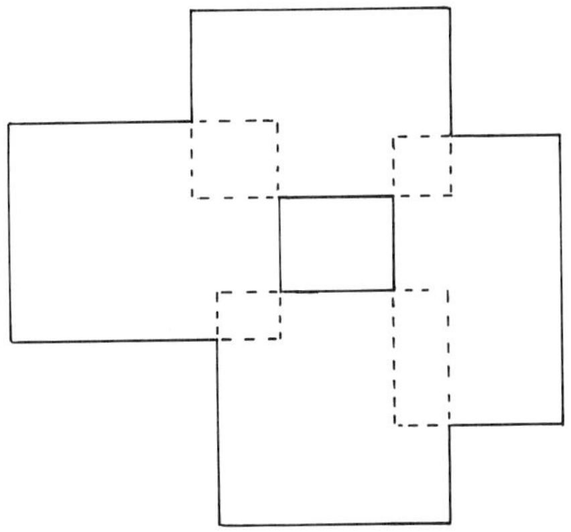

The main goal of this section is to develop an O(n log n + p) algorithm for the contour problem based on the divide-and-conquer paradigm. Here p is the number of straight line segments in the contour. It is also possible to achieve this optimal running time by a plane sweep algorithm which is however conceptually more difficult and computationally inferior.

The basic structure of the divide-and-conquer algorithm is again a hierarchical decomposition of the plane into frames. If $F = (f_1, f_2)$ is a frame, let RECT(F) be the set of rectangles having at least one vertical edge within frame F. We use V to denote the set of vertical edges of the rectangles. We want to compute two types of information about RECT(F): the first type, sets P(F) and STRIPES(F), describes the contour of the rectangles in RECT(F) within frame F, the second type, sets L(F) and R(F), supports the merge step. Let us describe the four sets in more detail: P(F) is the ordered set of y-coordinates of the vertices of the rectangles in RECT(F). Let $P(F) = \{y_1 < y_2 < \dots < y_m\}$, $m \le 2n$. The horizontal lines $y = y_i$, $1 \le i \le m$, divide frame F into a sequence of horizontal stripes. The i-th stripe $S_i(F)$ is defined by horizontal lines $y = y_i$ and $y = y_{i+1}$, $1 \le i < m$. For each such stripe we store an ordered list $LIST_i = LIST(S_i(F))$ of intervals $[x_1^i, x_2^i], \dots, [x_{2k-1}^i, x_{2k}^i]$ such that

1) $f_1 = x_0^i \le x_1^i \le x_2^i \le \dots \le x_{2k}^i \le x_{2k+1}^i = f_2$

2) the area (within the i-th stripe $S_i(F)$) between vertical lines $x = x_{2j-1}^i$ and $x = x_{2j}^i$ is covered, $1 \le j \le k$, and the area between vertical lines $x = x_{2j}^i$ and $x = x_{2j+1}^i$ is uncovered, $0 \le j \le k$, by the rectangles in RECT(F).

In other words

$$(\cup\{R; R \in RECT(F)\}) \cap ([f_1, f_2] \times [y_i, y_{i+1}])$$
$$= \bigcup_{j=1}^{k} ([x_{2j-1}^i, x_{2j}^i] \times [y_i, y_{i+1}])$$

STRIPES(F) is now the sequence $(LIST_1, LIST_2, \dots, LIST_{m-1})$.
The sets L(F) and R(F) are sets of intervals. L(F) is the set of intervals obtained by intersecting the rectangles in RECT(F) with the left boundary of frame F; R(F) is defined symmetrically. In other words, L(F) is the set of projections onto the y-axis of the right boundaries of those rectangles in RECT(F) which have their left boundary outside F.

The following diagram illustrates these definitions.

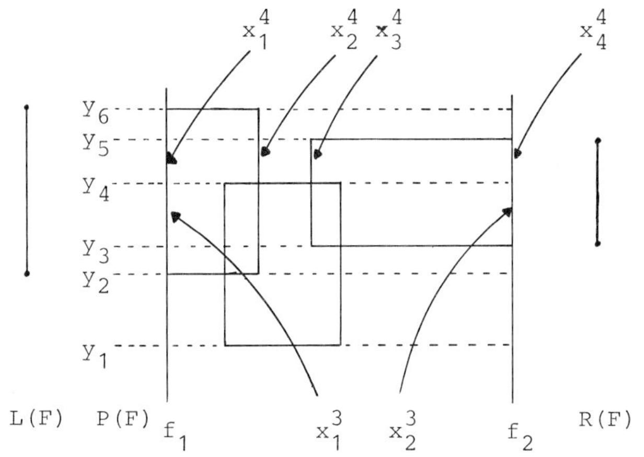

We will show below that the measure and the contour problem are easily solved once a suitable representation of STRIPES(F) has been computed for a frame F containing all rectangles. Before doing so we give a recursive procedure MC (for measure and contour) which given a frame F computes sets P(F), STRIPES(F), L(F) and R(F). We assume for simplicity that vertices of different rectangles have different x- and y-coordinates. The modifications required for the general case are as described in the preceding section and are left for the reader.

```
(1)   proc  MC(F,P,STRIPES,L,R)
(2)   if  F = (f1,f2) contains exactly one vertical edge, say
          ℓ = (x,y1,y2,s), where s ∈ {left,right}
(3)   then  P ← {y1,y2}
(4)         if  s = left
(5)         then  R ← {[y1,y2]}; L ← ∅ ; LIST1 ← (x,f2)
(6)         else  L ← {[y1,y2]} ; R ← ∅ ; LIST1 ← (f1,x);
(7)   else  choose a vertical line x = f which divides the objects in
            frame F in about equal parts and let F1 = (f1,f) and
            F2 = (f,f2);
(9)         MC(F1,P1,STRIPES1,L1,R1);
(10)        MC(F2,P2,STRIPES2,L2,R2);
(11)        P ← P1 ∪ P2 ;
(12)        LR ← R1 ∩ L2 ;
(13)        L ← L1 ∪ (L2 - LR);
```

```
(14)      R ← R2 ∪ (R1 - LR);
(15)      refine STRIPES1 according to P;
(16)      simplify STRIPES1 according to L2 - LR;
(17)      refine STRIPES2 according to P;
(18)      simplify STRIPES2 according to R1 - LR;
(19)      unite STRIPES1 and STRIPES2 to form STRIPES;
(20)      end
```

Lines (15) to (18) need some explanation. Note that in line (11) we combine partitions P_1 and P_2 to form the combined partition $P = \{y_1,\dots,y_m\}$, cf. the diagram below. In

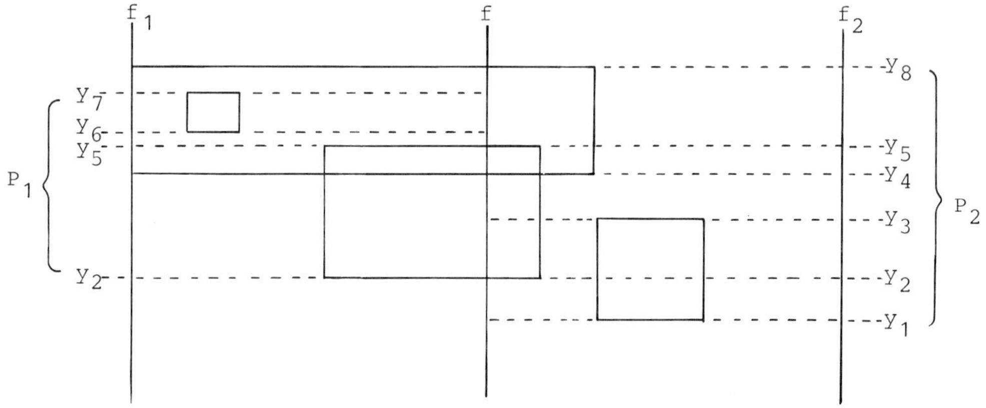

this diagram we have $P = \{y_1,\dots,y_8\}$, $P_1 = \{y_2,y_5,y_6,y_7\}$ and $P_2 = \{y_1,y_2,y_3,y_4,y_5,y_8\}$. In lines (15) and (17) we refine $STRIPES_1$ and $STRIPES_2$ according to the new partition. In our example, the stripe of F_2 between y_5 and y_8 is refined into three substripes: y_5 to y_6, y_6 to y_7, and y_7 to y_8. We obtain the lists LIST for these substripes by copying the list for the stripes between y_5 and y_8. In the actual implementation, the copy operation will be a pointer operation.

In lines (16) and (18) we simplify sets $STRIPES_1$ and $STRIPES_2$. Consider any interval, say $[y_i,y_j]$ in L_2 - LR. It represents a rectangle which extends all the way through frame F_1. We can therefore replace $LIST(S_h(F_1))$ of $STRIPES_1$, $i \le h \le j$, describing the stripe between y_h and y_{h+1}, by the trivial list (f_1,f) which indicates that the entire strip is covered. Set $STRIPES_2$ is simplified in an analogous way based on the intervals in R_1 - LR. In our example, we have $L_2 = \{[y_2,y_5],[y_4,y_8]\}$ and $LR = \{[y_2,y_5]\}$. We simplify $STRIPES_1$ by changing the lists of stripes $S_4(F_1),S_5(F_1),S_6(F_1),S_7(F_1)$ to (f_1,f).

Finally, in line (19) we form STRIPES from $STRIPES_1$ and $STRIPES_2$ by concatenating $LIST(S_i(F_1))$ and $LIST(S_i(F_2))$ to form $LIST(S_i(F))$, $1 \le i < m$, and combining the right interval of $LIST(S_i(F_1))$ and the left interval of $LIST(S_i(F_2))$ if both extend to the dividing line $x = f$.

With these definitions of line (15) to (19) it is easy to prove correctness of procedure MC. We leave the details to the reader.

It remains to analyse the running time. We represent sets P(F), L(F), and R(F) by ordered linked lists. P(F) is ordered according to y-coordinate and the sets L(F) and R(F) are ordered according to the bottom endpoint of the intervals. Then lines (11) to (14) take time $O(\bar{n})$ where $\bar{n}$ is the number of objects in frame F. For the representation of STRIPES we distinguish the measure and the contour problem. We treat the measure problem first because it is simpler.

For the measure problem a very simple data structure suffices. STRIPES is an ordered linear list of reals. If $P = \{y_1 < y_2 < \ldots < y_m\}$, then the i-th element of the list, $1 \le i \le m$, is the total length of the intervals in $LIST(S_i(F))$. No other information about $LIST(S_i(F))$ is maintained. It is now easy to see that lines (15) to (19) take time $O(\bar{n})$ where $\bar{n}$ is the number of objects in frame F.

<u>Theorem 12:</u> The measure problem for a set of n iso-oriented rectangles can be solved in time $O(n\log n)$ and space $O(n)$.

<u>Proof:</u> The discussion above implies that the running time T(n) of procedure MC satisfies the recurrence

$$T(1) = O(1)$$
$$T(n) = 2T(n/2) + O(n).$$

Thus $T(n) = O(n\log n)$. Let F be a frame containing all rectangles and apply procedure MC to frame F. The application yields P(F) and STRIPES(F) from which one can clearly compute the area of the union of the rectangles in time O(n). This proves the time bound.

The space bound can be seen as follows. Note first that the size of the representation of P(F), L(F), R(F), and STRIPE(F) is $O(\bar{n})$ where $\bar{n}$ is the number of objects in frame F. Note next that at any point of time there are at most log n incarnations of procedure MC, and that the number of objects in the associated frames form a geometric progression. Combining both observations we obtain the space bound. □

For the contour problem we have to work slightly harder. In this case we represent STRIPES(F) as a linked list of pointers. If P(F) = $\{y_1 < y_2 < \ldots < y_m\}$ then the i-th pointer points to the root of a search tree for the endpoints of the intervals in LIST(S_i(F)), $1 \le i \le m$. Again, we can perform lines (15) to (19) in time $O(\bar{n})$ where $\bar{n}$ is the number of objects in frame F. In lines (15) and (17) we extend the list of pointers and perform the copy-operations by setting pointers appropriately. Thus trees may share subtrees.
In lines (16) to (18) we redirect some pointers to trivial trees with only two leaves. The set of pointers to be redirected is easily found in time $O(\bar{n})$ by going through orered lists P(F) and L_2 - LR (R_1 - LR) in parallel. Finally, in line (19) we concatenate appropriate lists by creating new root nodes and defining the two son-pointers appropriately.

Theorem 13: The contour problem for a set of n iso-oriented rectangles can be solved in time and space O(nlog n).

Proof: The discussion above implies that the running time of procedure MC is O(nlog n) since the recurrence $T(n) = 2T(n/2) + O(n)$ can again be used.
We apply procedure MC as follows. We first sort all rectangle vertices by x- and y-coordinates and then replace the coordinates by integers 1,...,2n in a consistent way. This replacement does not change the topology of the contour but allows us to use bucket sort (cf. section II.2.1) in latter stages of the algorithm. Let F be a frame which encloses all rectangles, F = (0,2n+1) will do. Then MC applied to F yields (P(F) and STRIPES(F) in time O(nlog n). It remains to describe how to obtain the contour from P(F) and STRIPES(F).

The contour of a union of iso-oriented rectangles is a collection of contour-cycles. Each contour-cycle is a sequence of alternating horizontal and vertical contour-pieces. Every contour-piece is a fragment of an edge of one of the rectangles.
We show how to find the horizontal contour pieces from P(F) and STRIPES(F) in time O(nlog n + p) where p is their number. The vertical contour-pieces can then be found by sorting the endpoints of horizontal contour-pieces and the vertical rectangle edges by x-coordinate. Note

that time $O(n + p)$ suffices for the sorting step since bucket sort can be used. Recall that the x-coordinates are the integers $1,\ldots,2n$. Finally, the contour-cycles can be constructed from the contour-pieces by another application of bucket sort to their endpoints. Again, time $O(n + p)$ suffices.

The horizontal contour-pieces can be found as follows. Let $L = (x_1,x_2,y)$ be any horizontal rectangle edge.; x_1,x_2, and y are integers. We show how to find the k contour-pieces which are fragments of L in time $O(\log n + k)$. Assume that L is a bottom side of a rectangle; the other case being symmetric. Consider

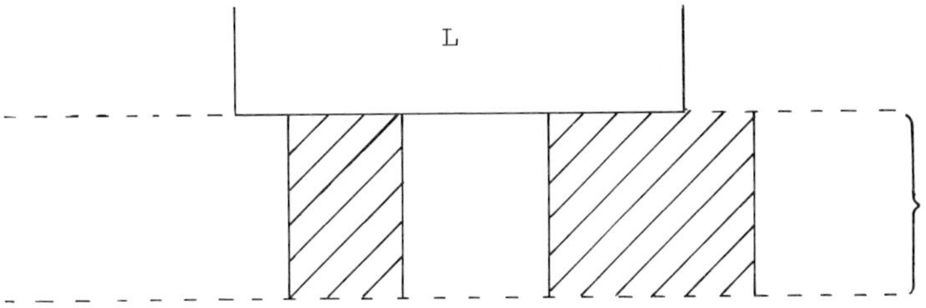

stripe $S_{y-1}(F)$ and let LIST = LIST($S_{y-1}(F)$). Recall that LIST is an ordered list of intervals and that LIST is realized as a search tree for the endpoints of the intervals. Also note that the tree has depth $O(\log n)$ since the height of the tree grows by one in every level of the recursion. In time $O(\log n)$ we can therefore find the first endpoint in LIST with x-coordinate $\geq x_1$; a simple linear search will then identify the k contour-pieces which are fragments of L in time $O(k)$. This finishes the proof of the time bound. The space bound follows immediately from the time bound. □

VIII. 5.3. Intersection Problems in Higher-Dimensional Space

In this section we will study intersection problems in higher-dimensional space. Let $S = \{R_1,\ldots,R_n\}$ be a set of iso-oriented objects in $\mathbb{R}^d$, i.e. each R_i is the cartesian product of d intervals one for each coordinate, $R_i = \prod_{j=1}^{d} [\ell_{ij}, r_{ij}]$. We allow that intervals degenerate to a single point.

We study the following two problems.

1) Report all pairs R_i, R_j with $R_i \cap R_j \neq \emptyset$. This problem was solved in two dimensions in time $O(n\log n + k)$ in sections 5.1.1 and 5.1.2. Here k is the number of intersecing pairs. We refer to this problem as all pair intersection problem.

2) Given iso-oriented query object $Q = \prod_{j=1}^{d} [\ell_j, r_j]$ report all $R_i \in S$ with $Q \cap R_i \neq \emptyset$. This problem comes in two versions: In the static version, set S is fixed and in the dymamic version, we also allow for insertions and deletions. We refer to this problem as the (static or dynamic) searching problem.

This section is organized as follows. We will first show how to solve the static searching problem by means of static range and segment trees, then extend the solution to the dynamic case by using the dynamic version of the trees. The all pair intersecting problem is finally solved by using a solution to the searching problem in a sweep algorithm. A solution to the searching problem can be based of the following

simple observations. For $R_i = \prod_{j=1}^{d} [\ell_{ij}, r_{ij}]$ we use $R_i' = \prod_{j=1}^{d-1} [\ell_{ij}, r_{ij}]$ to denote the projection onto the first d-1 dimensions.

<u>Lemma 14:</u> a) $R_i \cap Q \neq \emptyset$ iff $[\ell_{id}, r_{id}] \cap [\ell_d, r_d] \neq \emptyset$ and $R_i' \cap Q' \neq \emptyset$

b) $[\ell_{id}, r_{id}] \cap [\ell_d, r_d] \neq \emptyset$ iff either $\ell_{id} \in [\ell_d, r_d]$ or $\ell_d \in [\ell_{id}, r_{id}]$.

<u>Proof:</u> a) The direction from left to right is obvious. For the other direction, we only have to observe that $x_d \in [\ell_{id}, r_{id}] \cap [\ell_d, r_d]$ and $x' \in R_i' \cap Q'$ implies $x = (x', x_d) \in R_i \cap Q$.

b) obvious.

□

Lemma 14 suggests a recursive solution for the searching problem. For each fixed dimension we need to provide data structures which allow us to find all points contained in a query interval (range trees) and to find all intervals containing a query point (segment trees). The details are as follows.

Suppose first that d = 1. We have two trees. The first tree is a priority search tree (cf. section 5.1.2) and stores the n pairs (= points in $\mathbb{R}^2$) (ℓ_{id}, r_{id}), $1 \le i \le n$. It allows us to find all intervals containing a query point ℓ_d, i.e. $\ell_{id} \le \ell_d \le r_{id}$, in time O(log n + k) where k is the number of points reported. Furthermore, the tree uses space O(n) and can be constructed in time O(nlog n). The second tree is a balanced search tree for the left endpoints ℓ_{id}, $1 \le i \le n$, of the intervals. It uses space O(n), can be constructed in time O(nlog n), and allows us to find the k endpoints contained in query interval $[\ell_d, r_d]$ in time O(log n + k). We conclude that for d = 1 the static and dynamic searching problem has a solution with query time O(log n + k), prepocessing time O(nlog n) and space requirement O(n).

For d > 1 we have to work slightly harder. Again, we have two trees. The first tree is a segment tree for the intervals $[r_{id}, \ell_{id}]$, $1 \le i \le n$. For each node v of the segment tree we organize its node list NL(v) as a data structure, which solves the (d-1)-dimensional searching problem. Given query object $Q = \prod_{j=1}^{d} [\ell_j, r_j]$ this augmented segment tree allows us to find all R_i with $Q' \cap R_i' \neq \emptyset$ and $\ell_d \in [\ell_{id}, r_{id}]$ as follows. We search for ℓ_d in the segment tree. Then the node lists of the nodes of the path of search contain all objects R_i with $\ell_d \in [\ell_{id}, r_{id}]$. We use the secondary structures associated with those nodes, i.e. the data structures for the (d-1)-dimensional searching problems, to find all R_i' with $Q' \cap R_i' \neq \emptyset$.

Assume inductively that the search time in the (d-1)-dimensional structure is $T(n,d-1) = O(\log n)^{d-1} + k)$ where k is the size of the answer. This is true for d = 2. Then the search time in the d-dimensional structure is $T(n,d) = O(\log n \cdot (\log n)^{d-1} + k) = O(\log n)^d + k)$ since the (d-1)-dimensional solution has to be used at log n different nodes. Similarly, if the prepocessing time for the (d-1)-dimensional solution is $P(n,d-1) = O(n(\log n)^{d-1})$, then the preprocessing time for the d-dimensional solution is $O(n(\log n)^d)$. This can be seen as follows. Let n(v), where v is a node of the segment tree, be the cardinality of NL(v). Then $\Sigma\{n(v);\ v \text{ is a node}\} = O(n\log n)$ since every interval is split into at most O(log n) pieces and time $O(n(v)(\log n)^{d-1})$ is spent to construct the secondary structure for node v. Thus time $O(n(\log n)^d)$ is spent to construct all secondary structures. Finally, an identical argument shows that the space requirement of the d-dimensional solution is $O(n(\log n)^{d-1})$.

The second tree is an augmented range tree for the left endpoints ℓ_{id}, $1 \le i \le n$, of the intervals in the d-th dimension. Recall (cf. section VII.2.2) that in a range tree every point is stored in the node lists of all nodes along a path through the tree, i.e. every point is stored in $O(\log n)$ node lists. Let v be a node of the range tree. We organize the node list of node v as a (d-1)-dimensional search structure for those objects which have their endpoint ℓ_{id} stored in the node list. An argument similar to the one above shows that the resulting data structure has query time $O((\log n)^d + k)$ preprocessing time $O(n(\log n)^d)$ and space requirement $O(n(\log n)^{d-1})$. We summarize in:

Theorem 14: The static searching problem for iso-oriented objects in d-dimensional space can be solved in query time $O((\log n)^d + k)$, preprocessing time $O(n(\log n)^d)$, and space $O(n(\log n)^{d-1})$. Here k is the number of objects intersecting the query object.

Proof: By the discussion above. □

The extension to the dynamic version is not very difficult. We only have to replace static range and segment trees by their dynamic counter part. We have:

Theorem 15: The dynamic searching problem in d-dimensional space can be solved in query time $O((\log n)^d + k)$, insertion and deletion time $O((\log n)^d)$ and space $O(n(\log n)^{d-1})$. The time bounds for insertions and deletions are amortized.

Proof: The bound on query time and space is derived as in theorem 14. The bounds on insertion and deletion time are derived in exactly the same way as the respective bounds for range trees (with slack parameter 1) in lemma 4 of section VII.2.2. □

We turn now to the all pair intersection problem. We use the sweep paradigm, i.e. we sweep a (d-1)-dimensional hyperplane through $\mathbb{R}^d$. The sweep direction is the d-th coordinate axis, i.e. the sweep hyperplane is perpendicular to the d-th coordinate axis. We store the (d-1)-dimensional projections R_i' of all objects R_i with intersect the sweep hyperplane in a data structure which solves the (d-1)-dimensional searching problem. Object R_i is added to the data structure at transition point ℓ_{id} and deleted at transition point r_{id}. Thus 2n insertions and deletions with a total cost of $O(n(\log n)^{d-1})$ are required. Also, whenever an object R_i is added to the data structure we query the data sturcture and report all intersected objects. The total cost of all queries is $O(n(\log n)^{d-1})$. We summarize in

Theorem 16: The all pair intersection problem for n iso-oriented objects in $\mathbb{R}^d$, $d \geq 2$, can be solved in time $O(n(\log n)^{d-1} + k)$ and space $O(n(\log n)^{d-2})$.

Proof: Immediate from theorem 15 and the discussion above. □

VIII. 6. Geometric Transforms

Transformations (reductions) play an important role in computational geometry and in algorithm design in general. They allow us to classify problems according to their level of complexity and thus give us a more structured view of the area and also reduce the number of distinct problems by grouping them into classes. In more concrete terms, a transformation of problem A into problem B allows us to use an algorithm for B to solve A and allows us to transfer a lower bound on the complexity of A to a lower bound on the complexity of B. We used transformations extensively in this book for both purposes. Let us mention just a few situations. Most of chapter VI on NP-completeness is centered around the notion of a reduction, in chapter V we related the complexity of general path problems and matrix multiplication over semi-rings and at various places (e.g. in section 2 of convex hulls) we derived $\Omega(n\log n)$ lower bounds by reducing the sorting problem to a problem at hand.

Among the many geometric transforms we discuss only two: duality and inversion. The duality transform in $\mathbb{R}^d$ maps points into hyperplanes and hyperplanes into points. It can thus be used to transform problems about points into problems about hyperplanes and conversely to transform problems about hyperplanes into problems about points. We will have the opportunity to use both directions successfully in the sequel.

The duality transform in $\mathbb{R}^3$ ($\mathbb{R}^2$) transforms certain spheres (circles) into planes (lines) and vice versa. It can be successfully used to transform problems about circles and spheres into problems about lines and planes. One possible application of this transformation is the construction of Voronoi diagrams; note that vertices of the diagrams are centers of circles passing through at least three points of the underlying set. Thus the problem of constructing Voronoi diagrams can be viewed as a problem about circles.

VIII. 6.1 Duality

The duality transform in $\mathbb{R}^d$ relates hyperplanes and points and more generally k-dimensional subspaces with (d-k)-dimensional subspaces.

Let h be a non-vertical hyperplane in $\mathbb{R}^d$, i.e. h intersects the d-th coordinate axis in a unique and finite point. Let the points on h with cartesian coordinates $(x_1,\dots,x_d)$ satisfy the equation $x_d = p_1x_1 + p_2x_2 + \dots + p_{d-1}\,x_{d-1} + p_d$. Then the dual D(h) of hyperplane h is the point $p = (p_1,p_2,\dots,p_d)$ in $\mathbb{R}^d$. Conversely, $p = (p_1,\dots,p_d)$ is a point in $\mathbb{R}^d$ then h = D(p) is the hyperplane defined by the equation $x_d = -p_1x_1 - \dots - p_{d-1}\,x_d + p_d$.

An important property of the duality transform is the preservation of incidence and more generally of vertical distances, i.e. distances in the direction of the d-th coordinate axis. Let h be a hyperplane given by the equation $x_d = q_1x_1 + \dots + q_{d-1}\,x_{d-1} + q_d$ and let $p = (p_1,\dots,p_d)$ be a point. Then the vertical distance vd(h,p) is defined by

$$vd(h,p) = p_d - (q_1p_1 + \dots + q_{d-1}\,p_{d-1} + q_d)$$

We will also say that p lies above (on,below) h if vd(h,p) > (=,<) 0. We have

Lemma 1: Let h be a hyperplane and p be a point. Then vd(h,p) = - vd(D(p),D(h)). In particular, p lies on h iff D(h) lies on D(p).

Proof: Let $p = (p_1,\dots,p_d)$ and let h be given by the equation $x_d = q_1x_1 + \dots + q_{d-1}\,x_{d-1} + q_d$. Then hyperplane D(p) is defined by the equation $x_d = -p_1x_1 - \dots -p_{d-1}\,x_{d-1} + p_d$. Hence

$$\begin{aligned} vd(D(p),D(h)) &= q_d - (-\,p_1q_1 - \dots - p_{d-1}\,q_{d-1} + p_d) \\ &= -\,(p_d - (p_1q_1 + \dots + p_{d-1}\,q_{d-1} + q_d) \\ &= -\,vd(h,p). \end{aligned}$$

In particular, $vd(h,p) = 0$ iff $vd(D(p),D(h)) = 0$. □

We want to mention one more fact about the duality transform. For simplicity we restrict the discussion to $d = 3$. For p_1, p_2 distinct points in $\mathbb{R}^3$ let $L(p_1,p_2)$ be the line through p_1 and p_2. We have

Lemma 2: Let p_1, p_2 be points and let h_1, h_2 be planes in $\mathbb{R}^3$ with $L(p_1,p_2) = h_1 \cap h_2$. Then $D(p_1) \cap D(p_2) = L(D(h_1),D(h_2))$.

Proof: Since $p_1 \neq p_2$ and $h_1 \neq h_2$ we have $D(p_1) \neq D(p_2)$ and $D(h_1) \neq D(h_2)$. Thus $D(p_1) \cap D(p_2)$ and $L(D(h_1),D(h_2))$ are both lines. Furthermore, from $p_i \in h_j$ we conclude $D(h_j) \in D(p_i)$, $1 \le i,j \le 2$, by lemma 1, and hence the two lines agree. □

We are now ready for our first application of duality: the intersection of halfspaces. We will use duality to transform the halfspaces or rather the defining hyperplanes into points. The intersection problem is then transformed into two convex hull problems.

Let h_i, $1 \le i \le n$, be a hyperplane. We use h_i^+ (h_i^-) to denote the set of points which are on or above (on or below) h_i. The sets h_i^+ and h_i^- are halfspaces. Let m be an integer with $1 \le m \le n$. Our goal is to compute $S = \bigcap_{i=1} h_i^+ \cap \bigcap_{i=m+1}^{n} h_i^-$. We discussed this problem for $\mathbb{R}^2$ previously in exercise 6. In that exercise an $O(n\log n)$ divide-and-conquer algorithm is derived which uses the linear time intersection algorithm (cf. section 1) for convex polygons in the merge step. The analogous algorithm in $\mathbb{R}^3$ based on the $O(n\log n)$ algorithm for intersecting convex polyhedra (cf. section 4.3) has running time $O(n(\log n)^2)$. Duality will give us an $O(n\log n)$ algorithm in $\mathbb{R}^3$. From now on we restrict the discussion to $\mathbb{R}^3$.

Let $S^+ = \bigcap_{i=1}^{m} h_i^-$ and $S^- = \bigcap_{i=m+1}^{n} h_i^-$. In view of the $O(n\log n)$ algorithm for computing $S = S^+ \cap S^-$ from S^+ and S^- it suffices to show how to compute S in time $O(m\log m)$. Our algorithm is based on the following observation. The set S^+ is a convex polyhedron whose faces lie on some of the planes h_i, $1 \le i \le m$. We call plane h_i redundant (non-redundant) if there is no face (is a face) of S^+ which is contained in h_i. We will use duality to compute the non-redundant planes. Knowledge of the non-redundant planes will then allow us to compute S fairly easily.

So let us assume that plane h_a is redundant. Then $S^+ \cap h_a$ is either empty, a vertex of S^+ , or an edge of S^+ . In either case, let v be a vertex of S^+ which is closest to h_a. Then there are planes h_j, h_k, h_ℓ such that $v = h_j \cap h_k \cap h_\ell$ and $h_j^+ \cap h_k^+ \cap h_\ell^+ = h_j^+ \cap h_k^+ \cap h_\ell^+ \cap h_a^+$, i.e. planes h_j, h_k, h_ℓ witness the redundancy of h_a. Consider the duals $p_i = D(h_i)$, $1 \le i \le m$, of the planes. Then v lies on or above h_a and hence $D(h_a)$ lies on or below $D(v)$. Next observe that $D(v)$ is a plane which contains and hence is determined by points $D(h_j), D(h_k), D(h_\ell)$. This observation suggests the following lemma.

Lemma 3: h_a is redundant iff $D(h_a)$ is not a vertex of the upper convex hull of point set $\{D(h_i);\ 1 \le i \le m\}$. The upper convex hull of a point set consists of those faces (and incident edges and vertices) of the hull which have all points in the set on or below the supporting plane.

Proof: " ⇒": We have argued above that if h_a is redundant then there are planes h_j, h_k, h_ℓ such that $D(h_a)$ lies on or below the plane P determined by points $D(h_j)$, $D(h_k)$, $D(h_\ell)$. It remains to show that the projection of p_a into the xy-plane lies the triangle determined by the projections of points p_j, p_k, and p_ℓ. Let h_o be a plane which touches S^+ in vertex v and is parallel to plane h_a. Then $p_o = D(h_o)$ lies in plane P and lies exactly above point p_a. It therefore suffices to show that p_o lies inside the triangle determined by points p_j, p_k and p_ℓ.

The normal vector $\vec{q}_o = (q_1^o, \ldots, q_{d-1}^o, -1)$ of plane h_o lies in the cone defined by the normal vectors $\vec{q}_j = (q_1^j, \ldots, q_{d-1}^j, -1)$, $\vec{q}_k, \vec{q}_\ell$ of planes h_j, h_k, h_ℓ and hence $\vec{q} = \alpha\vec{q}_j + \beta\vec{q}_k + \gamma\vec{q}_\ell$ with $\alpha \ge 0$, $\beta \ge 0$, $\gamma \ge 0$ and $\alpha + \beta + \gamma = 1$. Also plane q_i, $i \in \{0, j, k, \ell\}$ is given by equation $x_d = q_1^i x_1 + \ldots + q_{d-1}^i x_{d-1} + c$ for some constant c. Hence $p_i = (q_1^i, \ldots, q_{d-1}^i, c)$ and therefore $p_o = \alpha p_i + \beta p_j + \gamma p_\ell$. This shows that p_o lies inside the triangle defined by points p_i, p_j and p_ℓ.
" ⇐ ". Suppose that $D(h_a)$ is not a vertex of the upper convex hull. Then there are vertices p_i, p_j, p_k of the upper convex hull such that $p_a = D(h_a)$ lies on or below the triangle with vertices p_i, p_j, p_k. By an argument similar to the one used in the only if part one can show that planes h_i, h_j, and h_k witness the redundancy of h_a. □

Lemma 2 leads to the following algorithm for computing S^+.
1) Compute $p_i = D(h_i)$, $1 \le i \le m$, and determine the upper convex hull of point set $p_i;\{1 \le i \le m\}$.
2) Use duality to obtain S^+ from the upper convex hull.

The computation of point set $p_i;\{1 \le i \le m\}$ takes time $O(n)$. The (upper) convex hull of the point set can be determined in time $O(m\log m)$ by exercise 13.
It remains to describe step 2) in more detail. Let f be a face of the upper convex hull and let h be a plane supporting f. Then $D^{-1}(h)$ is a vertex of S^+ by the proof of lemma 3. Also, if e is an edge of the upper convex hull separating faces f_1 and f_2 (supported by planes h_1,h_2) then $L(D^{-1}(h_1),D^{-1}(h_2))$ is a line which supports the edge of connecting vertices $D^{-1}(h_1)$ and $D^{-1}(h_2)$ of S^+ . (This is a consequence of lemma 2). We conclude that the structure of the upper convex hull gives us complete knowledge about S^+ and hence S^+ can be computed in time $O(m)$ from the upper convex hull.

<u>Theorem 1:</u> The intersection of a set of n halfspaces in $\mathbb{R}^3$ can be computed in time $O(n\log n)$.

<u>Proof:</u> By the preceding discussion. □

Our second example concerns problems about point sets in $\mathbb{R}^2$. We will use duality to transform them into problems about sets of lines which we will then be able to solve. Let $S = \{p_i;\ 1 \le i \le n\}$ be a set of points in $\mathbb{R}^2$. We consider the following two problems:

a) Decide whether any three of the points are collinear.
b) Compute the smallest area triangle which has vertices in S.

Note that the first problem is a special case of the second; it is tantamount to deciding whether the minimum area triangle has area 0. We derive an $O(n^2)$ algorithm for the first problem based on duality and then extend the algorithm to also solve the second problem.

Let $h_i = D(p_i)$ be the dual of point p_i; $1 \le i \le n$. Since duality preserves incidence we conclude that there are three collinear points in S iff there are three lines in set $H = \{h_i;\ 1 \le i \le n\}$ which have a common point. We decide the latter question by explicitely constructing the planar subdivision which is induced by the lines in H.

We construct the planar subdivision iteratively. Let SD_i be the planar subdivision which is induced by lines $H_i := \{h_1,\dots,h_i\}$. Then SD_1 has only two faces, one edge and no vertex and hence can clearly be constructed in time $O(1)$. We show how to obtain SD_i from SD_{i-1} in time $O(i)$.

Let us recall the representation of planar subdivisions. For each vertex we have the set of incident edges in clockwise order and for each face we have its boundary edges in clockwise order and for each edge we have pointers to its endpoints and the two adjacent faces. In addition to that we assume that for each line h_j we have the list of vertices and edges of the planar subdivision which lie on h_j. Finally, we assume that the lines are sorted by slope.

Suppose now that we have SD_{i-1} available and want to construct SD_i. In the diagram below h_i is shown as a horizontal line. If all lines in H_{i-1} are parallel to h_i then we can clearly construct SD_i in time $O(i)$

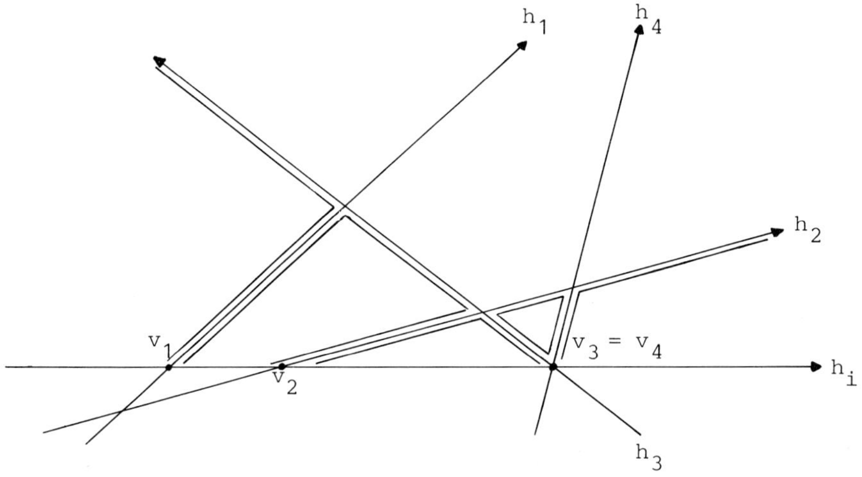

from SD_{i-1}. So let us assume that h_j, $j < i$, and h_i are not parallel. We compute $v_j := h_i \cap h_j$ and locate v_j in the planar subdivision by a linear search through the fragments of line h_j. This takes clearly time $O(i)$.

We locate the other points $v_k := h_i \cap h_k$, $1 \le k < i$, as follows. Line h_i

enters two faces of SD_{i-1}, say f and f', from v_j. We find the points where h_i leaves these faces by a linear search along the boundary of these faces. We make sure that we always follow that part of the boundary which is <u>above</u> h_i. In this way we locate two more points of the intersection. From these points we continue the construction in an analogous way. Note that faces above h_i which touch only in a single point are traversed completely. In the diagram above we have indicated the edges visited in this search by a double line. Let m_i be the number of edges visited in this search. Then SD_i can clearly be constructed in time $O(m_i)$ from SD_{i-1}. We have

<u>Lemma 4:</u> $m_i \le 5i$

<u>Proof:</u> Let F be the set of faces of SD_i (not SD_{i-1}!) which lie above line h_i and have a fragment of h_i on their boundary. Then m_i is the total number of edges bounding the faces in F. Let E be the multi-set of edges which bound a face in F. We partition E into three disjoint sets. In order to simplify notation and language we assume w.l.o.g. that h_i is horizontal and that all lines h_j, $j < i$, are oriented in the upward direction. It then makes sense to talk about the interior angle between lines h_j and h_i. It is always between 0 and π .

Let E_1 be the multi-set of those edges in E which have at least one endpoint on line h_i and let E_2 be the remaining set of edges. Since every face in F contributes at most three edges to E_1 (one having both endpoints on h_i and two having one endpoint on h_i) and since $|F| = i$ we conclude $|E_1| \le 3i$. It remains to count the edges in E_2. For this purpose, we partition the edges in E_2 into two groups E_ℓ and E_r. Let $f \in F$ be a face, let $e \in E_2$ be an edge on the boundary of f and let g be that edge on the boundary of f which is supported by h_i (g may be degenerated to a vertex). Edge e is supported by a line h_j, $j < i$. We put e into group E_ℓ if h_j intersects h_i to the left of g and we put e into group E_r otherwise. In the diagram below, the edges E_1 (E_ℓ, E_r) are indicated as solid (dotted, dashed) double lines.

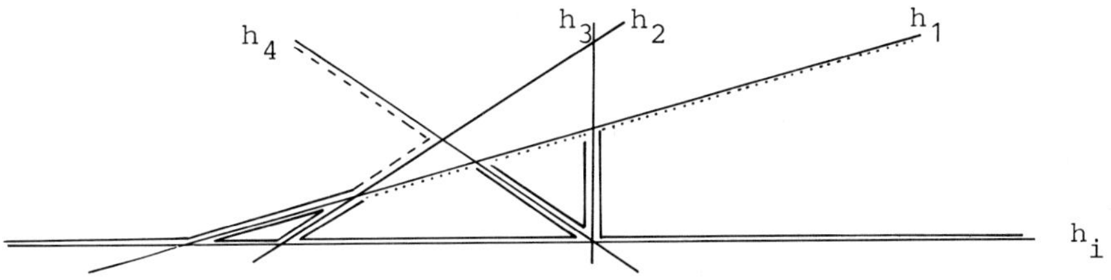

We show $|E_r| \leq i$. Then symmetry implies $|E_\ell| \leq i$ and hence $m_i = |E_1| + |E_\ell| + |E_r| \leq 5i$.

Lemma 5: $|E_r| \leq i$

Proof: We use induction on i. For $i \leq 2$ we have $|E_r| = 0$ and hence the claim is obviously true. So let us assume that $i \geq 3$. Choose j, $j < i$, such that $\measuredangle(h_i,h_j)$ is minimal. Remove line h_j from the planar subdivision and let E_r' be defined with respect to the resulting subdivision as E_r is defined with respect to SD_i. Then $|E_r'| \leq i - 1$ by induction hypothesis. It therefore suffices to show $|E_r| \leq |E_r'| + 1$. This can be seen as follows.

Note first that no edge which is supported by h_j can belong to E_r. This follows immediately from the fact that $\measuredangle(h_i,h_j)$ is minimal.

Observe next that removal of h_j merges some faces of SD_i. More precisely, there are two faces, say f_1,f_2, in F which are merged to a single face and every other face, say f, of F is either left unchanged or merged with a face which is not in F. In the latter case f (or the result of merging f with a face not in F) contributes at least as many edges to E_r' as it contributed to E_r. In the former case, the face obtained by merging f_1 and f_2 contributes at most one edge less to E_r' than f_1 and f_2 together contributed to E_r, since removal of h_j might combine two edges in E_r or combine an edge in E_r with an edge in E_1. Thus $|E_r| \leq |E_r'| + 1$ and the proofs of lemmata 5 and 4 are completed. □

We infer from lemma 4 and the discussion preceding it that SD_i can be computed from SD_{i-1} in time $O(i)$. Hence SD_n can be computed in time $O(n^2)$. Having computed SD_n it is trivial to check in time $O(n^2)$ whether any three lines in H go through a common point. We summarize in

Theorem 2: a) The planar subdivision induced by a set of n lines in $\mathbb{R}^2$ can be computed in time $O(n^2)$.

b) Given n points in $\mathbb{R}^2$ one can decide in time $O(n^2)$ whether any three of them are collinear.

Proof: By the discussion above. □

In the remainder of this section we extend theorem 2 to a solution of the minimum area triangle problem. The extension is based on the following simple observation. Let $p_1,\ldots,p_n$ be n points in the plane. For $1 \le i < j \le n$ let $Near(i,j) = k$ if point p_k has minimal distance from line $L(p_i,p_j)$. Since the area of triangle p_i,p_j,p_k is $dist(p_i,p_j)dist(p_k,L(p_i,p_j))/2$ we conclude that triangle $p_i,p_j,$ $p_{Near(p_i,p_j)}$ has minimum area among all triangles with vertices p_i and p_j. This shows that it suffices to compute function Near in order to solve the minimum area triangle problem.

Let us consider the dual problem. Let $h_i = D(p_i)$ be the line dual to point p_i, $1 \le i \le n$, and let i and j be arbitrary. Then point $h_i \cap h_j$ is the dual of line $L(p_i,p_j)$ by lemma 2; cf. the diagram below. Consider the line L which passes through p_k, $k = Near(i,j)$,

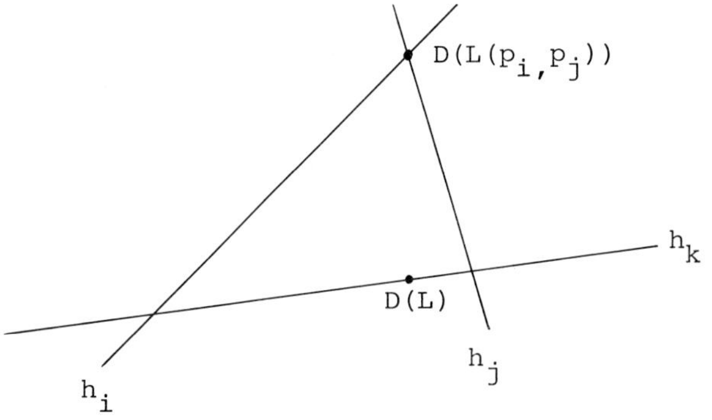

and is parallel to $L(p_i,p_j)$. The dual D(L) of line L is a point with the same x-coordinate as the dual $D(L(p_i,p_j))$ of line $L(p_i,p_j)$. This follows from the fact that the x-coordinate of the dual is given by the slope of the line. Since duality preserves incidence we conclude that line $D(p_k)$ passes through D(L). We also conclude that no other line h_l, $l \neq k$, can intersect the vertical line segment connecting D(L) and $D(L(p_i,p_j))$. Hence D(L) lies on the same face as $D(L(p_i,p_j))$. This observation immediately suggests the following algorithm:

Let $h_i = D(p_i)$, $1 \le i \le n$. Compute the planar subdivision induced by the h_i's and check whether any three lines have a common point. If not, draw a vertical line through every vertex v of the planar subdivision and find the closest intersection of this vertical line with an edge of the subdivision. This edge (supported by line h_k, say) defines Near(i,j), where $v = h_i \cap h_j$.

It remains to describe how the vertical lines are handled. We compute the intersection face by face. Since faces are convex polygons we can handle all vertical lines

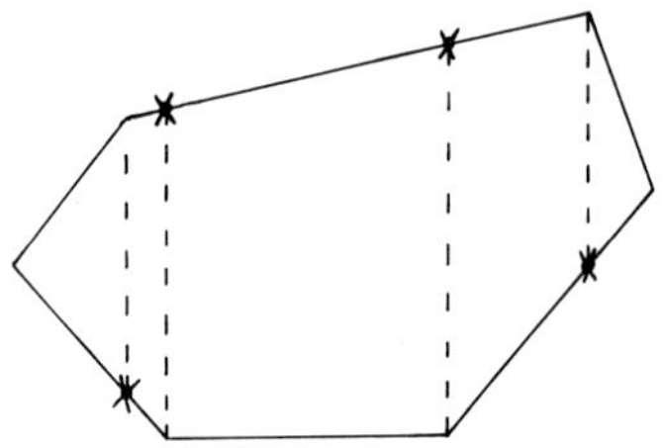

running inside the polygon in time proportional to the number of vertices of the face by a "merge" of the lower and upper part of the face. This shows that function Near can be computed in time $O(n^2)$ from the planar subdivision and hence proves

Theorem 3: The minimum area triangle problem in $\mathbb{R}^2$ can be solved in quadratic time.

VIII. 6.2 Inversion

We will now briefly discuss a second transformation which establishes a correspondence between lines (planes) and circles (spheres) in $\mathbb{R}^2$ ($\mathbb{R}^3$). It frequently allows us to transform problems about circles into seemingly simpler problems about lines.

Inversion in $\mathbb{R}^2$ ($\mathbb{R}^3$) is most easily described with respect to a polar (spherical) coordinate system. Let c be the origin of the coordinate system. Then inversion with center c maps a point p with polar coordinates (R,ϕ) (spherical coordinates (R,ϕ,ψ)) into point $(1/R,\phi)$ ($(1/R,\phi,\psi)$), i.e. it inverts the distance from the origin. An important property of inversion is expressed in

Lemma 6: a) For all p: $I(I(p)) = p$

b) Let C be a circle (sphere) which passes through the center c of the inversion. Then I(C) is a line (plane) which does not pass through c.

c) Let P be a line (plane) which does not pass through c. Then I(P) is a circle (sphere) which passes through c.

Proof: a) is obvious.

b) and c): We only give the proof for $\mathbb{R}^2$ and leave the three-dimensional case to the reader. We first express inversion in cartesian coordinates.

Lemma 7: Let (x,y) be the cartesian coordinates of point p with respect to origin c. Then I(p) has cartesian coordinates $(x/(x^2 + y^2), y/(x^2 + y^2))$

Proof: Let (R,ϕ) be the polar coordinates of point p. Then $R^2 = x^2 + y^2$ and $\tan \phi = y/x$. Let $\bar{x} = x/(x^2 + y^2)$ and $\bar{y} = y/(x^2 + y^2)$. Then $\tan \phi = \bar{y}/\bar{x}$ and $\bar{x}^2 + \bar{y}^2 = 1/R^2$. Hence I(p) has cartesian coordinates $(\bar{x},\bar{y})$. □

We are now ready for a proof of part c). Part b) is proved similarly and is left to the reader. Because of symmetry it suffices to prove part c) for a horizontal line.

Let h be a horizontal line given by equation $y = a$. Let p with cartesian coordinates (x,a) be an arbitrary point on line h. Then I(p) has cartesian coordinates (x/d,a/d) where $d = x^2 + a^2$. It is now easy to check that I(p) lies on the circle with center (0,1/2a) and radius $1/2|a|$. Also all points on this circle are images of points on line h. □

Our first application of the inversion transform uses lemma 6 directly. Let C_i, $1 \le i \le n$, be a circle in $\mathbb{R}^2$ and let $s_i \in \{+,-\}$, $1 \le i \le n$. We use $C_i^{s_i}$ to denote the interior (exterior) of circle C_i provided that $s_i = +$ $(s_i = -)$.

Lemma 8: If $C_1,\ldots,C_n$ are circles in $\mathbb{R}^2$ which all pass through point c and $s_i \in \{+,-\}$, $1 \le i \le n$, then $\bigcap_{i=1}^{n} C_i^{s_i}$ can be computed in time $O(n\log n)$.

Proof: Let I be the inversion with center c. Let $h_i = I(C_i)$, $1 \le i \le n$. Then h_i is a line which does not pass through c and $C_i^{s_i}$ corresponds to one of the halfspaces defined by h_i. We denote that halfspace by $h_i^{s_i}$. Let $P = \bigcap_i h_i^{s_i}$ be the convex polygon defined by the intersection of the halfspaces $h_i^{s_i}$, $1 \le i \le n$. We can compute P in time O(nlog n) by theorem 1. Also $I(P) = \bigcap_i C_i^{s_i}$. Furthermore, it is easy to compute I(P) since vertices of P are transformed into points and edges are transformed into "circular edges". Thus I(P) can be computed in time O(n) and lemma 8 is proven. □

Lemma 8 hinges on the artificial assumption that all circles have a common point c. This assumption can be dropped by investing one more idea: embedding into higher dimensions.

Theorem 4: Let C_i be circles in $\mathbb{R}^2$ and let $s_i \in \{+,-\}$, $1 \le i \le n$. Then $\bigcap_i C_i^{s_i}$ can be computed in time O(nlog n)

Proof: Identify $\mathbb{R}^2$ with the (x,y)-plane of $\mathbb{R}^3$. Let c be a point outside the (x,y)-plane, say c = (0,0,1) and let S_i be a sphere which passes through c and intersects the xy-plane in circle C_i, $1 \le i \le n$. Let $h_i = I(S_i)$, $1 \le i \le n$, be the plane obtained by inversion of S_i with respect to center c. Then $S_i^{s_i}$ corresponds to one of the half-spaces defined by plane h_i. We use $h_i^{s_i}$ to denote that halfplane. Then convex polyhedrom $P = \bigcap_i h_i^{s_i}$ can be computed in time O(nlog n) by theorem 1. Also $I(P) = \bigcap_i S_i^{s_i}$ and hence the intersection of I(P) with the xy-plane is the desired solution. We can compute I(P) ∩ (xy-plane) in time O(n) by transforming face by face of I(P). The details are left to the reader. □

Theorem 4 deals with circles in a very direct way. In Voronoi diagrams circles come up in a more subtle way. Let $S = \{p_1,\ldots,p_n\}$ be a set of n points in the plane and let VD be the Voronoi diagram of S; cf. section 3.1. Let v be any vertex of the Voronoi diagram . Then v is the center of a circle $C(v)$ which passes through at least three points of S and has no point of S in its interior. Conversely, the center of any such circle is a vertex of the diagram. As in theorem 4, we identify $\mathbb{R}^2$ with the xy-plane of $\mathbb{R}^3$, choose a point c outside the xy-plane and use $S(v)$ to denote a sphere which passes through c and intersects the xy-plane in circle $C(v)$. Consider the inversion I with center c. Let $h(v) = I(S(v))$. Then $h(v)$ is a plane such that at least three points in $I(S)$ lie on $h(v)$ and all other points in $I(S)$ belong to the same half-space with respect to $h(v)$. In other words, plane $h(v)$ supports a face of the convex hull of point set $I(S)$. This observation suggests the following algorithm for computing the Voronoi diagram of point set S.

Construct $I(S)$ and compute the convex hull of $I(S)$. This takes time $O(n\log n)$ by exercise 13. Let f be an arbitrary face of $I(S)$, let E be the supporting plane, and let $Sp = I(E)$ be the sphere obtained by inversion of E. Then either all points of S lie inside or on Sp or all of them lie outside or on Sp. The two cases are easily distinguished by testing one point of S (whose image under I does not lie on face f) with respect to Sp. In the latter case the center of the circle obtained by intersecting Sp with the xy-plane is a vertex of the Voronoi diagram (in the former case it is a vertex of the farthest point Voronoi diagram). In this fashion we compute all vertices of the Voronoi diagram in time $O(n)$, each vertex of the diagram corresponding to a face of the convex hull of $I(S)$. The edges are now readily computed. We connect vertices v and w by a (straight-line) edge if the corresponding faces of the convex hull share an edge. This proves

Theorem 5: The Voronoi diagram of a point set $S \subseteq \mathbb{R}^2$, $|S| = n$ can be computed in time $O(n\log n)$.

VIII. 7. Exercises

1) A sequence $P_0, P_1, \ldots, P_k$ of polygons is a balanced <u>outer representation</u> of convex polygon P if P_0 has at most 4 vertices, $P_k = P$ and P_{i-1} can be obtained from P_i by dropping every other boundary edge and extending the remaining ones. In the example, $P_1 = P$ is shown solid and P_0 is shown in dashed lines. Prove the results of section 1 using balanced outer representations.

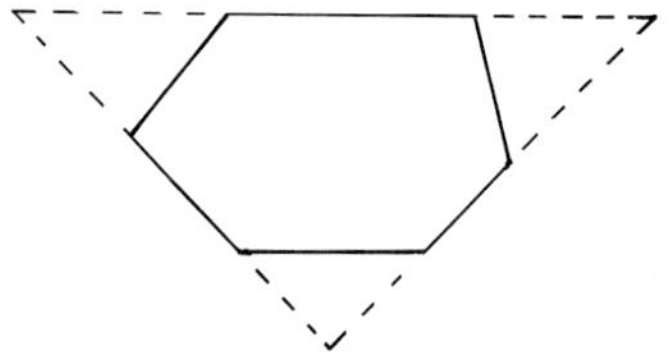

2) Let P be a convex polyhedron in $\mathbb{R}^3$. An <u>inner polyhedral representation</u> of P is an ascending chain $P_0, P_1, \ldots, P_k$ such that P_0 has at most O(1), say 100, faces, $P = P_k$, and P_i can be obtained from P_{i+1} as follows. Let V be a set of independent vertices of degree at most 10 of P_{i+1}. Then P_i is the convex hull of $V(P_{i+1}) - V$. Let n be the number of vertices of P.

a) Show that every convex polyhedron P with n vertices has an inner polyhedral representation $P_0, \ldots, P_k$ with $k = O(\log n)$. (Hint: Lemma 8 of section 3.2.1. implies that V can be chosen such that $|V| \ge a\,|V(P_{i+1})|$ for some constant $a > 0$). Show that the representation can be computed in time O(n).

b) Given a balanced inner polyhedral representation of convex polyhedron P and line L show that one can compute $P \cap L$ in time $O(\log n)$.

c) Given a balanced inner polyhedral representation of convex polyhedron P and plane E show that one can decide whether P and E intersect in time $O(\log n)$.

d) Given balanced representations of convex polyhedra P and Q show that one can decide in time O(n) whether $P \cap Q = \emptyset$.

e) Show how to compute $P \cap Q$ for convex polyhedra P and Q in time $O(n\log n)$.

3) Given balanced representation of convex n-gons P and Q show that one can compute $\text{dist}(P,Q) = \min \{\text{dist}(x,y);\ x \in P,\ y \in Q\}$ in time $O(\log n)$.

4) Given convex n-gons P and Q shows that one can compute max dist(P,Q) = max {dist(x,y); x ∈ P and y ∈ Q} in time O(n).

5) Given balanced representation of convex n-gon P and point p show that one can compute the balanced representation of CH(PUp) in time O(log n).

6) Show that one can compute the intersection of n half-spaces in time O(nlog n) (Hint: Use divide and conquer and theorem 5 of section 1).

7) Let P be a simple polygonal region. Let ker(P) = {x ∈ P; L(x,y) ⊆ P} be the set of points which can "see" the entire polygon. Show that ker(P) can be computed in time O(nlog n) (Hint: Show that ker(P) is an intersection of half-spaces one for each edge of P). There is also an O(n) solution.

8) Let $S \subseteq \mathbb{R}^2$ be finite. Show that CH(S) is a convex polygon whose vertices are points of S. (Hint: Let A = {(v,w); v,w ∈ S and one of the half-spaces defined by line L(v,w) contains all points of S}. Then CH(S) is an intersection of half-spaces one for each pair in A).

9) Let $v_0, v_1, \ldots, v_n$ be a simple polygon with $x(v_0) \le x(v_1) \le \ldots \le x(v_n)$. Simplify the algorithm given in the proof of theorem 1 of section 2 for simple polygons of this form.

10) Let $A, B \subseteq \mathbb{R}^2$. $|A| = n$, $|B| = m$. Show that one can decide in time O((n + m)log(n + m)) whether there is a line which separates A from B.

11) Let $S \subseteq \mathbb{R}^2$, $|S| = n$ and let $\varepsilon > 0$. Show how to compute in time $O(n + 1/\varepsilon)$ a convex polygon $P \subseteq CH(S)$ such that for all $x \in S$: $dist(x,P) \le \varepsilon \circ diam(S)$ where dist(x,P) is the minimal distance of x from any point of P and diam(S) is the diameter of S. P may be called an approximate convex hull (Hint: divide the plane into $k = 1/\varepsilon$ vertical strips of width $\varepsilon \circ xwidth(S)$ where $xwidth(S) = \max\{x(v);\ v \in S\}$ -

min $\{x(v);\ v \in S\}$. Determine the points with maximal and minimal y-coordinate in each strip and let P be the convex hull of these points).

12) Design an O(nlog n) divide and conquer algorithm for the convex hull problem in $\mathbb{R}^2$ (Hint: Use the algorithm which is implicite in the proof of Lemma 1 of section 2).

13) Design an O(nlog n) divide and conquer algorithm for the convex hull problem in $\mathbb{R}^3$ (Hint: the crucial subroutine takes two non-intersecting convex polyhedra P_1 and P_2 and computes the convex hull of $P_1 \cup P_2$ in linear time).

14) Let VD be the Voronoi diagram of some point set S, let $y \notin S$ and let $x \in S$ be such that $y \in VR(x)$. Show how to obtain the diagram for $S \cup \{x\}$ in time proportional to the "size of the change" of the diagram.
(Hint: Construct the perpendicular bisector of x and y first, say L. Find the intersections of L with the boundary of VR(x). Assume that one of the intersections lies on the boundary of VR(x) and VR(z). Continue to move along the perpendicular bisector of y and z,...)

15) Let VD be the Voronoi diagram of some point set S and let $x \in S$. Show how to obtain the diagram for $S - \{x\}$ in time O(slog s) where s is the number of edges on the boundary of VR(x).
(Hint: Let $e_1,\dots,e_m$ be the spokes of the Voronoi region of x in circular order as indicated in the figure. Let the spokes simultaneously grow into region VR(x) and find a "first" intersection (use a heap for that task); say it is the intersection of e_i and e_{i+1}. Replace e_i, e_{i+1} by the perpendicular bisector of suitable points and continue).

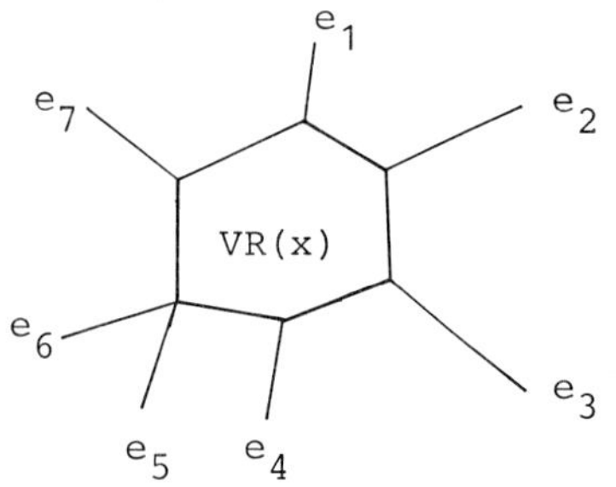

16) Let S and T be finite subsets of $\mathbb{R}^2$. Develop an algorithm for computing $VD(S \cup T)$ from VD(S) and VD(T) in time $O(|S| + |T|)$. (Hint: Use plane sweep).

The following exercises (17-19) treat alternative methods for the searching planar subdivisions problem. For all these exercises we assume that $\hat{G}$ is a straight line embedding of a planar graph with n vertices.

17) (Slab method). Let $x_1,\ldots,x_n$ be the x-coordinates of the vertices of $\hat{G}$ in increasing order. Divide $\hat{G}$ into n-1 slabs by drawing vertical lines through all vertices of $\hat{G}$. In order to locate a point $(x,y) \in \mathbb{R}^2$ in $\hat{G}$, first determine the slab containing point (x,y) by binary search for x in sequence $x_1,\ldots,x_n$. Then locate the position of (x,y) within the slab by binary search of the at most O(n) edges of $\hat{G}$ intersecting the slab. Note that no edges of $\hat{G}$ intersect within a slab and hence the edges can be sorted in a natural way within a slab from top to bottom. Show that this method yields a search structure of depth O(log n) and size $O(n^2)$. Find an example of a planar subdivision where the space requirement is $\Omega(n^2)$.

18) (Planar separator method). Since $\hat{G}$ is a planar graph the proof of the planar separator theorem (IV.10. theorem 3) guarantees the existence of a cycle $C = x_1,\ldots,x_m$ in $\hat{G}$ of length $m \leq 4\sqrt{n}$ such that removal of C cuts $\hat{G}$ into two subgraphs both containing at most 2n/3 nodes each. Use the slab method to decide whether a point lies inside or outside C. Then use the method recursively for both subgraphs. Show that this approach yields a search structure of depth $O((\log n)^2)$ and size O(nlog n).

19) (Trapezoid method) For the purpose of this exerxise define a trapezoid as consisting of two horizontal edges and two nonhorizontal edges. Moreover, the two nonhorizontal edges are subsegments of edges of $\hat{G}$ and there is no edge of $\hat{G}$ which intersects the interior of both horizontal edges. Refine a trapezoid into some number of trapezoids by

1) drawing a horizontal line through the vertex of $\hat{G}$ which has the median y-coordinate of all vertices in the trapezoid

2) refining the top and bottom half into trapezoids by using those edges of $\hat{G}$ which go completely through the top or bottom half.

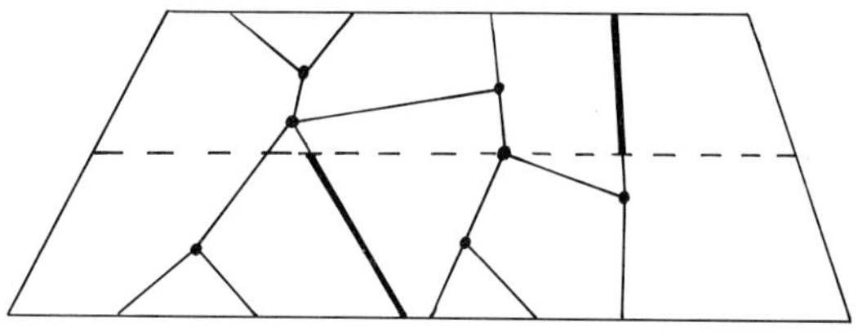

In our example, the top and bottom half are both cut into two trapeziods as indicated by the heavy lines.
Thus in each search step we first locate the point with respect to the horizontal dividing line and then with respect to the nonhorizontal dividing lines. Note that the latter number of dividing lines is not bounded by a constant and that the number of vertices in the various sub-trapezoids varies widely. Thus it is efficient to use a weighted binary search (cf. section III.4) for the search with respect to the nonhorizontal dividing lines; the weight of a sub-trapezoid being the number of vertices of $\hat{G}$ it contains. Show that this method yields a search structure of depth O(log n) and size O(nlog n). In fact, the depth can be shown to be bounded by 3log n + O(1) if the method of III.4. theorem 7 is used for the weighted binary search.

20) Let $S \subseteq \mathbb{R}^2$. Use the Voronoi diagram of S in order to find the largest circle C such that C's center is contained in the convex hull of S and the interior of C contains no point of S. (Hint: the center of C is either a vertex of the Voronoi diagram or a point of intersection of the convex hull of S and an edge of the Voronoi diagram).

21) Let $S \subseteq \mathbb{R}^2$. For $x \in S$ let $FVR(x) = \{z;\ dist(x,z) \geq dist(y,z)$ for all $y \in S\}$ be the set of points z which have x as their farthest neighbor. Show how to compute the farthest point Voronoi diagram in time O(nlog n).

22) Use the farthest point Voronoi diagram (cf. exercise 21) to find the smallest circle which contains all points of $S \subseteq \mathbb{R}^2$.

23) Given a set of n vertical or horizontal line segments show that one can compute all s intersections in time O(nlog n + s) (Hint: Use plane sweep; modify the algoritm given in section 4.1).

24) A circular segment is a segment of a circle. Given n circular segments show that one can compute all s intersections in time O((n + s)log n).

25) Given a set of closed polygonal curves show how to compute the regions defined by the union of these curves.

26) Let PP_1 and PP_2 be sets of simple polygons. Show how to compute all maximal regions which are covered by a polygon in PP_1 and a polygon in PP_2. Assume first that the polygons in PP_i, $i = 1,2$ are pairwise disjoint. Then drop this assumption. (Hint: Modify the algorithm for decomposing polygons given in section 4.1).

27) Let PP be a set of polygons. Compute the boundary of the union of the polygons in PP.

28) Let PP_1 and PP_2 be sets of simple polygons. Show how to compute all maximal regions which are covered by a polygon in PP_1 and no polygon in PP_2. Similarly, compute all maximal regions which are covered by at least three polygons in PP_1 and no more than two polygons of PP_2. For what other logical connectives will your algorithm work? Can you extend your algorithm to more than two sets of simple polygons?

29) Let $L_1,\ldots,L_n$ be a set of <u>non-intersecting</u> line segments. Line segment L_i <u>dominates</u> L_j if L_i intersects the infinite "strip" defined by L_j and the vertical rays (extending to $+\infty$) through the two endpoints of L_j. Compute an injective ordering ord: $\{L_1,\ldots,L_n\} \to \{1,\ldots,n\}$ such that $\text{ord}(L_i) < \text{ord}(L_j)$ if L_i dominates L_j (Hint: Use plane sweep. Augment the y-structure such that it records the restriction of ord to the active and dead line segments).

30) Give the details of the O(nlog n) algorithm for triangulation which is described in section 4.2.

31) Let P be a simple polygon. Compute a decomposition into a minimal number of convex parts. Use dynamic programming (Hint: Let P be $x_0,x_1,\ldots,x_{n-1},x_0$. Call pair (i,j) valid if either x_i or x_j is a cusp and $L(x_i,x_j)$ is inside P. For every valid pair (i,j), $i < j$, and ℓ, $i < \ell < j$, compute $\text{cost}(i,j,\ell)$ where $\text{cost}(i,j,\ell)$ is the minimal number of convex parts in any decomposition of polygon $x_i,\ldots,x_j,x_i$ which uses edge $L(x_\ell, x_j)$).

32) Let $P_1,\ldots,P_k$ be a set of non-intersecting simple polygons. Triangulate $P_1 \cup P_2 \cup \ldots \cup P_k$ using the edges of the polygons.

33) Let P be a simple polygon and let x and y be two points in the interior of P. Show how to compute a shortest path in the Euclidian

metric from x to y which runs completely inside P (Hint: Given a triangulation of P one can find the path in linear time).

34) Let $S \subseteq \mathbb{R}^2$, $|S| = n$. Prove an $\Omega(n\log n)$ lower bound on the time required to compute a triangulation of S.

35) Let P and Q be planar subdivisions all of which regions are convex. Let n be the number of vertices of $P \cup Q$. Show how to compute $P \cap Q$ in time $O(n\log n + s)$ where s is the number of intersections.

36) Consider the following memory allocation problem. A memory is an array of N cells. We want to dynamically maintain the free cells such that the following requests can be served efficiently. Given integer r (the size of the request) find a block of $s \geq r$ consecutive free cells. In the <u>best-fit</u> strategy we want s to be minimal, in the <u>first-fit</u> strategy we want the free block to start at the smallest free address. Show that prioritiy search trees can be used to implement either strategy (Hint: Represent a block of free cells by a pair (block-size, first address in free block)).

37) Let $\hat{G}$ be a planar subdivision with no vertical edge. A <u>zig-zag decomposition</u> of $\hat{G}$ is a sequence $P_1,\ldots,P_s$ of x-monotone paths such that

1) every edge of $\hat{G}$ belongs to exactly one path and only edges of $\hat{G}$ are used in the paths.

2) if $i < j$ and vertical line L intersects P_i and P_j then $L \cap P_i$ is not below $L \cap P_j$

3) s is minimal among all path systems which satisfy 1) and 2).

a) For a vertex v of $\hat{G}$ let indeg(v) (outdeg(v)) be the number of edges entering v from the left (leaving v to the right). Call v a start vertex of $\hat{G}$ if indeg(v) < outdeg(v). Show that every zig-zag decomposition satisfies

$s = \Sigma\{\text{outdeg}(v) - \text{indeg}(v);\ v \text{ is a start vertex of } \hat{G}\}$. Show how to compute a zig-zag decomposition in time $O(n\log n)$ and space $O(n)$ where n is the number of vertices of $\hat{G}$. Be careful that your algorithm not only computes a set $\{P_1,\ldots,P_s\}$ of paths but a <u>sequence</u> $P_1,\ldots,P_s$ of paths which forms a zig-zag decomposition.

b) Let $Q_1,\ldots,Q_m$ be a set of simple plane polygons in $\mathbb{R}^3$ with a total of n vertices. Let k be the number of edge intersections in the projection onto the xy-plane. Show how to use zig-zag decomposition to solve the hidden line elimination problem in time $O((n + k)(\log n)^2)$ and space $O(n + k)$.

c) For a zig-zag decomposition $P_1,\ldots,P_s$ let First be the set of first edges of paths $P_1,\ldots,P_s$. Design a plane sweep algorithm which runs in time $O(n\log n)$ and space $O(s)$ and computes set First and injective mapping num : First $\rightarrow [1\ldots s]$ such that there is a path decomposition $P_1,\ldots,P_s$ with $e \in$ First being the first edge of path $P_{num(e)}$ for all e in First. Moreover, design a plane sweep algorithm which given set First and mapping num maintains a mapping $\overline{num}$ during the sweep such that $\overline{num}$ is defined on the active line segments and $\overline{num}(e)$ is the path which contains edge e. The algorithm should run in time $O(n\log n)$ and space $O(s)$.

d) Use the solution to part c) to improve the space complexity of the hidden line elimination algorithm of part b) to $O(n)$.

e) Can you use zig-zag decomposition for the measure problem of a union of polygons?

38) Design an algorithm for hidden line elimination under perspective projections.

39) This exercise discusses a hidden line elimination algorithm of time complexity $O((n + k)\log n)$ and space complextiy $O(n + k)$. Let $Q_1,\ldots,Q_m$ be a set of simple plane polygons in $\mathbb{R}^3$ with a total of n vertices. Let Q_i' be the projection of Q_i into the xy-plane and let k be the number of intersections of edges of the Q_i''s. Obtain planar subdivision $\hat{G}$ with n + k vertices by adding the edge intersections as additional vertices. View every edge of $\hat{G}$ as a pair of two half-edges by conceptually introducing midpoints. For every vertex v of $\hat{G}$ assign labels locally visible and hidden to the half-edges incident to v. A half-edge is locally visible iff none of the polygons having v as a vertex covers it. Otherwise, it is hidden.

a) Assume that $\hat{G}$ is connected. Let v_o be the vertex of $\hat{G}$ with maximal z-coordinate and let S be the maximal connected subgraph of $\hat{G}$ containing v_o and consisting only of edges both of which half-edges are visible. Show that S is the solution to the hidden line elimination problem.

b) Derive from part a) a hidden line elimination algorithm with running time $O((n + k)\log n)$ and space requirement $O(n + k)$ for the case that G is connected.

c) Extend the solution of part b) to the case that $\hat{G}$ is not connected (Hint: Apply part b) to every component of $\hat{G}$. Use exercise 40 to decide containment of components and use this information to delete covered components).

40) Let $Q_1,\ldots,Q_m$ be a set of simple polygons with a total of n edges. Report all pairs of intersecting polygons (Hint: Use path or zig-zag decompositions and extend the algorithm given in section 5.1.1, theorem 2).

41) Given a set S, n = $|S|$ of points and iso-oriented rectangles in $\mathbb{R}^2$ report all pairs (p,R) of point and rectangle with $p \in R$. Design a divide and conquer algorithm to solve this problem in time O(nlog n + s) where s is the number of pairs reported (Hint: An algorithm similar to procedure INTERSECT of section 5.2.1. can be used. Let VERT be the set of projections of the points in the frame onto the y-axis and let LEFT (RIGHT) be the set of projections of rectangles which have their right (left) boundary in the frame but their left (right) boundary outside the frame.).

42) Use a solution to the preceding exercise and theorem 11 of section 5.2.1. to design an O(nlog n + s) algorithm for the rectangle intersection problem: Given n iso-oriented rectangles compute all pairs of intersecting rectangles.

43) Design a plane sweep algorithm for the contour problem of iso-oriented rectangles. Use segment trees. You should be able to achieve running time O((n + p)log n) fairly easily; an improvement to O(nlog n + p) is possible but quite involved. Here n is the number of rectangles and p is the number of contour-pieces.

44) Let S, n = $|S|$ be a set of horizontal and vertical line segments. Let pair (L_1,L_2) of elements belong to relation R if $L_1 \cap L_2 \neq \emptyset$. Compute the equivalence classes of relation R in time O(nlog n). The equivalence classes are also called connected components.

VIII. 8. Bibliographic Notes

Section 1 is based on Dobkin/Kirkpatrick (82), except that theorem 5 is taken from Shamos (75). The former paper also contains three-dimensional analogs of theorems 1 to 4; cf. exercise 2. A solution to exercise 7 can be found in Lee/Preparata (79).

McCallum/ Avis (79) gave the first linear time convex hull algorithm for the vertices of a simple polygon (theorem 1). Our proof follows Graham/Yao (81). Theorem 2 is by Graham (72) and theorem 3 is by Shamos (75). The lower bound to the convex hull problem in the algebraic decision tree model is by Yao (81) and Ben Or (83). Theorem 4 is due to Preparata (79) and theorem 5 comes from Overmars/v. Leeuwen (81). A solution to exercise 13 can be found in Preparata/Hong (79), and a solution to exercise 11 can be found in Bentley/Faust/Preparata (82). Finally, an O(nlog H) algorithm for the convex hull problem was recently given by Kirkpatrick/Seidel (82) where H is the number of vertices of the convex hull.

The O(nlog n) algorithm for constructing Voronoi diagrams is due to Shamos/Hoey (75). Theorems 5,6,7 and exercises 20,21, and 22 can also be found there. Lemma 7 and theorem 2 on searching planar subdivisions is due to Kirkpatrick (83). Section 3.2.2. combines work of Lee/ Preparata (77) who introduced the concept of path decomposition and proved lemma 10, Harel (80) who showed how to compute lowest common ancestors fast, and Edelsbrunner (83) who finally reduced search time to O(log n). Theorem 4 on searching dynamic planar subdivisions is joint work with O. Fries. The exercises are taken from Kirkpatrick (79) (exercise 16), Dobkin/Lipton (76) (exercise 17), Lipton/Tarjan (77) (exercise 18), Bilardi/Preparata (82) (Exercise 19). An algorithm for searching subdivisions with curved boundaries can be found in Edelsbrunner/Maurer (81).

The sweep paradigm was introduced by Shamos/Hoey (76). Theorem 1 and exercises 23 and 24 are taken from Bentley/Ottmann (79); Brown reduced the space requirement of their algorithm from O(n + s) to O(n). An $O(n(\log n)^2 + s)$ algorithm for line segment intersection was recently found by Chazelle (83). Theorem 2 and exercise 35 are work of Nievergelt/Preparata (82). Ottmann/Widmeyer/Wood (82) show how to solve exercises 25 to 28, and Guibas/Yao (80) solve exercise 29. The triangulation algorithm for simple polygons is taken from Hertel/Mehlhorn (83); some of the applications (theorems 5 and 6) are also from there. Theorem 7 and exercise 33 are due to Chazelle (82). Chazelle's paper also contains a seperator theorem for simple polygons. Exercise 31 comes from Green (83); a related problem was studied in Chazelle/Dobkin (79). The section of space sweep is based on Hertel/Mehlhorn/Mäntyla/ Nievergelt (83). Alternative algorithms for intersecting convex polyhedra can be found in Muller/Preparata (83) and Dobkin/Kirkpatrik (82); cf. exercise 2.

Interval trees were introduced by McCreight (80) and Edelsbrunner (80) and the proof of theorem 2 is taken from their papers. A first proof was given by Bentley/Wood (80). Priority search trees are due to McCreight (81) and all of section 5.1.2. and exercises 36 is taken from this paper. Segment trees were introduced by Bentley (77) as a method for solving the measure problem (theorem 7). Dynamic interval trees and segment trees were discussed by Edelsbrunner (82); the general discussion which also allows intervals to share endpoints is new. The idea of using path decompositions in plane sweep algorithms comes from Ottmann/Widmeyer (82), they used zig-zag decompositions in the sense of exercise 37. The algorithm of exercise 39 was developed by Schmitt (81). All of section 5.2. is taken from Güting (83), and all of section 5.3. is taken from Edelsbrunner/Maurer (81). A solution to exercise 43 can be found in Güting (82).

Geometric transforms are discussed at length in Brown (79) and theorems 1,4,5 are his. Chazelle (83) and Edelsbrunner/O'Rourke/Seidel (83) proved theorems 2 and 3. The latter paper treats the problem in higher dimensions also.

IX. Algorithmic Paradigms

There are basically two ways for structuring a book on data structures and algorithms: problem or paradigm oriented. We have mostly followed the first alternative because it allows for a more concise treatment. However, at certain occassions (e.g. section VIII.4 on the sweep paradigm in computational geometry) we have also followed the second approach. In this last chapter of the book we attempt to review the entire book from the paradigm oriented point of view.

Solving an algorithmic problem means to search for a solution to the problem within a set of possible candidates (= search space, state space).

Exhaustive search, i. e. a complete scan of the state space, is the most obvious searching method. Pure exhaustive search is rarely efficient and should only be used for small state spaces. We found several ways of improving upon exhaustive search, most notably branch and bound, tabulation, and dynamic programming. In the branch and bound approach (VI.6.2) to optimization problems one explores the state space in the order of decreasing promise, i. e. one has the means of estimating the quality of partial solutions and always works on the partial solution with maximal promise. The precision of the search depends on the quality of the estimates. It is usually quite difficult (or even impossible) to analyse the complexity of branch and bound algorithms in a satisfying way.

In more structured state spaces one can use dynamic programming and tabulation (III.4.1, IV.7.3, and VI.6.1). Dynamic programming is particularly useful when the problem space ist structured by size in a natural way and when solutions to larger problems are easily obtained from solutions to (all, sufficiently many) smaller problems. In this situation it is natural to solve all conceivable subproblems in order of increasing size in a systematic way. The efficiency of dynamic programming is directly related to the size of the state space. We encountered a large state space in the application to the travelling salesman problem (VI.6.1) and a fairly small state space in the application to optimum search trees (III.4.1) and least cost paths (IV.7.3). In some occassions, e. g. III.4.1, the search could be restricted to a suitably chosen subset of the state space.

Tabulation (III.4.1) is a general method of obtaining dynamic programming algorithms from top-down exhaustive search algorithms. The idea is to store the solutions to all solved subproblems in a table for latter look-up. We have used this idea for converting a backtracking algorithm for optimum search trees into the dynamic programming algorithm and for simulating 2-way deterministic pushdown automata in linear time on a RAM. The latter simulation led to the linear time pattern matching algorithm.

The divide - and - conquer paradigm is also applied to problem spaces which are structured by size. A problem instance is solved by generating several subproblems (divide), solving the subproblems (conquer), and combining the answer to the subproblems to an answer for the original problem instance (merge). The efficiency of the method is determined by the cost of generating the subproblems, the number and the size of the subproblems, and the cost of merging the answers. Divide - and - conquer algorithms lead to recursive programs and their analysis leads to recursion equations. We discussed recursion equations in sections II.1.3 and VII.2.2. The paradigm of divide - and - conquer was used very frequently in this book: in sorting and selection algorithms (II.1.2, II.1.3, and II.4), in all data-structures based upon trees (III.3 to III.7, VII.2.1 and VII.2.2, and VIII.5.1), in the planar separator theorem and its applications (IV.10), in the matrix multiplication algorithms (V.4), and in the divide - and conquer algorithms for computational geometry (VIII.5.2). Finally, the treatment of decomposable searching problems and dynamization (VII.1) has a very close relationship to the divide - and - conquer paradigm. In most applications of the paradigm a natural structure of the problem instances was used for the division step. For example, if the problem instance is a tuple then we can split the tuple into its first and its second half (merge sort, binary search, matrix multiplication,...) and if the problem instance is a set of objects from an ordered set then we can split the set into its lower and its upper half (the linear time selection algorithm, applications in geometry,...). The situation was slightly different in multidimensional divide - and - conquer (VII.2.2). There we frequently solved an instance of size n in d-dimensional space by generating two d-dimensional subproblems of size about n/2 and one (d-1)-dimensional subproblem of size n. Another interesting application of the paradigm is to planar graphs. We have seen two strategies. The first strategy is given by the planar separator theorem of section IV.10.2. It allows us to split a planar graph of n nodes into two subgraphs of about half the size by the removal of only $O(\sqrt{n})$ nodes. Moreover, the separating set can be determined in linear time. We used the planar separator theorem in several efficient algorithms on planar graphs, e. g. least cost path, chromatic number, ... The second strategy is given by the fact that a planar graph always contains a large set of independent nodes of small degree. We used this fact in searching planar subdivisions (VIII.3.2.1) and in the hierarchical representation of convex polyhedra (VIII, exercise 2).

Trees are a prime example for the divide - and - conquer paradigm. In trees one either organizes the universe (section III.1 on TRIES) or one organizes the set to be stored in the tree. The latter approach was used in sections III.3 to III.7 and leads to balanced trees. In these trees one chooses an element of the set for the root which balances the subproblems. In balanced trees for unweighted data balancing is done either according to the cardinality of the subproblems (weight - balanced trees) or according to the height of the subtrees (height - balanced trees). In trees for weighted data balancing is done according to the probability of the subproblems. We have also seen on two occassions (III.6.1 on weighted dynamic trees for multidimensional searching and VIII.5.1.3 on segment trees) that search structures for unweighted complex data can sometimes be constructed from trees for simpler but weighted data. The former approach, i. e. organizing the universe, was used in section III.1 on TRIES and in the static version of interval, priority search, and segment trees (VIII.5.1). The organization of the universe gives rise to particularly simple tree structures.

Closely related to trees which organize the universe are key transformation (=hashing) and direct access(II.2, III.2 and III.8). In these methods one uses the key or a transformed key in order to directly access data. This immediately implies small running times. Another application of the very same idea is presorting, i. e. transforming a problem on an arbitrary set into a problem on a sorted set by sorting. It is then often possible to identify the objects with an initial segment of the integers which opens up all methods of direct access. We used presorting in sections VII.2.2 on multi-dimensional divide - and - conquer and in section VIII.5 on orthogonal objects in computational geometry.

In graphs we studied two methods for their systematic exploration: breadth - first and depth - first search. Breadth - first search is particularly useful for distance type problems and was therefore used intensively in least cost path computations (IV.7). Depth - first search has the important property that components are explored one by one and is therefore the natural method of exploration in connectivity problems. We used DFS to determine biconnected and strongly connected components and to test planarity.

Frequently, solutions to problem instances can be found iteratively or in a step by step fashion. Examples are the construction of optimal merging patterns (II.1.4), network flow and matching problems (IV.9), the construction of least cost spanning trees (IV.8), and the construction of convex hulls (VIII.2). In some of these examples (e. g. least cost spanning trees or optimal merging patterns) each step performs an action which is locally optimal. This variant of iteration is sometimes called the greedy approach. In other applications of this paradigm (e. g. network flow) a solution is improved iteratively. Frequently, the concept of augmentation applies to these situations.

In the chapter on algorithmic geometry we discussed the sweep paradigm at length (VIII.4, VIII,5.1). Its power stems from the fact that it reduces the dimension of geometric problems for the cost of turning static into dynamic problems. In particular, two-dimensional static problems can often be reduced to one-dimensional dynamic problems which can then be solved using some sort of balanced tree.

The method of reduction also played a major role in other parts of the book. The entire chapter on NP - completeness is centered around the notion of reduction or transformation. We used reductions to structure the world of problems, to define and explore classes of equivalent problems (VI.1 to VI.5), to transfer algorithms (from network flow to matching in IV.9, from matrix product over the integers to matrix product over the set of booleans in V.5, from iso - oriented objects to general objects in VIII.5.2, and from straight-line to circular objects in VIII.6), and to transfer lower bounds (from sorting to element uniqueness in II.6, from decision trees to RAMs in II.3 and from boolean matrix product to matrix product over semi-rings of characteristic zero in V.7).

Balancing is also an important concept. In least cost path computations (IV.7) we balanced the cost of various priority queue operations by a careful choice of the data structure, in multi - dimensional trees (VII.2.1) we balanced the power of the coordinates by using them in the split fields in cyclic order, and in divide - and - conquer algorithms we always tried to balance the size of the subproblems. It is important to observe that perfect balancing is usually not required in order to obtain efficient solutions; approximate balancing will also do. In fact, approximate balancing is called for in order to cope with dynamic behavior. A typical example are balanced trees. In BB[α]-trees (VIII.5.1) we do not require each node to have root balance in the range [1/3,2/3] although such a tree always exists but leave more leeway and in height-balanced trees (VIII.5.2) we allow nodes to have between a and b sons. Introducing an amount of freedom beyond the necessary amount often has dramatic effects on the (amortized) behavior of these schemes. Again, balanced trees are typical examples but so are the dynamization methods of VII.1. For example, BB[α]-trees work for $\alpha \leqq 1-\sqrt{2}/2$, but $\alpha < 1-\sqrt{2}/2$ improves the amortized rebalancing cost dramatically. Similary (a,b)-trees work for $b \geqq 2a-1$ but choosing $b \geqq 2a$ improves the behavior considerably (III.5.2 and III.5.3).

Another way of interpreting approximate rebalancing is redundancy, i.e. to allow additional freedom in representation. The concept of redundancy can also be applied to storage space. We saw at several occassions, most notably range trees (VII.2.2) and dd-trees (VII.2.1), that storing objects several times can reduce search time considerably. In dd-trees multi-dimensional objects are stored without redundancy; they provide us with rootic search time and it was shown in VII.2.3.1. that this is optimal. Range trees store data in a hightly redundant fashion: they use non-linear storage space and provide us with polylogarithmic search time. In fact, the slack parameter of range trees allows us to trade between time and space.

Redundant structures frequently show good amortized behavior because rebalancing a node of a redundant structure moves the node away from the critical situations. Amortized analysis was used in the sections on dynamization and weighting (VII.1), range trees (VII.2.2), (dynamic) interval (VIII.5.1.1) and segment trees (VIII.5.1.3), BB[α]-trees (III.5.1), (a,b)-trees (III.5.3) and the union-find problem (III.8). A general discussion of the bank account paradigm for amortized analysis can be found in section III.6.1.

Worst case analysis (and amortized analysis which is the worst case analysis of sequences of operations) is the dominant method of analysis used throughout this book. Expected case analysis was done in only a few places; e. g. quicksort (II.3), selection (II.4), TRIES (III.1.1), hashing (III.2), interpolation search (III.3.2), weighted trees (III.4), self-organizing linear search (III.6.1.1),and transitive closure (IV.3). Expected case analysis rests upon an a-priori probability distribution on problem instances and therefore its predictions should be interpreted with care. In particular, it should always be checked whether reality conforms with the probability assumptions. Note however, that the expected running of many algorithms is fairly robust with respect to changes in the distribution. For example, a near-optimal search tree for distribution ß ist also a near-optimal search tree for distribution ß' provided that ß and ß' do not differ too much. Furthermore, a careful analysis of algorithms with small expected running time sometimes leads to fast algorithms with small wort case running time (e.g. selection) or to fast probabilistic algorithms (e.g. quicksort and hashing).

Self-organization is another important principle. In self-organizing data structures the items compete for the good places in the structure and high-frequency elements are more likely to be there. This results in good expected and sometimes also amortized behavior.

Generalization was the central theme of chapter V and also section VII.1. In chapter V we dealt with path problems over closed semi-rings, a generalization of least cost paths, transitive closure, maximal cost paths, and many other path problems. In section VII.1 we derived general methods for dynamizing static data structures for decomposable and order decomposable searching problems. Numerous applications of these general methods can be found in chapters VII and VIII.

The last two principles which we are going to discuss are approximation algorithms and probabilistic algorithms. These paradigms suggest to either change the problem to be solved (solve a simpler problem) or to change our notion of computation (use a more powerful computing machine). We observed at several places that a "slight" change in the formulation of a problem can have a drastic effect on its complexity: The satisfiability problem with three literals per clause is NP-complete but with two literals per clause it becomes fairly simple, the precedence constrained scheduling problem is NP-complete but if the precedence relation is a tree or there are only two machines then the problem is in P. Similarly, the computation of the convex hull of a point set takes time $\theta(n \log n)$ but if the points are sorted by x-coordinate then time $O(n)$ suffices. For optimization problems there is a standard method for simplifying the problem; instead of asking for an optimal solution we are content with a nearly optimal solution. This approach is particularly important when the optimization problem is NP-complete and therefore we devoted the entire section V.7 to approximation algorithms for NP-complete problems. We saw that some NP-complete problems resist even approximate solution but many others have good or even very good approximation algorithms. Even inside P approximation algorithms are important. A good example are the weighted trees of section III.4. The best algorithm for constructing optimum weighted trees has running time $\theta(n^2)$ and there is an $O(n)$ algorithm which constructs nearly optimal trees. Already for moderate size n, say $n = 10^4$, the difference between n^2 and n is substantial.

Probabilistic algorithms are based on a more flexible notion of computation, i. e. it is postulated that a perfect coin is available to the machine. (Less than perfect coins will also do for fast probabilistic algorithms as we saw in section I.2). We encountered probabilistic algorithms in many different contexts, e. g. the construction of perfect hash functions (III.2.3), universal hashing (III.2.4), probabilistic quicksort (II.1.3), graph connectivity (IV.9.2) and primality testing (VI.8). These applications may be grouped into two classes. In the first class coin tosses are used to randomize inputs (probabilistic quicksort, universal hashing). Typically, a random transformation is applied to the input and then a standard deterministic algorithm with small expected running time is used. The expected running time of the probabilistic algorithm on a fixed input then matches the expected running of the deterministic algorithm. The important difference is that the randomized algorithm controls the dices but a deterministic algorithm does not; the latter is at the mercy of its user who generates the problem instances. In the second class (construction of perfect hash functions, graph connectivity, primality testing) coin tosses are used to randomize the search for an element of some set with a desirable property. Typically, the property is easily checked and the elements having the property are abundant. However, no intimate knowledge about their location is available.

The design of an efficient algorithm is particularly satisfying if its performance matches a lower bound and hence the algorithm is optimal. Unfortunately, only a few algorithms have been shown to be optimal. We saw three approaches to proving lower bounds in this book. The first approach is the information-theoretic one and the typical argument goes as follows: In order to distinguish between N possibilities any algorithm requires log N steps. Of course in order to make this argument sound one has to define and study the primitive operations, the set of possible outcomes, and how the primitives operate on the set of possible outcomes. We used the information-theoretic approach in sections II.1.6 and II.3 on lower bounds for sorting and related problems, in section III.4 on searching in weighted sets, and in a modified form also in section VII.3.1 on lower bounds for partial match retrieval in minimum space. The second approach is by simplification which we used to prove the lower bound on the complexity of matrix multiplication (V.7). In this approach one designs transformation rules which allow to simplify an optimal program without increasing cost. The final product of the simplification process is then amenable to direct attack. The third approach uses combinatorial methods and was used in the sections on dynamization (VII.1.1) and the spanning bound (VII.3.2). In this approach one relates the complexity of an algorithm to a combinatorial quantity (the spanning complexity of a family of sets in VII.3.2 and various path lengths of binary trees in VII.1.1) and then analyses the combinatorial quantity.

Bibliography

We use the following abbreviations for journals and proceedings:

ACTA	Acta Informatica
CACM	Communications of the ACM
EIK	Elektronische Informationsverarbeitung und Kybernetik
FCT	Foundations of Computing Theory
FOCS	IEEE Symposium on Foundations of Computer Science
ICALP	International Colloquium on Automata, Languages and Programming
Inf & Control	Information and Control
IPL	Information Processing Letters
JACM	Journal of the ACM
JCSS	Journal of Computer and System Sciences
LNCS	Springer Lecture Notes in Computer Science
MFCS	Mathematical Foundations of Computer Science
SICOMP	SIAM Journal of Computing
STOC	ACM Symposium on Theory of Computing
TCS	Theoretical Computer Science

Alt, H., Mehlhorn, K., Munro, I. (1981): On the Complexity of Partial Match Retrieval, MFCS, LNCS 118, 156-161

Alt, H., Mehlhorn, K. (1982): Weighting and Weighted Dynamization, unpublished manuscript

Bentley, J.L., (1975): Multidimensional Binary Search Trees Used for Associative Searching, CACM 18, 509-516

Bentley, J.L. (1977): Solutions to Klee's Rectangle Problems, Carnegie-Mellon University, Dept. of Computer Science, typescript

Bentley, J.L. (1979): Decomposable Searching Problems, IPL 8, 244-251

Bentley, J.L. (1980): Multidimensional Divide-and-Conquer, CACM 23, 214-229

Bentley, J.L., Faust, M.G., Preparata, F.P. (1982): Approximation Algorithms for Convex Hulls, CACM 25, 64-68

Bentley, J.L., Maurer, H.A. (1980): Efficient worst-case data structures for range searching, ACTA INFORMATICA 13, 155-168

Bentley, J.L., Ottmann, Th. (1979): Algorithms for Reporting and Counting Geometric Intersections, IEEE Trans. on Computers C 28, 643-647

Bentley, J.L., Saxe, J.B. (1980): Decomposable Searching Problems I: Static-to-Dynamic Transformations, Journal of Algorithms 1, 301-358

Bentley, J.L., Wood, D (1980): An Optimal Worst Case Algorithm for Reporting Intersections of Rectangles, IEEE Transactions on Computers C 29, 571-577

Bilardi, G., Preparata, F.P. (1980): Probabilistic Analysis of a New Geometric Searching Technique, typescript

Brown, K.Q. (1980): Geometric Transforms for Fast Geometric Algorithms, Ph.D. Thesis, CS, Carnegie-Mellon University

Brown, K.Q. (1981): Comments on "Algorithms for Reporting and Counting Intersections", IEEE Transactions on Computers C 30, 147-148

Chazelle, B. (1982): A theorem on Polygon Cutting with Applications, 23rd FOCS, 339-349

Chazelle, B. (1983): Applications of the concept of duality to the smallest-area triangle and the halfplanar range query problem, International report CS-83-12, Brown University

Chazelle, B. (1983): Reporting and Counting Arbitrary Planar Intersections, Technical report CS-83-16, Brown University

Chazelle, B., Dobkin, D. (1979): Decomposing a Polygon into its Convex Parts, 11th STOC, 38-48

Dobkin, D.P., Kirkpatrick, D.G. (1982): Fast Detection of Polyhedral Intersections, 9th ICALP, LNCS 140, 154-165

Dobkin, D., Lipton, R. (1976): Multidimensional Searching Problems, SICOMP 5, 181-186

Edelsbrunner, H. (1980): Dynamic Rectangle Intersection Searching, Technical University Graz, Institut für Informationsverarbeitung, Report F 47

Edelsbrunner, H. (1982): Intersection Problems in Computational Geometry, Ph.D. thesis, TU Graz

Edelsbrunner, H. (1983): An Optimal Solution for Searching in General Planar Subdivisions, TU Graz, Report F 122

Edelsbrunner, H., Maurer, H.A. (1981): A space optimal solution of general region location, TCS 16, 329-336

Edelsbrunner, H., Maurer, H.A. (1981): On the Intersection of Orthogonal Objects, IPL 13, 177-181

Edelsbrunner, H., O'Rourke, J., Seidel, R. (1983): Constructing Arrangements of Lines and Hyperplanes with Applications, 24th FOCS, 83-91

Edelsbrunner, H., Welzl, E. (1983): Halfplanar Range Search in Linear Space and $O(n^{0.659})$ Query Time, Technical Report F 111, TU Graz

Frederickson, G.n. (1982): Implicit Data Structures for Weighted Elements, Report CS-82-04, Computer Science Department, Penn State University

Fredman, M.L. (1981): Lower Bounds on the Complexity of some optimal data structures, SICOMP 10, 1-10

Fredman, M.L. (1981): The Spanning Bound as a Measure of Range Query Complexity, Journal of Algorithms 1, 77-87

Fredman, M.L. (1981): A lower bound on the complexity of orthogonal range queries, JACM 28, 696-705

Graham, R.L. (1972): An efficient algorithm for determining the convex hull of a finite planar set, IPL 1, 132-133

Graham, R.L., Yao, F. (1981): Finding the Convex Hull of a simple polygon, Stanford University, Technical Report CS 81-887

Green, P.J. (1983): Convex Decomposition of Simple Polygons, typescript

Guibas, L.J., Yao, F.F. (1980): On Translating a Set of Rectangles, 12th STOC, 154-160

Güting, R.H. (1982): An Optimal Contour Algorithm for Iso-Oriented Rectangles, McMaster University, Report 82-CS-06

Güting, R.H. (1983): Conquering Contours: Efficient Algorithms for Computational Geometry, Ph.D. Thesis, CS, Univ. Dortmund

Harel, D. (1980): A Linear Time Algorithm for the Lowest Common Ancestor Problem, 21 FOCS, 309-319

Hertel, St., Mehlhorn, K. (1983): Fast Triangulation of Simple Polygons, FCT, LNCS 158, 207-218

Hertel, St., Mehlhorn, K., Mäntyla, M., Nievergelt, I. (1983): Space Sweep Solves Intersection of Two Convex Polyhedra Elegantly, ACTA INFORMATICA, to appear

Kirkpatrick, D.G. (1979): Efficient Computation of Continous Skeletons, 20th FOCS, 18-27

Kirkpatrick, D.G. (1983): Optimal Search in Planar Subdivisions, SICOMP 12, 28-35

Kirkpatrick, D.G., Seidel, R. (1982): The ultimate planar convex hull algorithm?, 20th Allerton Conference

Ladner, R., (1975): On the structure of polynomial time reducibility, JACM 22, 155-171

Ladner, R., Lynch,N., Selman, A.L. (1974): Comparison of Polynomial Time Reducibilities, 6th STOC, 110-121

Lee, D.T., Preparata, F.P. (1977): Location of a Point in a Planar Subdivision and its Applications, SICOMP 6, 594-606

Lee, D.T., Preparata, F.P. (1979): An optimal algorithm for finding the kernel of a polygon, JACM 25, 415-421

Lee, D.T., Wong, C.K. (1977): Worst Case Analysis of Region and Partial Region Searches in Multidimensional Binary Search Trees and Balanced Quad Trees, ACTA INFORMATICA 9, 23-29

Lueker, G.S. (1978): A Data Structure for Orthogonal Range Queries, 19th FOCS, 28-34

McCallum, D., Avis, D. (1979): A linear algorithm for finding the convex hull of a simple polygon, IPL 9, 201-206

McCreight, E.M. (1980): Efficient Algorithms for Enumerating Intersecting Intervals and Rectangles, Xerox Parc Report CSL-80-09

McCreight, E.M. (1981): Priority Search Trees, Xerox Parc Report CSL-81-5

Mehlhorn, K. (1981): Lower Bounds on the Efficiency of Transforming Static Data Structures into Dynamic Data Structures, Math. Systems Theory 15, 1-11

Mehlhorn, K., Overmars, M.H. (1981): Optimal Dynamization of Decomposable Searching Problems, IPL 12, 93-98

Monier, L. (1980): Combinatorial solutions of multidimensional divide-and-conquer recurrences, J. of Algorithms 1, 60-74

Muller, D.E., Preparata, F.P. (1978): Finding the Intersection of two convex polyhedra, TCS 7, 217-236

Nievergelt, I., Preparata, F.P. (1982): Plane-Sweep Algorithms for Intersecting Geometric Figures, CACM, 25, 739-747

Ottmann, Th., Widmeyer, P. (1982): On the Placement of Line Segments into a Skeleton Structure, Inst. f. Angewandte Mathematik und Formale Beschreibungsverfahren, D-7500 Karlsruhe, Report No. 117

Ottmann, Th., Widmeyer, P., Wood, D. (1982): A Fast Algorithm for Boolean Mask Operations, Inst. f. Angewandte Mathematik und Formale Beschreibungsverfahren, D-7500 Karlsruhe, Report No. 112

Ottmann, Th., Widmeyer, P., Wood, D. (1982): A Worst-Case Efficient Algorithm for Hidden Line Elimination, Inst. f. Angewandte Mathematik und Formale Beschreibungsverfahren, D-7500 Karlsruhe, Rep. No. 119

Overmars, M.H. (1981): Dynamization of order decomposable set problems, Journal of Algorithms 2, 245-260

Overmars, M.H., van Leeuwen, J. (1981): Maintainance of Configurations in the Plane, JCSS 23, 166-204

Overmars, M.H., van Leeuwen, J. (1981): Two general methods for dynamization decomposable searching problems, Computing 26, 155-166

Overmars, M.H., van Leeuwen, J. (1981): Worst Case Optimal Insertion and Deletion Methods for Decomposable Searching Problems, IPL 12, 168-173

Overmars, M.H., van Leeuwen, J. (1982): Dynamic Multi-dimensionsal Data Structures Based on Quad- and k-d Trees, ACTA INFORMATICA 17, 267-286

Preparata, F.P. (1979): An optimal real time algorithm for planar convex hulls, CACM 22, 402-405

Preparata, F.P., Hong, S.J. (1977): Convex hulls of finite sets of points in two and three dimensions, CACM 20, 87-93

Schmidt, A. (1981): Time and Space Bounds for Hidden Line and Hidden Surface Algorithms, Proc. of Eurographics, North Holland

Shamos, M.I. (1975): Geometric Complexity, 7th STOC, 224-233

Shamos, M.I., Hoey, D. (1975): Closest-Point Problems, 16th FOCS, 151-162

Shamos, M.I., Hoey, D. (1976): Geometric Intersection Problems, 17th FOCS, 208-215

Willard, D.E. (1978): New data structures for orthogonal range queries, Technical Report, Harward University

Willard, D.E. (1982): Polygon Retrieval, SICOMP 11, 149-165

Yao, A.C.-C. (1982): Space-Time Trade-off for Answering Range Queries, 14th STOC, 128-136

Subject Index

QUADPACK

A Subroutine Package for Automatic Integration

By **R. Piessens, E. de Doncker-Kapenga, C. W. Überhuber, D. K. Kahaner**

1983. 26 figures. VIII, 301 pages. (Springer Series in Computational Mathematics, Volume 1).
ISBN 3-540-12553-1

Contents: Introduction
Theoretical Background: Automatic Integration with QUADPACK. - Integration Methods.
Algorithm Descriptions: QUADPACK contents. - Prototype of Algorithm Description. - Algorithm Schemes. - Heuristics Used in the Algorithms.
Guidelines for the Use of QUADPACK: General Remarks. - Decision Tree for Finite-range Integration. - Decision Tree for Infinite-range Integration. - Numerical Examples. - Sample Programs Illustrating the Use of the QUADPACK Integrators.
Special Applications of QUADPACK: Two-dimensional Integration. - Hankel Transform. - Numerical Inversion of the Laplace Transform.
Implementation Notes and Routine Listings: Implementation Notes. - Routine Listings.
References.

QUADPACK presents a program package for automatic integration covering a wide variety of problems and various degrees of difficulty.
After a theoretical explanation of the quadrature methods, the algorithms used by the integrators are described, providing a detailed outline of the automatic integration strategies. The results for a set of parameter studies reveal efficiency and adequacy for wide ranges of problems. Applications are discussed for solving more complex problems, including double integration, computation of the Hankel transform, and inversion of the Laplace transform.
Apart from the explanation of the theory, the book includes the routine listings, the user's manual, and many detailed numerical examples and sample programs.
The documentation for use of the package is readable and clear for novice users. With the presentation of the mathematical methods and algorithms, however, some background in the area is assumed.

Solving Elliptic Problems Using ELLPACK

By **J. Rice, R. F. Boisvert**

1984. Approx. 53 figures. Approx 350 pages. (Springer Series in Computational Mathematics, Volume 2)
ISBN 3-540-90910-9

Contents: The ELLPACK System: Introduction. – The ELLPACK Language. – Examples. – Advanced Language Facilities. – Extending ELLPACK to Non-Standard Problems. **The ELLPACK Modules:** The ELLPACK Problem Solving Modules. – ITPACK Solution Modules. – **The Performance of ELLPACK Software:** Performance and its Evaluation. – The Model Problems. – Performance of Modules to Discretize Elliptic Problems. – Performance of Modules to Solve the Algebraic Equations. – **Contributor's Guide:** Software Parts for Elliptic Problems. – Interface Specifications. – Module Interface Access. – Programming Standards. – Preprocessor Data. – **System Programmer's Guide:** Installing the ELLPACK System. – Tailoring the ELLPACK System. – **Appendices:** The PDE Population. – The PG System. – The Template Processor.

This book is a complete guide to the ELLPACK software system solving elliptic partial differential equations.

ELLPACK consists of a very high level user interface to over 50 problem solving moldules. These modules are state of the art software for two and three dimensional problems and include finite difference, finite element, SFT, multigrid and many other capabilities. The book gives the practicing scientists the tools to solve a wide range of elliptic problems with minimum effort. It shows system programmers how to install and modify ELLPACK and experts how to adapt ELLPACK to a wide range of applications.

Springer-Verlag
Berlin
Heidelberg
New York
Tokyo